addicted.pregn

addicted.pregnant.poor

addicted.pregnant.poor

addicted.pregnant.poor

addicted.pregnant.poor

addicted.pregnant.poor

addicted.pregnant.poor

addicted.pregnant.poor

addicted.pregnant.poor

addicted.pregnant.poor

addicted.pregnant.poor

addicted.pregnant.poor

addicted.pregnant.poor

addicted.pregnant.poor

addicted.pregnant.poor

CRITICAL GLOBAL HEALTH:

EVIDENCE, EFFICACY, ETHNOGRAPHY

A Series Edited by Vincanne Adams and João Biehl

addicted.pregnant.poor

KELLY RAY KNIGHT

DUKE UNIVERSITY PRESS ■ DURHAM AND LONDON ■ 2015

© 2015 Duke University Press
All rights reserved
Printed in the United States of America
on acid-free paper ∞
Designed by Amy Ruth Buchanan
Typeset in Minion Pro by Copperline

Library of Congress Cataloging-in-Publication Data
Knight, Kelly Ray, [date] author.
Addicted.pregnant.poor / Kelly Ray Knight.
pages cm—(Critical global health : evidence,
efficacy, ethnography)
Includes bibliographical references and index.
ISBN 978-0-8223-5953-1 (hardcover : alk. paper)
ISBN 978-0-8223-5996-8 (pbk. : alk. paper)
ISBN 978-0-8223-7518-0 (e-book)
1. Pregnant women—Drug use—California—
San Francisco. 2. Poor women—Drug use—
California-San Francisco. 3. Cocaine
abuse—California—San Francisco.
4. Mission District (San Francisco, Calif.)—
Social conditions—21st century. I. Title.
II. Series: Critical global health.
HV5824.W6K65   2015
362.29082'0979461—dc23
2015015084

Cover art: A $600 per month rented room in
the Daya Hotel, San Francisco, November 2007.
Photo by author.

TO MOHER AND BARBARA —

For teaching me how to do the work

and showing me why it mattered

contents

acknowledgments

So many people supported me throughout this project. First, I would like to thank the women of the daily-rent hotels who shared so much with me. I would especially like to acknowledge Lexi, Ramona, Anita, and Monica. These four women literally took me under their wings while I conducted my fieldwork, and gracefully accepted my presence, my questions, and my tape recorder with wit, grace, tears, and irritability (to name just a few of the emotions we shared). As I hung out in the hotels or on the street many, many women went out of their way to make sure none of the dealers thought I was an undercover cop, which kept me safe. They teased me when I got propositioned for sex work, tried to borrow money, cried on my shoulder, asked about my kids, laughed with me and at me during our four years together. I hope my rendering of their stories will live up to the trust they placed in me.

Many physicians, program directors, psychiatrists, social workers, physicians, policy-makers, activists, pharmacists, neurologists, drug treatment counselors, and other professionals contributed to this project. With few exceptions, everyone I contacted for an interview responded promptly and answered my questions with candor. Many of these professionals agreed to be interviewed multiple times and were very patient with me as I pieced the story together. I was very fortunate to have their cooperation and engagement in my project, and any inaccuracies or misinterpretations that may have been made herein are entirely my own. I would like to thank the volunteer staff of the Women's Community Clinic Outreach Program, especially Leah Morrison, Ej Berhanu, and Laura Sheckler. Leah first escorted me into the daily-rent hotels in 2007. Ej and Laura continued to support my work while also working alongside me in the hotels. From the Ladies Night program I would like to acknowledge the support of Laura Guzman, Vero Majano, Mary Howe, Eliza Wheeler, Brit Creech, Lauren Enteen, and Emalie Huriaux.

This project started as a dissertation, and I would like to thank my committee members: Vincanne Adams, Philippe Bourgois, Charles Briggs, and

Lawrence Cohen. Vincanne Adams was a dedicated critic, a tough audience, and an avid supporter. She truly understood what I was trying to accomplish in this project and she helped me see a way to do it. I can truly thank Vincanne, returning draft after draft to me with extensive comments and challenging me at every turn, for making sure this book got written. Philippe Bourgois kept me honest to my own history—decades of public health work with women who use drugs in San Francisco. He challenged me to never lose sight of the structurally imposed social suffering that addicted women experience. Most important, Philippe encouraged me to identify—rather than to solve—the problem, and he pushed me to focus my work on pregnancy when I was initially resistant. Charles Briggs helped me to gain specificity about what I meant by "evidence," and to position my work within the larger canon of medical anthropology while remaining in critical conversation with the field of public health. Charles asked me to imagine how I would conduct my project if I didn't have decades of past experience with drug-using women in San Francisco. Lawrence Cohen supported my project from first hearing about it and steered me toward an analysis of neoliberalism in the sex-drug economy that would match my ethnographic experience. A generous and kind teacher, mentor, and colleague, Lawrence made sure I did not lose sight of the clinical realities that shaped life on the street for urban poor women, which later helped me identify neurocratic practices and their consequences. To all four of my committee members, who took my work so seriously and provided such excellent critique, I am happily and thankfully indebted.

I was privileged to study with many inspiring scholars at the University of California, San Francisco, and the University of California, Berkeley. I would particularly like to acknowledge Judith Barker, Nancy Scheper-Hughes, Sharon Kaufman, Deborah Gordon, Brian Dolan, and Donald Moore for helping to shape my studies in medical anthropology. I am fortunate to count them among my colleagues now. There are many additional colleagues at the UCSF Department of Anthropology, History and Social Medicine who have shaped my thinking, for which I am thankful, including Ian Whitmarsh, Seth Holmes, Aimee Medeiros, Nancy Burke, Galen Joseph, Dorothy Porter, Elizabeth Watkins, Akhil Mehra, and Kathy Jackson. Thank you to Carolyn Sufrin who has been a great sounding board and an ally for this project for several years. As a doctoral student I was surrounded by intelligent and challenging peers, who had a tremendous influence on my work. I would like to thank Jeff Schonberg, Liza Buchbinder, and Nicholas Bartlett from my cohort at the University of

California, San Francisco, as well as Suepattra May, Khashayar Beigi, Eric Plemons, Shana Harris, Robin Higashi, Jai-shin Chen, Elena Portocola, Scott Stonington, Xochitl Marsilli Vargas, and Theresa Macphail. Thank you to the students in the Structural Competence course at UC-Berkeley/UCSF and to Helena Hansen for her support.

I would like to thank my colleagues at UCSF, outside of anthropology, who supported my work on this project. Elise Riley, my epidemiological collaborator at the Positive Health Program at San Francisco General Hospital, helped write proposals with me and always sought ways to create interdisciplinary dialogue between our fields. Jennifer Cohen, Megan Comfort, and Andrea Lopez were part of a fantastic qualitative team; working with them stretched my thinking and improved my work. I would also like to acknowledge Cynthia Gomez and Carol Dawson-Rose because all that we shared together brought me to this point.

Working with Kenneth Wissoker at Duke University Press has been a privilege; his insights, feedback, and encouragement were welcomed and have contributed greatly to my work. Three anonymous readers provided me with invaluable feedback that helped to clarify my arguments and improved my manuscript immeasurably, and I am very thankful. I would also like to acknowledge Elizabeth Ault and Jessica Ryan at Duke University Press and thank them for all their support and shepherding through this process. I would also like to thank my research assistant, Kara Zamora, for helping to keep me organized and for proofreading multiple chapters of the manuscript in its later stages.

It is difficult to find enough words to express how thankful I am to my family. I would like to thank my sister, Holly Knight, and father, Mel Knight, who assuaged my fears about balancing my academic pursuits with my home life, and provided me with lots of encouragement when I needed it. I would like to thank Marti Knight for being a great mom. I wish that she could be here to read this book alongside me, but she is, of course, present on every page. I would also like to thank the Kral family—Audrey, Fred, John, and Marianne—for their ongoing support of and interest in my work. My husband, Alex Kral, and my children, Nathaniel and Annika, helped me through this project every step of the way. The three of them gave me the time to dedicate to it when I needed it and the distraction away from it when I needed that too. Many nights I left the house during dinnertime to work in the hotels, looking at the forlorn expressions on my children's faces. Lots of weekends were spent at the library or in front of my computer, and not with my family. It was possible thanks to Alex. For years, he canceled work trips, came home early, took the kids evenings, weekends, and on vacations so I could get through my studies, conduct my fieldwork, and write this book. I feel fortunate for and inspired by the love Alex, Nate, and Annika have given me from start to finish.

introduction

Pregnancy and Addiction in the Daily-Rent Hotels

CHANDRA HOTEL. MISSION DISTRICT, SAN FRANCISCO. NOVEMBER 2009

As I walk down the hallway, it is completely silent.[1] This isn't unexpected. It is about one o'clock in the afternoon, and most of the renters in this privately owned, $50-a-night hotel are either out trying to make rent or sleeping off the crack excesses from the night before.

I notice that the window you climb out of to reach the fire escape at the end of the hallway is open, but there is no breeze. The hotel smells like stale cigarettes, garbage, and Indian food (prepared by the management, who have access to the only kitchen, in their apartment on the first floor).[2]

Last night when I saw Ramona on an outreach shift, we talked briefly. Ramona was irritable and short with me. I asked if I could return today to go get something to eat with her, she said, "I don't care." Then, "OK, sure." At eight months pregnant she looked uncomfortable, and hassled. Her trick was waiting patiently for her to finish up with us. Her face was set in an angry grimace.

Today, I reach Ramona's room, end of the hallway on the right, number 26. I knock on the door. "Ramona, it's Kelly." Thud and a groan. Silence. I knock again. "Ramona, open the door, it's Kelly. Let's go get something to eat." It sounds like someone is crawling on the floor. Then I hear a sound that is difficult to describe. It is a grunt, several grunts actually, followed by a low moan. It is deep, animal sounding, but it also sounds almost muffled. More grunts. It sounds like she is trying to talk to me, to respond, but she can't.

Several things flash through my mind at once. First thought: stroke? Possible. She smokes a lot of cigarettes and a lot of crack, on top of her large heroin habit. She could have had a stroke and not be able to communicate. Second thought: Is she tied up? It sounds like she can't move very easily. She has a lot of regular tricks, but often needs quick money to make rent if they don't come through. Over the years I have heard more stories of sex workers being kidnapped and tied up in hotel rooms than I care to count. Tied-up is possible.

I knock again, and in a soft but urgent tone I plead, "Ramona, the door is locked, I am worried about you. Can you reach the door to let me in?" More groans, a bit longer. Third thought: labor! Shit, maybe she is in labor. I lean closer to the door to listen. The water is running. "Ramona, why is the water running?" No answer. "Ramona?" No answer.

I look at the fire escape. I know this room, room 26. Plenty of folks who haven't paid rent or who are banned from this hotel sneak in through the window off the fire escape. Hopeful, I tell Ramona, "I am going out on the fire escape to see if I can get in through the window." No answer. I walk the short distance from the door to the window and climb out. On the fire escape I lean over; the windows are locked, the curtains drawn. I can't see in at all.

I return to the door. "Ramona, can you open the door? I am worried that you are not OK. I don't want to get the manager." No answer. Now my heart is beating out of my chest. I am starting to panic. How long have I been at the door? Five minutes? Ten minutes? Maybe she already had the baby and is bleeding in there. That might explain the water running. Maybe she has OD'd. I really don't know what to do. I can't break the door down. If I call an ambulance without seeing her first, chances are likely she will be arrested "5150" and held for seventy-two-hour lockdown at the local public hospital's psych ward.[3] She will lose her housing and most of her stuff if she is gone that long. What if the manager kicks her out because of the problems I am causing? What if she is already dead? I can't leave without knowing what is going on, yet I am paralyzed by the potential consequences any of my actions might cause.

Weighing bad choice against bad choice, I decide.

"Ramona, I am going to get the manager to let me in. I will be right back." Back down the hallway, down the stairs. At the landing of the second floor about fifty parts of a broken vacuum cleaner are laid out on the floor. The manager, a South Asian woman in her early fifties, is bent over, trying to reassemble the machine. The manager has the desk guy looking over her shoulder. They are responsible for keeping things running for the owners of the hotel. They gain little from it, and tolerate little. They have heard it all before, and want the rent. They both look up at me. "I am worried about Ramona, she won't answer her door. I am not sure she is OK. "She is OK." The manager assures me dismissively, "I saw her this morning. She had a visitor." "Visitor" is daily-rent hotel code for a trick. Ramona was up working for her rent already. The manager turns back to the broken machine.

I go back to number 26. Knock on the door again. Louder now: "Ramona!! Ramona!! You need to open the door for me." There is no answer. I walk back to the manager. "Listen, I am really not sure if she is OK. And the water is running in her room."

"You know I can't open the door. I am not allowed to," the manager retorts.

"The water is running. It might be overflowing, I can't tell." This is a last-ditch effort on my part.

I walk back up. Still knocking. A small groan, but nothing else. I hear the sound of the manager coming, keys jingling. The water was running. That must have given her the excuse to open the door—water damage in the hotels is a huge problem. The manager is clearly annoyed with me. She sighs. With a high-pitched, very stern voice and a rap of the back of her knuckles on the door, she says, "Ramona!!!" No answer, but some movement maybe. The manager slips the key in the lock. As the door opens, it is immediately kicked back by Ramona, who is on the floor half-hidden behind it. "No," Ramona yells. Then Ramona looks up and sees me. She takes her foot off the door. I wedge myself through the half open doorway. "Ramona, it's Kelly. Are you OK?" The manager is already out of sight, halfway down the hallway, by the time I close the door. The manager isn't concerned, or perhaps more accurately, she isn't paid to be.

Ramona gets up on her feet, awkwardly. I quickly scan the room and her body for blood. She is naked from the waist down, with a short T-shirt on. Her legs are scarred, but I notice no bruises or blood. I walk two steps over to the faucet and turn off the water in her sink. When I turn around to face her again, she falls into my arms. Exhausted howls and screams come out of her. Her body heaves and shakes as she sobs in my arms. I hold her like a child, stroking her back, letting her cry on me. She sobs for a full minute. "It's OK," I keep repeating. "It's OK."

Then she looks up and appears to recognize her own vulnerability on my face. She separates from me and leans over the bed. Her swollen belly carries her forward so she needs to bend her knees. "I'm tired. I can't keep going on like this." She wails. "I feel like I am done."

I notice syringes on the bed and a bunch of other paraphernalia from last night's outreach strewn around. Condoms, gauze four-by-fours, medical tape, prenatal vitamins, an empty sandwich wrapper. She manages—barely—to get some underwear on and turn off the porn that is still playing on the suspended TV across from the bed. She isn't in labor, no stroke, no kidnapping.

She is just really high.

She stops crying. She wants to show me something. In a moment of lucidity she asks me if I have seen the mouse. "What mouse?" I ask. "The dead mouse. The baby. There." She is pointing under the bed. "I had to kill it. It wanted to sleep with me. It was crawling right in next to me on the bed. It had to go." Her face is plaintive. She is upset about killing the mouse and needs me to see it. I bend over and see a baby mouse dead on a sticky trap. "I have more," she says pointing to the remaining sticky traps on the low table near the door.

Now Ramona's high is coming back and she starts to phase out, meaning she is no longer talking to me. Trance-like, her body starts to gyrate, arms lift in stilted, choppy movements that don't seem intentional or connected to the rest of her body. Her eyes roll back in her head; she starts to sway on her feet, grunting again. I have seen Ramona a mess before, lots of times. Almost pissing in her own pants on the street, cursing the staff at the homeless shelter when the bathroom was closed. Yelling and running down the street chasing a high, with fiending eyes. Yet this is as high as I have ever seen her. She keeps bending over, low to the ground in a birthing pose, but she isn't in labor.

Not knowing how long this will last, and not knowing quite what to do as Ramona fades in and out of her high, I decide I have to wait it out. She is very fucked up, and she keeps getting too close to the wall and almost hitting her head and her arms against it. I get up several times to steer her gently toward the bed. Forty-five minutes of grunting and swaying later, she finds her flip-flops and heads to the door. I have suggested I get food and come back to her room because I was thinking she was too fucked up to walk down the stairs, but she has insisted on leaving. "I am starving," she says. "And I need to get out of here."

Down the stairs, stepping carefully over the vacuum parts, she says, "I'm coming back, OK?" She is trying to sound mean and strong. The manager has her key and could easily lock her out of her room, if she hasn't made rent yet.

She stumbles with me to the taqueria two doors down, where she attempts to eat her enchiladas two forkfuls at a time. Two young hipster men in their late twenties, with long beards and expensive sneakers, are staring at us from a few tables away. They are trying to eat and talk, but they are clearly uncomfortable watching Ramona as she moves between focused eating and almost falling out of her chair.

After about five minutes of eating Ramona says: "I am ready to go in (to treatment)." The food seems to be sobering enough to stop her fading out and grunting. "What did First Steps say to you when you left?" I ask.[4] Ramona was in First Steps, a program for pregnant women, one where you give birth and keep your baby if you live at the treatment facility and follow the rules. She left in August after only two days, when she was five and a half months pregnant. "They said they would always have a bed for me," Ramona comments. "When do you want to go?" I ask. "Tomorrow. Morning," she says. I have heard this before. Yet I still want to get her there. Is this really what she wants this time, or is this what she thinks I want to hear right now? "Call me if you want to go tomorrow. I will come down," I say.

I leave her to go pick up my daughter at school. I am terrified about what will happen to Ramona next and hugely relieved to get away from her. I wonder what reception she will get back at the Chandra Hotel. The manager will probably kick her out because of me being such a pain in the ass.

Ramona doesn't call me the next day.

Two weeks later

Ramona and I are riding in my car returning from the methadone clinic. She has had her baby, and he is still being held at the hospital while she decides whether and when she will enter drug treatment at First Steps. Getting on methadone through the pregnancy and postpartum program is a move toward that.

I ask her, "Did I get you in trouble when I had the manager open your door?" She looks kind of blankly at me. "You were groaning and grunting and I thought you were hurt," I apologize, unsure if she will see my intervention as a breach of her privacy.

"I was grunting? What do you mean?" she asks.

"You sounded like this." I imitate the sound to the best of my ability. She laughs a bit awkwardly. "Do you remember when we were together? And we went to eat?" I ask.

"Yeah, I remember eating. Yeah. I was grunting?" she asks again.

"Yeah, and banging your head against the wall, and flailing your arms like this" (I imitate as best I can while driving). "You were all over the place."

"Huh," she says, pensively.

She doesn't remember it.

"You should have taken some pictures," she says.

"I did," I reply, and we both laugh.

Life is tricky for addicted, pregnant women who live and work in the daily-rent hotels. Every day marks a battle against drug craving, housing debt, and potential violence.[5] All the while, the pregnancy ticks forward, ensuring multiple and complex institutional entanglements. The harsh everyday realties of poverty and addiction can open our eyes, while also forcing our gaze toward the complex bureaucratic and clinical configurations of care and treatment that protect and ensnare women, by turns. The goal of this ethnography is to tease out the threads that construct a web of apparent intractability for women who are categorized as addicted, pregnant, poor.

I seek to make connections between multiple audiences by telling the story of addicted pregnancy through the lenses of those figures enlisted to make truth claims about it—addicted, pregnant women, an anthropologist, public health epidemiologists, advocates, social policy-makers, treatment professionals, bureaucrats, and scientists. I take seriously what each of these figures says and does in relation to addicted pregnancy in order to ask: What forms of life are possible here? For women? For their children? For scientists and policy-makers? For drug treatment counselors and clinicians? For the anthropologist? Can we separate the madness of everyday life among addicted, pregnant, poor women from the social interventions designed to address these forms of life?

Through the examination of addicted pregnancy among poor women, I tell a larger story about how we understand addiction and mental illness in the United States today. I hope to demonstrate the ways that the experiences of addicted, pregnant, poor women challenge both emergent scientific paradigms and the ethical boundaries of socially condoned motherhood. The use of the term "addicted" to describe the pregnant women in this ethnography is intentional. "Drug user" is a more politically correct term, and for some persons, it is a more behaviorally accurate one. "Addicted" is a term frequently applied to persons experiencing physical and/or emotional dependence on a controlled substance who continue to use the substance despite negative consequences for themselves and others.[6] It references compulsivity and consequences in both scientific and lay contexts. I use the term "addicted" because it was how most of the women I worked with referred to themselves, which highlights important linguistic and political distinctions between how persons are named and how they name themselves. The use of the term can also help de-sanitize certain discourses about drugs and drug use that circulate in public health literature. The descriptor "women who use drugs" can be a very useful way to underscore the fact that women who are pregnant and use drugs in the daily-rent hotels should not be defined only in terms of their drug use. Yet this appellation's efforts to avoid reductionist categorization through a focus on behavior (drug use) can also erase the economic, social, and structural constraints that women who identify as addicted, or who are called "addicts" in media, public policy circles, and clinical settings, experience frequently. These experiences make "addicted" persons, so called, very different from middle- and upper-class drug users who do not experience the same structural consequences as a result of their drug use, and from those who do not experience drugs in their lives as a compulsive, problematic force.

I found "drug user" insufficient to describe the intensity and the suffering that many of the women I worked with were experiencing as a result of substances in their lives—in all their complex manifestations. Engaging the term "addicted" helps to link political and epidemiological discourses of addiction to emergent neurological debates that align addiction, as a brain disease, akin to other forms of mental illness. The messiness of "comorbidity" (co-occurrence of substance use disorders and mental illness) and its bureaucratic manifestations is a central theme in this ethnography. Today, posttraumatic stress disorder (PTSD) and bipolar disorder are diagnosed at very high frequency, and the prescription of broad-spectrum atypical antipsychotic medications is routine among homeless women. Clinically speaking, PTSD and bipolar disorder are difficult conditions to diagnose and treat in the presence of active substance use. Yet the symptoms of these conditions—trauma, despair, rage, and mania—are viewed by many clinicians as appropriate responses on the part of addicted women to experiences of poverty, social suffering, and housing instability.

In my time with women in the daily-rent hotels, pregnancy and addiction often stood in conceptual opposition. Pregnancy necessitates self-sacrificing behavior in a socially stable environment. Addiction, characterized as a chronic, relapsing brain disease, challenged notions of choice and free will. Further, addicted, pregnant women were framed by health and mental health providers, policy-makers, scientists, and themselves as traumatized figures of failed social reproduction living highly stigmatized and unstable lives. My use of the term "addicted" does not mean that I am aligning myself with punitive rhetoric and policies toward persons with drug addiction. Rather, it is a move to simultaneously acknowledge, engage, and interrogate the categories of addicted pregnancy, and the women who fall into and under those categorizations.

Temporality and Fact-Making

In the daily-rent hotels the concrete routines of living called on women to meet unrelenting, and often conflicting, temporal demands. Ramona, like all the other addicted, pregnant women who resided in the daily-rent hotels, operated in multiple "time zones" every day. She was on "addict time," repeatedly searching for crack and heroin and satiating her addiction to them. "Pregnancy time" reminded her that her expanding womb was a ticking time bomb. On "hotel time" she constantly needed to hustle up her rent through daily sex work. "Treatment time" demanded she answer: When was she going back? Was it too late? Could the baby be born "clean" if she stopped today? These are questions she asked herself and that were being asked of her. "Biomedical time" left a trace upon her—previous addicted pregnancies that followed her into subsequent births. Ramona had lost custody of her most recent child prior to this pregnancy. That child was now age three and in foster care. "Life time" operated to remind her of a life of addiction and involvement with institutions that had adjudicated her income-generating strategies and kept her unstably housed. It is difficult to hold the "whole story" of Ramona in a single, temporally fixed place, like an ethnography, in view of the stresses and

I.1. Anita's room the day of her child custody court date (Chandra Hotel, March 2010). Graffiti reads: "GOD hates sin, but LOVES the sinner"; "Checkout Time!"; "To many Aunts, to many Uncles"; and "you pay Now!!!" Photo by the author.

pressures that each of these temporalities placed on her. She appeared to be emotionally, physically, and structurally caught in a limbo state betwixt and between these temporal demands—negotiating the liminality of the everyday through both time and space.

In stark contrast, health and housing policies for the urban poor are built on efforts to erase the complexity of temporal demands in order to make them fixed and solvable. Most often this effort is accomplished through practices that try to stabilize the lives of addicted, pregnant women in and through numbers about them. Health statistics about disease and heath service utilization outcomes, as well as those about health economics and cost savings, are generated as "facts" that justify policy decisions. These facts stabilize problems of temporal incongruity, reifying problems as time-limited events that come with categorical, measurable behaviors. If Ramona's "behaviors" are driven by multiple different temporal demands, what sort of health and housing policy could aptly respond? When I discussed the phenomenon of multiple temporalities with a clinician, she replied:

Exactly. That is why words like "lying" and "knowing" don't apply here—not to these patients. I see my pregnant patients smoking crack, doing all kinds of craziness. And when they lose [custody of] the kid, they are *devastated*. I mean really traumatized, *retraumatized*. And I want to say, "Wait a minute, *come on*. You must have seen this coming?" But she didn't. She didn't see it coming. She didn't, really, *know* it was going to happen. Not before it did. I don't know if it is holding onto hope, or just the ability to compartmentalize the addiction from everything else that is going on.

The multiple temporalities at work in the lives of women like Ramona highlight how affective, behavioral, and material choices were structured in ways that felt literally impossible. Daily decision-making required making choices about the rent, dope, the baby, and the future that were temporally at odds with one another. Yet the ubiquity of hypervigilance, mania, stress, and depression, together with drug use, necessitated a new social actor, "the neurocrat," to emerge in order to facilitate women's acquisition of mental health diagnoses that could treat their poverty. "She didn't see it coming." And this clinician was right. She didn't. For many women, the present was imbued with future projections (the chance of motherhood, a future baby born tox-negative) and haunted by past ghosts (a traumatic childhood, years of addiction). These temporalities competed with the persistence of present needs: the next fix, a way to pay for one's hotel room, the next meal. The displacements happened all the time.

All the while, gaining recognition from governmental institutions, designed to help by providing material support and service acquisition, was structured by its own temporal demands. Worthiness for help was often determined by "time served" in treatment and "time clean" while pregnant. In clinical settings, mental illness diagnoses were determined by *current* symptoms, which often did not match onto time-defined, singular "events," such as those found in categorizations for PTSD and bipolar disorder of the *Diagnostic and Statistical Manual* (DSM). For epidemiologic purposes, behaviors were bound in time (often, within the last three, six, and twelve months) to be statistically analyzed. Finally, ethnographic narratives worked with their own sense of time; they produced evidence about the past and current experiences of addicted, pregnant women that were marked by both the everyday boredom of ongoing addiction and the urgency of health, mental health, and housing crises. In this sense, my effort to create a sense of the ethnographic present was constructed through witnessing, and through making editorial judgments about which times matter and why. Taken together, these diverse modes of veridiction, of affirming truth according to a particular worldview and according to the temporal demands they exact, make telling the collective story of addicted pregnancy in the daily-rent hotels challenging.

Addicted Pregnancy in the United States

The specificity and the generalizability of Ramona's situation should be placed in a broader US context. Science, politics, and social services interact in the US welfare state to create sympathetic opportunities for rehabilitation and redemption for addicted, pregnant women while also ensuring that adjudication and punishment will follow, should these fail. According to the US National Survey on Drug Use and Health, for all women in the United States, "the rate of current illicit drug use in the combined 2009–2010 data was 16.2 percent among pregnant women aged 15 to 17, 7.4 percent among pregnant women aged 18 to 25, and 1.9 percent among pregnant women aged 26 to 44."[7] When women are suspected, or admit to, prenatal substance use, their babies are tested for exposures to specific illicit drugs at birth. As a result of exposure to opiates/opiods (such as heroin or prescription painkillers), the babies can be given diagnoses such as neonatal abstinence syndrome (NAS), which enable health care providers to manage an infant's withdrawal symptoms postpartum. In 2012, the *Journal of the American Medical Association* reported that the incidence of NAS increased between 2000 and 2009, leading to a significant public health care cost burden in that "77.6% of charges for NAS were attributed to state Medicaid programs."[8] The article's lead author, in a national newspaper, described the findings in terms of "13,539 infants a year, or one drug-addicted baby born every hour."[9] These statistics are the reason that substance use during pregnancy is constituted as a "public health issue" in the United States, even as research on prenatal screening indicates that 75–90 percent of cases of prenatal exposure to tobacco, alcohol, and illicit substance use may be going undetected.[10] Thus, even though the percentage of US pregnancies that are marked by substance use is not exactly known, it is likely to be a considerable number.[11] I use the term "marked" deliberately because the processes by which women who use illicit substances prenatally are identified and what courses of action are taken as a result of that identification leave scars that linger far beyond the life of any one, singular pregnancy.

The epidemiological data cited here is not socially or politically neutral.

Every state in the United States has a surveillance system in place to identify prenatal substance use exposure; seventeen states consider substance abuse during pregnancy to be child abuse; three consider it grounds for civil commitment, or incarceration.[12] Even though the science about the short- and long-term effects of prenatal exposure to substances varies widely according to the types of substance (e.g., tobacco, alcohol, marijuana, opiates/opioids, cocaine, methamphetamine) and the timing and dosage of its use, scientists agree that prenatal exposure to any substance cannot be deemed "risk-free" for the fetus.[13] Moreover, from the perspective of moral adjudication and social stigma: any drug use during pregnancy is bad mothering. In the United States, it is morally anathema for a woman who is eight months pregnant to be seen smoking a cigarette, drinking a beer, popping a pain pill, shooting heroin, or hitting a crack pipe. Even as the physiological "costs" of the fetal exposure to those specific substances are not equally distributed, society applies increasingly rigorous forms of censure for illicit substance use when compared to alcohol or tobacco use. The biological nature of pregnancy, specifically in reference to the potential for shared illicit substance use through shared blood between a fetus and mother, shifts the ontological status of the woman and initiates legal, technical, and political limits on her as an individual.

In one recent court case, a pregnant woman from Wisconsin, Alicia Beltran, who admitted the use of opioid painkillers in a prenatal care visit, was arrested and detained in a treatment facility.[14] This case is one in a long list of others that debate prenatal substance exposure and what to do about it throughout the United States. These cases often gain national media attention.[15] Historically, criminal cases surrounding addicted pregnancy have centered on child neglect and abuse. Most recently, the adjudication of pregnant women who use substances has aligned more strongly with the fetal rights movement to contend that the "personhood" of the fetus is being violated through exposure to illicit substances without consent.[16] On the other end of the political spectrum, the forcible incarceration of women who admit to illicit substance use during pregnancy has been legally questioned and challenged on clinical grounds. As with many domains of pregnancy and addiction, the rights of a fetus to be unexposed and the rights of a pregnant woman to bodily autonomy are being juxtaposed and contested.

Returning to the epidemiology of addicted pregnancy in United States, the story of Alicia Beltran gives us pause. Given this cautionary tale, what woman would disclose drug use during pregnancy to her health care provider? As the report describes, Beltran was not using substances at the time of her admission and subsequent arrest. This allows her to be cast in a sympathetic public glow as the repentant addict. Yet, even in her struggle to get help with her drug use during her pregnancy, the fact of her drug use during pregnancy entangles her in carceral regimes in which the lines between care and coercion become significantly blurred. Even in her repentance, she is made criminal.

Scientific studies and clinical experts have emphasized the fraught relationship between drug use, drug abstinence, and pregnancy. Research indicates that the majority of women who decrease or abstain from substance use during pregnancy return to those substances postpartum.[17] Whether one adopts an understanding of addiction as chronic relapsing brain disease, a byproduct of a failed social environment, or a failure of will, there can be a great deal of slippage between the out-of-control addict deviant and the repentant, recovered citizen. In contrast to the picture painted here of Alicia Beltran, what are we to make of women who are less likely to be poster women in the ideological wars about how to respond to drug use during pregnancy? What can and what should be done about and for women who are sex workers, who are poor, mostly homeless, who get pregnant unintentionally and continue to use drugs despite the options for treatment, like Ramona? This book is an exploration of the predicament that we have collectively created in our attempts to sort through and also answer these questions. It examines the predicament of addicted pregnancy from the perspectives not just of policy and social science but also of the women themselves who are caught in these webs and are struggling to make a life for themselves inside them.

Hidden in Plain Sight

The specific neighborhood I worked in for this ethnographic research hosted multiple overlapping social groups and economies. The city streets were sites of both danger and possibility. Men and women in the drug-sex economy in this neighborhood mingled with working poor and middle-class Latino community members, along with middle- and upper-class residents and visitors who hoped to gentrify the area.[18] Addicted people, and the crime and poverty that often travels with the drug-sex economy, were both criticized and tolerated on these blocks.[19] These ambivalences reflected a broader public sentiment about how to manage the homeless in San Francisco, and the varied public perceptions about the rights of homeless and unstably housed persons to be "neighbors."

I.2. The Sixteenth Street BART plaza, near the daily-rent hotels, February 2007. Photo by the author. Photographs of women by Kari Orvik.

Figure I.2 speaks volumes about the changing political economy of the three-by-three-block neighborhood in which I worked. The women who participated in Women's Space, a local drop-in program for women, were given the opportunity to have beautiful portraits taken of them.[20] At the time, I remember the photography had a huge impact on the women who participated. They loved being able to put on makeup, have their hair done, and pose for the photos. It was a professional and serious endeavor, and it was also fun. Most women had never had a portrait photograph taken of themselves. One woman bragged happily when we first met about how many people in the neighborhood had complimented her on the photo while it was up in the Sixteenth Street BART plaza. The intention of the pictures was to increase visibility and knowledge about homeless women and the Women's Space program and to establish their rightful place in the neighborhood as well. Many of the people who were gentrifying this neighborhood worked downtown and utilized this subway stop to get to and from work, providing an opportunity for them to interact with this public art representing unstably housed and homeless women. Tragically, one of the women pictured in the exhibition was killed in an extremely violent rape and murder that took place in a local daily-rent hotel. The photo display offers insight into how poor women in this place are hidden in plain sight. They gained a physical and political visibility, speaking to multiple publics as representatives of homeless women, while the everyday violence of their lives in the daily-rent hotels still remained largely hidden.[21]

Gentrification and Policing

While I was conducting my four years of ethnography (2007–2011), it was not uncommon in the area of my study to find several store closure and for rent signs in older stores, which were rapidly "flipped" into higher-end restaurants and condos. The block parallel to Mission Street, where the majority of the daily-rent hotels were located, had successfully gentrified over the past ten years and now offered upscale condos and day- and nighttime businesses that catered to young hipsters and middle- and upper-class professionals. The drug-sex economies and the gentrification economies were both co-dependent and in conflict on these blocks. The gentrification economy was dependent on the "urban feel" of the area—to sell its businesses as young, hip, and exciting.[22] Since the early 2000s, the dot.com boomers had bought up office space in abandoned industrial spaces on the blocks to the east and west of the daily-rent hotels, but the impact on rental markets and long-term, local business owners was minimal compared to the "tech invasion" of the neighborhood that began occurring in force around 2009 and continues today.[23] Indeed, the Google bus, a large commuter bus with plush seats and Wi-Fi that whisks tech employees to Google's campus in Silicon Valley, has come to represent the intrusion of tech wealth, and the accompanying high rents and service prices, into the neighborhood.[24]

These changes have been met with activism from all sides. One group, with potentially controversial links to local real estate developers, conducted an online campaign in which they publicly marked homeless, poor, and drug-involved people in the neighborhood as a dangerous presence by identifying the place where they congregate (the Sixteenth Street BART plaza) as "deplorable" and a "blight."[25] In response to this sort of sentiment, a sidewalk posting appeared in front of the Nisha Hotel, which is situated on the boundary between a gentrified block and a block yet to fully gentrify, that reflected anger toward the neighborhood's new wealthy patrons and their declining tolerance

I.3. View from room facing Mission Street, Raman Hotel, April 2009.
Photo by the author.

for the urban poor. It read "Mission nite [*sic*] time patrons who harrass people who live on the street in this anti-poor city are worth less than shit."

One day I was sitting on the street with Anita discussing her postpregnancy plans and the terrible heroin withdrawal she was confronting. I asked her what she thought about the changing neighborhood. She told me a story that reflected awareness, savvy, and growing intolerance between the drug and gentrification economies: "I seen a dude—one of those new Mission dudes, a hipster—knocked off his bike [by a drug dealer]. He didn't run. He turned around and cursed the guy [the dealer] out. I couldn't believe it. These young people don't take any shit. Not anymore."

In addition to the drug-sex and the gentrification economies, the neighborhood also housed long-term San Francisco residents and business owners and formal and informal sector economies of immigrants and migrants, primarily from Mexico and Central America. These economies were various, including some shopkeepers and restaurant owners (although those are disap-

I.4. Spray-paint graffiti on sidewalk, Sixteenth Street, October 2008.
Photo by the author.

pearing as their shops are bought by gentrifying newcomers), informal tamale sellers, taco truck vendors, and stall operators. Some immigrant, and migrant, men also rent rooms in the daily-rent hotels, yet I documented very little direct interaction between them and the women sex workers in the hotels where I worked. One woman, Rebecca, commented to me that she tried "to keep those poor boys from getting eaten alive" in the Raman Hotel. She indicated that they often migrate to the United States from the rural areas of their countries of origin and get caught up in day labor, drinking and drugging in the hotels. She was making a protective, differentiating statement between young migrant men caught up by the dangers of the US ghetto lifestyle and the "regulars" (men from other neighborhoods buying sex and drugs) and the local men who were a regular feature of the drug-sex economy (dealers, drug runners, and other "third parties").[26]

Gentrification brought a massive police presence to the Mission District, and that has come to confine the drug-sex economies to a relatively small area.[27] The policing activity was constant. Often I would hear the whisper "Blue ghost" outside the shop where the majority of open-air drug dealing took place, to indicate that a plainclothes or uniformed officer was on the way down the street. Instantly, people would disappear into the hotels or the shops. I knew if I arrived on the corner and no one was around that the police had just been through. In 2009, I spent half a day on a bench at the Sixteenth Street BART plaza watching a sea of sex workers disappear and reappear like the tide as police cruisers circled or police officers on foot and on bikes patrolled.[28] An examination of the San Francisco Police Department statistics on violent and drug-related crime arrests provides a numeric understanding of the concentration of open-air drug market activity and police response in the area. According to the San Francisco Police Department Crimemaps website data, between March 9 and April 2, 2009, there were eleven arrests for (nonsexual) assault and sixty-six arrests for drug/narcotics charges. "Possession"—not sale or intent to sell—accounted for thirty-two of the sixty-six drug/narcotic arrests. The daily-rent hotels where I conducted participant observation stand on the blocks with the highest density of drug/narcotic arrests in the area.

Women living in the daily-rent hotels had mixed feelings about gentrification and the changes it wrought. Many women felt pushed out. Some women I spoke with felt the new businesses were "cleaning up the area," making it safer than it was. Others saw Mission nighttime hipsters as easy prey for "gaffle" sales—selling fake crack cocaine (gaffle), often made of soap, to customers the seller does not expect to see again or who will be too intimated to confront the seller once they realize they have been cheated. These multiple renderings of community ownership over these blocks paint a picture of interdependence and uneasy tolerance. On the one hand gentrification may be bringing a measure of increased safety. On the other hand high rents and high-end services inevitably push lower-income people, including tenants of the daily-rent hotels, further away from public access to community space. Indeed, battles over the price of space also referenced battles over tolerance of the drug-sex economy—an economy that had historically contributed, for good or ill, to low rental and housing costs in this neighborhood.

Just as many of the women in the daily-rent hotels expressed ambivalence toward the changes wrought by gentrification, they also described concern over the impact of the visibility of sex work and drug dealing on other neighborhood residents, particularly children. For example, Lexi explained to me that she did not want to be seen out working—doing sex work—during the day because many of the families with small children walking by might give her judgmental looks. "That is why I try to only work late at night, when the children are asleep," she told me. Many other women from the daily-rent hotels also expressed concerns about the neighborhood children being "exposed" to the drug sales and prostitution activities on the block. Our outreach clients would often ask us to move our activities if we were close to the entrances of one of several Pentecostal churches on these blocks that held family services in the evening. On an everyday basis, most families in the neighborhood tolerated and strategically avoided the drug-sex economy, especially shielding their children. The geographic configuration of the built environment aided in this separation: in this three-block area the daily-rent hotels populate the western side of Mission Street, while on the eastern side apartment buildings and grocery stores and other businesses predominate. The social effects of this distinction were significant. On the east side of the street, one could walk and shop buffered from direct awareness of the drug-sex economy; on the west side, walking the block meant passing by sex workers and being offered crack.

Although neighborhood groups were active in business councils and local schools, I only documented one public protest against the drug-sex economy in four years of ethnography. During this protest, in which children, teachers, and parents chanted and marched with signs down the western side of Mission Street to the Sixteenth Street BART plaza, women and men of the drug-sex economy scattered into hotels or hid in doorways with their faces turned down. Many were clearly abashed at being the object of protest, yet they were also clearly trapped, given that their livelihood and housing existed on these same streets. Similar to a police sweep of the neighborhood, the protest created momentary invisibility, followed by the immediate return of the open-air drug market. More recently local school groups, business owners, and advocates for the homeless in the neighborhood have joined forces to work against gentrification. They are trying to fight a large-scale market-rate housing development planned for a location across the street from the location shown in figure I.5, which detractors feel would create more intolerance for the poor and unstably housed in the neighborhood and negatively impact a local elementary school.[29]

Among all the various social actors in this contested and changing neighborhood, pregnant, addicted, poor women managed their basic needs and sought survival by paying for rooms in the privately owned daily-rent hotels. Very few anthropological studies of homelessness and urban poverty have

I.5. Public protest, Sixteenth Street BART plaza, October 2008. The middle sign reads "Please don't do drugs near our school." Photo by the author.

taken privately owned daily-rent hotels as their sites of ethnographic engagement.[30] Difficulty in gaining access might generally account for this lack. Unless one is willing to check in and rent a room for an extended period of time, one does not have a good reason to be there. This is often not financially feasible or necessarily desirable. Those who have engaged in ethnographic work in low-income hotels have limited their analysis to municipally funded hotels, in which tenants often have ongoing social service involvement, in the form of case management and home health visits.[31] I was primarily interested in life in the daily-rent hotels that were privately owned and not managed by governmental agencies or nonprofits and did not provide social service or case management components associated with the housing or the hotel. Privately owned and operated daily-rent hotels have been understudied as ethnographic sites in the United States.[32] The presence of many "unstably housed" women in these private, daily-rent hotels offered me the opportunity to investigate these spaces of habitation, which stand in the limbo between "sleeping rough," sleeping in the publicly funded shelters, and living in government-subsidized housing.

Getting Inside

*Never trust a bitch with your life story, because some day she might end up as
an eyewitness.*
—Graffiti inside Marta's room at the Daya Hotel, September 2007

My long history as a public health researcher and service advocate for women
who use drugs influenced my choice of field site. I had worked for over fifteen
years doing harm reduction work among the women in this community.[33]
Later, I began my participant observation at the Women's Space program,
which was held weekly for two hours in the evening at the homeless drop-in
center. As I was more interested in observing the hotels where women lived,
I began to volunteer for a weekly outreach program run by a feminist free reproductive health care clinic that served women, the majority of whom paid
daily for hotel rooms. The fifteen hotels in which I conducted participant
observation were not large, often housing about twenty to fifty rooms, on the
second or third floor above street level (see table A3).

Every shift night, the outreach team, usually two or three of us, trolled
through the hallways of the hotels, announcing "Condom ladies!!" We gave
safe sex and injection supplies to women who opened their doors or who
happened to be around. We would talk and laugh in the hallways, catch up,
confer, refer, and share stories. We were often called on to doctor wounds, assess the need for hospitalization (most often due to abscesses), and give pregnancy tests and prenatal vitamins, in addition to the free food and supplies
we offered (shampoo, tampons, soap, etc.). Through this initial interaction,
I came to identify women for ethnographic follow-up based on their social
interactions, housing situation, health needs, and willingness to talk. For four
years I was able to document the living conditions and social worlds in the
daily-rent hotels and the surrounding neighborhood firsthand.

There were specific forms of gendered economic exploitation that took
place in private hotels that were systematic—even as they were arbitrarily applied according the whim of the hotel management. These included forced
monthly evictions to deny women tenancy rights, extracting "visiting fees"
from paying sex customers to improve the profitability of the hotel as a brothel,
and creating ongoing indebted relationships with women while charging
exorbitant daily rental fees. Because I was known to the hotel management
as someone who had some form of institutionalized permission to interact
regularly with women, I was given basically unrestricted access to the daily-

rent hotels at any time of day or night, without having to rent a room or pay a visitor's fee. Without this sanctioned entree, I felt I would not have been able to document the realities of the lives of women in the hotels. Even with permission, however, hotel managers sometimes viewed me with suspicion or annoyance. My presence and interactions with women in these settings caused concern for me because I worried that I might jeopardize women's ability to stave off evictions. That said, my general experience with managers was one of tolerance, not open hostility.

I engaged with daily-rent hotel tenants for four years, experiencing, following, and describing twenty-three pregnancies among nineteen different women (see table A1). The women whose stories appear in these pages—Ramona, Lexi, Kitt, Cupcake, Dylan, Benz, Anita, and others—demonstrate how the daily-rent hotels are sites of a kind of insanity, where mediated and simplified political-ideological debates about neglect, rights, and governmental intervention are stretched to their breaking points by the chaos of addiction, pregnancy, and poverty. I often found myself in close proximity to the dangerous and violent stakes that were normative behind the walls of the daily-rent hotels. I was also often laughing along at the absurdity of an everyday life in which crisis, violence, memory, and hope intersected so dramatically. How would it be possible to reconcile, or even contextualize, the complexity of an ethical engagement with addicted pregnancy in this site? I turn, then, to the question of ethics.

When Vultures Surround You, Try Not to Die

FOLLOWING THE BLOOD.
RAMAN HOTEL. SEPTEMBER 2009

I am looking for the stain from the puddle of blood [on the floor of her hotel room], and then I see the faint outline. The way Lexi described it, when her water broke she was gushing blood all over the floor, right next to the bed. We are back from the hospital, and Lexi can barely walk. She wants to change the bloody pads in her underwear but discovers that the blood has already soaked through her jeans. "Shit!" she exclaims. Drawing on my limited gynecological knowledge, I ask what color the blood is to try and determine if it is newer bleeding (bright red) or clots (darker). She indicates that it is clots. Because she left the hospital against medical advice (AMA), she also left without the antibiotics she was supposed to be taking postsurgery.

"I have to get to work to pay for this room," she tells me.

"Lexi, I don't think you can," I respond. I can't imagine her pulling dates [doing sex work] in her condition.

She doesn't argue and goes to change her pad in the bathroom down the hall. Even if she does spike a fever, she won't return to the hospital. Because she came in on a 5150 psychiatric admit and left AMA, Lexi fears the hospital staff will commit her, to finish off her mandatory seventy-two-hour lockdown. Then no one would be at the bus station to meet her six-year-old son, Lionel, who is arriving, alone, in several hours. Lexi plans to bring Lionel back here to stay with her. When she returns from the bathroom she starts cleaning up syringes, empty cigarette packs, condoms, and old food wrappers from around the room. She arranges her and Pano's (her boyfriend's) shoes on the floor, near the door, and collects even more garbage mixed in with her welfare and child custody paperwork. When I leave about fifteen minutes later I loan her $20 for her rent. "I will pay you back," she says, "day after tomorrow."

The African proverb "When vultures surround you, try not to die" aptly characterizes the tensions between survival and vulnerability for addicted, pregnant women in the daily-rent hotels. Despite all of the good intentions of those who try to help, there is a culture of vulturism in urban sites of poverty that creates complex relations of power and interdependence for all social actors—pregnant women, their drug dealers, hotel managers, and social scientists and policy-makers alike. Urban poor people, in my case addicted, pregnant women, become targets for social scientific investigation and are ethnographically consumed because they are wounded and bleeding, metaphorically and sometimes literally. Social suffering is the necessary condition under which they become objects of study (not just for medical anthropologists but also for public health researchers, policy-makers, and journalists). The ethical stance of the ethnographer seeking to witness and then produce narratives about the social suffering in these sites of urban poverty is predicated on the extreme availability of suffering here: the addiction, sex work, violence, and poverty creating a perfect storm from which it is difficult to tear one's eyes away. The forms of suffering are also emplaced. They lie in waiting.

1.6. Room 43, Raman Hotel, May 2008. Photo by the author.

The anthropologist need only visit them at her convenience. Like the vulture she can circle around until the bleeding starts, and then she can engage.

It might be tempting to justify this consumption on grounds that there is an intention to "do good" or to "improve" the situation. Yet seeing the role of anthropologist as like that of a vulture offers a counter narrative—an up-close interpretation of ethnographic relations of give-and-take in which uneven power relations mask the extractive process of research as scientific altruism.[34] Social scientific vulturism also conjures older ghosts, from a time when many anthropologists were handmaiden to, even complicit in, colonial projects throughout the world. But on the ground, the complexity of the relationship between social scientist and research subject demands more nuance. It would be false to describe the relationship of urban anthropology and the urban poor as one of only exploitation. The witness here can play an important role of revealing the social and structural underpinnings of social suffering. Beyond that, my relationships with the women in the daily-rent hotels were more complex and ambivalent than a simplified political economic analysis of poverty would capture or, indeed, support. I was a vulture, an anthropologist seeking information, stories, and photographs to document the everyday suffering in the daily-rent hotels. But I was also an outreach worker, confidant, friend, chauffeur, and sometime "doctor." I did not have the clinical power to aid or cure or the social power to grant better housing or case management. This paradoxical subject position rendered me neutral, involved, and ineffective, by turns. I was present *and* distant. And I always went home at the end of the day, which in my case was to a house I owned fifteen blocks and a world away from the daily-rent hotels.

In a related form of complex vulturism, social relations between daily-rent hotel owners and managers and addicted, pregnant women are characterized by exploitation, care, conflict, and abuse. Occupying the housing status in between government-funded supportive housing and street homelessness, the daily-rent hotels were breeding grounds for poor health, physical suffering, and extreme mental stress for the women who lived in them. Yet the micro practices that occurred in the daily-rent hotels also demonstrated care and concern for the women tenants at times. Examples include allowing the outreach program to work in the hotels, allowing specific women to accrue debt, allowing women to leave their belongings stored at the hotel between temporary evictions. Taking a broader lens, the changing neighborhood also preyed on the women of the daily-rent hotels, as was reflected in increasing policing activity and decreasing social tolerance. Gentrification occurs in urban poor neighborhoods, like the one I studied, because the poverty of the ghetto is both edgy and, at least initially, cheap.[35] Wealthy citizens "eat up" the housing and businesses in the neighborhood because they are "dying"; they become "easy pickings." Ethnographic work in this setting demands a recognition that both the people and the place itself are available for knowledge production, exploitation, and rehabilitation because they are so poor. Can it also enable certain forms of care?

On that September morning, I was searching for the blood because Lexi had asked me to. She wanted me to bear witness to that terrible night: the traumatic series of events that included drug use, violence, and the loss of her baby. I was also searching for the blood because it was material evidence of the specific form of suffering that was happening in this place. Vaginal bleeding here stands in both for what is exceptional to life in the daily-rent hotels—an addicted pregnancy that could lead to a child growing up here—and for what is typical to it: having to continue to prostitute oneself for rent even under conditions of extreme bodily disintegration. Taking and giving are muddled in this scene. Lexi also knows she is helping my research by sacrificing her story to it, I know I am helping her with the $20 loan; we are both made needy and insecure. Yet one of us (me) is so clearly less at risk for terrible consequences as a result. The material conditions of consumption and insecurity at this sight demand an ethical evaluation of this complexity, one in which the vulturistic nature of the science is not eschewed yet the nuances of care, intimacy, love, and friendship are also not ignored. What interests me is the problem presented by holding all these truths, not the naming of only one of them.

Commitment, Writing, and Addicted Pregnancy

There is no question that my multiple attributions (as a public health researcher in the past, as an anthropologist in the present, and as an activist/ volunteer throughout) potentially created multiple social positions for me. These multiple roles, whether chosen by me or compelled upon me in the field, may have played a role in how women reacted to me and the information they shared. What isn't clear to me is how and in what way my multiple social positions changed the information given, and this problem came to inform my writing. I offer one early example, to explore the ways in which a perceived role might simultaneously appear to matter and to not matter. Alexandra, a woman I came to know well during my four years of ethnography, said something ironic to me the day after I had been introduced by the drop-in center staff as "a researcher," with the statement that "we value evaluation, it improves our programs." At the time I stated unequivocally that my project was not an evaluation, but it didn't matter. In some sense all research conducted in service settings, especially critical medical anthropology, one might argue, is evaluative. The following conversation indicates Alexandria's astute observation about my multiple roles, and also how her housing concerns—and my inability to really address her needs (housing)—rendered my "anthro-vulturing," in whatever form, largely irrelevant.

THE WOMEN'S SPACE DROP-IN CENTER. FEBRUARY 2007

I sit at the second table and see Alexandra. Alexandra is a large (three hundred pounds probably) and tall woman with a wide face and a vacant look about her. Her eyes seem overly open wide most of the time. She often sits but doesn't engage much and stares ahead of her.

Many of the women come into the drop-in like a hurricane and create a lot of energy and sometimes disruption. They announce themselves. Not Alexandra. My impression is that she is largely unnoticed, despite her size. I have taken a liking to her, partly because of her easy smile and gentle manner at the site. She doesn't intimidate me like some of the other women do.

When I see Alexandra she says, "You know, you look just like the woman from the other day, the researcher."

"Oh. That was me. You mean yesterday?"

"Yeah, you look just like her. I was thinking."

"Yeah. I am Kelly."

"Yeah. Alexandra. What are you doing here?"

"Well, I volunteer here."

"How can you volunteer and do research?"

"Hm. That's a good question. Well, I am interested in how women are managing their housing and dealing with their health, so that is what my research is about, and I thought Women's Space is a good place to talk to women who are concerned about that, so I come to help out."

"Oh. Can you get me some new housing? Because I have got to make a change!"

"Oh. No. Unfortunately I don't have access to any rooms. I am interested in talking to folks about their housing situations but I am not a case manager. I can't get people housing. Have you talked with Sophia [onsite case manager]? She might be able to help you. Where are you at now?"

"I am at the Omaha [hotel]. It's awful. See, I hear voices. And when I am in my room, I hear them outside and it makes me scared. And Michael, he's next door. He hears them too. We protect each other. But my worker at the hospital said 'Maybe they are real.'"

"Hm. Was he a psychiatrist?"

"Yes, a psychiatrist case worker. He said, 'Well, maybe there are people outside.'"

"What do you think?" I ask.

"I don't know. I don't like it. I feel scared when I close my door."

"That isn't a good feeling. Where would you like to be?"

"Get back on Section 8. Get something better for myself. I would like for Michael and I to go together, because he is scared too. Oh.

Food's up." Alexandra got up immediately to get a tray of food before it was all gone.

Alexandra raised several important concerns. First, she alerted me to the difficulty of marking the boundaries between research, care, and intervention in sites of social suffering. She helped me, early on in my fieldwork, identify the complex social and power relations that would develop between myself and the women. These relations would lead me to feel vulturistic, indebted, intimate, paternalistic, helpless, judgmental, empathetic, and confused over four years. The emotional responses I experienced toward pregnancy and addiction underscored a need for a self-reflective ethical stance—and writing style, in later analytic stages of the project; and a need to eschew completely the role of impartial witness and "write myself in" to the ethnography. It also informed my decision to include longer field notes of interactions with women. These field notes are constructed from verbatim conversations (I always had a recorder going) and reactions and analysis that I also recorded, speaking directly into the tape recorder, while driving home after fieldwork, which allow them to reflect the emotional immediacy of the interactions, as I experienced them.

The inclusion of longer field notes, extensive interactions between myself and my informants, and photographs in this book best captures the complex emotional tone of my four years of ethnography with women in the daily-rent hotels. Situations that often lacked ethical clarity seemed to magnify a deep commitment to demonstrate and document addicted pregnancy. This commitment was often shared between myself and the women with whom I became close. Ramona's initial comment to me after being reminded of her drug-induced state at the Chandra Hotel was: "You should have taken some pictures." This sentiment encapsulates that deep commitment: her showing me, up close, the chaotic challenges of addicted pregnancy, and me being there to capture it, through writing and photographs.

These commitments also carried risk. After much consideration, I have chosen to omit photographs of women (and their children) from this book. All the women gave me signed permission to publish any photographs taken, including those that were identifiable, and these photographs would have lent gravity and added realism to some of my descriptions. However, because many of the women were in ongoing legal cases and family conflicts in relation to their multiple addicted pregnancies, most with very uncertain outcomes, I felt the potential for negative consequences of circulating identifiable images was too great. Some women were angered by their omission and felt that part of their story was "being taken away."[36]

While I have chosen to omit photographs of women, or their children and partners, that are identifiable, I have chosen to reveal the neighborhood and city in which I worked (although all the daily-rent hotels and service agencies have been given pseudonyms). This decision reflects a commitment to bring addicted pregnancy out of the shadows, to not participate in the ways women remain hidden in plain sight. It also serves as a recognition that the Sixteenth and Mission corridor, with its overlapping and conflicting economies, is an important case study in the ways income gaps between the rich and poor are reshaping the US urban map and creating new challenges for civil society, urban development, and urban health. Masking the location would have prohibited me from using many of the newspaper articles and photographs that illustrate important aspects of the story of pregnancy and addiction for women in the daily-rent hotels. However, this is not a book about gentrification, and I do not claim to be doing a thorough ethnographic study of its dimensions and effects in this book. Revealing the site, but protecting its actors, allowed me to stay true to the anthropological veracity of the local while also unanchoring addicted pregnancy from this site to explore aspects of it that extend far beyond San Francisco.

Addicted pregnancy is replete with ambivalent, conflicted, and consequential actions for all the actors involved. The multipolarity of my emotional reactions to addicted pregnancy during my fieldwork mirrored both the conflicted emotional subjectivity of the women I encountered and the larger debates about federal governmental intervention in the reproductive and mothering lives of addicted women. Alexandra's comment helped me initially pay attention to how my ethnographic role produced knowledge while offering very little in immediate amelioration of suffering. The opening scene in Ramona's room reified a repeated experience I had throughout my four-year ethnography, one best described as a strong desire to rescue combined with a frustrated recognition of the insurmountable institutional, social, and personal barriers that addiction and poverty seemed to continually construct.

Placing my moral compass on this contested terrain, I attempt here to situate the ethical within the existential messiness of everyday circumstances and their responses, which are incomplete, made under duress, and often unsatisfactory.[37] In other words, mine is an ethics that is evoked in worlds marked by the scarcity and radical uncertainty of significant structural constraint. Contrary to first assumptions, however, the constraints of scarcity and insecurity do not operate exclusively in the daily-rent hotels that exploit and house pregnant, addicted women. These constraints move up and down the ladders of decision-making and power, permeating the expert speech acts of policy-makers, providers, and scientists who wrestle with naming the intervention, solution, and science that might "solve" addicted pregnancy.[38] In this sense, the ethical commitment of this ethnography is to write against an anthropology of easy enemies in which the tools of ethnographic engagement are wielded to attribute blame and produce affect in a manner that elides nuance and complexity. Critiquing a complex social problem like pregnancy and addiction requires a move away from simplistic categories, yet it cannot ignore the consequences of social policies, relationships, and behaviors that exact a terrible cost.

This study approaches addicted pregnancy as an everyday phenomenon in the lives of unstably housed women, as an object of scientific knowledge, and as a series of social interventions. Both the private, hidden experience of individual reproduction and the public, mediated social problem of addicted pregnancy strain the boundaries of simplistic renderings of subjectivity, science, and the state. Neither emergent neurobiological understandings of addiction nor social explanations contextualizing addiction in traumatic histories, current violence, and extreme poverty prove adequately responsive to the magnitude of the addicted pregnant woman as a social problem in this setting. Indeed, scientific and social explanations compete and collapse in on one another, while the elusive demand for efficacy in intervention remains constant.

In the social reproduction of pregnancy and addiction, a vital politics of viability is always at play. There are medicalized metrics of success offered by clinicians (methadone instead of OxyContin for the uterine environment) and by addicted women (days of infant detoxification after birth as a reflection of maternal achievement). And medicalized metrics of failure: a baby born with NAS, a stillborn baby, a low birth weight. When these metrics become aggregate they are statistics of the percentage of babies with prenatal substance exposure (for epidemiological research and governmental audit) and the percentage born substance-free (for program evaluation and fundraising). When these metrics are influenced by progressive liberal politics, the metric of success is keeping women from becoming Child Protective Services (CPS) cases, that is, keeping women far away from what is perceived as the most ill-informed and draconian form of state intervention for poor women and their babies. There are also metrics that measure the success of social controls: the number of drug treatment graduates and women who attribute their ability to maintain child custody to their undergoing incarceration (in a treatment program or a jail). There are social metrics of failure: addicted, pregnant women who smoke crack while discussing how all the crack babies born in the 1990s are now dangerous, predatory crack dealers with no conscience. In asking the question "What forms of life are possible here?" I seek to understand how a vital politics of viability operates to leverage claims of responsibility and neglect and to produce both hope and hopelessness in individual women and in the interventions designed and funded to respond to addicted pregnancy.

Addicted, pregnant women are biopolitical projects on which social and legal interventions are attempted as pregnant, addicted women travel between environments of drugs and hustling and institutions of care and coercion. Whether biological mechanisms or social-psychological histories are evoked to explain addiction, the path from pregnancy to mothering a child ultimately demands stability and abstinence. Neither the personal nor the social pathway to stability and abstinence was easily attainable for women in the daily-rent hotels. Risk was an organizing principle in the everyday lives of the daily-rent hotels, in how health and social service providers characterized women's traumatized histories, in how epidemiological public health studies categorized their victimization. Women were at risk, and so were their babies, as they sought to survive through addicted pregnancies in the larger landscape of the "risky city"—where homelessness, vice, and the diseases of urban health were perceived as rampant.

In the story of Ramona that opened this chapter, readers might recognize an image they already held of the "pregnant addict": a desperate figure who is both tragic and despised as the embodiment of social failure. Yet the specificity of Ramona's story reveals the harsh realities of housing instability, exploitation, and sex work; the complex personal conflict between a stated desire to quit using drugs and a continual need to respond to cravings; and the ethical conflicts that cause social actors close to pregnancy and addiction to toggle between care and coercion. Pregnancy and addiction in the daily-rent hotels was and is marked by a series of starts and stops, beginnings and endings, which traverse complex ethical terrains as women are forced to occupy the social roles of both victim and perpetrator. Daily-rent hotels emerge as specific sites of consumption and insecurity, in which the conditions of space and place give a concrete stability to the narratives of pregnancy and addiction. These narratives are anchored to a neighborhood, a set of hallways, and a series of rooms where I conducted four years of ethnographic research. The managerial and structural practices in the daily-rent hotels exploit women, but they also keep a roof over the heads of women who remain distal to progressive, liberal experiments in supportive housing. Follow me, then, into the worlds of the daily-rent hotels to see what might be made of the intractable and yet intolerable predicament of addicted pregnancy.

chapter 1. consumption and insecurity

When we first came in from the street, we saw Noah at the top of the stairs. She was really sick and begging the hotel manager's wife to let her through the locked gate. She said, "I really want to visit [number] 36. I have the ten dollars. I'll pay the fee. Just please let me come in." They wouldn't let her come in, and she was really distraught. The manager buzzed us through the doorway. While doing outreach on the floor above, I realized that no. 36 is Trina's room. Trina's room was far enough away from the front desk that Trina, if she was even home, probably didn't hear what was going on. Trina has told me that she's got a lawsuit going [against the hotel] because of them trying to raise the rent. Trina has also told me that the management withholds her mail, and won't tell her when she has visitors. I wondered if they wouldn't let Noah up because she wanted to go to Trina's room. Trina never comes out into the hallway when we are in the hotel.

As we were leaving, we checked in with Noah. She was now on the stairs near the door to the street, and she was crying and shaking. She told me she had cotton fever.[1] I asked her if she was thinking about going to the doctor. She said, "No, it'll pass." I felt her forehead and she was really hot.

Then somebody came through the front door and up the stairs next to us. An older guy, named Marcus. Noah asked if she could pay a fee and stay in Marcus's room for a little while. I think she just needed some time to rest. He ignored her. She said, "Come on, man!" as he bounded up the stairs. Noah said she wasn't sure what her plan was gonna be, "probably the street." She only asked us for wound care supplies. She wouldn't even take a sandwich, she was feeling so sick. It was very sad to leave her crumpled up like that on the hotel stairs. I don't know what ended up happening with her that night.

Consumption and Insecurity

Consumption

- The process of taking food into the body through the mouth (as by eating)
- Pulmonary tuberculosis: involving the lungs with progressive wasting of the body
- (Economics) the utilization of economic goods to satisfy needs or in manufacturing
- The act of consuming something

Insecurity

- The state of being subject to danger or injury
- The anxiety you experience when you feel vulnerable and insecure[2]

These definitions of "consumption" offer images of both gain (as through eating, or consuming) and loss (as through disease wasting, or utilizing goods). The experiences of consumption in the daily-rent hotels contained these same dualities. As Noah's experience attested, the consumption of everything (alcohol, drugs, food) in the daily-rent hotels was governed by the sense of both acquisition and loss. Insecurity reigned—even among women who did not appear emaciated or in active drug withdrawal. There was insecurity about money, drugs, food, cigarettes, housing, and violence. Women frequently described themselves as "starving" and were always "chasing a high," literally down the hallway. When visiting women tenants I would frequently hear the "Slam. Slam." of room doors closing. A woman would knock on a door. Someone would holler from inside, "Who is it?" Then the door would open and slam closed again. Sometimes I viewed this from outside the room (in other rooms or the hallway), sometimes from inside. Either way, the overall atmosphere was one of tension that seemed to pervade the hotel during the late afternoon and early evening, when most tenants were waking up or gearing up for the night ahead. An ironic feature of this tense atmosphere was its repetitive nature. While a low level of chaos came to feel normal and expected, neither I nor the women I spent time with ever felt relaxed. The doors slamming and the constant traffic were both expected and unpredictable. The needs of the women for food, drugs, water, cigarettes, were constant and inconsistently met. I never knew, on meeting a woman, where in the cycle of buildup and release she might be at any given moment.

Despite the whispers and near constant social interaction that characterized

1.1. Lexi's room, Nimish Hotel, June 2008. Photo by the author.

many women's daily lives in the hotels, the hotels did not create a communal environment for the consumption of alcohol, drugs, or food per se. Although women and men would often hole up in rooms to use drugs (especially to smoke crack) together, these were unstable arrangements. They often seemed to depend on which collection of individuals might have landed, or been forced to land, in that particular hallway or room on that particular day. A handful of examples illustrates the random and constantly fluctuating constellations of people, drugs, money, and food that formed life in the daily-rent hotels.

April 2008: I arrive to pick up Lexi at her hotel and find Pano [Lexi's boyfriend] on the stairs. We hang out while Lexi finishes with a (very loud) trick about ten feet down the hallway. "I am gonna make myself scarce, and get something to eat," Pano tells me sheepishly. "She should be done soon." I wait for about ten minutes, the trick leaves, and Lexi and I hang out for a bit. Pano returns with food for Lexi, after about twenty minutes. We all watch a movie together in the room, but people interrupt constantly for stuff: a hit of crack, a cigarette, to convey a message, whatever. Not two minutes goes by without an interruption.

September 2009: Ramona buys some crack after our interview, and we head up to her room for her to get high. After about fifteen minutes, she gets a call on her cell. "Remember that guy that you saw me talking to downstairs for a minute? Well, he wants to come up," she tells me after she hung up. I ask if he is a date, and whether she wants me to disappear for a while. "No. He is just getting a piece [of crack]. I can make some money off of him." She is going to sell him a piece of crack for a higher price but let him hang out in her room while he smokes it, which he does a few minutes later.

October 2009: Lexi and I return to her room. She opens the unlocked door, and a guy is masturbating on her bed to the porno on the TV. "Get the fuck outta here!" she yells. "Don't be like that," he calls back, walking down the hallway, while doing up his pants. "I don't even like that motherfucka!" she tells me after he has left, and we close her door. "He sneaks back [into the hotel], because he is eighty-sixed [barred from renting a room]. I try and be nice, but that ain't cool! [masturbating in her room]," she says, exasperated.

Materiality here is piled up in hotel rooms, the conditions of which are largely invisible to the intersecting social worlds that operate in public, just one floor below. Everyday "stuff" is also necessarily mobile, as women must drag possessions and necessities from daily-rent hotel to daily-rent hotel because they are perpetually displaced. The moral economies of debt that surround the drug-sex economy and the actual financial debts owed on daily-rent hotel rooms create social and physical relations that are unstable. Everyone was seeking something to consume (drugs, food, money for the rent), and constant insecurity bred specific forms of vulnerability. For women in the daily-rent hotels these forms of vulnerability included housing instability, mental and physical health complications, predatory violence, and food insecurity—all of which impacted both drug use and pregnancies. I argue that experiences of consumption and insecurity defined life in the daily-rent hotels, structured risk, and replicated larger debates about the dual, and often competing, demands of pregnancy and addiction.

Persons who are unstably housed are a distinct population whose physical and mental health are inextricably linked to the built environment and housing policies. Understanding the daily-rent hotels as specific ethnographic sites revealed that the term single room occupancy or "SRO" defines certain government policies that have converted private daily-rent hotel stock into publicly managed rooms and buildings for those who are eligible. The conversion of this housing stock and subsequent progressive interventions in the development of supportive housing in San Francisco created housing possibilities for the urban poor that were unfortunately not well matched to the needs of addicted, pregnant women. Even as unstably housed and homeless women were often targets of progressive housing initiatives, pregnancy and later child custody issues complicated their participation in these programs.

Housing Instability and Progressive Interventions

While women navigated their daily lives in the privately owned daily-rent hotels, several experiments in supportive housing were under way in San Francisco.[3] Historically, deinstitutionalization policies in California led to the reintegration of adults with disabling mental illnesses into the community, creating a housing need.[4] Due in part to geographic boundary limitations, housing stock in San Francisco was, and still is, chronically underavailable, which means that large, sprawling housing developments for lower-income single adults and families are not built outside the downtown area (as are,

1.2. Room in a new government-subsidized SRO building. Photo by the author.

for example, the *banlieue* of Paris). Thus, existing housing stock had to be repurposed to meet housing need. During this same period, the voting public and city officials expressed growing concern for the highly visible problem of chronic homelessness on city streets. Finally, public health policies promoting a "Housing First" agenda gained institutional support. Housing First argued that in order to address substance use disorders, respond to mental illness, and promote better health among the unstably housed, stabilization in housing had to be an essential first step. In sum, San Francisco's urban center saw a large growth of both chronically homeless men and women with comorbid mental illness and substance use disorders in need of housing during this period and a need to utilize existing housing stock to meet that need.[5]

The necessity of using existing buildings as sites for housing the burgeoning urban poor created a progressive housing opportunity for San Francisco health policy-makers and also created a parallel economy of privately owned hotels whose living conditions and management practices consistently exploited women tenants. The publicly funded buildings take two forms: (1) previously privately owned buildings whose master lease has been purchased by the City of San Francisco, and (2) new buildings built on the demolished sites of older buildings and in other urban spaces.[6]

1.3. Room in a privately owned daily-rent hotel.
Photo by the author.

During my ethnographic work in San Francisco as an outreach worker, and through several ethnographic projects that were contemporaneous with this one, I have worked extensively in both public and privately managed hotels. Clear differences between these housing settings were apparent. One feature of difference was the illegal practices of the daily-rent hotel owners and the variability in the regulation of these hotels, according to the degree of privatization of the particular hotel. Another difference was the way success, or efficacy, was measured. For the private daily-rent hotel owners, the metric of success is profit—the money garnered from exorbitant daily rental charges. In publicly managed hotels, public sector actors may measure a hotel's effectiveness by aspects of tenants' lives, such as "housing tenure"—the percentage of people who stay housed for at least two years in the same building—or by following indicators of health, such as adherence to prescribed psychotropic and HIV/AIDS medications, and consistency in keeping appointments with case managers, psychiatrists, and physicians. These numbers are then aggregated across buildings and programs as a whole to support ongoing city and state resourcing. Rent in the publicly managed hotels is government-managed and paid monthly. Access to publicly funded rooms is influenced by the health status of an individual and was often health provider–mediated; no such person-based evidentiary markers exist in the world of privately managed hotels. Access to private rooms is conditional on producing an identification card and having the money to cover the rent.

My ethnographic focus was on the private daily-rent hotels because I was interested in exploring the relationship between drug-sex economies and economies of temporary housing. In addition, none of the addicted, pregnant women I worked with successfully transitioned to affordable housing in government-funded hotel rooms during the course of my study.[7] The complex configuration of addiction, interpersonal relationships, entitlements, and mental health contributed to this fact. However, it was equally a by-product of the problematic role of pregnancy in this setting. Women could not return to either the private daily-rent hotels or many government-funded hotel rooms because neither of these were housing sites for families—they were intended to be SRO. Thus while progressive housing initiatives were being implemented in San Francisco, addicted, pregnant women often "fell through the cracks" of these policy effects. To begin to understand this complexity, one needs to explore how SRO hotel rooms and their payment structures are rendered in both policy discourse and on the street.

The "SRO" in Our Political Imagination, in Name, in Actuality

"SRO" does not mean what we—service providers, policy people—think it means. It is a term that is used in government, for policy. It is not a term that really works for the people who rent the actual rooms.
—Member of the Mission SRO Collaborative (October 2009)

The most direct rendering of the term "single room occupancy" is that only one person may occupy each room. There seems to be agreement that a "typical SRO is a single 8x10 foot room with shared toilets and showers down the hallway."[8] From the perspective of the epidemiological categorization, and in official language, privately owned daily-rent hotels would be included under the term "SRO." This is, in part, an artifact of history. Single room occupancy hotels began as temporary housing for low-wage workers and migratory laborers.[9] While rooms might well have been occupied by more than one person, they were not specifically intended for families or single women.

Currently the blurring between public and private management of individual hotel rooms and buildings makes "SRO" terminology problematic. Deeming a hotel, or a hotel room, an "SRO" because of its physical characteristics and layout does not reveal the important detail of how it is paid for, either daily, weekly, or monthly. All "SRO" rooms do not reflect an equal economic burden on their occupants. When progressive supportive housing movements began to take over the master lease on "SRO" buildings and rooms in buildings in order to manage them publicly, rents were stabilized at 30 percent of the occupant's income. Because the two managerial types—private verses public—had two divergent markers of success, these hotels were managed differently. Supportive housing hotel rooms did not have any daily or weekly rent and offered varying degrees of social and physical health services support onsite. Success in these programs was evidenced by persons staying housed, consistent with the original intention of the public takeover: to expand housing affordability in a geographic environment of chronic housing shortage and widespread housing instability among the urban poor. Privately managed buildings, running on a profit model, measured success by counting rooms filled.

My misunderstanding of this differentiation helped to explain why I had expected, when first approaching the "SRO" hotels I studied, to find their rental populations fairly stable. I had assumed the majority of the rooms (even in the private hotels) would be filled with welfare-entitled or other entitled renters because their access to a government subsidy ensured consistent rent payment, which I presumed to be desirable to hotel managers and owners. But this was only the reality for publicly funded hotels. Welfare-entitled clients, specifically tenants with access to Supplemental Security Income (SSI), could incur some portion of the rent cost, which balanced some of the cost of providing affordable housing. For private hotels, however, daily renters were a source of exceedingly more profit than welfare-entitled tenants who paid lower, negotiated weekly and monthly rates. Private hotels thus were run as de facto brothels, gouging renters and their visitors for fees, so that the notion of "single" occupancy at any particular moment was comical at best.

I learned that women were keenly aware of economic differences between publicly owned and private hotels, and some, like Ramona in the field note below, do not see the daily-rent hotels as "SROs." Whatever cachet the term had in relation to public subsidies, the SRO, according to Ramona, had little in common with the daily-rent hotel.

"THAT DUMP ISN'T AN SRO, I HAVE TO PAY DAILY."
SEPTEMBER 2009.

I meet Ramona in front of the Nisha Hotel. She is "starving" and eats the sandwich that I had brought for my lunch. She thinks the hummus is weird but good. She has never tried hummus before. She is seven months pregnant.

"I got an SRO," she tells me. "You are already in an SRO," I say, indicating the Nisha behind us. "That dump isn't an SRO, I have to pay daily," she quips, annoyed at my obvious ignorance. "People call it an SRO," I retort. "Well it isn't. If you pay daily it isn't an SRO. If you can pay for two [adult] people, it isn't an SRO," she barks back. "I got an SRO, a room at the European (Hotel). And I can keep my baby there [after the baby is born]."

"When do you move in?" I ask.

"I don't know. I have to talk to the case manager, deal with the paperwork. You got anything else to eat?"

Ramona points out that in the daily-rent hotels, with extra pay a renter can have more than one person sleep in his or her room. This is demonstrative of the fact that one is paying daily. If you have access to an SSI entitlement and have a monthly rental arrangement, then you are not allowed to house another person in your room. Having an extra renter or tenant paid for with SSI funds is illegal from a governmental perspective because the SSI benefits are linked to the mental and or physical health disability of the beneficiary, not to one's girlfriend, boyfriend, brother, or running buddy. Ultimately this links back to the evidentiary basis on which this system depends. Disability welfare entitlement cannot be shared because it is linked to the individual to whom it is granted. For this reason, persons who have housing benefit entitlements are monitored, and hotels (even privately owned ones) are supposed to enforce the "single" in SRO or risk possibly losing their payee status.

In fact, the term "SRO" could reference both privately owned daily-rent hotels (which are sites of illegal gendered exploitation) and publicly governed housing (which serve as sites of progressive housing policy implementation). Ramona's protest to me, to the contrary, was that if she was paying for her room with her SSI, and it was garnered through a governmental case management apparatus, then it was an SRO. If she hustled for the daily rent, it was not. These distinctions are not simply about linguistics. Many women (and men) lose access to entitlements and face eviction if it is discovered that they are harboring another person in their entitlement-subsidized room. Those who have subsidized "SRO" rooms have limited "overnights"—nights in which partners, friends, children, or others are allowed to stay the night without jeopardizing an entitlement benefit and risking the loss of housing. This limitation led Ramona to not pursue the "paperwork" she would need in order to garner the subsidized SRO room she mentioned. Although her baby could have roomed there with her, Duke, her partner and the baby's father, would not have been allowed to legally live with them under the conditions of the public housing allotment. She chose to put herself on a waiting list at a family shelter instead, a shelter spot for which she never became eligible postpartum. Ramona's experience points to the messy problem of housing, public support, and family eligibility in an environment where what she considered the best option was the most exploitative.

Daily-Rent Hotels as Spaces of Illegality and Debt

"THE BUSINESS." FEBRUARY 2008

Jackie was right outside the Grey Hotel, so I asked her how the Grey was. She said she liked it because the guy [the manager] ran "a really tight ship" and he was really strict. I asked about visiting fees, and this is what she described. She said, "If you lay down sixty bucks it's forty-five for the room, [the manager will say] 'plus five bucks for your late fee from last week, plus five bucks for your move-out fee, plus ten bucks for your stained pillow.' And so you have to be really careful to lay down just exactly the amount of money that you want to pay because he'll keep all the money and not give you any change based on whatever you give." The manager charged her $10 for taking a "too long" shower. He charges $5 for visiting [to bring a trick up to her room], but it's random when he's going to charge it, and he gets to decide how long visitors stay. Jackie says, "I like it 'cause it's got this controlled environment." She told me she thought it was safe, because the manager is such a cop about charging fees. But she was joking about it, she wasn't pissed, and she said it was just part of "the business." The trick is to be savvy enough to pay him the right amount of money if you didn't want to get ripped off. She gets two free visits a night [in which tricks do not have to pay extra visiting fees to hotel managers] if her rent is on time. To Jackie it was all about knowing the rules, but she described the rules as—her word—"inconsistent." She said, "He's [the manager's] totally inconsistent."

To housing policy-makers efficacy is measured by extended housing tenure of tenants in supportive housing; these tenants are often dually or triply diagnosed and usually engaged in health care. The metric that measures efficacy in the daily-rent hotels is money: cold, hard cash. A room can be rented if one has money to pay, and a valid form of identification. Otherwise, one is out on the street. Private hotels may have offered credit to some of the women I studied, but that debt eventually had to be paid. The insecurity of indebtedness produced risk for the women in their illegal activities, when they were frequently harassed to "get outside" (engage in sex work to pay for rent) by hotel management. Abstract behavioral constructs such as "sex work" lost their meaning, unless they were linked directly to the women's housing status.[10] The economic exploitation of the women in the daily-rent hotels was dependent on the built environment (the hotel itself) functioning as a de facto brothel, such that the hotel managers and owners made a profit off of the women's work. Hotel managers charged women fees for each "visitor" and regularly verbally harassed women and intimated them into engaging in sex work or risk eviction. The following field note excerpt provides further examples of the constraints of debt and sex work in the daily-rent hotels.

DALY HOTEL. MARCH 2008

The Daly Hotel is usually pretty mellow 'cause only Luisa's staying there. Now Cupcake and Marlena are there too, two kind of new women to this hotel. Usually Luisa's on her own. I heard the hotel manager screaming at Luisa, "You better get out there and make some money because you need some money." She was really mellow about being yelled at. Luisa's usually really pretty intense, rushing around and yelling, totally manic. But she was mellow. She was like, "Okay." Very submissive to the manager's yelling for her to get outside and start hustling [as a sex worker]; I thought this was unusual for her. Maybe she can't afford to get him angry with her.

The women frequently faced the fear of eviction from the hotels, which could lead to street homelessness and arrest by the police on solicitation charges. From hotel to hotel the application of charges for visitors, the extension of credit, and level of harassment by management varied—but not predictably enough to safeguard women in certain daily-rent hotels. All the daily-rent hotels in which I worked functioned as brothels, albeit with erratic degrees of arbitrary cruelty. It is important to note that Jackie's assessment of the exploitation as part of "the business" was absolutely correct. While I witnessed hotel managers harassing women and hostility between the managers and the women was frequent, it was hardly ever personal. It was about the rent. Indebted women would be targeted for more intense forms of harassment. When rent was paid, relations were friendlier in the hotels, or at least not fraught with conflict. However, because of addiction, debt, and exploitation, rents were rarely paid easily or on time.

The daily-rent hotels' metric of cash was inextricably bound to the gendered drug-sex economy, as was visually represented to me in the form of an edited sign posted on the door of the Chandra Hotel. The Chandra, like many daily-rent hotels, tried lowering its daily rates when the national economy entered a downturn in January 2009. The hotels also began, for the first time since I had begun my ethnography, to advertise not just vacancies but lower rates. Daily-rent hotel rooms that had cost as much as $45–50 in January 2008 had dropped to $35/night one year later. On one of the signs, someone had changed the lettering. Instead of reading "Daily Rate $35" it read "Daily Rape $35," poignantly capturing how violating the hotels can be for women managing the stress of addiction, sex work, and debt.

All the hotels had "gatekeepers," in addition to hotel managers. In the private daily-rent hotels the gatekeepers were often men in their twenties who would sit behind a heavy clear plastic window. These men had to buzz a visitor or tenant in through the door at street level. After being buzzed in, the person climbed the stairs and was interrogated on the first floor landing about

1.4. Chandra Hotel, January 2009. Photo by the author.

his or her presence in the hotel. These interactions were not overly intimidating, but they often had the hostile feel of an official checkpoint interrogation: no one was getting by the gatekeeper without an explanation, or some money for rent or a visiting fee. Even the police who occasionally raided the hotels checked first with management, often calling to announce their impending arrival. This forewarning allowed hotel managers to privilege certain guests with a warning that the police would soon arrive or were on the premises. Other guests got "hung out to dry" without a warning, especially if they had garnered disfavor with the management. Some of the gatekeepers worked in multiple hotels on the same blocks. The young male gatekeepers at some hotels were on the Internet and barely raised their heads in acknowledgment when we arrived to conduct outreach (not the case if I arrived by myself). At some hotels, children as young as six or seven years old would be in charge of the door buzzer, but a parent or relative was never very far away. In one hotel, it was not unusual to see several kids behind the glass, some on computers, some doing paper-and-pencil homework assignments, while all the action of the drug economy was unfolding on the landing above and a short distance down the hallway. Seeing young children in close proximity to drug deals and sex work negotiations helped to explain why the hotel owners and managers

1.5. Gatekeeper's desk, Grey Hotel. The board to the right of the desk displays a long list of hotel rules. August 2008. Photo by the author.

did not want the children or infants of tenants living in these hotels. This fact also left addicted, pregnant women with very limited housing options once their babies were born.

Hotel managers often lived in the hotels with extended family members in a section cordoned off from the other tenants. The hotel managers and staff seemed to know most of the women by first name in this three-by-three-block corridor. One reason for this familiarity was that the women were deliberately shuffled between hotels in order to deny them tenancy rights. This is a policy known as a "twenty-one-day." Technically illegal in San Francisco, the policy was widely practiced in the hotels in which I worked. Once a renter had occupied a room for over thirty days he or she would automatically gain residency status, and with that status the tenant became harder to evict. Hotel managers required that individuals move out for two to three days when they approached the thirty-day limit, usually after about twenty-one days of renting a room. The "twenty-one-day" is also referred to as "musical rooming," in reference to the children's game of musical chairs. In the daily-rent hotel version, everyone gets displaced, and often someone ends up without a room (homeless) and out of the game. If they had a congenial relationship, the hotel management would sometimes offer to store a woman's belongings while she was not occupying a room, or make promises to return the tenant to the same room after the necessary hotel rotation had taken place.

Few women felt it was worth it to fight a twenty-one-day request, often because they were fearful of making relations more strained with hotel management. The management could mete out privileges and punishments in overt and subtle ways to express their displeasure about the hassles a woman might be causing them. Suddenly, debts could be called in, the boyfriend who was just home from prison could become unwelcome, the rent could increase, or the hot water could be turned off. The constant displacement and resettlement to a new hotel meant the woman had to renegotiate social relationships and quickly become abreast of the drug and sex work politics in order to get her needs met in a new setting. However, this was often preferred to the more systemic discriminatory punishments that might await a tenant activist who protested a twenty-one-day eviction.

The relationships between hotel managers and gatekeepers and the women renters were inflected with racist, classist commentary that flowed in both directions. For example, one hotel manager disclosed to me: "I no longer rent to black women." I have documented hotel management being openly hostile toward women who were very physically sick, yelling at them and kicking them out of the hotel on multiple occasions. Frustrations over the daily exposure to drug use and sex work was frequently expressed by hotel management and gatekeepers, even as these same persons appeared to gain financially from these same behaviors.

I have heard many rumors forwarded by women tenants about the owners and the families that manage the daily-rent hotels. These rumors were sometimes spoken to support racist rhetoric, sometimes to underscore the rationale for management's brutal behavior, and sometimes to convey empathy and solidarity. For example, it was rumored that the hotel owners imported managers from India, had them trained to be tough on drug users and sex workers in their hotels in Los Angeles, and then had them come to San Francisco to work. It was rumored that the managers were paid no salary other than visiting fees so that they were encouraged to run the hotels like brothels— because they too were being economically exploited by the owners. It was rumored that one owner of many of the hotels, whom many women knew and had interacted with, had a very powerful lawyer against whom one could never win an eviction case. It was rumored that all the management families were "low caste" and working as managers in the hotels in San Francisco was an improvement on what their lives would have been in India. Although I documented consistent gendered exploitation of women in the daily-rent hotels, the rumors and other witnessed interactions supported the interpretation that the hotel managers were the adjudicators of these structural discriminations while not profiting to the same degree as the owners. Hence, sentiments of conflict and occasional solidarity passed between women and managers, particularly if managers balanced privileges with punishments.

The hotels made a tremendous amount of money from charging renters daily, accruing renter debt, and charging clients of sex workers visitor fees. Charging visiting fees, like musical rooming, was and is illegal in the city of San Francisco, yet it was widely practiced in the hotels in which I conducted participant observation. This is how it worked: a woman rented a room for the day, paying $50. Every trick she brought into the room had to pay the manager a $10 fee to visit, plus pay for the cost of the sexual service. The cost of the service varied by a variety of factors, including the price of specific sex acts, how much the sex worker thought she could charge the trick, the degree of desperation of the sex worker, the pressure of needing to share a cut of her profits with "third parties," and how the sex worker was feeling mentally and physically at that moment (dope-sick, depressed, energetic, exhausted).[11] While a tenant in a government-subsidized hotel room paid on average $500/month for a room, a sex worker, caught in this daily-rental hotel arrangement, would pay $350/week. Assuming only five tricks a night, another $350/week in visiting fees was garnered from her labor for the hotel. She kept whatever money was gained from the sex work, minus her rent, payouts to others, and money for drugs, food, and any other necessities. The relationship between the hotel managements and the women engaged in sex work in their hotels reflected a mutually dependent yet exploitative labor market. This could be equally applied to women who were dealing drugs out of daily-rent hotel rooms in which buyers could be charged visiting fees, although I witnessed much less of this type of charging.

The everyday economic reality of women in the daily-rent hotels was one of perpetual indebtedness. The message from hotel management posted to tenants of the Visha Hotel, "Please Be Good, Don't Ask For Money Loan," offered one indication of the way structural policies in the daily-rent hotels contributed to a moral economy of strained social relationships and everyday tension between the women and the managers, and between the tenants. Debts were often called in by hotel management, but different women were able to negotiate different lines of credit with their hotels. Some hotels were known to be more lenient about letting women accrue debt. Other hotels were

1.6. Message from the hotel management, Visha Hotel, January 2008. Photo by the author.

very strict, and still others seemed arbitrary in their decisions. For example, on a single floor of one hotel, on a single night, it was not unusual to have one woman struggling to find enough tricks to pay down her hotel debt and avoid a night outside, another woman unfazed by owing the hotel several hundred dollars, and yet another woman calling in the debts of others (boyfriends and friends) to pay down her own debt to the hotel. Hotel management would also often "employ" the women to clean bathrooms or work the front desk, sometimes in exchange for paying down debts. In several cases, it appeared that women were feeling threatened that they would lose favor with the hotel management and performed this labor in addition to paying approximately $50/day in rent, and even when they were not in debt. Women were frequently intimidated by hotel management and fearful of their arbitrary actions. I witnessed heated verbal exchanges, curses, and name calling back and forth, but these were typically more show than action. Women who were overly angry with the hotel management ran the risk of getting kicked out of the hotels with all of their possessions thrown out for others to rummage through on the street out front. On the other side of the equation, I also frequently witnessed women spending all the money they had for rent on drugs and then expressing anger at hotel managers for demanding the rent.

The conditions of the hotels, and their individual rooms, varied from unsanitary to outright dangerous. None of the rooms had bathrooms, and most looked like the two pictured here (figs. 1.7 and 1.8): stained walls, dirty, broken furniture, chipped and peeling paint, often with bloodstains and graffiti on the walls. Most rooms had terrible infestations of bedbugs, rats, and mice—there were flies everywhere and often garbage in the hallway, along with broken TVs, dirty bed sheets, old mattresses, and other odds and ends.

Women faced the stress of rental debt, of imminent displacement from a twenty-one-day eviction, and street homelessness. The living conditions of the daily-rent hotels also produced stress, manifesting itself in sleeplessness, hypervigilance, and near-constant anxiety. Bathrooms were often occupied for sex work, and rooms were often shared (against hotel policy) to save money and reduce debt. This could mean a woman slept on the floor, or chose not to sleep at all during the nighttime hours when sex work was most frequent and lucrative. The cumulative effect of the structural policies and physical conditions of the daily-rent hotels, in combination with active drug addiction, contributed to poor mental health and frequent health complications.

Doctoring Women in the Daily-Rent Hotels

Physical and mental health outcomes are uniformly worse for homeless persons than for their housed counterparts.[12] Interestingly, epidemiological studies have generally failed to capture the physical and mental health consequences related to specific housing types. There are several reasons for this. The first is that definitions of homelessness can often vary from study to study. Some studies deploy the label "homeless" not just for persons living on the street, or even only in a public shelter, but also for persons using daily-rent hotels for part or all of the month, but without stable housing beyond each day of rental payment. This is not always the case, though. Researchers sometimes want to compare the effect of sleeping inside—even in a daily-rent hotel—to outside. Then those women who are housed in daily-rent hotels become "housed," while women on the street and in shelters are labeled "homeless." To further blur the categories, some epidemiological studies use the terminology "homeless," "sheltered," and "housed"; others categorize per-

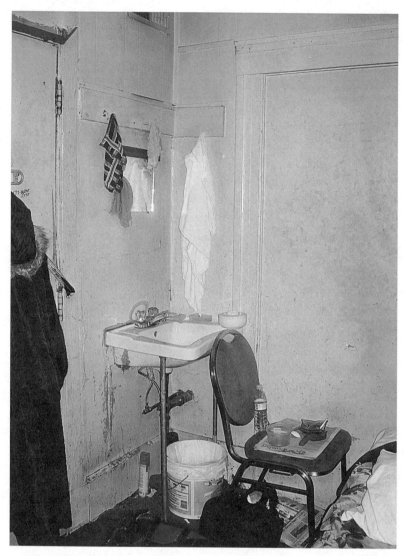

1.7. Room in the Daya Hotel. Cost if paying daily: $1400/month. November 2007. Photo by the author.

1.8. Floor stained and eaten away from a bedbug infestation. The carpet has been pulled up. Raman Hotel, October 2009. Photo by the author.

sons as "permanently housed" versus "transitionally housed" in their comparisons. Despite this lack of categorical uniformity, the epidemiological data is consistent: any way that "homelessness" is operationalized scientifically, it is extremely unhealthy.[13]

What was clear ethnographically was that the women in the daily-rent hotels, like Noah, whose cotton fever opened this chapter, often eschewed health care services unless they considered themselves in critical condition.[14] Some women worried that their health concerns would be dismissed by medical providers if they were identified as drug users, through their own disclosure or through documentation on a previous medical record. Problematic relationships to health care institutions provided some explanation for why addicted, pregnant women largely avoided prenatal care once their pregnancies were discovered. Kitt described her experience after my prompting her to see a doctor.

I am walking down Mission Street, and I catch up with Kitt, whom I haven't seen in a month. I ask, "How have you been? I haven't seen you for a while."

"I was in jail. I caught a [prostitution] case. Now I am back and my lip is fucked up. It won't heal right. Look at it. Do you think its staph?"

I take a look. Her upper lip is split and swollen. It looks like it might have scabbed over and then she picked it open again. "I don't know," I say. "I am not a doctor. But you should go have it looked at if you are worried."

"Yeah." A woman who has walked up to us agrees. "Staph don't do that. Staph's all over [your body]."

Kitt says: "I can feel something moving in there. Side to side. Like a worm. It is like there is something in there. Do you think there is, or am I just trippin'?" she asks.

"You might be just trippin'. I don't know. I am not a doctor," I say, looking at it.

"What happened?" I ask.

"Some girl punched me, split my lip, over some dope. It was payback," she states matter-of-factly.

The next day, I see her again. She says, "I went to the doctor, like you said. They told me it was '*nothin'*.' They didn't even give me any cream or anything. They just thought I was a crackhead. I spend a bunch a time in the ER for nothin'."

During my participant observation in the daily-rent hotels, I was routinely called upon to fulfill the role of "doctor." Often the role of doctor involved being asked advice about whether a condition—frequently an STD or a wound—necessitated a visit to the hospital. Even when some form of medical intervention seemed imminent, women were reluctant to access care unless it was deemed absolutely necessary. This was not because they wanted to wait until infections reached the point that they would be guaranteed a hospital stay. Rather, women feared losing their rooms in the daily-rent hotels, their livelihood (if they were selling drugs or doing sex work), and their possessions should they require hospitalization. Stacy made this clear to me when I suggested that she might need to go to the wound clinic for an abscess that was causing a fever: "If I go in [to the hospital] they are going to keep me on a [antibiotic] drip for two days. I know it. Who is going to move all this stuff [drugs she needs to sell]?" she asked me. Another woman, Maria, ended up in the hospital at the same time as her husband. He had endocarditis, and she had a lung infection. She told me that even though they were gone a week from their hotel room, the management would not offer them a discount. "We had to pay $50 every day [when we were in the hospital]!! Even though we have lived here for years!" she remarked.

Pragmatically, women sought out my doctoring services for temporary treatment. On my part, this involved attempting to clean and bandage wounds with gauze and medical tape that we provided on our outreach shifts. My aid was often a mere extension of the self-doctoring practices women routinely engaged in to avoid formal institutions of care, to keep working, and to maintain housing. Abscesses, the most common wound, were treated by women themselves or by other women, but if this was too difficult or inconvenient I might be asked to help out. One evening, a woman beckoned me into her room because she was trying to clean a deep bite puncture that she had received on the back of her neck during a drug fight with another woman. On another day, just before we left for Anita's child custody hearing, an abscess on her back shoulder opened up and started to bleed. I was able to quickly clean and bandage the wound with the supplies she had in her hotel room, so she could put on a jacket for the trip to the courtroom. Crysanne's experience offered another example.

CRYSANNE'S HOSPITAL VISIT. SEPTEMBER 2008

As we walk down the hallway, Crysanne's door opens. I can hear the noise of several other women inside, but the door is only opened a little. Crysanne says she is "always taking care of everyone." The man across the hall, whom Crysanne openly dislikes, has been banging on her door to get her to come out for a couple of minutes. "The girls [outreach team] are here, get the bandages. The girls are here," he repeats, yelling at the door. "OK, OK," she yells back.

"Do you have the good ones [bandages]?" she asks. "I can barely walk." She is on the floor, on her knees. Her ankles, lower calves, and feet are bandaged and covered with a pair of the white tube socks that we pass out sometimes. She says, "It's really bad. I don't know what

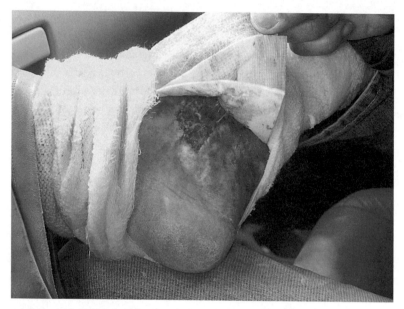

1.9. Crysanne's infected ankle, outside the Bridgit Hotel, April 2008.
Photo by the author.

to do. I am taking a bottle of ibuprofen a day for the pain. I don't think
that is good for my liver."

"Look at it," she says. She takes off one of her bandages, as she
usually does, to reveal the bloody, pus-filled open wounds on both her
ankles.

"Do you want me to take you in [to the hospital]?" I ask. "We could
go to [the public hospital's wound clinic]. I can pick you up so you don't
have to walk there."

"No. No. I am afraid they are going to take my legs. They are always
threatening to operate. They're the reason I have this shit, because of
those crazy antibiotics they put me on."

I ask her what she means. She says she was treated at the hospital for an infection from an abscess with an antibiotic that was being
tested in a clinical trial. She walked out of hospital before the trial was
over. Later, she says, she received a letter indicating that the medicine
caused "diabetes, coma, and death," and she was asked if she wanted
to sue. "I ignored this, of course," she says.

"Now, I think that is why I can't heal, that's why my feet won't heal.
My immune system is shot. I have no immune system. Any infection I

have won't heal. And this place has bugs everywhere. Terrible. Look at all the marks on my arms."

Crysanne shows me the small bumps on her arms as she is scratching them. She says, "The medical people always think we are just picking, but it is the parasites around here." Crysanne is referring to the itching and picking of scabs that people on crack and methamphetamine will often have, which sometimes get dismissed in medical settings. Everyone in her hotel complains about the bugs, even urging us not to sit down in the hallway or on the beds while we are doing outreach, for fear we might catch them too.

"And did I tell you? I am not paying rent. My sink doesn't work. I can't even brush my teeth. And I have told them so many times to move me [to another room on the same floor]. I can't sleep, because that crazy motherfucker is up screaming and yelling on crack all night long." Crysanne is referring to the guy across the hall who is now bouncing up and down on his bed, with his door open, staring at us while we are talking. "They won't move me. They said no, even though the hotel is half empty. Fuck them. What would you do?" she asks me, directly. I am not sure how to answer; despite the bugs, I don't know what will happen if she is kicked out of her hotel room.

Frustrated, she asks for more bandages, and we move on down the hallway.

The following week, I run into Crysanne on the street. She has been evicted for not paying rent. She is staying with one of her children in a nearby neighborhood. She told me she went to the doctor to try and get some pain medication for her feet.

"The woman I saw was like twenty-five," she frowns. "I'm in my sixties. I have been out here [on the street] a long time, taking care of myself. They told me [years ago] that I was going to lose my legs, that they had to operate. Look at me now, I am walking."

"Getting away from the bugs in those nasty hotels has helped," she says. "Anyway, I tell the girl, the doctor, I say, 'You going to give me some of the good medication, the stuff that really heals what I have?' Because they had given it me once, remember I told you. I healed right away. The doctor told me maybe at the end of the visit. And she wouldn't give me pain meds. I just left. I said, 'You don't waste the good stuff on people like me, do you?'"

For eighteen months, Crysanne needed to clean and bandage the severely infected wounds on her ankles, which did not heal until she moved out of the daily-rent hotel. Many health care providers I interviewed also indicated their frustration with attempting to treat wounds and infections in the presence of ongoing stimulant use. One clinician told me: "Patients who use crack all the time don't heal. It is terrible for them and it is terrible for us. And they pick, so the surface skin wounds don't heal either. It is practically the mark of stimulant abuse." In Crysanne's situation it is difficult to distinguish between health problems exacerbated by drug use and those induced by the conditions of her daily-rent hotel. Crysanne's self-care strategies, her worries about the health problems caused by the conditions in her daily-rent hotel, and her hospital visits provide an example that is emblematic of many women's interactions with housing and health care institutions.

Residential Transience and Food Insecurity

The women were rarely found in the same daily-rent hotels from week to week. Multiplying the number of women I knew (approximately seventy-five) who regularly rented rooms in daily-rent hotels by the number of available rooms (roughly three hundred) conveys a sense of the possible combinations of people who could end up on any hallway on any given day. As a result, new social arrangements were constantly being established, dismantled, and re-established throughout the week. This changing social configuration caused moments of tension and solidarity between women while also heightening the overall levels of insecurity. No one, including the other women on a floor, me, or the hotel management, really knew who was going to turn up, with what to offer, or with what demands.

"Residential transience" is a public health construct derived from research among the homeless that has recently gotten some attention. Residential transience argues that the disruption of changing housing situations may be as significant a factor in housing-related poor health outcomes as the location itself (e.g., public shelter, street, daily-rent hotel). Residential transience could be precipitated by a forced eviction after twenty-one days of tenancy, which often led to displacement from one daily-rent hotel to another, or a housing downgrade from a daily-rent hotel to street homelessness. This epidemiological framing has its contextual appeal. It matches more closely with the experience of housing disruption on the ground, in my ethnographic experience. The women cycled through multiple forms of housing throughout the year, with the level of residential transience being extremely high between the daily-rent hotels, creating specific forms of disruption to daily life. In this way women not only followed the "institutional circuit" through jail, treatment center, shelter, flophouse (daily-rent hotel), street, and hospital that Kim Hopper so astutely identified in his ethnographic work; they also followed the daily-rent brothel circuit, moving and being moved from hotel to hotel constantly as a result of a twenty-one-day eviction by hotel managements, accrual of debt that could not be repaid, and/or interpersonal conflict and rule breaking.[15]

The epidemiological research on residential transience indicates that it increases depressive symptoms, especially for women, even after homelessness, as one form of transience, is taken into account.[16] Residential transience has also been linked to injection-related HIV risk behaviors, when studied by the same group of researchers.[17] Lexi provided one example of the links between sadness, risk, and housing transience after her eviction from her daily-rent hotel:

LEXI'S EVICTION. MAY 2008

Lexi is outside. She got evicted from the Daya. She went to go dose [to her methadone treatment program], and when she got back the sheriff was there. She was so upset. She was crying, and she said she was "regressing." She said she doesn't want to go back to a time when she had to "wear two or three pairs of pants" [because she was sleeping on the street]. But last night she did it because she was so cold. It was really hard to see her so down when she's such a strong person. She hasn't been street homeless in a long time. She talked about having to do car dates [sex work in tricks' cars] even though she doesn't want to and it's not safe and she can't make that much money. But there it is. That's what she's gotta do to get herself back inside. But first she needs an ID, which was stolen while she was sleeping outside. She was looking for Wisdom, who is holding Lexi's ID. Lexi has spread her documentation out between like four or five people on the street, so if something happens and her stuff gets lost, somebody has a backup copy, in case she can earn rent for a room in one of the daily-rent hotels.

As "residential transience" is gaining purchase as an epidemiological categorization that may better capture the experience of housing instability and its health effects, one must ask: why? This shift may reflect the frustration that even after years of epidemiological studies of homelessness and its effects, it is still problematic to compare evidence between studies because the construct ("homelessness") is unstable. Another possible contribution is the effect of the globalization of public health. Many quantitative researchers who specialize in injection drug use, HIV/AIDS, and urban health began to work outside the United States when injection drug use–related HIV epidemics surfaced in the late 1990s and early 2000s, in places such as Thailand, China, India, Russia, and Eastern Europe. Connections that might have otherwise not gained traction were made between the ill-health effects of "internal displacement" (a World Health Organization concept, which is used a great deal in refugee/migration health to refer to health results of war, conflict, natural disaster, or political repression) and US domestic homelessness. "Residential transience" offered a different way to measure homelessness, by assessing the experience of displacement, or housing disruption. It offered a more globally informed construct for managing the relationship between sociostructural risks for disease and environmental instability.[18]

The relationship between place and violence has also been examined from an epidemiological perspective, comparing the effects of both housing type and residential transience. Margot Kushel and her colleagues conducted research with unstably housed women in San Francisco and found what many women in my ethnography corroborated: being outside is typically more dangerous than anything that might happen in a daily-rent hotel.[19] This does not mean that the hotels are safe; they are merely safer than being on the street. Compared to the risk of "abject homelessness"—literally sleeping on the street, camping out under a bridge, or sleeping in a car—the daily-rent hotels were eminently safer for women. They offered the women a measure of safety from attack and robbery because they conceivably provided a door that a woman could lock, and bathrooms with showers, which offered women sex workers the opportunity to clean up and negotiate better paying dates. Hotels may have offered the potential for a reduction of violent sex work encounters because of close, neighboring witnesses—like Pano staying on the stairs just outside while Lexi was with a date. Hotels, particularly daily-rent hotels, may exact a cost for that added perception of security, however. Women in larger qualitative cohort studies have reported that the crowding, chaos, and instability in these hotels can trigger mental health symptoms such as hypervigilance, disordered sleep, social withdrawal, and anxiety.[20] These symptoms, many of which are associated with PTSD, might be protective for reducing violent encounters.[21] But they also take an emotional toll.

Yet another construct from global public health appears to be traveling with epidemiologists from the global South to the inner-city North: "food insecurity." The role of "food insecurity" (what anthropologists often theorize as "hunger") has gained momentum as a factor to be measured and assessed among unstably housed urban poor populations in the United States.[22] Much research has concentrated especially on HIV-positive persons who are part of the US urban poor, perhaps because research in Africa has shown a considerable effect of food insecurity on HIV treatment success and mortality rates.[23] Research conducted in San Francisco among HIV-positive homeless and marginally housed individuals reported that "among 250 participants, over half (53.6%) were food insecure. Higher odds of food insecurity were associated with being white, low CD4 counts, recent crack use, lack of insurance, and worse physical and mental health."[24] Similar results have been shown among crack smokers who are HIV-positive in Atlanta and Miami and among families with young children, especially when the mother is experiencing mental health problems.[25]

In a large study, the "Prenatal Risk Overview" (PRO), of factors that contribute to poor birth outcomes, 1,386 prenatal patients were screened at four community health clinics. The results indicated a strong overlap between housing instability, food insecurity, depression, and drug and alcohol use: "The PRO classified 48% at moderate or high risk for housing instability; 32% for food insecurity; 75% for lack of social support; 7% for intimate partner violence; 9% for other physical/sexual abuse; 18% for depression; 23% for cigarette use, 23% for alcohol use, and 25% for drug use."[26] The material facts of food insecurity among addicted, pregnant women point toward a significant problem of unmet basic needs that has also been identified among unstably housed women in general.[27] These facts also numerically capture a biological marker that researchers of the outcomes of prenatal drug exposures on infants and children assess through an "adversity index." The "adversity index," which includes a range of sociostructural and personal measurements, such as degree of poverty and mental health status, seeks to capture the role of the environment outside the uterus on uterine stress.[28] This sophisticated research asks questions about both illicit drug exposures and exposures to a variety of environmental stressors that could impact fetal growth and development, such as food insecurity.

1.10. Ramona's room. Cell phone, crack pipe, biohazard bucket, and needles. Very little food. Robert Hotel, August 2009. Photo by the author.

Every ethnographic conversation I conducted was prefaced by the offer of food, even if it was just gum. While we also provided food on outreach shifts, I began coming to do fieldwork with tangerines, granola bars, nuts, and cookies. Any food I could find that might be easily carried was placed in my bag with my tape recorder and camera as I headed out for a day of fieldwork, moving with the women from the street up into their rooms and back out onto the street. My descriptions of the importance of healthy food, and its lack, appeared in a very early field note about an outreach shift:

OUTREACH. NISHA HOTEL. JUNE 2007

We had a food bag with peanut butter and jelly sandwiches and juice boxes, and chocolate. Ruth [another outreach worker] told me about how her first thing she had tried to change in the outreach program was the food that we give out—to make it more nutritious. Then her first night out, when she brought all this health food, and women were like, "I'm coming down [off drugs] and I really need sugar." So she basically was still trying to figure that out. She told me that kind of was a way of excusing the fact that there's so much sugar in what we give away.

For Benz, who was eight months pregnant, making the connection between her hunger, her drug use, and her baby's well-being was a concern:

Benz tells me that she is "starving." She asks me for extra food from the outreach bag. She is so tiny. Her belly is getting big, though. She asks if I want to feel the baby move. I smile; she lifts her shirt a bit. I feel a kick and a roll. "The baby is bouncing around so much today," she tells me. "And I haven't even smoked that much [crack]." She takes the prenatal vitamins and the extra food, and heads back into her room.

Later in the same week, after my meeting with Benz, the *What to Expect When You're Expecting* website sent me a friendly reminder about eating healthy during pregnancy. As an experiment in juxtaposition, I had signed up on the website by entering a date of my last menstrual period, essentially feigning an online pregnancy contemporaneous with those of many of the women in the daily-rent hotels. I wanted to see how the email monitoring of a digitally connected, upper-middle-class professional's pregnancy would compare to the experiences of the women renting rooms in the daily-rent hotels. The notice I happened to receive that week was about healthy eating habits during pregnancy:

Best Foods to Eat While Pregnant

Twelve superstar foods that should headline in your diet

At 11 weeks pregnant, these twelve pregnancy power foods pack an amazing amount of nutrients into just a few bites, making them especially effective when efficiency is a priority (as when you're too sick to eat much, when you're gaining weight too fast, or when you're not gaining quickly

1.11. Tylenol advertisement, Sixteenth Street BART plaza, April 2008. Photo by the author.

enough). Put all of the following "it" foods on your A list: (1) Avocados (2) Broccoli (3) Carrots (4) DHA eggs (5) Edamame (6) Lentils (7) Mangoes (8) Nuts (9) Oatmeal (10) Red pepper (11) Spinach (12) Yogurt.

While reading the email, I reflected. Lexi did order the yogurt parfait thing at McDonald's once when we were there, when I was paying for it. Otherwise, I could not recall any pregnant women in the daily hotels consuming any foods on this list. They could not cook in their rooms and had no refrigeration. That potentially ruled out numbers 2, 4, 6, 9, and 12. An avocado cost about 70 cents to a dollar; spinach was about $1.50 a bunch. The women whom I worked with were very intermittent users of free food programs. They did not participate in weekly meal delivery programs for elderly and disabled tenants that deliver food to some hotels in other San Francisco neighborhoods. The weekly outreach shifts that I participated in provided a peanut butter and jelly sandwich and salty/sugary snacks. We always offered visibly pregnant women more of that food.[29] Given the level of food insecurity I was able to document

1.12. Poster for the Women, Infants, and Children program reads "Everything comes with nutritional information. Except her." Daily-rent hotel window can be seen above the billboard. August 2009. Photo by the author.

ethnographically, did the placement of the Tylenol advertisement at the Sixteenth Street BART plaza (fig. 1.11) signal an insensitive disregard toward the poor, drug addicted people who frequent this corner, or was it perhaps an invitation to medicalize their experience of food insecurity?

While none of the women were accessing prenatal health websites that provided weekly email updates, pregnant women in this neighborhood did get reminders about nutrition during pregnancy.[30] The form these took was not specific nutritional advice so much as educational admonishments for not taking responsibility for their children's nutrition, and encouragement to sign up for a federally funded food program. The poster in figure 1.12 is one of these advertisements directed at poor women in the neighborhood.

My interaction with Ramona at the hospital offered a sense of the challenges that poor women can face connecting with food securing services. It also demonstrated the way drug addiction can compete directly, and coexist, with the desire to secure nutrition for oneself and one's baby. An overwhelming reciprocity between the stress of food insecurity, addiction, and a baby on an opiate detoxification treatment was in operation here.

At one point Ramona disappeared from the hospital and left me with her newborn son for about thirty minutes. I thought she was out smoking a cigarette. Things were really charged and tense between her and Duke [Ramona's boyfriend and the baby's father] today. I thought maybe they were fighting out of earshot from me and the nurses on the ward. I rocked the baby back and forth, singing softly, watching him sleep. At one point the nurse came over to give him his injection, part of his detox off the methadone. She inserted the needle into the splinted IV. He didn't wake.

Ramona finally returned with a handful of paperwork. "Sorry. I tried to text you, but my cell wouldn't work. I had to get my WIC [Women, Infants, and Children] stuff together, so the baby will be set when he leaves [the hospital]. I didn't have the right form and it took forever. How is he doing?" she asks a bit anxiously. I hand him carefully to Ramona—carefully because he is attached to the IV line that is treating his neonatal abstinence withdrawal symptoms.

"He has been sleeping the whole time. The nurse gave him his shot," I tell her reassuringly. "He is so beautiful," I add. "Yeah," she sighs, smiling. She sits with him, totally absorbed for the moment. I step away from her into the hallway to give her some time with her son.

Later I drive her back to her daily-rent hotel.

A few weeks after that, I asked Ramona's baby daddy, Duke, about accusations I had heard of drug use during Ramona's hospital stay. He says, "Yeah, she was smoking crack. She was stepping out for that. We both were."

Residential transience and food insecurity are two embodied experiences that created disruption, stress, anxiety, and suffering among the women who lived and worked in the daily-rent hotels. Privately managed hotels profited indirectly from these forms of destabilization. These hotels also engaged in specific forms of gendered economic exploitation to directly profit off women involved in sex exchange. All these factors increased women's risk for poor health. Addicted, pregnant women were placed at increased vulnerability because while pregnancy was tolerated within the daily-rent hotels, bringing children home from the hospital (should a woman maintain custody) was discouraged. Imagining the "SRO" or "homelessness" as they are currently categorized in the majority of epidemiological studies did not capture the complexity of the social worlds that existed within the daily-rent hotels, yet recent studies of residential transience and food insecurity offer ways to numerically calibrate the role of environment stressors, outside of substances alone, on the development and health of both mother and child in this setting.

Taking a wider view, one can see that multiple predatory practices were being engaged in the lives of women. Social scientific vulturism extracts data to document specific forms of insecurity made manifest through the exploitative rental practices of the daily-rent hotels. The daily-rent hotels themselves are being slowly and systematically consumed by the practices of gentrification escalating in the neighborhood. This site and its inhabitants, particularly addicted, pregnant women, are enactments of and metaphors for the larger US economic context of growing insecurity—a context in which access to credit and housing have been increasingly linked to predatory lending and the amassing of unpayable debts and where health and well-being are linked ever more strongly to one's zip code and the environmental stressors of the built environment. Some people, like the women in the daily-rent hotels, are being left behind to fend for themselves as best they can.

chapter 2. addicted pregnancy and time

The medical clinic is going on at the drop-in tonight, and the first conversation that I had was with Kitt, who told me she was "gonna go have
an abortion tomorrow." I gave her a pregnancy test a couple of weeks
ago on outreach, and she said that was how she confirmed it. She's
twenty weeks pregnant, now. She's missed the appointment [for the
abortion] a couple of times, and I'm wondering if she's not sure if she really wants to go. It seems like it. "If I don't do it now, it is going to be too
late," she sighs. I haven't seen her this down in a while.

We didn't have a lot of time to talk. She wanted to go up to the clinic,
because she said she was "kind of smelling down there." It seemed
like it might be a yeast infection. But it could also be another STI [sexu-
ally transmitted infection]. I asked her if she had somebody to go with
her tomorrow to the [abortion] clinic, and she said, "I have a couple
of girlfriends who'd said they would go, but you never know." I said,
"Yeah, you know, that can be a hard thing to do on your own," and she
said, "Yeah, I think that they're gonna come with me tomorrow." It was
hard to see her so sad. I am not sure how reliable her friends are. After
our brief conversation, Kitt went up to the medical clinic. I went to go
find her later that night, and she was already gone. I made a mental
note to check in with her on Tuesday [night on the outreach shift]. On
Tuesday, I didn't find her in the hotels.

One week later

I just ran into Kitt, and she told me that she lost her place to stay—that's
one of the reasons why we didn't see her on outreach. It sounds like
she came into some money, somehow—her husband's in jail . . . and
his dad just passed away. So, because there was a settlement there,
Kitt came into seven thousand dollars, somehow, through her hus-

band's father. She gave the money—five thousand dollars of it—to her mom, because her mom's raising two of her kids, and then her sister's got another one of her kids. She had called her mom the night of her abortion, to tell her about the money, and found out that her son, Daniel, who's seven, was in the hospital [getting a minor operation]. So Kitt went out to the hospital to see him.

When Kitt is staying in the hotels, she has to move every twenty-one days, so she is frequently displaced. Here, the timing was terrible because she was coming up on her twenty-one-day at the Nimish [Hotel] when she went in for the abortion. She said she had $15 credit with the hotel. She told the hotel management that she would be gone for a night, and they had agreed to hold her room, but when she got back to the hotel they had packed up her stuff. Kitt found this out because she saw another hotel guest selling her belongings out on the street. She freaked out and got into a fight with the hotel manager, and the manager called the police. Kitt threatened the manager, saying that "something bad was gonna happen," and the hotel manager called her a "bitch." It sounds like it was a huge incident.

Even now, Kitt's really upset and really high and spinning. She went outside to take a hit of crack before she could come back in the drop-in and tell me the rest of the story. But she was still really charged up. She lowered her voice to a whisper and said to me, "I took care of that problem," indicating that she had the abortion. She looked really upset about it, still. She said that she didn't have a place to stay that night, but this is where she knows the [drug] dealers and works [does sex work]. She looked really upset. She said she was still going through a lot, and she just really wanted to talk to me—she was talking a mile a minute, about everything. She showed me a picture on her cell phone of her son when he was in the hospital after his operation. She just seemed really overwhelmed after having the abortion, seeing her son in the hospital, getting a bunch of money that she needed to redistribute to her mom, and then having lost her hotel room, and all her stuff, on the twenty-one-day.

After about fifteen minutes, she said, "I gotta get out there and make some money before the cops are all over the place," as she rushed out the door.

In the story of Kitt's abortion/eviction many things appear to be happening *at the same time*. The everyday physical realities (of hunger, drug withdrawal, and pregnancy), the social interactions, and institutional involvements pulled women into and out of different temporalities.[1] And at all times for an addicted, pregnant woman, the clock was ticking as she moved ever farther into her pregnancy, closer to the birth of her child, and an inevitable collision with medical and carceral institutions. Kitt's story provided an example of how multiple temporalities intersect and collide during the week of her abortion, underscoring the importance of documenting the relationship between addicted pregnancy and time.

Not "Who Is She?" but "When Is She . . . Due?"

When I interviewed Cupcake during her third pregnancy in 2009, I asked about her own childhood. She told me: "I can't remember too much. I moved so often between the [foster] homes and the juvies [institutions for juvenile offenders and runaways]. I couldn't even tell you all the places I have been, the when and the where of it. I was a bad kid, and I got in trouble a lot."[2] Cupcake, in her retelling, was a person whose subjectivity was predicated on time spent in institutional settings; her temporal anchors to family were no longer recoverable. Ramona provided a counterpoint to a lack of access to memory. During her intake with her methadone counselor, she was given a health history, during which she lied, knowingly. When questioned about a series of psychiatric symptoms, she answered impatiently and dismissively, saying, "Yes. Yes. Yes to all of it!" When the counselor left the room, Ramona turned to me and, smiling, said, "Whatever it takes to move things along." The temporal referent for this interaction with the intake counselor was the burden of answering a laundry list of questions. It differs significantly from Ramona's discussion of "her history" being used as a weapon against her gaining custody of her newborn baby. With the intake counselor the temporal pressures of "treatment time" were in play. Ramona understood the demands of this routine. Answering yes to the majority of the symptoms might translate into benefits or services at a later point. Or maybe it would just get her more quickly to her dose of methadone, the true meaning of her treatment visit from her perspective. After she was dosed on methadone, then she could visit her son in the hospital.[3]

Shifting the question from "who" to "when" is a deliberate provocation meant to unhinge, and reconstitute, ontological debates about the homeless as a population of study in anthropology. Many anthropological engagements with the homeless have focused critical energy on questions of the veracity of characterizations of mental illness and addiction.[4] Several pronouncements have caught my attention, including (1) that the majority of the homeless are not in fact mentally ill; or that (2) if the homeless are mentally ill, it is because they have been made so by shelter workers who transform their poverty into illness; or that (3) the homeless must lie about mental illness diagnoses to gain sympathy and services even though they may or may not be traumatized and/or have a mental illness; or that, finally, (4) the categorization of the homeless is politically contingent on social constructions of "mental illness" and "addiction" that serve no utility beyond the bureaucratic control of socially undesirable people. My concern with these analyses does not stem from disagreement. As I demonstrate with my own data, I share an intellectual starting point of unpacking the socially and politically constructed diagnostic contexts of mental and health diagnoses. Where I have found issue with these debates is in their often totalizing commitment to an either/or perspective that must be settled on and defended. Either the homeless are being labeled (incorrectly) as mentally ill, or they are not. Either they are all "addicted," or "addiction" is a ruse. The question always seems to return to the validity of claims about "who." Who are the homeless, really?

I am less invested in arguing whether or not comorbidity with substance abuse and mental illness is real among the pregnant women living in the daily-rent hotels. Indeed, addictive behaviors and mental health symptoms that psychiatric diagnosticians would label with disease categorizations were commonplace across the women I studied and throughout the many years I conducted participant observation. In fact, women talked about themselves and their social world as "crazy," and called themselves "addicts," all the time. What I am interested in asking is something else: what temporal registers matter here? Bringing time into the equation can help to unseat the temptation toward binary categorization and forward the conversation. I want to explore how understanding the demands of multiple temporalities can expand our epistemology of comorbidity into everyday life and demonstrate the ontological fluidity that addicted, pregnant women in the daily-rent hotels were forced to embody.

An ethnographic attention directed toward temporal constraints helped to explain why the pregnant women I encountered sometimes seemed crazy, sometimes lucid—a distinction that often depended on the pressures of temporally bound social circumstances. Rather than deny that crazy things were being said and done by and to the women in this setting, I suggest here that we pay attention to time. A desire to make some sense of the "mass of observations in front of me" led me to describe the exercises of making temporality rational.[5] The temporalities that mattered for making sense of addicted pregnancy were addict time, hotel time, pregnancy time, jail time, treatment time, epidemiological time, biomedical time, memorial time, and life time.

Addict Time

Addict time was the hourly repetitious cycle of "seeking and scoring" behaviors that one enacts in order to access and use drugs of addiction. Every day was essentially the same from the perspective of addict time, paradoxically characterized by both crisis (withdrawal or craving) and monotony (seek, score, repeat).[6] Women who were actively using drugs gave an impression of lives filled with endless repetition. This temporal description maps seamlessly onto the renderings of addiction as a brain disease in which people who are addicted to drugs do not make decisions to use or not use drugs so much as respond, unconsciously, to neurological cravings that persistently recur.[7] But scientific descriptions of addiction run counter to the women's own claims of agency and control in relation to their drug use. Connecting the biological experience with the social specificity of types of drugs was of key importance. Heroin, cocaine, and alcohol may share some similar neurochemical pathways, but addict time in the daily-rent hotels was largely defined by crack cocaine.

Although many women used heroin, and sometimes prescription opioid analgesic pills they bought off the street, or even alcohol (despite the expense), crack was the drug that all the women used every day in the hotels, often all day and night. Every time I returned to the hotels I found women perpetually seeking and scoring crack. My observations of these behaviors were not typically accompanied by narratives about attempts to reduce or regulate drug consumption on the part of most women. For example, I completed a long interview with Ramona in 2009, two days after she had left a residential treatment program when she was five and a half months pregnant. In the interview, she discussed "not being ready" to stay in the residential program. She adamantly insisted that her use of crack cocaine was "purely psychological" and that she could stop at any time. "If I want to get high, I am going to get high," she said. "It is that simple." Yet, as I watch her leave my car and immediately spend the money I have given her to complete the interview, she

2.1. Ramona preparing to cook her crack before smoking it. Chandra Hotel, August 2009. Photo by the author.

does not appear to be casually *choosing* to smoke crack on that occasion.[8] She is "jonesin'" for crack the minute the money hits her hand. She is yelling at a dealer up the street, "I told you I would get it, now hold on!!" He walks away, and she is pissed. She approaches another guy and buys the crack, and we head upstairs. Back in her room at the Chandra Hotel, Ramona prepares her crack. She rests her spoon on a flyer for the women's health study I worked for during the time of my ethnographic fieldwork. The flyer was given to her the previous evening (not by me but by another staff person) in hopes of recruiting her into a study about victimization, HIV risk, and housing instability.

Ramona, at this moment, is arguably unable to discuss and definitely uninterested in discussing her drug use behaviors in survey-friendly language. Instead, she wants me to document her into a future. She invites me to record her progression from this moment of addiction and pregnancy into a future moment of recovery and motherhood: "You can video the whole thing, Kelly. You can tell the story of me and this baby, follow me when I go back into treatment. Watch me get out of this mess."

People who are in recovery from drug addiction often describe "being in my addiction" as a temporal location, a time when drug seeking and con sumption trumped all other concerns. The power of addict time (the ability of an addiction to distract people from services and relationships) was reiterated multiple times by the health care providers I interviewed, specifically in relation to pregnancy and mothering among women who use drugs. The power of addict time was also the most frequent form of excuse provided by epidemiological survey workers for why participants fail to show up for service appointments at the assigned time: "The drugs got in the way." Read this statement as "the drugs control the time." One health care provider described how pregnant women who may be trying not to use drugs still have their "time taken away," when they get "caught up on the street" and pulled back into smoking crack. Cupcake described her newfound sobriety from crack in terms of time during her third pregnancy: "I got my time back. I can go to the movies, I can just enjoy life. I see things now that I never had time to see before when I was always running around. Always crazy. Never stopping."

Those who foster addict time are also bound by its temporal constraints. Dealers, runners, and other go-betweens lose profit if they are not available to the people seeking their product. One woman, Monique, who was a young pregnant drug dealer whom I knew briefly over a couple of weeks in 2007, was funny and sarcastic when I suggested she go to the Women's Space drop-in one night: "Yeah, sure. Maybe I can take some time off for that," she quipped.

Addict time determined how addiction looked and was enacted in the daily-rent hotels. In contrast to ethnographic studies conducted in drug treatment facilities in which the phenomenon of addiction consisted of "talk about addiction," addict time in the daily-rent hotels looked desperate and encompassing.[9] Less words, more action and chaos. The telos of treatment settings, which seek to disrupt or stop "addict time," can mask the reality of the multiple temporal constraints on the lives of those who are dependent on substances, presenting a picture in which addiction is an out-of-context behavioral choice. An awareness of the operations of addict time in real-world settings may explain why many treatment programs promote the management of "environmental triggers" known as "people, places, or things" that might pull the user struggling with abstinence from drugs or alcohol back into "addict time"—a seemingly endless, repetitive cycle of scarcity and (temporary) satiation.

Hotel Time

Hotel time, like addict time, was daily. It started at 10 a.m., when a woman could pay $35–60 for a room in a daily-rent hotel, and continued until morning checkout the following day, when the same amount had to be garnered for the next evening's stay inside. Hotel time also operated on a monthly cycle, in that tenants were forcibly evicted prior to earning enough consecutive days in a hotel to earn tenancy rights.[10] Next to addict time, hotel time was the single most frenzy-producing temporality women had to respond to on a daily basis. The pressure of hotel time was constant. The women, who rarely chose to stay in shelters for extended periods, or even for one night, were bound by hotel time. Lexi described multiple instances of working late into the night until she could finally earn enough for a room in a daily-rent hotel. In this way, addict time and hotel time are co-constitutive. If one found herself in one temporality, one was often stuck in the other as well.

The political economy of welfare entitlements played a key role in who suffered the ill effects of hotel time. However, the story was not a straightforward one. In other words, having access to welfare benefits did not equal protection from housing exploitation. No institutional intervention, whether potentially protective (such as welfare entitlements) or structurally violent (such as police harassment), had the expected consequences when filtered through the competing concerns of addiction and complex social relationships. Entitlement access worked in such a way that the only people who were stable, those who were not evicted monthly and who got a monthly rent charge (as opposed to a daily charge), were on Supplemental Security Income (SSI). But not all people on SSI were paying monthly, which presented a puzzling conundrum. On the one hand most drug users I encountered did attempt at various points to access SSI benefits. Many were denied, sometimes for years. But the official position of the city government was to facilitate their move, when medically indicated, off the city and state welfare rolls (General Assistance) and onto the federal welfare program (SSI).[11] According to this logic, one would assume that most of the women would be receiving SSI and that all those who were receiving SSI would secure monthly rent rates. This was not the case—in part because living in addict time often precluded the women's ability to negotiate these more stable housing arrangements.

The illogic of this situation perplexed me. Take Ramona's situation. She had been on SSI for several years. She had never had a monthly rental deal with a hotel. When she was offered an SSI-subsidized room in an SRO where she could return with her newborn, in a hotel that was full of working poor mothers with young children, not drug users and sex workers, she didn't take it. It may have been because she wasn't ready to quit using drugs. However, she offered another explanation: she resented the hotel taking part of her ssi benefits money. This did not really make sense, because paying into a publicly funded hotel room would be less expensive than paying daily. While publicly supported sros can only take 30 percent of a person's income, the private hotels' daily rental charges often exceed the amount of an ssi-supported monthly income. There wasn't a lot of money left over for drugs or food, or anything else at that point. But without the monthly rental deal, Ramona paid $1000–1800 for the same room, unless she could manage to double up with another sex worker, have Duke pay it, or bargain with a trick to include the room in the price of their transaction. The result of paying daily, in whatever form, meant more hustling, more sex work to pay not only for the hotel but also the drugs and food. And it is every day, all day. Here addict time and hotel time were at odds with the rational logic of progressive housing policy initiatives. The recognition that the multiple temporalities were not experienced in linear progression, but rather all at once, may help to explain why apparently straightforward housing solutions, such as a subsidized room in a building or a monthly rate in a hotel, were often not successfully adopted by Ramona or other women.

It was under the constraints of addict time and hotel time that women found themselves to be pregnant. Rental debts often spiraled out of control if women experienced any sort of crisis in relation to a pregnancy, be it their own or another woman's in the hotels. Kitt, who paid daily for her hotel room through sex work and other hustles, lost her housing when she had an abortion and then needed to attend to her elder child who was hospitalized. Lexi accumulated rental debt when she agreed to accompany Dylan to the hospital for the birth of Dylan's child. The hospital Dylan chose was not in the neighborhood, and Lexi was gone for two days during Dylan's long labor and delivery. The vast majority of the women who became pregnant during my ethnography did not become so intentionally. Instead, the discovery of a pregnancy introduced an additional temporal mode on top of those already in play.

Pregnancy Time

Conventionally, pregnancy time is nine months, split by trimester. From an institutional perspective, pregnant women who are homeless and using drugs become biomedical time bombs once pregnancy is discovered. Time started to work backward from the projected due date. The women, themselves, asked: How much time can I keep using (drugs) before I have to stop? When will it be obvious to others that I am pregnant? How much, and of what substance, is too much?

A pregnancy diagnosis put women on a train; whether it would end up in a wreck or arrive at the station unscathed and on time was unknown and highly contingent. However, the clock was ticking, and it would end—one way or another. Kitt's 2007 pregnancy was stopped by her decision to have an abortion at twenty weeks. For Cupcake in 2008, an ultrasound at six months revealed that her "fetus" was actually only a mass of cells. The baby had not materialized, and the pregnancy was terminated with a D & C. Tara's pregnancy ended in late miscarriage at five and a half months, rumored to be the result of a violent fight between her and her boyfriend. He disapproved of her drinking at the bar while pregnant.

The train wreck metaphor of pregnancy time could not have been more clearly embodied than in Lexi's case. Knowing Lexi prior to my ethnographic work, and having known her pregnancy history, made me sensitive to the particular medical issues she faced. Because her cervix had opened midpregnancy in 2004, leading to the death of her baby, we both knew, in 2009, that her pregnancy time could stop at around six and a half months. While other women like Dylan, Ramona, Danell, Anita, and Benz were able to ride out pregnancy time—still using until late in their pregnancies (seven to nine months)—Lexi was on another schedule. No amount of prodding by me seemed to help Lexi get to prenatal care. She did not want her methadone program to know about her pregnancy, for fear they would place her in a pregnancy-linked treatment slot, which would cause her to lose her methadone if she lost her baby, a repeat of her experience in 2004. Throughout her pregnancy, Lexi vacillated between concern and ambivalence about her pregnancy, the demands of her pregnancy in direct competition with the demands of drug and alcohol addiction: addict time verses pregnancy time.

When asked about when women seek out drug treatment services, one provider described to me two "typical types" of women who use drugs who enter treatment programs. First, there are women whose pregnancy serves as "a wake-up call." These women tend to come into treatment earlier in their pregnancies, or when they first find out they are pregnant. Many women who use heroin do not menstruate, or at least not regularly, so detection of pregnancy through that traditional means is often not available to them.[12] Women with considerable opiate dependencies frequently do not discover pregnancy until more advanced symptoms appear. Regardless, women in this first "group" (according to the provider) become future-oriented immediately. Pregnancy time becomes a clock ticking toward a better future, a chance at motherhood, drug-free. There is a second group of women, according to the provider, who wait. "They are in denial about the pregnancy. They are using [drugs] throughout their whole pregnancies," the provider told me. Even as their bodies swell, and other women begin to ask or comment about them, they continue with their everyday life, to the extent possible, as if they are not pregnant.

I can recall an interaction with Ramona that captured this dichotomous life. She was seven months pregnant, and we were talking on the street in front of her hotel. A woman came by, someone Ramona knew but I didn't. The woman stopped, looked at Ramona's stomach, and said, "Oh! Are you pregnant?" "No," said Ramona flatly and stared her down. "But . . ." the women trailed off. "Oh, I just thought . . ." "Well, you thought wrong," Ramona corrected abruptly. This was patently absurd. Ramona was hugely pregnant. Is this an example of the denial the provider described? Ramona fit the provider's behavioral profile, but her social negotiations on the street were actively protective. When the woman left, I asked, "You didn't want her to know?" "No. Way," she responded. "I don't need her up in my business. Why does she need to know? What good would that do? I don't want no one knowing out here." I witnessed many such public disavowals, and a general lack of discussion about pregnancy, even between women. Dylan, who was hugely pregnant, was still hustling on the street days, even hours, before her baby was born. These denials and omissions allowed the women to adequately respond to the demands of addict and hotel time while avoiding acquaintances' intersubjective involvement in their futures, whether they might judge them or wish them well.

Jail Time

Jail time came to women in multiple ways. All the pregnant women that I worked with had interactions with the police. The years of my ethnography were marked by a period in which one local police chief was replaced by another who targeted "drugs and prostitution" as his main areas of focused resourcing.[13] This increased surveillance has expanded and intensified since 2010, now taking the form of a growing online neighborhood watch program that has monthly meetings with the police chief and local city government and organizes frequent meetings and events to discuss sex work, drug dealing, and violence in the neighborhood. One evening in June 2008 I ran into Abril, a younger sex worker, and she described how the police had been "all over her" the night before. She said that she had told the police: "I gotta be out here to pay for my rent. If I don't work I don't get to sleep for the night [inside a hotel room], so can you leave me alone."

When Kitt described her time inside jail and her time outside jail, she spoke more broadly about her family history, her feelings of failure as a mother, her rage, and her racialization on the streets. During this extended conversation she represented herself in multiple temporalities—through jail time, explaining the possibilities she felt she had had in jail, her sense of being trapped on the streets, and her concerns about the inevitability of reincarceration.

KITT. ON JAIL TIME. SEPTEMBER 2008

Kitt has just returned from an unsuccessful and demoralizing visit to the hospital ER, and we sit down to talk on a bench at the Sixteenth Street BART plaza. Dealers, women from the hotels, commuters, and local resident families are all rushing past us, attending to their differing needs.

"The thing is," Kitt says, sighing, "I have outgrown it out here. I don't know why I came back [to the neighborhood]. I was in a treatment program in jail. I asked to be in it. I volunteered. And it was good, and when I got out I went to a residential [program], but I only stayed a night. And I came back out here and I got caught up [in hustling and drug use]. I am mad at myself. I am kind of punishing myself for being back out here, you know. And my self-esteem is pretty low right now."

Kitt starts crying.

"Where else could you go?" I ask.

"Well, that's the thing. I get lonely. I mean I still got my family. But I feel like if I can't do right by my kids. I got four kids. If I can't do it right with them, then I can't do it at all. I can't go home."

"And it is harder now. I want to do a swap for [jail] time, but I have to have a stable residence to do it. It's hard to prove that [residential stability]. And every day I am out here I am just uppin' my chances of getting another [sex work] case, of getting violated [on probation]. I just did my first date in a week out here last night because I was hoping not to go that route. I have a lot of anger, at these men coming at me with twenty dollars and ten dollars. Because it [the money] is so low and I know I am worth more than that. And these white girls out here. It is so much easier for them to get dates."

"Why do you say that?" I ask.

"It's just society. The other day, I am out, and I think I am look-ing good, I am dressed, you know, dressed up. And this car pulls up and there is a white girl, dirty, all curled up in a blanket. And he goes with her, because she's a white girl. And she is all strung out and not charging nothin'. I'm just, I am too old for this shit."

"Do you feel like the police target you because you are black?" I ask.

"No. They treat us [sex workers] all the same!"

In March 2009, Kitt is back in jail. Back out and then in jail again in September 2009.

Kitt was a woman who was wholly unsuccessful at avoiding jail time. As the quote here indicates, she blames herself for that lack of success. Perhaps her explanation of her positive experience with drug treatment in jail provides some explanation for her frequent recidivism—or perhaps the massive in-creased presence of the police on the street, targeting sex workers and drug dealers in the neighborhood. Even though she felt the police were not racially targeting her for arrest, Kitt felt her ethnicity played a role: because she was black, she couldn't get easy dates. Because of this, she may have been taking more risks, which could have made her more vulnerable to arrest. Her vio-lence could also have played a role, because Kitt was someone people paid to beat on other people that owed them money or had slighted them. Her crack use was in part linked to that social, and financially profitable, role of "enforcer" that she occasionally played. Many social services coordinated with the jail, so arrest could become a key temporal access point for social services.[14] As one senior policy official said to me, "Many women get the mental health screening in jail. [Pause and a sigh.] God forbid, but we are actually incarcerating women in order to get them hooked into services. Jail time is one way in." All these factors seemed to create a perfect storm of recidivism for Kitt, in which jail time became a significant and determining temporality for her.

At Ramona's postpartum intake appointment, she waxed philosophical to her old counselor: "You go through a lot of pain and a lot of sorrow [going through drug treatment]. But it is worth it in the long run." Her counselor did not reply directly to this emotional-motivational confession. Instead the counselor asked knowingly, "How much jail time did you do this time around [during this pregnancy]?" "Not too much," Ramona said equivocally, shifting gears. "Maybe a month." "Oh, that's good," said the counselor. The counselor knows jail could lead addicted, pregnant women directly to the treatment program, and this was the narrative she was fleshing out. Ramona provided it. "But that [the jail time] was a couple of months ago. And from there I went to First Steps. You know, I was court-ordered. And, you know, I didn't stay," Ramona told her counselor. When I interviewed one provider in the drug treatment program, he described the relationship that the program had with the jail. "If a pregnant woman is picked up and suspected to be an opiate user, they [the jail] will call us right away. They don't want them [the pregnant women]. They don't want them to miscarry or to go into labor [while in custody]. They don't want the liability. We get about half of our women through the jails. Sometimes we have wondered when we have a lot of jail referrals if there are changes to arrest rates going on out on the streets or something. We ask, 'Why did we get six women from the jails this month, when last month we got none?'"

Unlike Kitt and Ramona, Cupcake was able to avoid jail time during her brief pregnancy in 2008.[15] She was on probation and staying at the Brigit Hotel, paying daily, when she called my cell phone to ask me for a letter. She had been stopped by the police, who had found condoms in her husband's car (hundreds of condoms). The police wanted to report this as a probation violation, based on the condoms being proof of her engaging in sex work. This type of policing of sex work was not unusual; it reflected a systematic problem for suspected sex workers in San Francisco.[16] If the outreach program could provide a letter saying that we had distributed the condoms, then she could bring it with her to the court date. I referred her to the outreach program, and they provided the letter. Although her husband got incarcerated, she did not get a violation on her probation record. After the trial she told me about trying to get a job. "I went to the Salvation Army. The woman there was really nice, but she said, 'It hasn't been enough time. Come back when you have a few more months [on probation] behind you.' She felt like I hadn't had enough time in my probation. It was too risky for her [to hire me]. I can't get anything [no jobs]! I went to McDonald's, I have been everywhere. And with the baby coming, I just want to get work." The pressure of jail time and pregnancy time intersected, as Cupcake was unable to secure a legal job before her baby was born, which meant on going sex work.

When I interviewed Cupcake and her husband, Marco (now out of jail), in 2009, she was pregnant again. They told me the story of the arrest with the condoms. It turns out he was picked up by the police initially for solicitation. He was picking Cupcake up in his car, and the police thought he was a paying date. Then when the police discovered that Cupcake and he were married (they have the same last name and address on their licenses), they searched the car and found the condoms. Cupcake and her husband told me this story with laughing disbelief: "How could the cops think I was her date??!" It is funny. However, Marco was serving as a protector that day, watching out for Cupcake while she was doing sex work. Because of his long-term involvement in the drug economy, Marco was too well known to the police in the neighborhood and thus a target for interrogation and arrest. He felt he could not circulate frequently outside their hotel room, even just to walk around, or the police might "jack him up" on a parole violation and reincarcerate him. Since she couldn't find another job, they felt it was easier for her to make money for them as a sex worker, even risking arrest, than for him to be sent back to jail. Neither of them was using drugs at this time (November 2009)—she had stopped smoking crack, and he had never used. ("I am addicted to money," he told me by way of explanation.) They planned to move out of state to get away from the probation violation issues with local police and to avoid Cupcake getting pulled back into addict time. Until they did, Marco was on hotel time, and Cupcake could be facing jail time.

Treatment Time

Treatment time operated like a revolving door. Women who were using drugs and pregnant could get access to drug treatment programs. The women I worked with stayed between one night and eighteen months in residential treatment programs. These residential programs provided "transitional housing," where a woman could stay while pregnant with her newborn while her child custody was still under state surveillance. If treatment funding was linked to a pregnancy and the pregnancy was discontinued—through elective abortion or pregnancy loss—the treatment ended as well. In this sense, the child was receiving drug treatment and the mother was not—or at least not without the unborn child to justify her access.

Time served in treatment was a benchmark for worthy motherhood as judged by institutions, such as Child Protective Services (CPS), that managed custody for the majority of women's children at birth if they were flagged for drug use during pregnancy. Benz stopped and restarted her methadone treatment throughout her pregnancy. At one point a hospitalization gave her the impetus to start methadone treatment again. She often apologized to me about not going to methadone treatment and made a point to say that she "needed to get back there" every time we would see each other. While she was and had been a heroin user, her crack use was her self-expressed biggest concern when it came to her baby's well-being. Privileging fetal crack exposure over opiate exposure was a consistently expressed folk belief among women, reflecting both the awareness of media portrayals of the stigma of "crack babies" and the experience of the effects of ongoing crack use on one's own body as opposed to heroin use. On the street, people would say, "Heroin is a preservative; stimulants ruin you [your body]."[17] There is no treatment for crack addiction that parallels drug replacement therapy (such as methadone or buprenorphine for opiate/opioid dependency). For Benz, methadone treatment offered a way to establish a record of making an effort to reduce or stop her drug use during pregnancy, a record that would be shared with CPS later when her child custody was at stake.

For providers who worked with opiate-dependent women who delayed seeking methadone treatment, managing the addicted pregnancy could become an exercise in "putting out the fire." The treatment goal quickly shifted from the cessation of drug use during pregnancy to getting the woman as clean a drug tox screen as possible, and the most social services, prior to the baby's birth. One provider told me:

Pregnancy isn't a long time. It may seem like nine months is long time. But to get women stabilized on methadone, to get them prenatal care, to deal with their housing issues, get them to sign up for Medi-Cal, get a psych evaluation and follow-up if they need it, so they can deliver a baby with only methadone onboard and not get a CPS case? It is rarely enough time. If women arrive to us at seven and half months, eight months, chances are they have all of the issues that will get you tagged by CPS: they have been using throughout their pregnancy, they might have a severe mental health issue, they are in denial about the pregnancy, and they are probably unstably housed. At that point, we are just barely able to put out the fire—to get them on methadone and off everything else.

For Ramona, putting out the fire became her strategy once she was arrested and brought to the hospital. She told me:

> The police, they came up to me, and said I looked like someone who had a bench warrant. It was such bullshit. I was just sitting there. But then they [arrested me and] took me to the hospital. Because I was pregnant they needed to get me [medically] cleared first before they could take me to jail. Well, they [the hospital staff] admit me. And they put me on methadone. And then after a whole day, like at two o'clock in the morning, the cop comes in and I say, "What the fuck? Am I going to jail or what?" And he says, "No. You cleared. You cleared like an hour ago. You can go." But see I was already on my way at that point. I thought, well, if I stay, he will be born clean. I only got like two more days, and his tox will be clean. So I stayed. Went into labor two days later and out he came.

The choice to enter into treatment time is not only determined solely by pregnant women. One service provider described her unhappiness with a social worker who did not jump to the assistance of a mutual client when the pregnant woman expressed interest in residential treatment. Personality, prejudice, and cumulative negative past experiences can inform providers' decisions, and their technocratic roles offer them the authority to grant or withhold access to drug treatment. The provider I interviewed was able to override the case manager's authority and get the woman into residential treatment. The story was relayed to me as a cautionary tale: when treatment time comes, the door better be left open:

> I had a client who was admitted to the hospital. She was having severe medical complications with her pregnancy and needed to be hospitalized. In the hospital, she refused a bunch of tests; they said she snuck out of the hospital to use drugs—which will happen. When I met with her a month or so later she said she was ready to go to residential. I called the social worker to help facilitate. Her response was, "That is a waste of time, she won't go." Well, I followed up. I got her a spot and guess what? She just won custody back of her child. She is doing excellent. She is very happy. It goes to show, you can't give up. Don't write people off. If you keep offering [drug treatment] one hundred times, maybe the one hundredth time she will take it.

Epidemiological Time

Most of the women in the daily-rent hotels actively engaged in public health studies, participating in survey interviews whenever they were eligible. Sometimes they were targets of study recruitment, as Ramona was when she was given a study flyer (later used as makeshift placemat for her crack spoon). Equally often, the women proactively sought out enrollment, asking us when we conducted outreach shifts, "Do you know of any studies?" Studies were a route to material compensation, through payment for interviews and surveys, and a means to gain access to testing and counseling for various health conditions.[18] When women participated in research studies, and when they were asked to fill out forms in clinic offices, they were enlisted into epidemiological or "epi" time.

In general, epi time marked the ways study respondents were time-frozen into classifications during statistical research in order to bound and thus compare descriptive categories. Bounding time for generalizablility is the hallmark of validity in statistical research.[19] If persons can be said to have the same reported behaviors within a specific time frame then they can be given a categorical slot. For example, "crack smokers" are those individuals who report smoking crack cocaine *in the last thirty days*. If we agree on that understanding of what a crack smoker is, then we can compare other things about those people we have named "crack smoker"—their ethnicity, gender, housing status, access to drug treatment, arrest history, and so on. Notice that all of the comparative characteristics also require decisional points in relation to time. Even ethnicity and gender can change in subjective appellation over time. It is not identifying what is fixed but rather making fixed what is not that epidemiology finds as its challenge. This is a challenge it takes seriously for the most part. My goal is not to mock that exercise. Rather, I place it in conversation with the other temporalities that bear weight on the everyday experiences of women living in the daily-rent hotels.

As I engaged in multimethodological, federally funded research projects while simultaneously conducting my ethnographic project, I frequently experienced the clash of multiple temporalities in the research study context. One example came in a staff meeting discussion about the recruitment of a qualitative interview sample. The staff meeting consisted of those persons working on the survey development for the epidemiological measures and those who primarily work on the qualitative substudy. The problem of temporality came up in the survey measure of victimization. We grappled with the following question: for women living in social worlds in which verbal conflicts and verbal abuse are ubiquitous and sexual and physical violence are frequent, how could we measure the "degree" of victimization? A measure of "ever" (as in lifetime) was not very informative, as 100 percent of respondents might respond yes. So what kind of violence could really "count" when violence is normative? How could temporally bounding events of violence help or hurt our understanding of their role in women's health?

On the one hand violence against women was being extensively dissected and temporalized.[20] On the other hand the measure here is inclusive and broad because of the need to document, to make visible through numbers, the extent and nature of the victimization women are experiencing. Measures such as these have helped pave the way not only to further studies of violence against women, especially violence against women during pregnancy, but also to the provision of safe housing and social services to respond to this now visible social problem. We did not make up the measure; it is a "validated" measure used in many previous epidemiological studies. It frustrated all of us to try and discern meaning from the measure, given the ubiquity of violence and victimization among unstably housed women. We settled on reporting contextual data that explored the linkages between the built environment, past trauma and perceptions of safety, as well as quantifiable data linking mental health status to experiences of violent victimization.[21]

Epi time, in contrast to the other forms of temporality that made demands of the women in the daily-rent hotels, raised the question of whether the "violence of counting" can ever be undone through better measurement.[22] Acknowledging that statistics generated from public health research help to elucidate social problems under the veil of methodological objectivity does not solve the problematic way time-bounding can stand in for history and elide current material and affective experiences of addiction, poverty, and stress. Epi time, like all other times, was significant and partial.

Biomedical Time

Biomedical time often existed elsewhere: in the offices of CPS, at hospitals, and at drug treatment clinics. It was inscribed in the form of legal custody files that outlined, in techno-clinical language, assessments of the fetal outcomes of a specific pregnancy. As the material remainders of the audit culture of addicted pregnancy, these adjudicating documents were continually referenced without being present.[23] A woman's pregnancy history preceded her into the present, and it also left a biomedical trace.

Of the nineteen women in this study who had twenty-three pregnancies during my ethnographic fieldwork, only two were first-time mothers. Most women had a history of multiple past pregnancies—Dylan had her third child, Kitt was pregnant with her fifth, Lexi was pregnant with her third, Anita had her fifth, Cupcake with her third, and Ramona her sixth. None of the multiparous women were living with their children in the daily-rent hotels. The pregnancies I documented were constructed relative to pregnancies and children past. Anita made a point of mentioning, repeatedly, that it was not until her father died that she had a baby with a positive tox screen for illicit drugs; her first three were born "clean," even though she had used drugs early in those pregnancies. Cupcake discussed how she was young and crack addicted when her first two daughters were born.

Ramona was furious that the CPS worker could use her "history" of child custody loss against her in her current [2010] custody case. After sending her daughter DeLoni to a relative, Ramona met Duke and became pregnant with a son, born in 2007. This son was placed in foster care almost immediately after birth because Ramona did not enter drug treatment. Ramona relayed her anger to me and her counselor at her methadone intake appointment, a counselor who had worked with her and DeLoni but not her subsequent sons.

RAMONA AT INTAKE. JANUARY 2010

Ramona is talking rapid-fire, angry and adamant. She is describing to Mary—her old counselor—an argument she had with the CPS case worker who came to the hospital when her son was born a few days earlier.

"His tox screen was clean! You hear what I am saying? The CPS worker is a straight bitch. She said, 'We are going on your history.' 'That's the only reason why I have a case! His tox screen was clean!' '*Your history*,' she said. I mean, I had been using up until then [just before his birth], but I knew he would only have methadone [if I stayed in the hospital after being arrested]. She [the CPS worker] said, 'He can come to see you at First Steps in three weeks.'

"I said, 'That is not up to you!'

"She [the CPS worker] said, 'Well, that is my recommendation.'

"'Well I don't give a fuck about your recommendations. So what are you gonna do about that. And stay on up out of my business! And by the way I have custody of my other daughter [DeLoni].'"

DeLoni does not actually live with Ramona, but she was making the point about keeping custody to provoke the CPS worker by demonstrating that CPS does not have unilateral control over her as a mother or her children. Ramona "gave up" custody to a relative in another state in order to not have DeLoni placed in foster care. The "history" the CPS worker is referencing is in relation to DeLoni and Ramona's older son, now three years old.

Ramona tells us that the CPS worker said, "You have custody! What do you mean?"

"I said, 'None of your damn business! I don't have a CPS case so you don't need to know about that!' Oh, I went off on her bad, Mary." Ramona stops talking for a minute.

The counselor (Mary) asks, "Which CPS worker did you go off on about what kid?"

This is damage control on Mary's part. Mary is trying to assess whether she might be able to intervene on Ramona's behalf. But Mary does not recognize the worker's name when Ramona says it.

"Which kid?" Mary asks again.

Ramona responds, "About my son, about the one I just had."

"And how old is that baby?" asks Mary—she does not know that Ramona has been pregnant very recently. Mary is trying to catch up with Ramona's story.

Ramona says, "five days old. I just had got discharged yesterday out of the hospital! And DeLoni, remember DeLoni was on six. She was on six DTO [a detoxification treatment to manage opioid withdrawal symptoms]. He [her newborn] is only on 2.5. So he is doing really good, you know what I mean? But that [CPS] worker is a straight bitch. How can they go on my *history* when his tox screen was *clean*?"

Ramona's story demonstrated how the social mantle of failed motherhood could attach itself to addicted, pregnant women in ways that the women could not easily undo. Biomedical time created "proof," quantifiable markers of poor mothering. However, this proof was given an inconsistent social reading at the bedside. The relative scores (6 v. 2.5) are presented as significant, ascribed through Ramona's reading as the essential difference between "dirty" (drug-exposed and problematic) and "clean" (not meriting a CPS case).[24] Yet the numerical exactitude had little actual bearing on Ramona and her son's subsequent adjudication.

It has been argued that women who use drugs may be more averse to seeking prenatal care earlier in their pregnancies because of fear that doing so will be accompanied by state-level adjudication and the loss of child custody.[25] This fear is well founded. Some researchers have shown that this fear and its associated lack of prenatal care has had direct impacts on the fetal health outcomes (such as low birth weight) of women who use drugs during pregnancy.[26] The current level of sophistication in the scientific understandings of prenatal drug exposure includes measurements of exposure to substances (illegal drugs, tobacco, alcohol) along with exposure to "adversity" in the personal and social environment (maternal mental illness, homelessness, unmet basic needs). This methodological inclusivity is a promising corrective. Previous scientific literature focused on drug exposure (especially crack cocaine) to the exclusion of all other factors that might impact infant/child health and development. Much of this early prenatal substance use exposure research was discredited, but not before creating a legacy of media-generated moral panic that survives today.[27] What is disheartening is how little this scientific literature is read or translated down to the decision-makers in custody cases.[28]

The level of control women have over how a custody case will be decided, if CPS is alerted when a baby is born, was not attached to this science but to child welfare workers' interpretations of it. In the complex world of maternal drug use within environments of adversity, a lack of medical sophistication, and personal bias, among CPS workers could affect custody decision-making. Yet CPS workers may also have been using the numerical justifications provided by the biomedical time of a specific pregnancy, and pregnancies past, to legitimate a case in which "adversity" (poverty, housing instability, maternal mental health) was a pressing concern in relation to child welfare. In either situation, such deployments of biomedical time could effectively nullify treatment system efforts at support and reassurance.[29] CPS has the authority, even without the scientific expertise, to make such crucial custody recommendations. One physician shared her frustration with me at her inability to provide a clear road map for women once they enter drug treatment:

CPS involvement depends on the case worker, the range is huge. Some will look at the dose of methadone and make a decision to pursue the case. Even though good research shows that the degree of infant abstinence syndrome is not determined by the mother's dose of methadone. She could be taking sixty milligrams and the baby could detox for six weeks, she could take one hundred and twenty milligrams and the detox for the baby could be shorter. So the CPS worker could make this very important decision based on false assumptions. The fact that my client [the pregnant woman] is working so hard, and has done everything right, but can't get housed—this might not be the deciding factor. [It might be her CPS case worker's assessment of her methadone.] And she [the pregnant woman] is terrified, terrified that she will lose the baby. And I can't tell her unequivocally that she won't.

The construction of fetal histories through state intervention and surveillance used temporal frames that worked for and against women. A woman's immediate custody and longer-term custody were calibrated by how her child came into biomedical time. The biomedical tracking of drug exposure and poor prenatal care provided a technocratic trace. Yet biomedical time was itself scientifically unstable. Crack exposure in newborns could lead to immediate temporary termination of parenting rights with the child becoming a ward of the state. Yet there is a great deal of scientific controversy about the short- and long-term effects of crack cocaine on fetal health. In terms of intrauterine opioid/opiate exposure, there was a wide variability in neonatal abstinence scores and detoxification treatment pathways—some women's children were born with higher scores, but still detoxified relatively quickly. Other babies had lower neonatal abstinence scores but required longer treatment periods before their withdrawal symptoms dissipated. The numbers mattered. To CPS workers those numbers indicated the degree of exposure and were used as one quantifiable reflection of a mother's potential parenting competence. And having a previous baby born "dirty"—with a positive tox screen—carried implications into subsequent parenting custody negotiations.

Memorial Time

The emotional trauma of the loss of child custody was so acute that many women could not even speak of it. They would begin to talk about what had happened when custody had been severed, and then they would clam up or start to cry, before saying, "Let's talk about something else." The loss of children to the system was an ultimate source of shame and a mark of failure. Ongoing sex work, drug addiction, arrests, and poverty—circumstances that often stigmatize women into social exclusion—simply did not compare. Lexi's description of the night she gave up custody of her son and met the father of her next two children reflects the duality of the singular traumatic event and the everyday violence of the drug sex economy. She told me:

> The night I gave up Lionel. I was a wreck. I had called my sister, and asked her to come pick him up. 'Cause I had relapsed and I knew I would lose him to the system [CPS]. [After she picked up Lionel] I was just sitting on the ground. On the curb. Just loaded [very high], and crying my eyes out. I felt dead. Then Pano comes up, and he asks me if I have a place to stay. He's being so nice. I didn't even care at this point. I don't remember nothin'. I was just so distraught. And then when I woke up the next morning I was in his [hotel] room. And I still had my clothes on! I couldn't believe it! He didn't even try anything. He didn't take advantage. 'Cause I think he knew. He knew how blown away I was behind losing Lionel.

The expected trauma of waking up naked after sex that she doesn't remember with a stranger in a hotel room is surprisingly (in Lexi's telling) trumped by the recognition of her vulnerability as a drug-using mother who has just lost custody of her child.

Just as biomedical time produced a material trace in the form of neonatal abstinence scores and CPS case files, "memorial time" had a material representation: the memory object. Memory objects allowed children lost to the state to be reenlivened in the everyday.[30] Memory objects included photographs, recordings of children's voices on cell phone messages, and children's gifts, which served as tokens of separation.[31] In memorial time, the trauma of child loss that occurred when custody was severed was reconfigured through memory objects into an imagined present (the child is still here) and an imagined future (custody could still be regained). This reimagining allowed women to "live again" in the temporal and spatial contexts of the daily-rent hotels. Memorial time stabilized motherhood in sites of radical uncertainty produced by homelessness, drug use, and ongoing participation in the drug-sex economy.[32]

One of my first encounters with memorial time crystallized the ongoing traumatization of child loss for the women living in the daily-rent hotels. This

2.2. Memory objects, including photographs on the wall of a daily-rent hotel room and stuffed animals, April 2010. This photograph has been altered so faces are not recognizable. Photo by the author.

happened very early on in my fieldwork. I had heard stories, narratives from women who use drugs about the experiences of losing their children and their feelings of failing as mothers, over and over and over again during the hundreds of qualitative interviews I had done with drug-using women since 1995. So prevalent was the narrative that my anecdotal recollection is of having done very few qualitative interviews with a drug-using woman that did not include it. The routine appearance of child loss trauma narratives could be largely attributable to what Judith Butler calls the "symbolic violence" of interviews of this type, especially when these interviews take place in institutional settings.[33] According to Butler, women conform to the unwritten "rules" of confession with institutional representatives who expect this trauma narrative and the associated retributional interactions it produces: sympathy on the part of the interviewer and the relief of moral burden on the part of the respondent.[34]

The narrative is one thing. Seeing the symbol so matter-of-factly presented before me, in an ethnographic setting, was an entirely different and greatly more emotional experience. This next field note carried both aspects: the construction of the stigmatized mother-failure on the part of a drug-using woman, who interpreted my nervous smiling as judgment, and the way she carried an enlivened memory object, traumatically, and literally, attached to her body.

THE PICTURE FRAME. MISSION STREET. JUNE 2007

I didn't feel strange doing outreach, even though it was my first night. I feel like I integrated really well. People were friendly and easy to talk to. One woman—I did have a bad reaction with a woman who was embarrassed. This is important, and I forgot it the first time [in my notes]. She was somebody we [the outreach team] met on the street. Ruth [an outreach worker] didn't know her previously. The woman was really high on speed, or crack. She kind of singled me out as somebody who was laughing at her. I was smiling—Ruth and I talked about it later—I was smiling at her because I felt really, really awkward that she was so embarrassed about how high she was. She wanted stuff [supplies and food] from us, but she was definitely embarrassed to have us see her in "that way."

And then she opened her coat and showed me a picture of her daughter. It was in a four-by-six frame that she was carrying around with her, in her hand, the whole time we are talking. "I always keep her here," she said, cradling the picture carefully, very close to her body. She didn't hand the picture to me, for a closer look. As if she was afraid I might drop it. She never let go of the picture.

It was such a sad gesture, a physical, material connection for her to a life that she wasn't living anymore. And, she sort of, in a quiet voice, said, "You know, it's not a, it's not a good time, for me to be with her, right now. This isn't me" . . . which is something I've heard a lot. Women don't want their kids to see them when they're high or when they're out on the street, when they're working (doing sex work), and they describe it in a way of saying, "This isn't me." Which is a real statement about what drug use, and the associated sacrifices that come with it, can do to change who you are and who you think you are, your subjectivity. Especially how you can be as a mom, and fail as a mom, and what are okay ways to show up for your kids.

So after all that, she says, "I know you are laughing at me." Not in a harsh way, but in a more embarrassed way. I was mortified. I said, "No, not at all." But what else could I say? "I am sorry you are so embarrassed? You shouldn't feel bad?" That would all sound like bullshit, given what a personal, sad thing she had shared with me. Plus I just met her. It is very painful to see women who are so low, and kind of wearing their shame in a litany of excuses, and the picture in the frame just put me over. Like that is all she has left of being a mother is to carry around the picture. I am sure she could see it in my eyes, my sadness about that. So it was awkward, and then she just shuffled off.

This early encounter with a memory object became a searing image for me as I explored the experiences of addicted pregnancy over the following four years. It demonstrated the interplay of affective states of motherhood for women who use drugs and the temporal demands of everyday addiction and relationships with the state.

The women did not consider their symbolic mementos of their lost children to be the same as the child himself or herself.[35] However, the memory objects were very alive material representations of what the women could no longer care for—at least during their "addict time." The child who cannot be here—right now—*is* very much *here* in the photo. Participating in memorial time was an essential feature of mothering through addicted pregnancies, as Ramona demonstrated to me one afternoon. On our way to the hospital to visit her newborn son, prior to checking into residential treatment, we stopped at McDonald's. As we sat at the table, Ramona asked me, "Take a picture of me and DeLoni." I was a bit confused by this request at first. DeLoni wasn't with us. Then she pulled out a picture of DeLoni, her daughter now seven years old, who lived with a relative in another part of the state. She held the picture very close to her face. "Make sure it is just us," she said. I took the picture, and she wanted to see it. I showed her, and she frowned. "No, that is not what I meant. Just us, our faces." She told me. I took another picture. "No, that's not right," she said, viewing the second picture. "I want it to look like she is here. With me." I finally got it. She wanted the picture to create the illusion that her daughter was there in McDonald's, with us. She wanted to document her and her daughter in the same place, *at the same time*, which they could not be, due to Ramona's drug use and the state's adjudication of her mothering. "My camera won't do the trick. I can't get that close," I said. I was unable to create the memory object that Ramona desired.

When Allan Young describes the construction of the diagnosis of Post-traumatic Stress Disorder (PTSD), he outlines the importance that time and event play in differentiating PTSD from other mental illnesses that shared the same or extremely similar symptoms.[36] Here, I would like to introduce how PTSD was originally constructed in relation to temporal constraints; the very temporal constraints that the use of memory objects seeks to undo by materially "freezing" lost children in time. The specificity of the social and political context that produced PTSD is directly recognizable in the unique relation that PTSD diagnosis has to time. This relation also reveals larger tensions between the clinical recognition of psychosocial suffering as experiences of trauma and the scientific need to isolate the trauma as occurring from a set of time-delimited social events that simultaneously produce legitimate and illegitimate forms of PTSD. If on the one hand homeless women have traumatic events in their past and on the other their current everyday life is filled with ongoing traumatic violence, how can the trauma be temporally bound?

In March 2010 Anita told me a story about running back into her hotel room to get some books she had purchased for her young son. The books were Anita's memory objects. She bought books for her son with whom she was court-ordered not to have any contact unless she entered drug treatment. When her aunt brought her son to the street in front of her daily-rent hotel, Anita was able to give her son the gifts that she had been carrying around with her for over a year.[37] To Anita, the books held the potential for a future of family reunification. By buying the books, Anita had been able to enact mothering, even as she was deauthorized to do so by the state.

ELMO AND THE SKY. MARCH 2010

Anita is crying. "Kelly you would not believe it, she [the aunt] told him [Anita's son] that I was his mommy! She told him! And he said, 'That is my mommy,' and he pointed at me. It was beautiful." Anita is really crying now. Her son who visited is now three years old. "You know how I always buy him stuff but I can never give it to him, because she [the aunt] won't let me see him? Well I ran back up here in the room and found two books, one with Elmo and one about the sky. And he was so happy to have a present from his mama."

___

For Anita, the unrelenting demands of opiate and crack addiction, and housing instability, coexisted with an imagined future of mothering that was materially anchored to the everyday through memory objects in memorial time.

Life Time

The concept of life time summarizes how women talk about childhood memories, addiction and mental health problems in their biological and foster families, and legacies of poor parenting that they experienced as children. It also encompasses women's narratives of "the life"—often traumatic and violent stories of involvement in drug-sex economies and multiple, parasitic relationships with men. These forms of life time appear initially divergent, but they in fact overlap and inform one another. They form a lengthy, intergenerational narrative of trauma, neglect, and violence.[38]

Stories abound about homeless women's lifetimes of trauma. When Cupcake was describing being unable to remember all of the institutions that she had lived in throughout California during her youth, she also mentioned that she and her brother had been dropped off at CPS by their mother at the ages of two years (Cupcake) and six months, respectively. Cupcake remembers nothing about her biological mother. Dylan, who had seen her mother twice in her entire life, described being raised by her maternal grandmother and hitting the streets at age fifteen when her grandmother died. Kitt ran away from home after her mother excommunicated her from their church after her pregnancy at age thirteen and subsequent abortion. Monica described tensions with her mother over Monica's sexual molestation in foster care. Anita blamed her grandmother—her father's mother—for the death of one of her children and for her father's drug overdose death. Crysanne described her extremely violent partner convincing her to "get out on the streets" (to start prostituting and using drugs) while beating her up. Crysanne left her children under her mother's care and never returned to parent them while they were children.

One day in April 2009, I spent the afternoon with Pano and Lexi in their room at the Chandra Hotel. At one point, Lexi left the room to talk to her brother, who had just come out of prison and rented a room next door. This proximity to her brother made Lexi uncomfortable, but she also felt "responsible" for him. While Lexi was absent, Pano told me, "You know, Kelly, I know Lexi isn't dumb, but she trusts people. And she shouldn't. They take advantage of her." I was thinking to myself that this is how Lexi has described Pano, that he "takes advantage." Pano went on, "You know the reason why she has the bipolar? And she should be taking her medication? Because she had a rough road. I know she did. When she was young and her mother made her take care of that baby—she lost her own childhood. She lost her church. She lost everything to what her brother did. And it is just sad." Lexi returned, and Pano and I stopped discussing Lexi's childhood.

Later, in September 2009, Lexi tells me the whole story. When her mother was working during the day, Lexi was responsible for taking care of the kids. At sixteen, she was fixing dinner, and she went upstairs to find her two brothers naked and playing "games" with her nine-year-old sister. "They all thought it was funny," Lexi told me. When Lexi and her sister got the physicals for school a few months later, they were both given blood tests. Lexi's sister's test came back pregnant. Because Lexi's sister was so young and had been impregnated by her brother, Lexi's mother forced Lexi to claim the baby was hers, after it was born. She was publicly humiliated when she arrived at her church with the new baby and was excommunicated. The brother who had returned from prison to stay in the hotel next door to Lexi and Pano was the same brother who had got Lexi's sister pregnant. Pregnant herself, Lexi was still nervous about his unpredictable behavior but felt forced to take him under her wing. This is Lexi's life time, what she has to deal with. Pano felt that the madness of this life time had contributed to her bipolar disorder. For most women, life time functioned as a backdrop, a referential set of experiences that were both explanatory for the women at the same time they were shrugged off as normative and typical.

The Ethnographic Present/Presence

At the most rudimentary level, the multiple temporalities that shaped and constrained the lives of pregnant women in the daily-rent hotels offer a lens into how knowledge about the social problem of the addicted pregnancy is produced and circulates.[39] As I critique epi time for its social elisions, so too does ethnographic accounting need a balanced rendering. It can reveal temporalities hidden by other methodologies, even as it does so through allegiance to the systematization of rumor and the subjective experience of witnessing. Following Veena Das, pregnancy can be construed as an "event." Through both the construction of speech about and the silence or denial of pregnancy, one can see the proliferation of meanings that women attach to their past, future, and present. The way the pressures and characteristics of all the modes of temporality intersect is reflected in a field note I recorded in March 2008. The note also reveals that the narrative is revelatory of both the speakers and the subject. The talk about the event, the retelling of Marta's death, reveals the rich ability of ethnographic methods to expose the story of the story as embedded truth, as "situated knowledge."[40]

MARTA'S DEATH. MARCH 2008

There are many versions of Marta's death. The fact that there are many indicates both how much it mattered (because people talked a lot about it) and how stories travel and change on the street. Different people have different understandings of blame and responsibility. There are spoken logics about safety, protection, and exploitation that operate locally, and in unexpected ways.

Marta was someone I knew fairly well from doing outreach in the daily-rent hotels for almost a year. Tall and strong, and equally strong-willed, Marta was typically pretty well-dressed and put together, on her game, in her early twenties.

I first heard this story secondhand from another outreach worker.

She told me: "We [the outreach team] arrived at the Nisha Hotel and climbed the second set of stairs. At the end of the hallway Marta's boyfriend Axel was screaming at her, 'I don't care how bad you feel you need to get out there and work!' He wanted Marta to get up and out on the street and start turning tricks [to make money for the night's rent and drugs]. Axel had a cane, and he was menacing, threatening to beat her up.[41] Marta was lying on her bed, looking unwell, feverish and in a tucked, fetal position. We tried to get her a shelter bed, but the DV [domestic violence] shelter that does twenty-four-hour intake was full."

The DV shelter won't take women who can't be clean and sober, and Marta had a large heroin habit. I was told she also had a huge, visible abscess on her right arm. Perhaps this had been causing her fever?

The outreach team thought about calling the police but wanted to check with Marta first. Axel threatened again and then stormed out; "I am going to get something to eat! Get to work!"

When the outreach team asked Marta, they found out that Axel was in violation of his parole, and getting him arrested was not what Marta wanted at all. It would bring up other problems: the need for her to do even more sex work, without him offering protection.

Unable to offer her a shelter bed, the outreach team briefly discussed a safety plan, which Marta dismissed: "He's fine. I am just [dope] sick. He will calm down." They said, "We will check back at the end of the night if we can find a place."

A few days later, I returned to the hotels with the outreach worker who had been with Marta when Axel had threatened and stormed away. We learned that Marta was in the hospital in a coma. She was dead within twenty-four hours of our hearing the news. While we were searching for another woman, also for a DV bed for that evening, I started asking people if they knew what had happened to Marta. In the following week, I asked many more women that I regularly saw on the street and in the hotels.

Everyone I spoke to agreed that Marta had been pregnant. I also learned that when Axel had left "to get something to eat," the police had arrested him on the parole violation and he had been taken into custody for forty-eight hours. Because Axel never returned, Marta was forced to leave her room and search for money (to pay for the hotel room) and heroin to stave off withdrawal and treat her abdominal pain.

Marta went to the Bottoms, a nearby homeless encampment. There, according to one story, she was hanging out with a couple of guys. One of the guys, Winslow, returned to the hotels and said, "I just left Marta down in the Bottoms with CJ, she isn't looking good, we couldn't wake her up. I hope CJ don't try nothin'." Winslow was worried that CJ might try and rape Marta while she was in such a deep heroin nod.

It turned out the "nod" was a coma. I never heard who called the ambulance or how Marta got to the hospital.

In the days that followed I heard that Marta's death had been caused by the following:

1. "That nasty abscess."
2. "She was pregnant and after her miscarriage she wasn't right."

[This story also includes theories about a botched abortion and a potential ectopic pregnancy.] Various people held differing beliefs as to whether Marta knew she was pregnant or not.

3. "She got staph." She did in fact get a *staphylococcus* infection. I had heard that from a service provider who had spoken to the hospital. It was said that "she went septic." She was in a coma for one week prior to dying.

Despite the violent threats witnessed on the outreach shift, most folks on the street believed that if Axel had not been arrested on a parole violation, Marta would still be alive.

When I attended Marta's funeral a few days later, Axel was crying and crying, staring at the altar made in Marta's memory at the local homeless drop-in. He was so distraught that he had to leave the small gathering and stumble out onto the street and disappear for a while.

Marta's story raises, in a practical sense, the problem of authorization.[42] It provokes a self-reflexive examination of the role of time and multiple temporalities in the production of evidence about pregnancy and addiction, including the evidence produced by me. My ethnographic present consisted of both witnessing and reconstruction, as the note about Marta's death indicates. This was not only an outcome of doing anthropology as "homework," as Brackette Williams has referred to ethnographic engagements that anthropologists conduct between other daily activities in their hometowns.[43] I was, during my fieldwork, decidedly housed and distracted by coursework requirements, work requirements, parenting responsibilities, and a life outside anthropology. During my four years of fieldwork I was not there *all the time*, living in the village, so to speak. Yet the temporalities that came to bear on the women I worked with emerged as critical to my analysis, despite my lack of constant observation and despite the many events I did not see or hear about.

Multiple temporalities bore weight on pregnant women's daily lives, self-care, and interactions with institutions. I suggest that social scientific debates about the categorization of the homeless (as mentally ill and/or addicted) might be better unpacked through a consideration of multiple temporalities. The relationship between multiple temporalities and the women's meaning-making elucidated their social roles as pregnant women in their everyday lives and the technocratic adjudication of their mothering potential. The personal, the social, and the biomedical were made temporal, through symbolic practices of recording time as rent paid, drugs taken, children documented in photographs, surveys completed, and time served. Ethnographic engagement in this setting offered access to the personal, the familial, and the auto-biographical as I recorded the narratives the women told me about themselves as children, women, and mothers, growing up in their families, and their current status in and out of relation with family members. That engagement also afforded me access to the ways women's reproduction and motherhood were biomedicalized because of their identification as addicted, pregnant, and poor.[44]

chapter 3. neurocratic futures in the disability economy

I am on-site to recruit women and men into a small qualitative study about the impact of Care Not Cash (San Francisco's welfare deferral and housing policy) on HIV risk behaviors. I meet a woman, about my age, midthirties. She is very eager to be interviewed. I ask if she is on GA (General Assistance) and she says, "Not anymore."

We go upstairs to the room the drop-in center is loaning me for interviews nearby and talk for several hours. Lexi is homeless, sleeping with her boyfriend, Pano, off and on in the parking lot of a bread factory three blocks away. The bread factory tolerates the homeless as long as they clean up and disperse when the morning shift starts. Lexi has a tent; she says it is pretty okay, as long as the men don't get too drunk and start to hassle her when Pano is gone. We talk about welfare, drug use, housing, and family. These are all connected to a recent painful experience for Lexi: she lost a baby in October. She describes her confusion about why the hospital couldn't save her daughter, born at six and a half months when Lexi's cervix opened prematurely. "When they handed her to me, I thought she would just be a . . . I don't know, I didn't think she would be a *baby*. A full baby, with hands and feet and . . ." She starts to cry.

Lexi's access to methadone maintenance treatment was linked to her pregnancy through a special program seeking to expedite pregnant women into drug treatment for opiate addiction immediately on request. When she left the hospital after her daughter died, she was detoxed and had to scramble to find another funding stream to pay for her methadone. As her health status changed from "pregnant addict" to just "addict," so did her ability to make claims on the state for drug treatment access. She was put in touch with a social worker who could process her needs, and immediately the social worker encouraged her toward SSI [Supplemental Security Income]. Lexi told me: "The case worker said, 'You have PTSD . . . you haven't dealt with the death [of your baby]; you are in trauma, and you can't work.' I said, 'No,' because I have always worked. I came to this life late, to drug use late. I used to work. I didn't want to give up like that. But that was it. I had PTSD. And you know I did [have PTSD]. I mean, of course I did. But I just didn't want it to mean something for the welfare."

The addicted, pregnant women in the daily-rent hotels found themselves enmeshed in a complex web of addiction, mental health diagnoses, and housing instability in which specific forms of social recognition were in operation. As the foregoing field note indicates, I initially recognized this phenomenon on the day I met Lexi in 2004, when conducting a study of a welfare reform measure in San Francisco. The frequent co-occurrence, or "comorbidity" in the biomedical language, of substance use disorder and mental health conditions is widely documented in the public health and clinical literature.[1] The National Survey on Drug Use and Health of the US Substance Abuse and Mental Health Services Administration estimated that nearly two million women aged eighteen or older had both serious mental illness (SMI) and a substance use disorder.[2] However, as Lexi's example demonstrated, teasing out the causal relationship between mental illness symptoms and substance abuse behaviors was complex on the ground. This difficulty was an unforeseen consequence resulting from the collision of neoliberal federal welfare reforms seeking to defund addiction as a disease and complementary actions taken on the local level to diagnose mental illness in order to treat poverty. Following João Biehl, mental health diagnostic practices in this setting have become "displacements," pivotal bureaucratic events designed to manage material suffering that reference larger ongoing ideological and political debates in the United States about health care access equity and the entitlement rights of the urban poor.[3]

If the temporal demands of life for addicted, pregnant women were overwhelming, the rhetorical, discursive practices of interventions toward health and housing were equally so, and equally debilitating. The assessment of disability status played a central role in bureaucratic interactions with women substance users in general and addicted, pregnant women specifically. Historic changes in the welfare entitlement structure gave rise to a specific social actor responsible for the biomedicalization of poverty whom I call the "neurocrat."[4] Neurocrats helped grant monetary attribution to drug users whose diagnoses met beneficiary criteria. The neurocrat was, and is, an advocate-cum-bureaucrat. He or she is responsible for the documentation that distinguishes mental illness from addiction and enables health claims to become economic claims as they travel from the street to the clinic to governmental bodies. Mental illness/substance use diagnosis, suffering, and reproductive biology have combined in a new moral economy of disability, or what I call the "disability economy."[5] In order to understand the logics and consequences of the disability economy, I left the daily-rent hotels and conducted ethnography with those who are responsible for constructing and implementing neurocratic practices.[6]

Where a woman using drugs might land on the spectrum—from "mentally ill and disabled" to "merely addicted and just poor"—was highly contingent in this setting.[7] Among the women in the daily-rent hotels, few of the women I interacted with had a diagnosis of schizophrenia or showed outward signs of schizophrenic behavior. There were no nightmare visions of the asylum: women muttering, randomly yelling at people not seemingly present, lost in psychotic reverie or staring blankly, socially disconnected. Rather, spending time in the daily-rent hotels in the early and later evening meant experiencing a high degree of tension and hypervigilance among and between women and men—women yelling at people who were very much present, sharing their despairing complaints about hotel management, their manic and not-so-manic laughter, and their general frenzy. The routine chaos of the drug-sex economy was omnipresent, and I frequently felt unable to predict the dynamics of constantly emerging and dissolving social configurations at "peak hours." In contrast, coming to the hotels in the morning or in the middle of the day was like a being in the eye of the tornado. The hallways were often near-silent, with many women still passed out, exhausted from nights of smoking crack and turning tricks, a few quietly working on the acquisition of money to ensure the hotel room for that night. The hypervigilance, depression, and mania that I regularly witnessed in the daily-rent hotels matched the mental health diagnoses women gave to themselves and were given by medical professionals—PTSD and bipolar disorder.

These were "new configurations of madness," made manifest in the daily-rent hotels. While PTSD and bipolar disorder are not "new" mental health problems, these diagnoses have an emergent, and currently shifting, social history among homeless women.[8] Trauma, sorrow, rage, and mania provided an existential register for the gendered abuse, institutional interactions, and everyday housing instability these women suffered, and, through diagnosis,

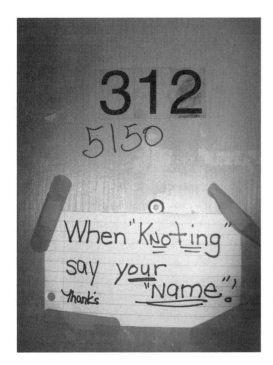

3.1. Doorway has been altered to read "5150," the police code for a mandatory seventy-two-hour lockdown for psychiatric evaluation. Metropica Hotel, April 2009. Photo by the author.

opened up doors to social legibility. The politico-scientific trajectories of these mental health diagnoses parallel this social history. Among women who use drugs, for example, PTSD is one compensatory avenue by which advocates and care providers can create a space of social recognition and gain stabilizing economic and housing benefits. The prevalence of PTSD is well documented in epidemiological studies.[9] The manifestation of PTSD symptoms is widely recognized by providers who interact with unstably housed, addicted women on a regular basis. The up-and-down presentation common to bipolar disorder maps directly onto the social experience of chronic stimulant abuse. Yet PTSD and bipolar disorder have slippery scientific pathways. Both illnesses are difficult to diagnose in the presence of active stimulant use (e.g., crack cocaine or methamphetamine). Newly minted atypical antipsychotic medications have contributed to an increase in these diagnoses among the homeless, in part as a result of a full court press from pharmaceutical companies to utilize these "broad spectrum" medications.

Most of the women in this ethnography experienced a "neurocratic pregnancy." These pregnancies included the social, governmental, and medical management of pregnancies among women who were unstably housed, with complicated histories of neglect and abuse in childhood, as well as active stimulant use, and who are assumed to have or to have been diagnosed with depression, bipolar disorder, and/or PTSD. However, to contextualize an addicted pregnancy in the disability economy, I first describe how the changing social and scientific renderings of disability gave specific character to everyday life for the San Francisco homeless.

"Disability": The Target That Moved

To understand how "disability" became a moving target, one must engage with the simultaneous relevance and irrelevance of "comorbidity"—the co-occurrence of mental illness and substance abuse—as a significant characteristic shared among the urban poor. Comorbidity is an epidemiological given among the homeless and a key construct that circulates in governmental discourses. For example, epidemiological data from national study samples of adolescents and adults entering drug treatment state that approximately 70 percent report a co-occurring mental health problem.[10] One health official I interviewed recounted the high rates of comorbid substance abuse and mental illness among the San Francisco homeless population to underscore their need for health and social services—particularly supportive housing. He told me: "Of the people in supportive housing in San Francisco, 93 percent have a major mental illness that we can name. That is very, very high. Eighty percent use cocaine, speed, or heroin every thirty days, or get drunk to the point of unconsciousness. There are no more-disabled people in this country."

Nora Volkow, the director of the National Institute of Drug Abuse and a pioneering proponent of a neurological understanding of addiction as a brain disease, has affirmed the common sense of comorbidity by reinforcing the notion that addiction itself is a mental illness. She highlights the complex pathways of causality between addiction and mental illness:

> To help explain this comorbidity, we need to first recognize that drug addiction is a mental illness. It is a complex brain disease characterized by compulsive, at times uncontrollable drug craving, seeking, and use despite devastating consequences—behaviors that stem from drug-induced changes in brain structure and function. These changes occur in some of the same brain areas that are disrupted in various other mental disorders, such as depression, anxiety, or schizophrenia. It is therefore not surprising that population surveys show a high rate of co-occurrence, or

comorbidity, between drug addiction and other mental illnesses. Even though we cannot always prove a connection or causality, we do know that certain mental disorders are established risk factors for subsequent drug abuse—and vice versa. It is often difficult to disentangle the overlapping symptoms of drug addiction and other mental illnesses, making diagnosis and treatment complex.[11]

Here comorbidity is mapped: addiction and mental illness are characterized spatially in the brain and epidemiologically recognized across populations. In addition to quantifying comorbidity, the San Francisco health official quoted earlier qualified the population in supportive housing as the "most disabled in the country" to make a related but separate point. One physical or mental illness may be clinically relevant at an individual level, but comorbidity, with its multiple, overlapping conditions, could create route to housing. While not all poor substance-using men and women will expend ssi benefits to pay for rent, garnering such a benefit can help to decrease chronic street homelessness overall.[12] Both clients and policy-makers viewed ssi acquisition as a social investment in housing stability. One policy-maker told me, "With harm reduction and the integration of the mental health and substance use treatment services, I think there is more knowledge. Specifically in relation to ssi there is an understanding that if you can get someone housed [as a benefit of entitlement advocacy] you can work on those [mental health and substance use] issues much more effectively than if they are not housed."

This policy-maker is appropriately standing behind a series of epidemiological studies that demonstrate the differential benefit to the target population and the cost-effectiveness of supportive housing interventions for the homeless mentally ill men and women.[13] In this political economic context drug addiction was not only a problem that carried emotional and financial costs to the individual person and/or his or her family. The related health and mental conditions that are documented to travel along with substance abuse, *when you are poor*, cost society a fortune. Health policies for the urban poor that attend to both treatment efficacy and cost are hardly unique to San Francisco. On the global stage, assessing the "global burden of disease" attributable to illicit drug use and mental disorders is produced through an evidence-gathering partnership between several major universities in the United States and the World Health Organization. A recent meta-analysis included "epidemiological reviews of all diseases, injuries and risk factors and estimates of mortality and cause of death for all countries in the world," in which mental illness and illicit drug use are prevalent.[14] At the local level, the San Francisco Department of Public Health (SFDPH) directly funded the generation of epidemiologic and clinical data from the largest public hospital about "frequent flyers"—homeless and marginally housed persons, often with substance use problems and mental health issues, who monopolize public resources with frequent trips to ERs and preventable hospitalizations.[15] For local health providers and policy-makers the questions arose of how best to ensure appropriate care and treatment in the most cost-effective manner while maintaining the city's commitment to a mental and physical health care safety net for the urban poor. The fiscal burden of the urban poor's health and mental health problems propelled the public health officials in San Francisco to investigate the mass movement of this population from city- and state-funded welfare entitlements onto the federal welfare rolls. The history of that local policy evolution relates to drug users in a very specific way, stemming from a nationally expressed political need to delink addiction from mental illness, in order to make comorbidity irrelevant because of costs. The federal government's move to no longer recognize drug and alcohol dependencies as disabling diseases helped to initiate a redoubling of attention toward mental illness and its relationship to housing instability and poor health.

The bureaucratic delinking of addiction and mental illness began in the late 1990s with fiery national debates about the worthy and unworthy poor. In 1996, Congress approved a set of welfare reform policies, the Contract with America Advancement Act, that were signed into law by then president Bill Clinton. Many reforms were included in Public Law 104–121, but chief among them, from the perspective of San Francisco urban health, was the decision to deny access to SSI and Social Security Disability Insurance (SSDI) for those individuals who had claimed drug and alcohol dependence as their primary disabling diagnosis.

Briefly, SSDI is a federal entitlement program supported by the Social Security tax deposit withdrawals from working persons' monthly paychecks. The program does not pay for short-term benefits or partial disability, and one needs to have a work history to claim benefits, the duration of which depends on age (called the "duration of work test"). Supplemental Security Income does not have a "duration of work test" requirement to claim benefits and does not require any work history. Rather, one has to be over sixty-five years of age, blind, or disabled. To meet SSI eligibility criteria one must also prove a limited income, citizenship, and residency. The residency requirements can be difficult to prove for women in active addiction with documented mental health disorders. They must find a local agency, individual, or even a daily-rent hotel manager who can be assigned the status of "representative payee" (rep payee) through the Social Security Administration. Rep payees agree to sign for ssi checks, pay bills and sometimes rent, and disburse the money to beneficiaries.[16] Also a federal entitlement, ssi is paid for through the Social Security general fund.

Several political economic developments led to the change in ssi and ssdi eligibility criteria in the late 1990s. First, the number of persons applying for ssi under a drug and alcohol dependency category had increased dramatically from 1989 to 1995 (from 16,100 to 130,924), so the net federal payout had increased substantially.[17] Second, the political climate during this same period supported broad measures of criminalization for people who use illicit substances (mandatory sentencing laws, restrictions on housing and job training for persons with drug-related criminal offenses) that amounted to "zero tolerance" for any public support programs serving persons with drug and alcohol dependence issues.[18] Multiple national media stories reinforcing the suspicion that drug "addicts" were using federal welfare dollars to buy drugs also emerged during this period.[19] A physician offered clinical evidence of the added harm of federal entitlements for people with substance use disorders in the public media and in a peer-reviewed public health journal.[20] Finally, one epidemiological study found that ssi entitlement enrollment was associated with increased drug use.[21]

After January 1997, the complex relationship between addiction and poverty was reconstituted from a disabling medical condition (addiction as a disease) to an immoral, malingering set of criminal behaviors (using welfare funds to buy drugs). Detractors argued that the fact that some drug-addicted people might choose to spend money on substances rather than on a place to live proved the point that addiction was, in fact, a compulsive, progressively detrimental disease that overtook the minds and bodies of addicted people. The general public and congressional policy-makers did not share this view of addiction as a disease or of addicted people as disease sufferers. It was argued that ssi benefits were enabling, not helping to stop, addiction. The public sentiment that was expressed was that addicted people were capable of working in paid employment; they just chose to spend the government's money on alcohol and drugs instead.

Thus, an individual could no longer claim disability based on the medical evidence of drug or alcohol dependence. One could, however, reapply under another diagnosis, if it was adequately documented in medical records, and win back SSI entitlements. As the Social Security Administration's website describes it, "substance addiction disorders," known as code 12.09, are no longer causative but rather are "referential" disorders. Addiction does not satisfy evidentiary criteria: "The structure of the listing for substance addiction disorders, 12.09, is also different from that for the other mental disorder listings. Listing 12.09 is structured as a reference listing; that is, it will only serve to indicate which of the other listed mental or physical impairments must be used to evaluate the behavioral or physical changes resulting from regular use of addictive substances."[22] A policy brief from the National Poverty Center made the case that most health providers, be they physicians or drug treatment counselors, recognized that persons with substance use disorders also had mental health problems: depression, trauma, schizophrenia, mania, and so on. However, *documenting* and distinguishing between those medical conditions had not been a clinical priority prior to the SSI disallowance of addiction. After the change in eligibility, it became both a clinical reality and political necessity to document other physical or psychiatric qualifying conditions to regain access to SSI benefits. The policy brief claims that "by April 1999, only 35.5% of former [drug and alcohol dependent] recipients had re-qualified for SSI under other medical conditions, most often a psychiatric disorder."[23] With the changes to disability entitlement eligibility, the neurocrat was born.

Going Mental: The Rise of the Neurocrat

The neurocrat is the person who amasses an assemblage of evidentiary documentation—clinical diagnoses, medical history, employment history (or lack thereof), proof of poverty, and other certifying paperwork—that must be collated—to claim federal SSI disability benefits. What is significantly different about neurocratic practices, as opposed to other forms of beneficiary advocacy (which are certainly not new or specific to twenty-first-century San Francisco), is that neurocrats must provide evidence of serious mental illness *in exception* of substance use. Since 1997, SSI and SSDI disability documentation has included a box in which neurocrats must testify (evidenced through the accompanying documentation) that the individual in question is suffering from a mental illness that is not induced by his or her substance use. This box becomes the technocratic trace that delinks addiction from mental illness and renders comorbidity bureaucratically irrelevant.

Neurocratic practices have become formally institutionalized into city policy over time. I remember working at the women's needle exchange program in the Mission in the fall of 1996, when women would arrive in a panic clutching letters of denial from the Social Security Administration, worried about what would happen to their housing and their ability to meet their basic needs when they were kicked off ssi in January 1997.[24] The effort to get people reenrolled was frenetic at that time. Needle exchange volunteers tried to reassure people and hooked them up to benefits counseling or case management. The impression on the street at that time, however, was that unless you had an HIV-positive diagnosis with many associated health complications, or AIDS, you weren't getting your disability benefits back.[25] Within several years, however, a concerted effort to move all the persons potentially eligible for ssi and ssDI onto (or back onto) the federal rolls became an organized political effort on the part of the sFDPH. In 2004, the sFDPH produced a cost-benefit report that sealed the "ssi advocacy" programs' ongoing support. The report discovered that there were over five thousand San Franciscans potentially eligible through mental health disability for ssi who were not receiving those benefits. Policy-makers were faced with a large population of urban poor persons in need of services and a complex bureaucratic morass of agencies and processes, as one provider told me:

> The policy climate has shifted significantly since the ssi advocacy program began in 2002. Because at that time the director of public health was like "Get these people off my back! Somehow, fix this!" Because the [ssi] advocates were pissed off. The clinicians were pissed off. The Human Services Agency was agitated, and the Social Security Administration was agitated. So all these people were brought together to discuss even "What is ssi?" and sort it out because it is very, very complicated. It is like acronym hell. Have you ever seen an award letter sent to a client? How could anyone understand that? So it is extremely complicated and it was made more complicated because it is very legalistic and you have two bureaucracies involved in it.

There are many complex moral, social, and scientific reasons why neurocratic entanglements became so common among drug users in San Francisco in the late 1990s and early 2000s. The necessity to stave off the loss of needed services resulting from ssi defunding was the driving force, but the reduction in health care costs was also an impetus. In 1998, the sFDPH adopted a "single standard of care" as its mental health policy, meaning that the uninsured would have the same level of access to mental health care as the insured. In the state of California, when SSI is awarded, Medi-Cal (California's version of Medicaid) is also granted. Therefore, hospital-based costs, other health care costs, and costs for mental health services could be billable to the federal government by the city, if the persons receiving those services were attached to a federal disability program. The unrecouped profit for the city of not getting those five thousand eligible persons onto SSI amounted to $27 million.[26] According to one provider, "costs matter, money talks" in city government.

The SFDPH study assessed the barriers among patients and their providers. It found that would-be SSI recipients could not independently manage the complex paperwork successfully to "win" SSI cases. Medi-Cal's and mental health providers' concerns were both practical (the paperwork takes too much time away from providing care) and moral (handouts do not equal health). According to the report:

> The workgroup identified that to reach such a goal [of moving eligible recipients back onto SSI], the recommendations would have to address the SFDPH clinical staff's real and perceived problems with not only the application process, but the entitlement itself:
>
> - The process is complicated, time-consuming, and often futile;
> - Advocates try to tell me [the provider] who is disabled and how to diagnose my clients;
> - The benefit is contrary to the "recovery model," it is a permanent label, and the money "enables" clients with their substance addictions.[27]

A pilot program was developed in which nonclinical staff would amass the evidence and complete the paperwork needed to make a good case for a would-be SSI recipient. The outcomes of the study changed the practices of SSI advocacy, and the way "success" was measured. One policy-maker close to the process explained:

> We attached advocates to specific clinics. They did education, they assessed the issues, and we found one hundred people whom we could agree should be on SSI. The dynamic was shifted. Instead of serving the client, the advocate was now serving the clinic and the clinician. They [the advocates] were making it easier for the clinician to get their client onto SSI. We were measuring not just client satisfaction but satisfaction with the referral source [the advocacy]. It really shifted the conversation:

now the advocates were serving the clinician, not [the advocate saying to the clinician] "My client, you give me what I need." Now the advocate amasses all the proof, and the clinician can say if they agree or don't agree. Now they [the clinicians] have just turned the whole process over.

Because the city had identified a large proportion of people who were mentally ill and not receiving SSI, resources went into this newly instantiated neurocratic endeavor. One mental health provider told me: "Most of our clients are dual-disordered [substance use and mental illness] or *at least* dually disordered. We are able to purchase about one million dollars' worth of SSI advocacy services because we found that the return on that investment to our mental health services was five to one." Relationships of solidarity were built between clinicians and the advocates (neurocrats), who now provided training about disability and completed the bureaucratic paperwork. Shifting the target of the advocacy services from patients to physicians ("now the advocates were serving the clinician") acknowledged the structural constraints on clinicians who had previously needed to assess the care and treatment needs of patients while also managing payment structures and benefits eligibility regimes. SSI advocacy, then, highlighted the benefits to the individual (housing stability), to the clinician (reduction in paperwork burden, refocus on clinical care), and to the city (reimbursable health and mental health care). All the while the federal government demanded that substance use be bureaucratically sidelined in favor, largely, of mental health diagnoses. A policy-maker said: "I think organically, and by training, and through relationships [between advocates and clinicians] who might qualify for SSI has changed [since 1997]. Because it has been proven, the success rate [of winning cases] has shown that even though they have a substance-using issue, that we are able to get them SSI, if we frame it a certain way."

Accompanying forms of fiscal management for persons receiving SSI were put in place to mitigate the concerns that clinicians had over their drug-using patients being granted large amounts of cash every month. First, a "rep payee" was often required for persons with substance use and mental health disorders. This individual could be designated by the SSI beneficiary or could be assigned through a nonprofit social service agency that does financial management and case management and sometimes offers transitional and permanent housing. In this scenario, the drug-using beneficiary is not in complete financial control of his or her welfare entitlement. Often rent is paid, and sometimes other basic needs are taken care of, and the payee only gives the individual a nominal amount of the remaining check per month for expenses. Rep payee services can charge beneficiaries fees, but the mental health system created a program to offer the service free of charge to encourage its utilization. Rep payee services were put into place to help provide financial management support for those who want it and to prevent the misuse of entitlements on drugs, alcohol, or other purchases. I have interviewed many men and women over the years who have had to use the rep payee system. Some of them have expressed gratitude in having someone else to manage their money and prevent them from spending it on drugs or alcohol, and some of them feel they have been abused by rep payees who wield an unequal power over their financial freedom. In the world of the daily-rent hotels, this could result in private hotel managers serving as rep payees, who might also have been charging women higher rents than those charged in public government-funded rooms. Another scenario was to have the liquor stores or convenience stores, which sell expensive, unhealthy food and cigarettes, serve as payees. Second, lump-sum, retroactive ssi payments have been discontinued in favor of spreading out retroactive payments in smaller amounts. In the past, once ssi was granted, if the disability could be proven to have existed for months or years prior to the granting date, back payments were issued. This could amount to tens of thousands of dollars and could trigger people in recovery from drug addiction to return to drug use and/or lead to reckless spending among active users. I have seen both in my ethnographic experience: women returning to their old neighborhoods with money burning a hole in their pockets, and women describing "burning through" large checks in one week, or even a weekend.

Even as rep payee polices have been applied, and sometimes poorly regulated, the overall shift toward embracing addiction as a disabling, organic disease in the mental health field in San Francisco is partially responsible for the lessening of clinician resistance. One physician explained the emphasis on distinguishing the substance use disorder from the mental health condition: "The advocates write the [ssi] letters for us about our patients. And they [the advocates] have been clear that the letter must say that the mental health issue is not caused by the substance use. They feel that this is very important. We have to check a box on the form attesting to that for the ssi application." In the next chapter, I discuss how that testimony is difficult in many cases, particularly for those mental health conditions that tend to be attached to homeless women—bipolar disorder and ptsd. First, however, a further investigation into neurocratic practices will capture the on-the-ground management of the evidence that constitutes mental health disability, to answer the question "How is unproductive madness made visible?" In the spirit of the dual, triple, quadruple diagnoses that are constantly evoked in relation to homeless, drug-using people by advocates, bureaucrats, physicians, even anthropologists—we need to begin by addressing the hierarchy of diagnoses that has served as a catalyst for the development of neurocratic expertise.

"Posttraumatic Benefits Syndrome"

A strong case for ssi benefits due to mental illness disability is certainly not the only route to ssi qualification. Physical health conditions, such as HIV/AIDS, also count. Yet the eligibility stability has changed over time. Earlier in the HIV epidemic in the United States, documentation of an HIV diagnosis had been sufficient to prove a disability case for ssi. Those persons who had an HIV diagnosis and drug and alcohol dependence as their disability conditions quickly reenrolled in ssi after the drug and alcohol dependence disqualification in 1997. However, with the advent and subsequent mass rollout of protease inhibitors in the late 1990s and then even more effective medications in the following years, HIV eligibility shifted. The Social Security Administration then came to perceive HIV as a chronic illness that might or might not be disabling. At a national conference of HIV prevention and care service providers in a city in the US Midwest, I attended a strategy-based, three-hour training session in which a benefits professional informed everyone in the audience about the "how to" of winning ssi and ssDi cases when HIV may not be the primary disability. The trainer numerically justified her expertise: "My average for getting a disability case approved is three months, where nationally it takes an average of 1–3 *years* and 70% of cases are initially denied."

The room was packed with social workers and benefits counselors from all over the country. As the presenter whipped through slide after PowerPoint slide, it was clear that she was an absolute professional. "I give hundreds of these trainings a year," she mentioned at one point. With humor, compassion, and aplomb, she revealed the sociocultural logics of the Social Security Administration's disability program, by laying bare the definitions and details that matter. To that end she was direct about the lack of value added to maintaining any politicized perspective on the illness experience when entering into the process of pitching an ssi case. She said:

Now the definition of disability is that an individual is unable to engage in any substantial gainful activity due to a medically determinable physical or mental impairment or impairments [and] the result of that impairment has lasted or is expected to last for twelve months or is expected to result in death.

Now I have been working in HIV/AIDS back from years ago. Back when people were dying, you know, within a year or two. When you deal with Social Security you have to realize that, even though we know that HIV/AIDS could result in death, they [Social Security] have never acknowledged that portion of it. I have never seen them acknowledge that. [Pause] Okay. When you have someone who is dealing with a form of cancer [pause], they will acknowledge that [the disease could be fatal]. If you have someone dealing with another life-threatening illness, they will acknowledge that. I am just telling you what is. I am not telling you it is right or wrong, good or bad. I am not going to tell you how to politically change things. I am just going to tell you what is, so you are successful [at winning SSI/SSDI cases].

She continued:

You see, [SSI] benefits are very much like a dysfunctional family. Don't make any common sense. Never have. Never will. It is just the way they are run. You know, they are made by lawmakers who mean well. And they create law, after law, after law, after law, after law. And then what you've got is what we have today as a benefits system. And the consumer goes to access that system and they go, "Whoa." And the sad thing is that so many people who should be able to access Social Security wind up with what I call a diagnosis of "posttraumatic benefits syndrome."

In other words, if you didn't have a mental illness before, you might get one trying to get your disability approved.

The trainer shared with us the fact that the Social Security Administration has diseases that constitute "listing levels of impairment" in "the Blue Book," which is published on the administration's website. The Blue Book, which ironically shares the same name as the nationally recognized guide for pricing a used car, is a "living document," according to the trainer, of "medical conditions that automatically qualify someone if they have met the requirements for step 1 [limited income] and step 2 [their condition is severe enough that they cannot perform their regular work]. If you find a listing level of impairment for your consumer, whether it is HIV or not, then you are automatically granted." Neurocratic practices involved a shift away from the clinical recognition of a disease. This new instantiation is materialized by applying a numeric code, making it "clear" and "concrete" that everyone is speaking the same language about the body and the mind. The trainer pulled up the website and began to guide the audience through the Blue Book. Evoking a bureaucratic logic that attends to auditable categorizations, she offered advice about the work culture of SSI case auditors in order to help us outwit an overwrought government paper-slave into not feeling harassed when an applicant's case came across his or her desk. The trainer coached us:

> Notice the numbering when you are in the Blue Book. They have a numbering system. When I do a case I use their number system, because I want their [the administration worker's] job to be so easy, that when they see my case they say, "This one is gonna be a piece of cake. I am gonna go ahead and start working on this right now." Think about it. If you get a situation presented to you that is straightforward or one that is really complicated and messy, and you have a choice of what you are gonna work on today, which one are you gonna go for first? [We answer, "The easy one."] Most people will go for the easy one. So you want to make your case so clear, so concrete that they say, "Wow, they are even using our terminology. I can't wait to get the medical records and see if this case is gonna get granted." So become familiar with the Blue Book, which is the book of automatic qualifiers that Social Security has for all disabilities, that at step 3, in the sequential evaluation process, is gonna get somebody granted.

As the training wore on, it became increasingly clear that the task of enabling social stability for the women I worked with—and ultimately health and mental health insurance coverage—was an exercise in imposing rationality onto an irrational system. The politics of recognition that benefits advocates needed to learn and deploy focused on reconstituting the experience of poverty, joblessness, despair, and poor health into legible diagnoses within a mentally unstable benefits system. Drawing out the trainer's analogy, benefits advocacy was an exercise in moving poor women substance users from one dysfunctional family—their families of origin, their home life in the daily-rent hotels—into another "dysfunctional family"—an SSI home. It would be a mistake to assume this was only a lateral move, however. Moving onto SSI might not solve all the problems that women drug users face and have faced, but it does, more often than not, give them some financial stability and increase the likelihood that they get better housing and mental health care.

Lexi provided an extraordinary description of how biomedicalized categorizations of mental health circulated in her everyday life, when I quite accidentally discovered her neurocratic paperwork.

CATEGORIZING THE EVERYDAY. SEPTEMBER 2009

Lexi and I are going to pick up some paperwork on her son, Lionel, who is in her mother's care. We park in front of the Child Protective Services [CPS] building while Lexi is telling me about a regular (a long-term trick), Gregory. She is afraid he will be picked up by the police because he always parks in the same place, every day. She explains that she "has trained him not to want to have sex too often." But she still gives him a blow job or a hand job every day for forty dollars. Gregory is upset that Lexi hasn't been available since her recent hospitalization. I wonder if he is also worried about her. I have met Gregory, and he takes care of Lexi by giving her food, gifts, and clothes constantly, as well as money. He sees himself as her benefactor. He even celebrates both his own birthday and hers with parties, which her boyfriend, Pano, is invited to as well. Pano, Gregory, and Lexi hang out often.

Lexi suddenly realizes she doesn't have her phone. "Pano was just waiting for me to leave my phone," she tells me. She fears that if she has left her phone in her hotel room, Pano will sell it for crack. She gives me a piece of paper to hold while searching for her phone in her bag.

"What's this?" I ask, looking at a form with a bunch of numerical category codes on it and boxes to check. The codes look like diagnostic codes for mental, physical, and behavioral health conditions.

"I was just doing my 'research,'" she says. "I was pretending like I was a drug counselor. I was filling this stuff out here. [Shows me the form, pointing to a question] I pretended like I was a social worker or something. [Laughs] See, I was actually trying to figure it out. See on the back. [Flips the form over to where a list of numbers and associated diagnostic conditions are listed] See, I was pretending I had a client in the mirror, and I was talking. 'OK. What's your name? How long have you been using alcohol?' And then I fill in the code on the front of the paper. This is for the Department of Public Health. It is confidential patient information. You see this [pointing to the place on the form where it says 'confidential']. This is for data and shit."

She finds another form in her purse that is filled out. "I just did this for myself. Primary diagnosis, OK? So my primary is '294AA.' But see, I should have put 'three' in there because I was referred by myself, not by the police. I was just playing [pretending], though. Because those numbers aren't right. See the way to do it is [pause] . . . OK, Axis I. Mine is [flips the sheet over] a 303.0X. No, wait, that isn't alcohol, that's heroin. But anyway, you get it. There's codes for all that shit."

She continues: "See, there are a bunch of them: 'In the last thirty days: Visit to the emergency room?' [Indicates her answer on the form] 'Yes.' 'Visit to the psych ER?' 'Yes.'"

She quickly mumbles through several other questions: "Jail, twelve-step, physical health problem, diagnosis TB, hepatitis, children in placement, children in the home. This is a trip! Living arrangement, primary source of income. This is a trip."

She hands the paper back to me and, returning to her purse, she finally finds her cellphone. "Thank God!" she says, clutching her phone as we leave the car to enter the CPS office building.

Neurocratic claims, those without a visible injury or obvious physical disability, prove to be a unique testing ground for SSI advocacy. The benefits trainer, without irony and perhaps not by coincidence, chose "bipolar syndrome" as her case example when it came to mental health diagnoses and claims. "They [bipolar cases] can be a challenge [audience laughter], and they [the SSI cases] are really hard to get granted, unless there is really, really good evidence and really, really good supportive documentation about the hospitalizations." She continues, "And it is not uncommon with people with bipolar syndrome to minimize as much as they possibly can with their medical providers, so the medical records many times aren't really true depictions of how truly disabled they really are, because many of them have shame around that disability." Here emotional and social experience reenters the arena of evidence production and the neurocrat's role is to make visible what a patient might be reluctant to attest to and what a provider might not document. Ultimately,

3.2. Benefits and child custody paperwork spread out on Lexi's bed. Nimish Hotel, November 2009. Photo by the author.

the lack of a clear biologic marker makes these cases difficult to win. The trainer explained how the technocratic trace can be problematic in mental health cases:

> So bipolar conditions are some of the hardest cases to get granted not because Social Security is trying to deny them, it's because the evidence is something that is [Pause] . . . There is no test you can do for bipolar condition. You can't do a certain test. Now I have some of my bipolar people who are so impaired, and bipolar is just one of their disabilities, so that I can throw out [the bipolar disorder]—I mean not throw out, but I can have a neuropsych eval[uation] done, which is a comprehensive two-day test. And through the neuropysch eval I have one bipolar client who's got probably three other disabilities on top of it, and we had no medical evidence to work with. She wouldn't see the doctor, she is deathly afraid to see the doctor. I did the neuropsych eval and I got so many disabilities, I got her granted right away. So, sometimes getting a neuropsych eval is the way to get the cases. The trick is knowing when to use a neuropsych eval or not. It's really difficult. You need to know that there is something *cognitively* going on that is going to be captured in the array of tests that a neuropsychologist does.

Without a clear biological marker to "test" for a mental health condition, we were told, it could be more instrumental to find qualifying assessments (like a neuropsychological evaluation) that could detect additional disabilities. Clinician experts emphasized that among their patients—homeless and marginally housed persons in San Francisco—close to 100 percent of their patients were dually or triply diagnosed. Frequently this translated into (1) a substance use disorder; (2) a mental illness; and (3) a third diagnosis that was often a physical problem that would also be acceptable in an ssi beneficiary audit, such as HIV/AIDS, epilepsy, cancer, arthritis, lupus, or chronic liver disease. Clinicians were well aware of the disjunction between their clinical tasks of caring for and treating their patients and the difficulty of providing the neurocratic documentation necessary to obtain reimbursement for their services and stabilize their patients' social worlds through housing access and disability income. One clinician told me:

> DOCTOR: There are two different directions, unfortunately, that we have to go. When they [patients] show up in our clinics we need to emphasize their psychiatric disorder as the primary problem, and that's so that we get paid. But *clinically* their primary issue may be alcohol use, and that is what I spend my time working on them with, even though they also have a mood disorder. That may be secondary to their alcoholism.
> KELLY: How do you determine what is secondary and what is primary?
> DOCTOR: Anyone who gets referred to me, 99 percent have an Axis I disorder [primary psychiatric condition bringing a patient into mental health care] and a substance use problem.[28] So when they show up, I know they have a stimulant problem and a mental illness that is separate from that. And you really can't say that one is worse than the other, one caused the other. You need to manage both of them aggressively. And when they co-occur, your treatment for either one is a step up. It is easier to treat depression in someone who is not using substances. It is easier to treat alcoholism in someone who is not depressed. When you have them both together it is just that much more difficult. So my approach is, it's more counseling, it's more group therapy, it's more time with me, it's more medications, higher doses. Sometimes it impacts what medications I give them, because there are some medications which may make their substance use disorder worse, and some medications that might make the substance use disorder better. Sometimes you get a two-for-one deal.

The neurocrat translated one form of clinical reality—the documentation of diagnoses—into a materially legitimate, social categorization that leveraged material gains, both for people who use drugs and the city itself. Neurocratic, ssi-advocacy-generated evidence did not cancel out the clinical, DSM categorization; on the contrary, it multiplied its significance. The bureaucratic demand for such evidence was pushing physicians and psychiatrists toward new ways to document mental health disability. Disability for the drug-using, urban poor population in San Francisco was a diagnosis of intersecting poor health and poverty. Interestingly, when diagnoses were at stake in neurocratic claims, the diagnostic hairsplitting over DSM categorical specificity appeared to largely disappear.[29] Instead, our trainer emphasized the importance of building bridges toward ssi linguistic categories:

> You've got your DSM, what is it? Like twelve now? [Everyone laughs; "DSM four," we answer back] Four. Is it four now? They keep changing it. So you have got your DSM. And you have got your way that you describe it [bipolar disorder]. Well, you see they [ssA] don't use that. Because there was a little group of attorneys who got together and decided that they are going to create a blue book. And *that's* how they are going to determine disability, and they got medical people involved with [pause] lawyers. And that's why you have to learn how your normal way of describing something is actually described by Social Security. Period. You make that bridge, and you are going to get cases won.

Lexi perceived herself to be "bipolar" based on a clinical diagnosis and because of the importance of getting the numerical category correct for entitlements and services. Each appellation categorized her subjectivity in a different way. On the one hand she worried about her traumatic experiences with child loss being reconstituted to "mean something for the welfare." On the other hand, she wanted to play the role of drug counselor, attempting to make her experiences with drug use, psychiatric symptoms, hospitalizations, and housing instability "count" through their numerical translation.

The neurocrat in this ethnographic setting served as the go-between. The neurocrat was dependent on the veracity of "technologies of truth" that privilege medical evidence above all other forms.[30] Yet the neurocrat also produced evidence by translating clinical diagnoses and symptom terminologies into entitlement legibility. The neurocrat's job was not to identify potential labor, or to reveal a potentially productive poor population. Rather, the role of the neurocrat was to make the madness of poverty legible. The neurocratic constitution of the madness of urban poverty limited the potential for the beneficiary to productively participate in society, while at the same time legitimizing the government's role of compensating individuals suffering from illnesses widely thought to be produced, or worsened by, the structural vulnerabilities of poverty and housing instability. One medical provider explained to me the mechanism for getting on SSI: "They walk in to the GA office and on the bottom of that form there is a box that says 'Can't do workfare.'—forever![31] [Laughs] Check that off, and then they are referred to SSI advocacy." Another physician shared her attempts to avoid Social Security Administration hairsplitting about the causality of disability, and debates about the worthy and unworthy mentally ill. In clinic she asks herself one question: "Would I hire this person?" She said, "I consider the physical and mental health of the patient *in front of me*, and I ask myself, honestly: 'Can this person *currently* do a job, any job, for eight hours a day, five days a week?' The answer is often 'No.' The question for me, is—and it should be for everyone because this is about *work*, being *able* to work—'Can this person work? Would I have them work for me?'" Last, I spoke with a psychiatrist about bipolar disorder and SSI eligibility. She was dismissive: "SSI. [Sighs] SSI is a bureaucratic exercise, it is over here [she motions away from herself with her hand]. It is important. It stabilizes people, it might keep them housed. It doesn't heal anyone. What *I* am concerned about is the patient." These descriptions help us to see how providers and neurocrats alike were bound by the structural constraints of mental health care and entitlement eligibility schemes. Many clinicians struggled to remain on task with the endeavors of health and mental health care for their urban poor patients despite bureaucratic challenges.

Neurocratic "futures" in the disability economy emerged after both drug and alcohol dependence were discontinued as medical conditions that afforded persons federally funded disability benefits in January 1997. This discontinuation, which necessitated increased focus on the documentation of mental health disorders among men and women who use drugs, changed the practices of evidence production and affected practices of care and treatment between patients and providers. In the context of perceived resource scarcity and in a federal climate in which addiction is not recognized as a disabling disease, care and stability still needed to be offered and maintained. Care and stability came at the price of operating within neurocratic logics. The practices of recognizing trauma, mania, and depression as mental health diagnoses, such as PTSD and bipolar disorder, institutionalized the desperation of homeless women. But they also got them inside, off the streets and into daily-rent hotels, or in some cases into supportive housing. In this way, participation in neurocratic practices became, and still is, a key avenue to garnering future stability and on going engagement with mental and physical health services.

In the world of the neurocrat, because of ssi laws and policies, addiction cannot *count* as a disease. This creates a discontinuity in the governance of addiction and mental health, and contradicts science and public health discourses that claim addiction and mental illness are co-influencing, organically based conditions. Addiction *cannot* be the disease that is making someone crazy, despite research and policy expertise that underscores the co-constitutive relationships between substance abuse and mental illness. Neurocratic logics create the ongoing separation of clinical and bureaucratic reality for both patients—homeless and poor persons seeking disability aid—and their physical and psychiatric caregivers. Because of emergent understandings of the addicted brain, psychopharmacological treatments for a "broad spectrum" of mental health diagnoses, and the presentation of symptoms that overlap between mental illness and active substance use, accurate psychiatric diagnoses can be extremely difficult to make from a clinical perspective. Difficult—but they are absolutely essential to leverage socially stabilizing benefits afforded through access to federal disability entitlements.

chapter 4. street psychiatrics
and new configurations of madness

I STOPPED TAKING MINE, JUNE 2008

Monica and I are walking down Mission Street on a sunny afternoon in June 2008. We come across a poster on a building for lease, one of the many businesses that will most likely transition into a high-end restaurant or bar as part of the ongoing gentrification of these blocks. The poster, reading "Against Psychiatry," catches my attention, so I pause to read it and take a picture. The fine print claims that psychotropic medications actually cause the mental illnesses that are visible in brain scans, because all the scans are taken of people on medications. The poster reads: "Look! Kids! This is your brain on psych meds!"—playing off the antidrug campaigns of the 1980s, which implied that a user's brain became "fried" (like an egg in frying pan) as a result of drug use. I ask Monica what she thinks about it. "Hmm," she says, "I don't know. I stopped taking mine [her psych medications]. They were giving me really bad dreams. I didn't feel right. They made me sleep all the time and then the dreams came."

Both of Monica's trips to the psychiatric ER have been the result of 5150 arrests after sexual assaults. Remembering these incidents, Monica has described herself as "so traumatized, so out of my mind," that being in psychiatric lockdown on a seventy-two-hour hold felt like a "relief." She said she "almost didn't want to leave." A psychiatrist I interviewed backed up Monica's experience. For a crack smoker—traumatized and hysterical in the midst of a mental health crisis—the focus of the psych ER was temporary stabilization and release. As this psychiatrist affirms, substance use can stand in the way of further mental health care, particularly among stimulant users:

> [The mental health system's] excuse is always that it is the substance use. We blame the substance use, and don't look further than it. And [psychi-

4.1. Poster on Mission Street, June 2008. Photo by the author.

atric emergency services] is designed for that. The most common presentation that they deal with, the most common presentation is intoxication with a stimulant. So all they do is give them a benzodiazepine [tranquilizer], let them sit around for ten hours until they clear [the drugs]. And they often look a lot better and they are no longer suicidal and they send them out the door. It doesn't mean that they don't have other [mental health] problems. It means that the acute syndrome has passed. And with crack, it lasts not very long at all. As soon as they [the doctor and patient] can develop a coherent plan, they kick them [the patients] out. And they don't look beyond their crack use, and that is unfortunate because there is a lot underneath. Trauma. PTSD is ubiquitous [among women who smoke crack]. And part of it is that we don't have a lot to offer them, unless they have something else [an identified mental health problem]. You can't come into the emergency room and say to me "My primary issue is that I am a prostitute and a crack addict" and expect me to have any good answers for you. Or a place to put you. Or treatment. And that's sad, because there is nothing. It's like "Oh, okay, here's some condoms." I mean, that is where we are at as far as an intervention.

According to this clinician, stimulant use can mask symptoms of mental illness. Yet with a stimulant use presentation alone, very few mental health services will be offered to women. In this sense, psychiatric emergency services could become a site for respite.[1] Although Monica had been on SSI disability for an intellectual disability (not a mental illness) since she was a child and experienced a range of serious mental health symptoms, she had no consistent psychiatric care or follow-up.[2] Monica was not perturbed by this and didn't consider herself particularly in need. Her SSI benefit kept her stably housed, and she didn't want to be on psychiatric medications. She said, "I can't live. I sleep too much [on the medications]." She told me that crack use made her symptoms—paranoia, panic attacks, anxiety—much worse. But she tried to control that on her own.

May presented a different picture. She was much more threatened by what she experienced as the insinuation that she was mentally ill and might need mental health medications. When I saw her in August 2007, she was seeking new housing. Having accepted a room in a hotel in another neighborhood, she had felt frightened. She attributed her constant crack smoking to her need to stay up all night because she was so concerned about her safety. She was wheelchair bound and awaiting an operation to help her walk. Her case manager recommended a psych evaluation for paranoia, but she rejected the idea that anything was wrong with her mind: "I am smoking crack all night because I am terrified. My place is scary. I am afraid someone is going to break in. I don't feel safe. I can't get out easily because of my legs. I feel trapped. And [names outreach worker from city mental health] wants me to go on medication—she thinks I am paranoid. I told her, 'I messed up my leg, not my head.'"

From May's perspective, there was a clash between what made her visible to health care providers and also a very expensive patient (her injury and impending leg surgery) and what made her more manageable to persons seeking to place her into housing (psych meds). Despite her rant, within several months May had successfully transferred back into the neighborhood and told me she was content with her new housing funded through a city program, for which her SSI paid 30 percent of the rent. One year later I ran into May on the street, and she approached me looking very worried. She was "tweaking" (on a stimulant) and convinced that a guy in a car across the street was following her. She had me watch the guy in his car for a half hour until he finally drove away. She was usually low-key, and this was the first time I had seen her acting really paranoid. When I hung out with her later that week in her new room, she told me a long story about the murder of her partner and her own history of multiple sexual assaults. She said she is still worried about people breaking in through her door. Does May need psych meds for her paranoia? Support to process her history of trauma? Better housing? To smoke less crack? All of the above?

Cupcake told me that going through the process of getting on ssi or any other form of welfare that might stabilize her housing would force her to be under the control of "authority figures" too much. She said, "I have a problem with authority, you know. I don't like rules. That's why I was always in trouble, always in jail. But I qualify [for ssi]. I qualify for sure because of all my childhood experiences, and because of my behavioral problems. Shit, why do you think I got involved with crack in the first place? But we [my husband and I] feel like if we went that route [and got on ssi], we would never get out of here [out of the daily-rent hotels, out of the Mission, and out of San Francisco]." In Cupcake's view, a future—being drug-free from crack and having a child that she could retain in her custody—did not include a neurocratic disability. Marco, her husband, concurred: "Even though I spent a lot of time inside [in jail and prison], I always worked. I was always able to work to make my money. Even if it was hustling. I never took no handout."

For Cupcake, crack use was a common-sense response to childhood trauma: "Why do you think I got involved with crack in the first place?" This anecdotal experience is supported by epidemiological evidence: survey research showing an association between substance use and trauma in larger cohorts of unstably housed women.[3] Monica, Cupcake, and May's descriptions of their crack use reflected a frequently expressed sentiment among women in daily-rent hotels: crack use cut both ways. While chronic crack use inevitably increased fear, anxiety, and vigilance, this heightened state could sometimes be useful, given historic and current environmental stressors. But the poverty and institutional entrapments of longer-term crack use, including the need for a mental health diagnosis to stabilize housing, created dead ends.

Kitt's explanations of her stimulant use were even more sophisticated and contextually specific. Kitt connected her stimulant use to her past and current emotional and financial needs. Her first pregnancy happened the first time she got high on speed. She had sex with a grocery clerk in exchange for the drugs when she was thirteen and ended up pregnant as a result. In 2009, she was paying child support for her four children, who were under relatives' care, out of her ssi check. During one lengthy visit together, she discussed with me her family history, her pregnancies, her self-medication with crack and speed, and her mental health history, each subject blending seamlessly into the next. Kitt explained how speed use helped her to calm down but crack was what kept her angry enough to manage the life of the daily-rent hotels. Addict time, life time, and jail time all coalesce to contribute to her structural vulnerability, drug use, relationships, housing instability, and self-identity.[4]

KITT, TWO PEOPLE INSIDE. MISSION STREET. SEPTEMBER 2008

Kitt can't really go home. Her mother wouldn't accept her, and she would need to get her own place. Kitt has been in and out of juvenile detention since she started running away at age thirteen. That was the same year she first got pregnant and started using speed.

When she got out of jail last week, Kitt was told by a local service agency that they could get her an SRO room in the Tenderloin [neighborhood] for $470 a month. This is considerably less than the $50/night she would pay in a daily-rent hotel. However, because she pays child support out of her SSI check, paying $470 for rent would only leave her $100 left over.

She doesn't feel she could survive with her drug habit and basic needs on that amount of money.

Kitt was diagnosed with bipolar disorder at age nineteen. She was 5150'd after what she called a "speed psychosis." She is currently off all her psych medications. She likes speed because it calms her down—unlike crack. "It [speed] makes me feel peaceful and sociable. Crack helps me feel angry, helps me act out about this lifestyle, this life that I am living down here. I get to fight on crack, and beat up other people, be tough and stay tough. But there are really two people inside me. One is really quiet and shy. But she can't show up out here."

Trauma is understood to be a ubiquitous experience among homeless women and PTSD to be a normative diagnosis reflecting current and childhood experiences. Yet the constant, repetitive nature of trauma exposures in this setting created a dynamic in which women often did not seek mental health care. Even if they did, they could not easily enter the system as stimulant users and access social support programs (treatment, counseling) unless they had been given a mental health diagnosis and/or were willing to accept one. Thus, providers theorized (and many of the women reported) that the women engaged in street psychiatric practices. They self-diagnosed and "self-medicated" with stimulants, opiates/opioids, cigarettes, alcohol, and other substances as a form of psychotropic treatment that kept them productive. Street psychiatrics could temporarily stave off feelings of panic, anxiety, and despair about the insecurity and violence that permeated everyday life. Many of the drugs, particularly stimulants, used for self-medication paradoxically also exacerbated these same feelings.

One service provider told me:

> I don't blame [women] for using stimulants. The mania is functional. It allows you to hustle, to get your work done. Smoke crack and it puts everything on hold, so you can be focused and energized to do what you need to do. Whether it is turn tricks or hustle up money in some other way."

Another medical provider acknowledged the downside by rejecting the term "self-medication." He told me,

> Oh, I know plenty of women who "self-medicate," who have experienced and do experience terrible trauma and abuse. But I don't like the term "self-medication." I am a physician, and I expect that when you talk about "medication" you are speaking about something that will improve health, or relieve symptoms. I have never seen crack do that. I have never seen it work. It always makes everything worse.

Women were self-diagnosing mental health conditions and self-medicating their symptoms in response to historical and current trauma, and to maintain the energy and aggression needed for self-preservation. While this may have been adaptive for survival on the streets, it was also a strange by-product of the clinical difficulty of parsing out mental health symptoms from those induced by stimulant use in the diagnosis of bipolar disorder and PTSD. This diagnostic difficulty had to be overcome to enable neurocratic futures.[5] Thus, bipolar disorder and PTSD were at once problematic to diagnosis from a psychiatric perspective among drug users yet essential to a bureaucratic reading of life in the daily-rent hotels.

New Configurations of Madness: Bipolar Disorder and PTSD

Nearly 10% of participants in an urban general medicine clinic screened positive for lifetime bipolar disorder. This is one of the highest reported lifetime estimates of the rates of bipolar disorder in primary care. Past primary care studies [done in 1985, 1988, and 1997] have estimated the rate of bipolar disorders between .07% and 1.2%. . . . The high estimated prevalence in this clinical setting may be related to the low socioeconomic status of the population.

—A. K. Das et al., "Screening for Bipolar Disorder in a Primary Care Practice," *Journal of the American Medical Association* (2005).

How are we meant to interpret the findings from this study, published in the *Journal of the American Medical Association*? Does poverty make you crazy? Are the poor more likely to be labeled as such? Similarly strong arguments have been made in the social scientific literature about the homeless: that the behaviors needed to survive in street settings—social withdrawal, aggression, hypervigilance, theft, and rage—are medicalized into mental health diagnoses for the better social management of these populations.[6] I don't disagree with this broad assessment. I also don't discount that the experiences that many women talked to me about, using the language of psychiatric symptomology, were real to them and very debilitating. It was the micropractices of behavioral assessment and mental health diagnosis on the part of homeless women and their institutional interlocutors that I found more revealing of the coconstitution of power and control. I documented the constant back-and-forth of translation from experience and behavior in the daily-rent hotels into disease manifestation through the neurocratic practices and clinical care that shaped this messy terrain. In the world of addicted, pregnant, poor women, the convergence of multiple representations of biology and social suffering occurred in relation to both bipolar disorder and PTSD.

Bipolar Disorder on Drugs: Making Sense of Mania

My curiosity about the diagnosis of bipolar disorder among women first emerged in 2004. At that time, I had been a qualitative health researcher with women who use drugs for a decade and had conducted and analyzed hundreds of life history interviews. When I began a study in 2004, I noticed something. As I was discussing women's lives, drug use, and everyday experiences, almost all the women I was interviewing reported that they were "bipolar." This was different from how I was used to women discussing themselves and their emotional experiences of health or mental health. Prior to those 2004 interviews, I had often heard recovery rhetoric—narratives of regret about drug use, sadness and despair over the inability to change drug-use behaviors, difficult family histories, and current social and housing problems. No diagnoses, at least not for mental illness. All of a sudden (from my perspective) everyone was bipolar. This trend has continued both in my ethnographic work with women in daily-rent hotels and in several other studies with women who use drugs.[7] I began wondering, what has changed?

One contribution to the change was the development of neurocratic advocacy on the part of San Francisco city officials in order to stanch the loss of revenues caused by the changes in ssi eligibility criteria and to reengage those who were dually and triply diagnosed back into systems of care. One result of these shifts could have been that women had greater access to psychiatric assessments, increasingly their likelihood of garnering diagnoses. In other words, the political economy of health care funding might have made mental illness more statistically visible. Another change arrived in the form of new medications—atypical antipsychotics—that could treat a "broad spectrum," or wide range, of mental health symptoms. These pharmaceuticals can be used even if a clear diagnosis of mental illness is confounded by active stimulant use. Finally, both bipolar disorder and PTSD reflect a medically and institutionally valid avenue to transform the mania, depression, trauma, and rage of homeless, women who use drugs into recognizable and legitimate social suffering that qualifies for aid.

To further explore what I perceived to be an increase in bipolar diagnosis, I asked a question in an email to a list of psychiatrists and physicians who practice in three major US cities: "Have you seen any changes in the diagnosis of bipolar disorder among the homeless since the late 1990s?" One physician said, "No." Another said that she had noticed more people self-diagnosing bipolar disorder, especially stimulant users who "identified with the symptoms." A third physician indicated an unequivocal "Yes." When giving reasons why, the physician stated:

> I think that most of us have seen an increase in bipolar diagnoses in patients with primary personality disorders and substance use disorders (both common in the homeless populations). This has been related to a confluence of factors.

1. More clinician/research focus on the "bipolar II" diagnosis, which has had softer criteria than "bipolar I" and is prone to overdiagnosis. [Bipolar II involves milder episodes of mania, or hypomania.]

2. New indications for the treatment of bipolar disorder using brand-name psychotropic drugs (lamictal, zyprexa, risperidone, abilify, seroquel, geodon). This has led to an all-out campaign by the pharmaceutical manufacturers to overemphasize bipolar disorder.

3. The deemphasizing of psychotherapy and the emphasizing of medication management. Psychotropic medications have limited efficacy in either personality disorders or substance-use-related mood instability. On the other hand, psychotropic medications can have a tremendous benefit in the treatment of bipolar disorder. As the old saying goes, if the only tool that you have is a hammer . . . everything looks like a nail.

When I raised these issues in a conversation with a local clinician, he concurred:

CLINICIAN: The increase in the diagnosis of bipolar disorder is due to the pharmaceutical industry, because now there is a "plethora of treatments for bipolar disorder." Physicians are much more likely to diagnosis people with bipolar disorder because they think that will help.

KELLY: The medications will help?

CLINICIAN: No. The label ["bipolar"] will help because they can put a medication on it.

Atypical antipsychotic medications have morphed from treatments for schizophrenia to treatments for most, if not all, mental health symptoms typically occurring in a population of urban poor substance users.[8] From a treatment perspective, the fact that these medications do not decrease feelings of pleasure (anhedonia) or cause sedation make them ideal of people who already crave stimulants. Another physician described the proliferation of diagnoses for which these medications are now prescribed.

The newer antipsychotics are very broad spectrum. They work for just about every serious mental illness. They work for depression, they work for schizophrenia, they are mood stabilizers for bipolar. Some of them have anti-obsessional components. If they [patients] have a mental illness and you give them a medication from that class it [the medication] is probably going to benefit it [the mental illness] to some degree. That is what we have found over time. They were first launched to treat schizophrenia only, and then bipolar, and now augmentation of depression, anxiety, insomnia, PTSD. It's everybody. It is just going to keep going.

This apparent panacea effect is fortunate from a pharmacological perspective. If an individual actually has bipolar symptoms (mania as well as depression) and is treated only with a selective serotonin reuptake inhibitor (SSRI) antidepressant drug, they may be "pushed" into mania, and they may experience an increased craving for stimulants. In that case, their pharmacologically managed treatment for mental illness symptoms is essentially working against their recovery from stimulant abuse. I asked one physician to describe the complexity of medically managing stimulant use and psychiatric medications.

PHYSICIAN: An example would be someone with schizophrenia who uses meth [methamphetamine]. If you give them Haldol, which is an older antipsychotic medication, it may increase their cravings for stimulants. Because one of the side effects is that it causes anhedonia, when you don't feel any pleasure, which can also be a symptom of depression.

KELLY: So the experience would be that they feel like they are coming down [off of meth]?

PHYSICIAN: Or withdrawing. Not just coming down, but crashing completely. And that is often a persistent feeling that they try to escape. Chronic meth use burns out the part of their brain that experiences pleasure. So without meth they have no pleasure. And I am giving them a drug that prevents them from experiencing *any* pleasure. Because they burnt that circuit through meth use, and even through recovery, I am giving them a medication that will make that worse. . . . For every symptom that leads them to use in the first place, there is a [psychopharmacologic] medication that might make that worse. So I have to be very careful not to do that. And even sedating medications that don't cause anhedonia can worsen their cravings for meth.

Emily Martin points out that in France, in the mid-nineteenth century, manic depression was known as "la folie circulaire" (circular insanity) by the Alienists, who were seeking to diagnosis and treat it. She writes: "Falret described [bipolar disorder] in 1854 as an illness in which this succession of mania and melancholia manifests itself with continuity and in a manner almost regular."[9] Among the women living in the daily-rent hotels, addict time worked in much the same way. Addict time was marked by the continuous repetition of the embodied experience of craving and temporary satiation.[10] Of all the women I worked with, Ramona gave me the most concise description of the overlap between the experiences and symptoms of bipolar disorder and stimulant use. She said, "Listen, here's me with my bipolar, right? And I am racing, and I am paranoid. I am uncomfortable and pissed, really angry. I am depressed. And here's you coming down off crack. We *act the same*. It looks *just the same*. How you gonna say that you *know* [if it's the crack or the bipolar disorder]? You can't tell the difference." Another physician went so far as to call bipolar disorder a "garbage diagnosis," especially for stimulant users.

> PHYSICIAN: [Bipolar disorder] has a tendency to be a garbage diagnosis. When you don't know what else it is, especially when they are on stimulants.
> KELLY: So you have a woman who is smoking crack . . .
> PHYSICIAN: You can't ever assess them adequately, so [doctors] have a tendency to come out with a label of bipolar disorder. And no one is doing them [the drug users] any favors because it is a bad diagnosis to have. . . . One of the reasons that antipsychotics are so popular is because antipsychotics actually do pretty well across all three diagnoses, especially the newer, the more activating antipsychotics. So [the provider decides] "Give them [the patients] some [atypical antipsychotic medication]." [And the provider sees], "Oh, look, they are doing better." What I am saying is getting the diagnosis right in those settings is very important, and very hard in someone who has not stopped using stimulants, or is still feeling the effects of stimulants. People who are two years out of speed use can still have the effects of them because of the impact of amphetamines on the brain. [Their bodies] will continue to kick or tweak [demonstrate involuntary movements of the arms and legs and jittery restlessness commonly seen in people who are intoxicated with stimulants]. They [the former speed users] are agitated, and that is not their baseline [how their nervous system would be working without the stimulant use history]. So they will come across as bipolar or psychotic. [The doctors] just don't get what is going on, to try and figure out what medicines will help them.

The physician points out that an individual may appear mentally ill when the residue of chronic methamphetamine use is still impacting their brain.

A person may be using stimulants and have crack-induced manic episodes. These diagnostic quandaries are clinically challenging and become legally important to differentiate for neurocratic purposes. Yet there are widely used newer pharmaceuticals that can both treat and mask differences in the etiology of the symptoms. These medications are not without physical side effects. One provider commented on the irony of stabilizing someone's mental health while introducing physical health risks. This provider said:

> There are significant risks with the newer class of medications. They cause metabolic complications: weight gain, diabetes, high cholesterol. We are talking about a population that tends to die early, significantly earlier, and from a cardiovascular cause. And now we have [atypical antipsychotic] medications that cause cardiovascular disease. So it is a bit risky. Twenty years ago we were giving [patients older anti-psychotic medications and they had all these movement disorders. You could see that this person was being medicated on an antipsychotic. They looked like it. They had the facial grimacing, the shuffling walk, the blank face. But they weren't overweight and they didn't have diabetes. Now, we give them the new class of medications, and they have bellies that are fifty inches around, their cholesterol is through the roof, their blood sugars are out of control, and they are dying from heart attacks. At least they run that risk.

However problematic to diagnose and convenient to medicate, bipolar disorder has become a mental health categorization that is increasingly attached to the everyday realities of women living and hustling in the daily-rent hotels. Concurrently, PTSD has become instantiated as the diagnosis that captures the familial and social history of these same women and their current experiences of violence and abuse.

Trauma Is the New Black

Trauma is the major signifier of our age. It is our normal means of relating present suffering to past violence.
—Didier Fassin and Richard Rechtman, *The Empire of Trauma: An Inquiry into the Condition of Victimhood* (2009)

Ninety-nine percent of my patients in supportive housing have PTSD. With the women it is 100 percent.
—Clinician, San Francisco (2010)

In *The Empire of Trauma*, Didier Fassin and Richard Rechtman describe trauma as "one signifier for a plurality of ills signified."[11] Fassin and Rechtman provide an anthropological investigation into the "historical construction and the political uses of trauma" by uncovering the scientific genealogy of trauma's diagnoses as well as its "moral genealogy." Being attuned to the moral genealogy allows Fassin and Rechtman to understand how the veracity attached to the concept of trauma could be utterly transformed in three decades, so that what was viewed with suspicion of malingering is now seen as a normative and expected response to the collective and individual violence pervasive in modernity.[12]

This line of inquiry, which considers scientific and moral changes to be coconstitutive, is of particular utility here. New configurations of addiction and mental illness publicly circulate and influence forms of clinical and regulatory governance. The addicted, pregnant poor woman sits squarely upon this nexus. She lives at the intersection of currently accepted truths about her: as the embodiment of a traumatic past, at constant risk for everyday violence, as a person in need of a diagnosis that will give a "traumatic/manic" reading to her life and make her socially legible. One physician with over a decade of experience treating women who use drugs provided a view into this clinical reality when I asked her about "trauma."

> KELLY: I wanted to ask you about trauma.
> PHYSICIAN: What kind of trauma? There is the trauma that shows up in ER, most often as a result of a motor vehicle accident. There is the violent, intended trauma, like "I got beat up," or "I broke my leg because I jumped out of a building." Then there is sexual trauma, which a lot of my patients have had. There is emotional trauma, which is usually attached to all of those above. So, trauma is like a very nonspecific word. When I hear that word, I always have to think in my mind: "What is the person who is using that word referring to?"
> KELLY: What do you see as the cumulative effect?
> PHYSICIAN: The cumulative effect of trauma is *huge*. And not just with the women, the men too. And some of it is just living where we live—in a city where there is a lot of everyday violence in the streets, and there is a lot of poverty. There is a lot of desperation, in certain segments of the patient population. So there is a lot of trauma. More, I suspect, than you would see in other places or other social strata.

KELLY: How does knowing that affect your approach to those patients?

PHYSICIAN: [Pause] I want to think that it doesn't. But it often helps to extenuate those things [the traumas] when I am trying to get services for them [patients]. [Laughs quietly] You kind of play on that compassion-producing response. In trying to get someone into a program, or to get them a service. Yeah. Or to get them, say, an appointment with a specialist. It helps to kind of provide more context for [the referral, to explain to the other service provider] "Why am I trying to reschedule this patient for the fifth time when they have missed all their referral appointments with you?" "Why should you even bother to set some time aside for this patient who has consistently no-showed?"

KELLY: How do you convey that?

PHYSICIAN: There is this really abbreviated language that physicians use to get their points across. We talk about people being "status post trauma" or "sexual assault childhood." "Sexual assault, CSA [child sexual abuse]." When we give their history, we usually describe people using these one-liners: "forty-seven-year-old, male-to-female transgender, HIV-positive, CD4 count x, viral load x, on antiretrovirals, with significant history of childhood sexual trauma, recent rape." It is all this comma, comma, comma.

"Comma, comma, comma": a succinct description for how the suffering produced from familial and social histories could enter into the medical record as an additive, as a contextualized proxy anchoring future mental health diagnostic claims. The sequential arrangement of emotional, physical, and social vulnerabilities could be explanatory of asocial behavior (not showing up for appointments, not accepting "help"), while it also activates exception (further opportunities to engage) by facilitating care. The "comma, comma, comma," reflective of cumulative vulnerabilities among the urban poor, is *expected*. And the impact of cumulative trauma is also expected to be visible in and on the bodies of patients, and reflected in their behaviors. In this way, perspectives on cumulative trauma mirrored circulating neurological assumptions about comorbidity, that mental illness and addiction both impact and change dopamine pathways in the brain, and frequently co-occur. These perspectives also reflected extensive clinical expertise among the physicians I interviewed; expertise that bred a keen awareness about the chaotic and stressful social realities of their urban poor patients. The physician needs to translate the impact of cumulative trauma into a medical language which relocates the structural vulnerability of housing instability and intergenerational poverty into chartable disease.[13]

"Comma, comma, comma" also caught my attention because it mirrored the way Tara had spoken about herself. Tara was a young woman I had met in early 2008 when she was six months pregnant. She liked to go to one particular bar in the neighborhood and would often show up in Monica's hotel room after fights with her violent boyfriend. Monica called Tara her "daughter," and Monica was Tara's "mom." Monica had a couple of "street daughters," younger women whom Monica relied on, and whom she could mother, because her sterilization at a young age had disallowed the possibility of her having her own birth children. Tara and Monica had a kinship bond that helped ground Tara in her relationships with men and provided someone in the neighborhood who would keep track of her. Tara's biological parents had introduced her to speed, through injection, at age twelve. She had also experienced "a lot of abuse, not nice stuff," she told me, without elaboration.

I had heard from Monica that Tara had lost her baby as a result of her boyfriend beating her up after she had come home drunk one night from the bar. "She knew she shouldn't have been drinking. He didn't like her drinking with the baby," Monica said to me. "But I don't like that man anyway." I was never able to confirm with Tara anything about the details of her late pregnancy loss. One day in late 2009, I ran into Tara at the homeless drop-in. She was explaining to another guy that she was homeless now. She had finally left her "asshole" boyfriend, because he wouldn't stop beating her up. She said, "I just want to go home [to another state]. But I can't go back and live with my folks. And they won't help me get an apartment. They don't even want me in the same city [with them]. Or my boyfriend. Fuck him." She sighed and looked over at me, half smiling, head cocked: "Trauma, trauma, trauma," she said, half-sarcastically.

Comma, comma, comma; trauma, trauma, trauma. The common-sense understanding expressed by women living in the daily-rent hotels and their medical/mental health providers was that any marginally housed woman who was using drugs would have a history of trauma, typically chronic and severe adult and childhood physical and sexual abuse, and often an additional mental health condition. One epidemiologist told me, "When we first tried to publish our data on PTSD symptoms among homeless women, the [research journal] reviewers kept sending the papers back because they didn't believe our numbers. They said, 'They couldn't be that high. The prevalence of these

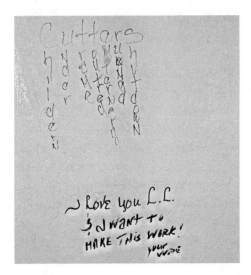

4.2. Graffiti on the wall in a Daya Hotel room, January 2008. Photo by the author.

symptoms could not be that high.' But it was." Indeed, haunted childhoods and current relationship conflicts about love and loss were written on the walls of the daily-rent hotels. Here is one example.

"Cutters" is a slang name for people, mostly women and teenage girls, who intentionally cut their arms and other parts of their bodies. Figure 4.2 shows how a daily-rent hotel tenant has created an acronym to reflect the experience of childhood trauma and its lasting effects: Children Under Trama [*sic*] Toutred [*sic*] Enternaly [*sic*] Runed [*sic*] Shutdown. Below the CUTTERS acronym there is a plea for reconciliation: "I love you L.L. and I want to make this work."

Allan Young most famously analyzed the interconnection between the development of the scientific diagnosis of PTSD and the specificity of its social history. He described how the need for scientific validity in psychological assessment created a technique of diagnostic measure, the use of the DSM, which established rigid criteria for what is "true" in terms of mental health diagnoses. In an active effort to allay criticism about the "soft" science of psychology and create institutional credibility for psychiatric diagnoses, the DSM-III was revised using the following claims: "(1) Mental disorders are best understood by analogy with physical diseases . . . (2) the classification of mental disorders demands careful observation of visible phenomena . . . [and] (3) empirical research will eventually show that the serious mental disorders have organic and biochemical origins." The scientification of PTSD, which had the same parentage as the "DSM-III Revolution," functionally sidelined psychoanalytic clinical criteria and introduced multiple forms of statistical validity (face, predictive, and independent), which were consciously "indifferent to vagaries of content and context."[14] This process is a diagnostic manifestation of what Ludwik Fleck refers to as the false assumption of a determinative logic between conceptualization and evidence.[15] That is, in the case of PTSD, what the disease was became inextricably tied to how the disease was being categorized and quantified.

While it is not the ethnographer's role to reach a final judgment about what is "real" and what is "true" about the experience and diagnosis of PTSD, the clinical-level hairsplitting has dissipated in relation to unstably housed women who use drugs. According to the providers I interviewed, all women met the diagnostic criteria for symptoms in screening; they all told narratives of childhood and adult exposure to trauma and violence. However, there are concrete material and social consequences that today are inherent in a PTSD diagnosis, and it is important to recognize the subtle circularity at work.[16] PTSD is produced and deployed in response to specific social and political circumstances—the traumatizing effect of childhood abuse and adult homelessness. Yet the need to clinically legitimatize claims of trauma subsumes and reconstitutes the conditions under which traumatic dysfunction can be claimed and appropriate medical and social services can be requested. Among the women in the daily-rent hotels, PTSD was political, economic, and social in etiology. Its intimate links to social benefits could not be easily disentangled. The site of diagnosis provided the terrain on which these epistemological shifts were realized in moral, practical, and financial terms.[17]

It was difficult to attempt to distinguish and bound the sheer magnitude of the trauma-inducing events that unstably housed women experienced, over a lifetime and within the years of my ethnographic engagement.[18] The "comma, comma, comma" of cumulative suffering in this setting served to overdetermine the naturalization of trauma while also euthanizing its collective emotional response. In the everyday worlds of addicted, pregnant women, multiple temporal demands interacted to produce a form of constant antagonistic stress, the symptoms of which manifested in street and institutional settings. It was difficult for the physicians, the outreach workers, the anthropologist, and the pregnant women to account for the impact of specific traumatic events. In short, traumatic events never ended, or appeared not to—like a perverse orgy of misfortune.[19] The provider quoted at the beginning of this chapter claimed that stimulant (crack)–using women would not receive mental health treatment because the mental health system was not set up to meet their needs. On the other hand the mental health system did recognize (in accordance with all health providers I interviewed) that the physical and social environments in which women lived created and exacerbated emotional traumas. Trauma, again, was recognized as ubiquitous, yet somehow poorly managed in response. The result, in one's physician's experience, was self-medicalization with substances.

> PHYSICIAN: If they [women who use drugs] walk into a mental health clinic, they are not going to feel comfortable. They may or may not have a mental illness. If you walk in with schizophrenia, there is a group for you! If you walk in and you are a crack addict, there is no group for you.
>
> KELLY: What about for PTSD?
>
> PHYSICIAN: We aren't the VA [Veterans' Administration]. We aren't prepared for it. At the VA it's the first question, everyone gets screened for it. We don't do a good job with trauma. Perhaps if there is a sexual assault that enters into the ER, [services exist] to put [the patient] in position [to get mental health follow-up]. But that is different than someone who is essentially raped every night, or assaulted in some other ways on a daily basis. The chronicity of it is much more damaging. Kind of like a combat vet. And it is much more [pyschotropically] treatment resistant as well. It also doesn't bring them in for treatment because it is repetitive. It's like, "OK, this is my life. I live on the street. Yeah, people are going to beat me up and take my money. Happens all the time. Happens to everyone around me. Why should I seek treatment for it? I just drink [alcohol] instead. Or smoke crack." I think that [crack] is one of the most common forms of self-medication for PTSD.

I found that an individual woman's emotional connection to traumatic events and her acceptance of mental health treatment was influenced by her degree of social and economic desperation. Poverty, and other ongoing structural vulnerabilities, continually informed acceptance into diagnostic categories. Two of Lexi's pregnancies illustrated this point. In 2004, when we first met, Lexi had recently lost a baby under tragic, emergency circumstances. Her daughter had been born prematurely when she was six and a half months pregnant. Her cervix had opened up. The hospital officials were unable to resuscitate the baby at birth. Lexi always felt that the providers had not done enough to save her baby because she was a drug user and she is black. A case manager insisted that Lexi apply for disability because of "PTSD" after her baby died. She resisted having her trauma "mean something for the welfare," even though she recognized that she was, indeed, traumatized.[20]

In 2008, I accompanied Lexi to an appointment to try and get her Section 8 housing reinstated. She had applied while in jail, when pregnant with her son, Lionel (now age seven). "I couldn't believe it when my sister called me and told me I got the letter. It took *that* long [seven years]," she told me. We drove to another county for her appointment. When she was in jail she had filled out applications for every county in the Bay Area, and one out of San Francisco had finally come through. "I am going to get my housing figured out and I am going to have Lionel move back here," she tells me on the drive. "We can finally be back together." Lexi was excited. When we get to the appointment, the official asked her a bunch of questions. One was about disability. I noticed Lexi emphasized that she had PTSD. The official looked up and nodded, making a note of it. Later, Lexi had to mail back more paperwork, but she didn't do it. I asked why several times and she was dismissive about it, saying, "Yeah, I got to get that stuff together."

Soon after the Section 8 eligibility visit, Pano was back out of jail. Then I realized that she had not followed up on the paperwork because she didn't want to live so far away from Pano, who would remain in the neighborhood. Pano was only briefly out of jail, though, just long enough, according to Lexi, to get into a money-related conflict with her daily-rent hotel manager. Lexi ended up facing eviction from her room for nonpayment of rent. She tried to fight the eviction by using the advocacy services available to "SRO tenants." During an attempt to "stay" her eviction, the case worker asked her if she had any "disabilities." Knowing that saying yes would increase the chances of getting more time to fight the eviction, she said, "Yes, PTSD." The eviction worker made a note of it. She was evicted anyway and spent eight months on the street, homeless, after which Pano returned from jail. Lexi became pregnant again shortly afterward, in early 2009.

In Lexi's case, her PTSD diagnosis did and didn't matter. In her initial resistance to the diagnosis, PTSD marked a boundary for her. She did not want to be marked as someone who could never work (her perception of what receiving SSI meant), and she didn't want her personal trauma medicalized. Later, when Lexi's situation became more materially desperate and her drug and alcohol use more entrenched, PTSD became a potential lever. On the one hand it served to make her a legible "victim," a person rendered more vulnerable in the eyes of governmental housing agencies than someone without such a diagnosis. On the other hand it did not instrumentally translate into some form of psychiatric care or social support that could stabilize her housing or income.[21]

In early 2010, when I spoke to Lexi, she was trying not to smoke crack or drink alcohol—and had received her first clean urine tox at her methadone program in four years.[22] She said to me, "I am finally getting housing. I am getting on SSI. But I am doing it all myself. I went to the SSA [Social Security Administration] office on my own, 'cause I can't get anyone to help me. Now I just need a psychiatrist. Everything else is in place, because they [the SSA] have a record of my PTSD from way back in 2004! I just need a psychiatrist but I don't know where to get one." Lexi was surprised that her case had just been sitting there, at the SSI office, for six years. Although she had a paper trail, she was forced to serve as her own advocate.

Neurocratic Pregnancies

One hundred percent [of the pregnant women in drug treatment pro-grams] have a treatable mental health issue. Most will report either PTSD or bipolar disorder, but they have not been clinically assessed for those disorders. They are familiar with the symptoms. They have friends who have these diagnoses. They look at their own histories, especially the severe, just horrible, histories of trauma that these women have gone through, and these disorders seem like a fit.
—Health care provider (2009)

Craving pickles during pregnancy is fine. Craving crack is not. This social reality can be extremely problematic for pregnant women if one is to "treat" addiction as a brain disease. In the biological model of addiction, pregnancy status would have no causal bearing on "learned addictive behaviors," and the stress of a pregnancy within the context of the daily-rent hotels may in fact increase drug use. According to a neurobiologist of addiction I interviewed, reactions to stress that are organic mechanisms in the brain—that have nothing to do with choice and everything to do with chemistry—can trigger a return to drug use behaviors, particularly in environments where people have used drugs in the past: "It's in the brain. It is all in the brain. And there is no question that if you read the literature everybody agrees that stress can reinstate drug taking in animals that have had that behavior extinguished, or who are abstinent. So stress will do it [initiate drug taking]. Sometimes a small dose of the drug will do it. Sometimes going into an environment where you have previously had the drug will stimulate you to take the drug again." This catch-22 quandary extends to issues of emotional well-being. Moods that swing from angry to happy to deeply sad are normal in pregnancy. They are the result of hormonal fluctuations. Bipolar disorder, PTSD, and the medications often used to manage those conditions can be problematic during pregnancy. Ten to 20 percent of pregnant women experience depression during pregnancy; 10–15 percent report postpartum depression.[23] Women who are depressed prior to getting pregnant run an increased risk of postpartum depression.[24] Among women who have a bipolar diagnosis prior to pregnancy, 25–50 percent experience a severe affective puerperal (postpartum) psychotic episode.[25] Women who have mental health diagnoses and are already engaged in a health care system can face the difficult decision of continuing on psychotropic medications that may have helped their mood state and daily function but now place their fetuses at risk. As one clinician pointed out, women who have bipolar disorder have an evitable risk of "psychotic episodes" after their babies are born.

> Atypical antipsychotics are actually fairly safe in pregnancy. But the other component is that you have to be prepared for their symptoms to get worse if you change medications. So if somebody becomes pregnant and they were on [names a medication], I might say, "Well, it's the first trimester, it is pretty risky that your child will have a neural tube defect, and not be born viable. So I can stop this medication. But now you're pregnant and I am changing your medications around. The risks of you becoming unstable during your pregnancy increase, but the safety to your child may be more favorable. And then once you deliver, we are going to go back to something that worked." But that is also another high-risk period for postpartum psychosis. And women who are bipolar are at by far the highest risk for having postpartum psychosis. It is almost diagnostic for bipolar. It can happen outside of bipolar disorder, but it is kind of a telltale sign that you have bipolar disorder if you have postpartum psychosis.

Some of the women, like Lexi (who had diagnoses of both bipolar disorder and PTSD), just quit taking their psychotropic medication on their own when they discover they are pregnant, and they leave the health care system.

For the addicted, pregnant women I worked with for this ethnography, mood states mixed regularly with drug use and the work (hustling) necessary to meet basic needs and stay housed. Pregnancy destabilized mental health, through fluctuations in mood, sleep, hormones, and anxiety. Pregnancy was additive. It was an add-on stressor to an already stretched-to-breaking emotional inner world and an irrationally violent and exploitative social world. Notions of "pregnancy as disability" and the disabling aspects of pregnancy for homeless, women who use drugs are interrelated. None of the pregnant women had jobs for which they were eligible for short-term disability benefits as a result of their pregnancy status. Some were already granted ssi disability for mental and physical health conditions. All of the women who did not enter residential treatment went back to (sex) work shortly after giving birth. Lexi needed to turn tricks to pay down her hotel debt immediately after she left the hospital. She worked even though she had not healed properly from her hysterectomy. Ramona was pulling dates down the street when I came to accompany her to her methadone intake appointment, five days after her baby was born, also because of hotel debt, underscoring how "hotel time" dominated women's lives in this setting. These experiences provided an extension to the concept of stratified reproduction.[26] Not only are some women discouraged from reproducing; some women get to claim disability as a result of childbirth and some don't.

Indeed, the discussion over what neurocratic futures might be possible for pregnant women never left the political economic domain, because battles over scarce public health dollars were constant, and continually renegotiated. The costs of care and treatment for addicted, pregnant women emerged in most conversations I had with clinicians, regardless of how scientifically technical they may have been at the outset. The argument was made that pregnancy and addiction would do well to plead its case in relation to health care costs. The lion's share of mental health resources for stimulant users in San Francisco were deposited into programs that served the health needs of men who had sex with men. Men who have sex with men and who use methamphetamine are at very high risk for HIV infection.[27] And HIV infection and AIDS are very expensive diseases. But as one clinician pointed out, women who use drugs, are unstably housed, are working as sex workers, and get pregnant are also at risk for HIV infection. Focusing on the cost of caring for their infants postpartum was suggested to me as an appropriate strategy to bring attention and resources toward this neglected group. The clinician said:

Gay men plus meth equals HIV. That is just how the funding calculus works. Now, women plus sex work plus crack *does* equal HIV but it does not get the same level of resources. And I don't know why. Even if it isn't the same level of risk [for HIV] it still seems that the funding is too uneven. We can even break it down to costs; look at the dollars. What happens when those women get pregnant and show up at the hospital? These are kids that are in the NICU [neonatal intensive care unit] for days afterwards [postpartum]. There is a lot of resources that go into the follow-up for babies that are born to mothers that use heroin. We need to look at the [health] outcomes. I think that [allocations of funding] become arbitrary without looking at the outcomes.

The reality of comorbidity (dual, triple diagnoses) made the compartmentalization of intervention responses to addicted, pregnant women almost immediately inadequate. How is the decision made to try and respond to the addiction before the mental illness, or vice versa? Diagnosing and responding to (1) a substance-use disorder (with a replacement drug therapy), (2) a mental health condition (with a mood-stabilizing drug), and (3) a social environment bereft of support or future orientation (with stable housing) was a complex task. I discussed this challenge with a clinician who had a broad knowledge of both psychopharmacological agents and the everyday lives of addicted women and men. I mentioned that many women whom I knew who were pregnant did not necessarily have an opiate/opioid addiction, so they did not have access to one of the drug treatment programs offering psychiatric evaluation. She reflected:

> There is no place for them [crack-using women] to show up. Unless they get pregnant. And that is unfortunate, that the first time that we [the mental health system] catch them is when they are pregnant. If they get court-ordered late in pregnancy, it is partially because there is not a lot that is available to them before that. We used to have a program that was defunded and may not even exist anymore. When I started, I worked with a program that was a place that women who were crack smokers could show up.
>
> But with cocaine, though, it doesn't matter if it is in methadone or through the mental health clinics. At no stop along the way do they have anything [in terms of a pharmacological replacement therapy] to offer somebody that uses, abuses stimulants, whether it is crack or meth. We don't have a drug [a psychotropic medication] that works for stimulants.

4.3. "2 Do" list written on the wall in a Chandra Hotel room, March 2010. People have annotated the original list, which is focused on buying hygiene supplies: guaze (*sic*) and tape for treating abscesses, lotion, clothing. Additional things to acquire are drugs, pussy, and a new man. Next to the list someone has written: "Crazy? No Mother I'm awake." Bloodstains from blood shot from used syringes can be seen on the bottom right. Photo by the author.

If you have mental health symptoms, if you are depressed, I will treat your depression and I will do it aggressively with the hope that it will have an impact on your crack use.

And that is our approach: to take whatever else we can do something about—whether it's their opioid addiction, their depression, their bipolar—and treat it really aggressively to put them in the best place to engage in therapy or counseling for their cocaine addiction. That is the best we can do. And that can be important because their life is often so chaotic because of the combined effects of, you know, being bipolar, untreated, and a crack user, that they are never gonna stick in a counseling program for their crack use, until we stabilize their mood, stabilize their housing, hook them up with medical services. And give them a lot of support so they can show up [to addiction counseling] on a daily basis for group.

The evidence that counted to make addicted, pregnant women socially legible was shaped by practices of addiction and mental health treatment that assumed that both conditions were brain diseases that were heavily influenced by each other and by the environment in which the addiction, trauma, mania, and depression were being experienced. Clinicians (physicians, clinical pharmacists, and psychiatrists) sought medications that could manage both substance use and mental health symptoms. It was hoped that a psychopharmacological pathway could displace narratives of moral failure. A focus on disease offered that possibility. Yet current treatments for addicted, pregnant women were still organized around notions of personal responsibility. One provider told me: "The problems of responsibility and accountability are huge. We are a drug treatment program. We expect accountability; we expect people to admit they have a problem, and that they need to take responsibility for it. Especially pregnant women: they need to take responsibility for the fact that she is going to have a child."

Medicalization and personal responsibility were strongly linked in programs that could offer a "drug substitution" for addiction (methadone for heroin, for example), and this may be cause for deserved critiques about the governmentality of addiction and the social control of "addicts."[28] For pregnant women who used crack—for which there was no drug substitution—drug treatment and mental health services were much more limited.

Mental Health Transience

"Residential transience" (the movement between dwellings and changes in types of housing) is a risk for poor physical and mental health among drug users that has been documented in the public health literature and was an ever-present weekly reality for the women in the daily-rent hotels.[29] These same women also suffered from and leveraged mental health transience.[30] Mental illnesses moved. Diagnoses became an essential legitimizing force for making entitlement claims on the state. Diagnoses attached themselves to practices of recognition for gendered physical and sexual violence in childhood and adulthood, through PTSD. Bipolar disorder captured the often despairing, yet also maniacal, social landscape of everyday life. Residential transience was conceptualized as an aggregate risk—not, by definition, affecting each individual in exactly the same way. Mental health transience successfully swept up some pregnant women into moral worlds that felt explanatory of their familial history (Kitt making the connection between running away from home, getting pregnant while using speed, and getting a bipolar diagnosis), and even comforting (Monica's 5051 after being raped). Other women utilized the social benefit opportunities that mental health transience offered (Ramona at her methadone intake, May to get rehoused in a better hotel, Lexi modifying her appropriation of her PTSD diagnosis over time).

Addiction, mental illness, pregnancy, and disability formed a complex assemblage of biological and social markers that enabled state recognition and required governmental regulatory management. Neurocrats emerged out of a dual need on the part of city health policy-makers. On the one hand neurocratic recognition practices were designed to ensure economic stabilization for drug- and alcohol-dependent persons. Renewed SSI was meant to stave off street homelessness within the larger political context of welfare reforms that punished poor women, particularly poor, pregnant women and mothers, and an increasingly virulent War on Drugs campaign. City health officials also needed to support SSI advocacy for mental illness eligibility in order to bill for services delivered within the health and mental health safety net. Diagnoses of bipolar disorder and PTSD among drug-using, unstably housed women occurred in a service context in which mental health diagnoses were needed and valued. These diagnoses followed a pharmacological logic. Atypical antipsychotic medications entered the market and appeared to successfully treat the broad spectrum of symptoms of mania, depression, rage, and despair that characterized women's lives, even if ongoing crack use confounded the majority of diagnostic attempts. These complex interactions between addiction and mental illness gave a specific valence to how pregnant women experienced stratified reproduction in the context of the daily-rent hotels.

chapter 5. stratified reproduction and kin of last resort

Reproduction: Social/Actual

"I got two kids . . . both my daughters got adopted. The first one was born in 1999. I was too young, I was like fifteen, just turned sixteen. I didn't have a place to go so they [CPS] took her. I wasn't able to get custody back of her because they said I wasn't stable . . . [I feel that] I was too young. I wasn't ready. She's better off. Not better off, better off's not the right word. But I think she's all right. I didn't feel like it [her being taken away] was a good decision at that time, because a mother, well, every—well, not every [pause], but a mother wants to be with her child. And I look back on it now and it is probably good that she has had something stable, because ever since then, you know, I have been through a lot of shit."

"And then my other daughter. I had her in 2004. I was in a [drug treatment] program and then I relapsed and lost her [to CPS]. I had been court mandated to the program at three or four months [pregnant], and I stayed there my whole entire pregnancy. But I was on drugs too [before the program], so it was good that I got clean when I did [early in the pregnancy]."

"Did you catch a case [a sex work arrest]?" I ask.

"Yeah, but I got treatment, through Prop 36.[1] You know when they give you like twenty chances [to enter drug treatment and stop using drugs]. I had pretty much expended every chance that they gave me. You know, like I was just one [chance away] before they would have canned my ass [sent her back to jail]. [We both laugh.] If I wasn't pregnant, I don't know, I think they would have given me [jail] time. 'Cause I just didn't care, like I said. I didn't like rules."

"You were smoking a bunch [of crack] at that time?" Cupcake nods, yes.

Attention Drug Addicts And Alcohol...

Get Birth Control Get $300 Make
The Call Today
1-888-30-CRACK
Every Baby Deserves A Sober Start!

5.1. Project Prevention Facebook ad.

"Were you thinking about treatment?" I ask.

"No. Not before I knew I was pregnant. Not before they tested me in jail. But I didn't want to have no crack baby either. So once I tested pregnant I thought maybe this is my chance to straighten up. So 'Fine, give me the program.' So I was *willing*. But I still wasn't completely [pause] giving up [on drug use]. I didn't like the rules. I got lots of consequences, but still, I stayed [in treatment]. But after she was born it was a big jump from the program to transitional [housing] for me. I wasn't ready. And I relapsed and lost her."

"How did that work? Were there [CPS] case workers coming to see you?" I ask.

Cupcake: "Yeah. They are *always* coming to see you. And you got to go in on your certain days and you can't be late and all that. Same thing as like a probation officer. [Pause] I got overwhelmed I guess, and it was a lot and I was trying to find employment. You know, I never had had a job before, you know what I mean? It was just a lot of different stuff. And so I went to another [drug treatment] program, but you couldn't have your kids there, but you could have visits [with your child]. And I did that, and I graduated from that program. The judge said I had to do a six-month program, without her [Cupcake's daughter], and that was part of the stipulations of getting my daughter back [into Cupcake's custody]. So I did the program. But once again I did it for *her* [for her daughter]. I wasn't doing it for myself. And that is where a lot of my whole thing was, was not doing it for me, you know?"

The image of the child in the Prevention Project's advertisement for paid birth control and sterilization of women who use drugs (fig. 5.1) and Cupcake's narrative of her experiences with incarceration and drug treatment during pregnancy tell two different stories in two different ways. On the one hand pregnancy and addiction is reduced to a disturbing image of a suffering baby, with a paid offer to avoid a similar future tragedy. On the other hand we see the complex world of Cupcake, at sixteen years old and pregnant, but initially unaware of it, attempting to manage the pressures of addiction, poverty, and motherhood under the adjudicating eyes of the state.

The multitude of ways the addicted, pregnant women I worked with interacted with and avoided systems of care and control throughout their pregnancies is demonstrative of the phenomenon of "stratified reproduction" at work in the United States. "Stratified reproduction" was first coined by Shellee Colen and was applied broadly by Faye Ginsberg and Rayna Rapp in their work to "transform traditional anthropological analyses of reproduction and to clarify the importance of making reproduction central to social theory."[2] Stratified reproduction is a concept used to "describe power relations by which some categories of people are empowered to nurture and reproduce, while others are disempowered" from doing so.[3] Examples of stratified reproduction are plentiful in the United States and throughout the world.[4] State-funded efforts to forcibly sterilize women in communities of color, particularly poor African-American women, offer a poignant and shameful example that is both historical and currently circulating in political discourse in the United States.[5] For example, state representative John LaBruzzo has proposed to pay poor women in Louisiana $1,000 to undergo surgery to have their fallopian tubes tied in order to "reduce the number of people going from generational welfare to generational welfare."[6]

I am interested in exploring the divergence between the complex experience of addicted pregnancy (such as Cupcake describes) and its representation in the wider public (through advocacy programs and the media). While the concept of stratified reproduction applies to varied groups of women, the specific vulnerabilities of women who use substances while pregnant or parenting has been highlighted by several authors. Nancy Campbell offered an astute and thorough examination of the historical construction of women drug users in the United States in *Using Women: Gender, Drug Policy, and Social Justice*. Campbell describes the seedlings of ideological constructs that have taken root in current debates about pregnancy and addiction. In order to examine how historical debates about substance use during pregnancy are currently scaffolding onto new scientific imaginaries of addicted pregnancy, we first need to visit the past.

By historically situating women who use drugs, Campbell offers critiques of both positivist renderings and narrative representations of drug users in the United States. A lack of methodological transparency and ideologically driven pronouncements about pregnancy, women, and drug use have created a dangerous, widespread influence in policy arenas: "Women who use illicit drugs embody both individual deviance and social failure; the difference between drugs and their users have been racialized and their meaning encoded in the 'figures' of women who use drugs on which political discourse relies. . . . Such gendered and sexualized meanings of women and drugs . . . show how public constructions are produced, how they circulate, especially in public policy, and the assumptions that shape them."[7] By analyzing media representations and public court cases involving women drug users and, importantly, critiquing ethnographers who study women who use drugs, Campbell makes the case that women who use drugs have been construed as "spectacular failures." She argues that all these forms of representation contribute to the "governing mentalities" that underpin drug policies: "Basically how we 'know' drug addicts matters for how we govern them."[8]

According to Campbell, then as now, "addicted women are understood to reproduce their own (in)humanity, as well as offspring who are not fully human."[9] The fact that women in general bear the brunt of responsibility for social reproduction lies at the heart of medical intervention and state management strategies that seek to exert control over the lives of addicted, pregnant women and their offspring. In her analysis of *Born Hooked*—the published transcripts of congressional debates and expert testimony about drug-using, pregnant mothers and their children that were held before the House Select Committee on the Welfare of Children, Youth and Families in 1989—Campbell demonstrates that the divisive political climate over fetal rights between feminists and conservatives in the United States forced a new form of biopolitical management of addicted, pregnant women to emerge.[10] She writes: "Anti-abortion advocates forced feminists to defend 'unfit' mothers and occupy an almost (but not quite) indefensible position." Through these intricate acts of deferral, political consensus came to rest on the health of the fetus over the course of these hearings, and what Campbell calls "postmodern progressivism" was born. "Postmodern progressivism occurs with 'the redefinition of coercive measures as compassionate rehabilitation—and the inevitability of punitive sanctions. [Campbell states,] I call this reconfiguration 'postmodern progressivism,' distinguishing the expansive Progressivism of the earlier twentieth century from today's version, which takes place in the context of the ideological contraction of the state's responsibility for social provision."[11]

Several women in my ethnography experienced a current addicted pregnancy, while also remembering changes that occurred historically in the adjudication of prenatal substance exposure. Anita had given birth to her eldest child, then twenty-one years old, when laws were changing toward pregnant women who were suspected of using drugs. She told me a story of a baby the hospital staff had put on "hold" in the neonatal intensive care because the mother had admitted to smoking crack while pregnant. She said, "My daughter was born clean in 1989, but she had meconium and could not breathe well at first. So she went to the ICU for a while first. I remember I went there to see her, and I saw this other baby, a big baby, who looked perfectly fine. I asked the nurse why the baby was in the ICU, and she said, 'Oh, that baby has a drug hold on it.' I was so glad not to be in that situation, because that baby looked just fine, but the mom got caught using [drugs]." This story of Anita witnessing the shift toward increased social control over apparently healthy babies was in juxtaposition to Lexi's description of a hospital where the ideology of family unification trumped biomedicalization, at least for a period of time. One day when Lexi and I were driving back from her methadone program, she pointed to a hospital nearby. She said, "This is where all the women [who used drugs] would come to have their babies back in the day [in the 1980s and 1990s]. You know I had Lionel late, I wasn't pregnant until 1999, but I remember hearing stories about this hospital. You see the folks there [at that hospital] never took no mama's baby away [because of a mother's drug use]. If you had your baby there, you could keep it."

As pregnant women, drug users became increasingly criminalized during the late 1980s and early 1990s in the United States. For a period of time, feminists fought back successfully against criminal measures to arrest and incarcerate women who used drugs while pregnant. According to Campbell, winning this battle meant advocating "postmodern progressivism," which included feminists supporting increased involvement on the part of the drug treatment and child protective services institutions in order not to appear as if they were laissez-faire about drug use during pregnancy, or ignoring the potential adverse consequences of prenatal substance exposure. "Feminists had to argue for increased access to treatment, gender-specific treatment, and parenting education, even though these techniques lend themselves to a form of social discipline and surveillance. By broadening the analysis to what pregnant drug users need from the state and society, feminists were paradoxically placed in the position of arguing for the expansion of postmodern progressivism as the lesser of two evils."[12]

Medical sociologists Marsha Rosenbaum, Sheigla Murphy, and Paloma Sales, with their qualitative work in two studies that span the years 1991–1998, have offered a critique of neoliberal policies directed toward pregnant women that mirrors aspects of Campbell's thesis.[13] To Murphy and Sales the construction of pregnant drug users as irresponsible citizens was part of an "ideological offensive," created through media-generated portraits of "welfare queens"— women who only get pregnant in order to receive welfare funds from the state—and pregnant crack smokers who deplete public health and welfare resources by producing sick offspring.[14] These two socially constructed figures (the welfare queen and the crack mom) allowed neoliberal social welfare and health policies to be pushed forward in the mid- and late 1990s. For example, the Personal Responsibility and Work Opportunity Reconciliation Act of 1996, informally known as "welfare reform," instantiated the individualization of responsibility for poverty and its consequences.[15] The percentage of low-income, substance-using women receiving cash assistance declined from 54 percent in 1996 to 38 percent in 2001, and states were then authorized to perform urine drug screenings on welfare recipients and deny benefits to adults convicted of drug-related felonies.[16]

According to David Harvey, neoliberal projects create groups of persons who are included and persons who are excluded. By "attacking all forms of social solidarity" (such as trade unions), dismantling the social welfare systems, and privatizing public institutions (such as social housing), neoliberal policies were able to maintain the power base of "a new class of entrepreneurs" and elites.[17] In this frame, unemployment and poverty were constructed as the result of *individual choice* rather than structural forces.[18] Neoliberal policymakers deemed the inability to effectively participate in the "free market" a personal failure of the poor.[19]

The dual forces of (1) a postmodern progressivism that focused social support on the fetus and not the pregnant woman and (2) neoliberal welfare reforms caught up with Lexi in 2004, shortly after her daughter had died. While she had been able to access methadone during her pregnancy, other benefits (GA and food stamps) were jeopardized because she had a drug-related felony on her record. Lexi explained this to me by describing how she had needed to produce a "seeable child"—she needed to have already had her baby—in order to access material resources that might have stabilized her pregnancy:

> What happened was, I got off GA because of the fact that I was pregnant, I am trying to remember exactly how this happened . . . I got pregnant, I went on methadone, but they told me I couldn't be on GA, that I had to apply for AFDC [Aid to Families with Dependent Children]. But AFDC told me . . . When I went down there AFDC told me I could not receive AFDC because I was a felon. I could only receive AFDC once the baby was born. . . . I was only six months pregnant, and I was a felon. If you have other kids and you are not pregnant, fine, then you are eligible for it. Fine. But being a felon, I am not eligible unless I have a seeable child.

Lexi also lost her methadone maintenance treatment slot when her daughter was born prematurely and died.[20] No longer pregnant, Lexi went through a rapid methadone detoxification, because the public funds that supported her access to drug treatment were linked to her fetus and not to her. Both examples demonstrate the ways the social and health needs of women who use drugs became legitimate and visible through pregnancy. The "seeable child" justified the interventions of care and coercion, access and loss.

For those living at the stigmatized outer boundaries of "Main Street," such as those living in the daily-rent hotels, individual responsibility for social welfare entitlements became entrenched during this period in the United States. Murphy and Sales report that the women they studied repeatedly tried and failed to perform the "technologies of the self," the sets of individual practices through which citizens must discipline themselves that Foucault has argued became a requirement of neoliberal regimes:[21]

> [Pregnant drug users'] mothering standards and values resonated with most American mothers: mothers should protect their children from harm; keep them fed, warm, presentably clean; and see they are educated, prepared for the work world and shown right from wrong. These goals are a tall order under conditions of lifelong victimization, lack of skills and education, unplanned childbearing, single parenting, violent and unsafe housing and scarcity of resources, not only for the child's play and learn-

ing but for the basics, such as food, clothing, and shelter. Nevertheless, our interviewees tended to hold themselves personally accountable for their poverty and for caring for their children.[22]

How access to welfare support interacted with drug treatment access became muddled in Ramona's retelling. She explained how her drug treatment was being paid for during her pregnancy, indicating that she didn't need welfare support to pay for her treatment, but she was certain that the drug treatment program would take a portion of her ssi disability payment. "I don't need ssi to get into the [drug treatment] program. No. They have to let me in [as a postpartum, drug-using woman trying to maintain custody of her newborn son]. But they [the program] will sure as hell take all my money. They will take it *all*."

Lexi's experience of the loss of drug treatment in 2004 became a key determining factor in her refusal of prenatal-associated methadone maintenance and prenatal health care during her pregnancy in 2009. Sales and Murphy argue that the structural violence of the Clinton era welfare measures sacrificed poor women—especially black, crack-smoking mothers—on the altar of "reform." Funding linked to biological status (pregnancy) served to stabilize and then ultimately destabilize Lexi during two pregnancies. Lexi's reconstitution as disabled by PTSD became the only viable source for state recognition through welfare acquisition available to her after the death of her child. Lexi's experience provided a proximal convergence of multiple forms of biological citizenship, knitting mental illness (PTSD), addiction, and pregnancy together into a complex web of service claims and denials for unstably housed women.[23]

As Jeanne Flavin explains, pregnancy and addiction currently serve as a site of ongoing state intervention to criminalize women's behavior.[24] The nature and extent of the crime committed by pregnant women in the United States varies a great deal by locality, throwing into relief the political variability of ethical and legal engagements with women, their reproduction, and their drug-use behaviors. In a recent report the Guttmacher Foundation summarized this variability across states, while outlining the formal modes of adjudication that juridical, health care, and welfare entities use in the monitoring of addicted pregnancy:

> Since the late 1980s, policymakers have debated the question of how society should deal with the problem of women's substance abuse during pregnancy. In 2014, Tennessee became the only state to specifically criminalize drug use during pregnancy. However, prosecutors have attempted

to rely on a host of criminal laws already on the books to attack prenatal substance abuse. The Supreme Courts in Alabama and South Carolina have upheld convictions ruling that a woman's substance abuse in pregnancy constitutes criminal child abuse. Meanwhile, several states have expanded their civil child-welfare requirements to include prenatal substance abuse, so that prenatal drug exposure can provide grounds for terminating parental rights because of child abuse or neglect. Further, some states, under the rubric of protecting the fetus, authorize civil commitment (such as forced admission to an inpatient treatment program) of pregnant women who use drugs; these policies sometimes also apply to alcohol use or other behaviors. A number of states require health care professionals to report or test for prenatal drug exposure, which can be used as evidence in child-welfare proceedings. And in order to receive federal child abuse prevention funds, states must require health care providers to notify child protective services when the provider cares for an infant affected by illegal substance abuse. Finally, a number of states have placed a priority on making drug treatment more readily available to pregnant women, which is bolstered by federal funds that require pregnant women receive priority access to programs.[25]

This lengthy and varied description of state responses reveals how the adjudication of pregnant women, through forced service utilization and/ or criminalization, is operationalized at the nexus of scientific evidence, reporting practices, choice, and personal responsibility. Localized politics and state social landscapes play a role in the interpretation of scientific evidence to produce the variability in the criminalization of prenatal substance use by geography. Flavin and others argue against the "false assumptions" made about the effects of prenatal substance use on fetal and child outcomes. These assumptions are being equally and carefully questioned by scientific and clinical communities as well. In March 2013, for example, an international group of physicians, drug treatment providers, and research scientists composed an "open letter" to major US news networks and policy-makers calling for an end to "Alarmist and Inaccurate Reporting on Prescription Opiate Use by Pregnant Women" through the misinterpretation of scientific evidence about prenatal exposure. The letter argues: "A great deal of experience has been gained over the course of almost 50 years regarding the effects of prenatal opiate exposure on expectant mothers and their babies, and guidelines have been established for optimal care of both. And yet, reporting in the popular media continues to be overwhelmingly inaccurate, alarmist and decidedly harmful to the health and well-being of pregnant women, their children, and their communities."[26]

The intersection between science and questions of criminalization is further destabilized and reconfigured when a biological understanding of addiction is considered. The emergent understanding of addiction as a "complex brain disease characterized by compulsive, at times uncontrollable drug craving, seeking, and use despite devastating consequences" runs directly counter to liberal notions of free will that apply broadly to matters of criminal intent or negligence.[27] According to this definition of addiction, women could choose to continue a pregnancy but would have little or no choice over choosing to continue addictive behaviors. Yet the question of choice, whether to stop or to continue using drugs, maintains social traction even as the current science of prenatal substance use exposure and emergent neurobiological understandings of the course of addiction complicate questions of both "willpower" and "environment."[28]

New Sciences of Addicted Pregnancy

Since the days of *Born Hooked*, research on prenatal exposure has diversified in terms of its targets. This science resulting from such research now acknowledges the role of polysubstance use in complicating outcomes for children exposed to substances while in utero. Yet this epidemiological intervention does not easily displace the media-generated representations of a specific drug—first crack, then meth, and now prescription opioid medications—as the latest threat to familial unity and maternal love. The science of prenatal exposure is also sympathetic to the collapse of neurological categorizations between addiction and mental illness in epigenetic studies focused on uterine stress and increased vulnerability for poor health outcomes through hereditary linkages. While scientifically advanced, these renderings of prenatal exposure also harken back to earlier psychoanalytic renderings of mothers as a causal link for mental illness and addiction among children. Finally, the science of prenatal exposure is taking a sociological turn in its efforts to index "adversity"—to account for the role of poor social environment and poverty in the child outcomes of substance-using pregnant women while also quantifying the impacts of substance exposures.

Although the scientific study of children prenatally exposed to substances is not new, the shifts toward accounting for polysubstance use, maternal mental health, and adversity have a social history linked to the invention and proliferation of the "crack baby" and historic welfare reforms that demonized the drug, its female, pregnant user, and her children. My interest is to explicate how this social history currently haunts the media-generated knowledge about addicted pregnancy, scientific inquiry about pregnancy and addiction, and the everyday lives of the pregnant women in the daily-rent hotels.

Polysubstance Use in the Context of Cocaine Exceptionalism

When animals have free availability of cocaine, the animals stop eating, they stop sleeping, and 100 percent of them die. If they have free availability of nicotine or, for the same matter, heroin, the animals survive.
—Nora Volkow, quoted in "A Conversation with Nora Volkow: A Scientist's Lifetime of Study into the Mysteries of Addiction" (*New York Times,* August 19, 2003)

In social theory making about women who use drugs and in biomedical renderings, cocaine—specifically crack cocaine—has occupied the "savage slot."[29] It is perceived to be the drug that is most dangerous, most racialized, most wild and primitive, most other, and most in need of a colonizing, bioclinical intervention. Science demonstrating a racial bias in the reporting of substance use among pregnant women did little to dissuade the racialized political and popular discourses surrounding crack during the late 1980s and 1990s, and this legacy continues today.[30] So entrenched is the association of crack use with blackness in the United States that an article was published in the *Journal of the American Medical Association* reporting on the use of statistical methods to refute a biological connection between ethnicity and crack addiction. The article's conclusion read: "Findings of race-associated differences are often presented as if a person's race has intrinsic explanatory power. This analysis provides evidence that, given similar social and environmental conditions, crack use does not strongly depend on race-specific (e.g., biologic) personal factors. . . . It provides evidence that prevalence estimates unadjusted for social environmental risk factors may lead to misunderstanding about the role of race or ethnicity in the epidemiology of crack use. Future research should seek to identify which characteristics of the neighborhood social environment are important and potentially modifiable determinants of drug use."[31]

Potential confusion over the representation of statistical facts about blackness and crack created a necessity to conduct statistical analyses to prove that "neighborhood social environment" played an important role in who used crack. My experience of the ethnically diverse sample of women living in the daily-rent hotels was that I did not interact with a single woman who was not smoking crack or did not have a history of chronic crack use.[32] Many substance users, including pregnant women, are polysubstance users.[33] One health care provider I interviewed described the problem this way:

> "There isn't a lot of data that shows that cocaine causes birth defects."
> "There is quite a bit about alcohol," I respond.
> "Yeah, but it's for the crack baby you have to get qualified data. No one smokes crack who doesn't drink, anyway. But one of the reasons the data about crack and fetal outcomes is so tricky is because many people believe that there are too many other environmental things that might be playing a role. And they can't [statistically] control for all of those things, because things are so out of control [socially]."

Unfortunately, in epidemiological research the impact of one drug can be overdetermined as a result of the particularities of the research questions and approach, while the potential effects of the integration of many substances can go underrecognized. The tendency to privilege the effects of one substance—what I call "drug siloing"—is very common in the media-generated representations of the consequences of neonatal substance exposure. One effect of drug siloing is that it focuses attention on a specific drug and its user and away from the social environments whose conditions increase the likelihood of drug use in general. Early media representations were driven by scientific studies of cocaine-exposed infants, in which crack exposure was privileged as the single causative agent for problems in infancy and early childhood. These "landmark" studies were later debunked when it was revealed that the prenatal exposure consisted of multiple substances (including tobacco and alcohol) and environmental factors impacting the pregnant women who participated in those studies.[34] Drug siloing can make cause-and-effect relationships seem more straightforward than they are, while demonizing certain drugs and, by association, the people thought to use them. If modern media representations of addicted pregnancy find their point of origin in "crack babies," they have now traveled onward to discover "meth babies" and, more recently, "oxybabies."[35]

These new forms of fetal victimhood reflect emergent national anxieties about rising rates of methamphetamine use among women of childbearing age, particularly poor white women in rural areas, and current mounting concern over the misuse of opioid analgesic medications—prescribed or illegally bought.[36] The science that seeks to accurately assess the impact of substances on fetal and child development must take extreme measures to isolate the impacts of specific substances. These epidemiological studies also try to pay the social debt for the construction of the "crack baby," a construction now debunked by science itself.[37] In other words, if "bad science" created the "crack baby," then the new science that says anything further about prenatal exposure had better be "good."

The damage done by the media creation and scientific authorization of the "crack baby" continues to be felt today, and little has been done to redress the families torn asunder and criminalized in its wake during the 1980s and 1990s.[38] As one pediatrician stated in a recent *New York Times* article about the public legacy of crack baby science, "society's expectations of the children [exposed to cocaine in utero] . . . and reaction to the mothers are completely guided not by the toxicity, but by the social meaning of the drug."[39] Even as polysubstance use has gained traction in scientific studies of prenatal exposure, crack is still a central referent for current concerns and knowledge production about pregnancy and drug use.[40] Researchers may have multiple new tools and databases at their disposal to try and answer specific questions, such as: What difference does drug use make during pregnancy? Which drugs? How much exposure? When during pregnancy? Women in the daily-rent hotels created folk categories to assess their own risks and manage their fears.[41]

> KELLY: When you said you didn't want to have a crack baby, what does that mean?
>
> CUPCAKE: You seen them commercials on TV? And those babies that are addicted and stuff. And I shit you not, I thought about that kind of thing. Like that is what my baby—because I didn't know that I was pregnant until I went to jail [at three to four months pregnant]. And that hit me like, wow, like hard. And I seen them commercials in my head. [I was thinking] "I don't want to have a kid like that." You know what I mean? So that's why I got clean. Because I didn't want to have a crack baby. It wasn't like, "Oh I am gonna be a mom, and it's gonna be great." No. I just didn't want to have a crack baby. You know. [That's] my reality.

The media frenzy that was produced around the phenomenon of "crack babies" has been well documented.[42] The gravest accusation in this media portrayal of the available scientific data was the one that was least related to controlling fetal risk through abstinence from crack smoking. The accusation was that crack use makes women, especially African-American women, incapable of maternal love. Murphy and Sales write: "The image of poor, inner-city African-Americans whose mothering instincts had been destroyed by crack was highly publicized and widely accepted."[43] Campbell asserts that discourses about the effects of addictive drugs on the maternal instinct are heavily influenced by concepts of women as both biological and social reproducers for society. I wish to take the discussion in a slightly different turn, by examining the socio-structural contexts of the daily-rent hotels, which placed limits on the possibility of maternal love, and how the expression of those limits might be captured (as in Cupcake's statement above) as recognition of what forms of motherhood might be socially available in "reality" to addicted, pregnant, poor women.[44]

Addiction and Mental Health Convergence in the Toxic Mom

The scientific technologies mapping addiction as a brain disease and suggesting genetic connections between mental illness, heredity, and addiction have been gaining mainstream media and institutional support. Examples of this recent sea change include the proliferation of mainstream media articles on the biological foundations of both addiction and mental illness; the appointment of Nora Volkow, a research psychiatrist who did groundbreaking research on magnetic resonance imagery (MRI) to map drugs' effects on the brain, as director of the National Institute of Health's National Institute of Drug Abuse; and the fact that in the decade 1997–2007 psychotropic medications ranked highest for "most promotional spending" by pharmaceutical companies in direct-to-consumer advertising.[45]

While the idea that addiction and mental illness share neurological co-location is emergent, it has a parallel social and psychoanalytic history. In this history American visions of mothering and responsibility—heavily influenced by psychoanalytic constructs—haunt and clash with current scientific understandings of addiction and mental illness among women. Debates, both publicly mediated and within scientific circles, about the effects of maternal drug use on fetal development and later child health and behavioral outcomes began to emerge in the United States as early on as the 1830s, when physicians first documented infants with withdrawal symptoms from maternal opioid use during pregnancy. Yet the gaze turned away from congenital concerns and toward theories of addiction causation, in which mothers took center stage as the causal agents for their children's addictive behaviors.[46]

Campbell describes the historic situatedness of discourses of blame that implicated the mother's role in raising drug-addicted children. Up until the mid-twentieth century, addiction was considered "adaptive" for male addicts, who were supposed to be struggling under the constraints of their mothers' overcontrolling behavior. Women addicts were largely left unexplained by this psychoanalytically informed focus on dynamics between mothers and sons.[47] During this same period another form of the toxic mom emerged. "Schizophrenogenic mothers" produced children (again mostly males) with schizophrenia, whose root cause was located in the mother's assumed coldness and neglect.[48]

Expert constructions of addiction and mental health in the United States have centered on the dysfunctional family (with the mother at the helm) as the breeding ground for madness and drug-addled criminality.[49] Research focused on mother-child dyads has underscored these concerns, citing parenting difficulties among substance-using women that can include difficulties establishing attachment with newborns and providing adequate parenting through responsive and engaged behavior.[50] Other epidemiological studies have privileged social disadvantage over biological exposure as the determining factor in child development.[51]

The causal linkage between addiction, mental illness, and mothers has a significant sociohistorical resonance that informs current nature/nurture debates. The pregnant homeless women I worked with shared concerns about "passing on" psychotic, addictive, or other negative personality traits from themselves to their children. Lexi often described her son, Lionel, as "hyper," and she fretted about how her drug and alcohol use during her pregnancy might have contributed to his "too high" energy. Crysanne described her mother's alcoholism and addiction to pills, as well as her grandmother's alcoholism, as factors contributing to her turning to drug use and becoming "anxious." Crysanne believed both "bad behavior and bad luck" might be hereditary. When I drove Duke back to the subway station after we dropped off Ramona at residential drug treatment, he shared his concerns about hereditary disadvantages:

I am riding with Duke, the baby daddy of Ramona's son, born in December 2009. He begins to discuss Duke Junior, the baby Ramona had in 2007—who was "full of crack."

"Is that the baby Ramona was speakin' about when she said, 'I let the other one go'?" I ask, repeating a conversation we all had on the way to dropping Ramona off at First Steps [the residential drug treatment facility]. "Yes." He sighs. "We couldn't keep that baby, because he was loaded up with drugs. We couldn't have kept him. We were off the hook [using a lot of crack] at *that* time."

"Did he get adopted?" I ask.

"Yeah," he says. "But anyway I told Ramona, see I have ADHD [attention deficit hyperactivity disorder]. I have ADHD, and I told Ramona, with the drugs [the crack use] and me having ADHD, that that baby would probably get that too. I was worried about that because it works like that, through the parents to the kid."

Duke was restating an argument about genes and the environment. He linked his diagnosis of ADHD with stimulant exposure, calculating that the hereditary disadvantage that he brought to the table would only be made worse by Ramona's drug-use behaviors during pregnancy. Scientific optimism about the technological ability to bridge connections between mental health disorders and other conditions influenced by heredity abounds in current neuroscientific literature. As described in the following scientific abstract, unpacking the puzzle of environmental adversity and genetic propensity is central to locating the etiology of mental disorders.

Just as research during the Decade of the Brain (1990–2000) forged the bridge between the mind and the brain, research in the current decade is helping us to understand mental illnesses as brain disorders. As a result, the distinction between disorders of neurology (e.g., Parkinson's and Alzheimer's diseases) and disorders of psychiatry (e.g., schizophrenia and depression) may turn out to be increasingly subtle. That is, the former may result from focal lesions in the brain, whereas the latter arise from abnormal activity in specific brain circuits in the absence of a detectable lesion. As we become more adept at detecting lesions that lead to abnormal function, it is even possible that the distinction between neurological and psychiatric disorders will vanish, leading to a combined discipline of clinical neuroscience.[52]

What this scientific optimism can look like on the ground is a layperson's calculus of risk probability based on degree of exposure, type of exposure, interaction with specialists, and increasing prevalence of diagnostic categorizations that collapse ADD/ADHD with addiction, impulsivity, and compulsivity. Website postings from support groups reveal parents' lay assessments of how their adoptive children's current and potential intellectual and social abilities are causally demarked in relation to prenatal exposure. For example, in one mother's description of her four children, the writer travels between diagnoses linked to prenatal substance exposure, "neglect" in the home environment, "attachment" (a psychoanalytic construct), and neuropsychiatric diagnoses to create a complex and collapsed picture of causality and dysfunction.

> My 4 adopted children were all prenatally exposed. Two were born addicted.
>
> Our oldest adopted child was exposed to unknown amounts of at least alcohol and meth. No real documentation available. He was also neglected during the first year. He's doing well. He does have some ADD [attention deficit disorder] kinds of issues, and was formally dx'd [diagnosed] with attachment and sensory integration problems. At age 11 he is doing well, is at grade level academically, and is in general a very happy, healthy little boy. I do feel that he likely has FASD [fetal alcohol spectrum disorder] and that the ADD would fall under that umbrella.
>
> Second adopted child was born addicted to pain killers and exposed to other drugs, including alcohol. He was significantly delayed the first year, and had a significant speech delay, along with reflux and some food sensitivities. He continues to be a bit developmentally delayed. He is now 8 and does pretty well in school, but he is not reading yet. I think overall he functions somewhere between the developmental ages of 5 and 6. I suspect he also would be dx'd with FASD if we went through the evals for that.
>
> Third adopted child was born addicted to meth and exposed to everything else, including alcohol. She had some significant delays the first year and reflux problems. At age 4 I would describe her as a bit ADHD. Okay, more than a bit. She's pretty wild at times and we struggle to deal with

her level of noise and activity. She's often pretty happy, especially when things are going along to her liking. She is learning to not throw things or have a screaming melt down when she is told "no." I think she (we!!) have made some progress as she doesn't have a melt down EVERY day now.

Youngest adopted child is 3 and doing well. Don't know what he was exposed to, but suspect some level of alcohol and know tobacco. Unsure of any other things, but suspect. . . . Seems to be on target, for the most part. We've had to do some work on attachment with this one, due to a few moves during the first year in foster care, but overall is doing well and meeting expected milestones appropriately.

Generally my kids are happy and play well, are social and engaging in an appropriate way. They are progressing and haven't [reached] a plateau in development. So far, anyway.

I do wonder if one or two of them will be totally independent as adults, but . . . we don't expect that they'll be out on their own at age 18 anyway, so we'll see how they're doing when they get to their 20s. We have time to work toward those goals now and we do parent with that in mind (learning to live independently).

The tendency to attribute undesirable intellectual and social-behavioral characteristics to children who were exposed to substances in utero was as common a practice in the daily-rent hotels as it was in wider social media forums. As discussed earlier, it is not a viewpoint based in the current science of the impacts of prenatal drug exposure, which argues that while no degree of exposure can be assumed to be risk free, the adversity of the prenatal and subsequent parenting environment plays a significant mediating role in how these impacts come to be expressed emotionally and behaviorally. One adoptive mother's post offered an interesting counter-discourse in which the desire for explanatory models and diagnostic categorizations was questioned with an antimedicalization perspective on her child's behavior and a rejection of the term "disability." She wrote:

my middle son is now 10. born addicted to meth. he had many problems as a baby, but now is a normal healthy child with adhd. his doctor says it is most likely related to his exposure, but i hate to even call adhd for him a disability. . . . because while it does hinder his ability to sit in a chair 8 hours a day at school . . . i believe it is also the reason that he has an eye for detail which makes him an amazing student . . . and the reason he is so smart because he never stops asking questions about things. after what his doctors have told me over the years, i am pleasantly surprised by his behaviors and ability levels.

The limited options for pregnant women in the daily-rent hotels gave emphasis to the role of the environment and the ability to nurture within it. These options also predicted children's futures, alluding to the mothering or parenting that might be possible or impossible in this setting of material deprivation, violence, and substance use. One program provider for substance-using pregnant women described in the following way how the intersection of poverty and problematic behavior can foretell a child's future: "If a family stays on the street, if the parents remain addicted, if the parents continue to abuse the children, if the parents continue to neglect their children, then the child does not stand a chance. The child *will* become like the parents because that is all the child knows."[53] The new sciences of addicted pregnancy attempts to measure the role of factors in the social environment along with prenatal exposure to substances to paint a comprehensive picture of the vulnerability both mothers and children may experience.

Indexing Adversity

The current science of prenatal substance use exposure seeks to parse out the complex social worlds of mothers and their children by measuring how personal and social factors (not only biological ones) play a role in the infant and child outcomes. For example, in the "adversity index," a measurement tool that is used in sophisticated studies of the impacts of prenatal substance use, maternal mental health, "poor quality of the home," and "poverty" are all factors weighed against the impact of methamphetamine exposure in utero.[54] Studies that index adversity are able to quantify the additive risk for poor child outcomes in ways that early studies of crack exposure ignored entirely. Much of this research is now gaining traction in epigenetic studies, which study how biological and environmental factors exert stress on the uterine environments to alter gene expression and create vulnerability to poor health outcomes.[55]

Dysfunction—personal, familial, and social—comes to be writ large when science measures uterine stress at the biological and social levels. The womb of the addicted, pregnant woman is reinvisioned as a site for stress absorption. The material realities of the daily-rent hotels, along with the substances shared from mother to fetus and the mental health states of pregnant women, all pose potential toxicities. Indeed, the reactions that women expressed to their pregnancies were heavily influenced by the bereft material realities that characterized their lives in the daily-rent hotels. Active addiction often meant living most waking moments in relation to substances. A pregnancy discovery could translate into an additional stress in an already compromised social world. In a mainstream sense, pregnancy necessitates planning for an uncertain future. Among women in the daily-rent hotels, pregnancy often meant adding another uncertainty to a long list of the unstable relationships and risky endeavors required to ensure housing and ongoing access to substances. Thus pregnancy evoked feelings of ambivalence and fear, and a deferral of action, at least among the women whom I knew were pregnant.[56]

Like the majority of the women I studied, Kitt reported that her pregnancy was unplanned. She had "makeup sex" with her husband after they had been fighting. He lived in a different city, and I never met him. Even though Lexi was deeply in love with Pano, as she repeatedly pointed out to me, she was "shocked" to discover she was pregnant. She said that her religion forbade her to get an abortion. Tara was pregnant with her boyfriend's baby and also ambivalent, as was Benz initially. Toward the end of her pregnancy, Benz became very invested in entering treatment to maintain custody of her baby, and this desire increased after her daughter was born. Benz's husband, the baby's father, was serving time in jail when Benz entered treatment. Both Danell and Dylan got pregnant from sex with paying customers. Dylan said simply, "I made a mistake" in reference to her pregnancy as a result of unprotected sex with one of her regular customers. Cupcake's pregnancy in 2008 ended with a D & C procedure because it was a "false" pregnancy (a cyst); throughout 2009 she was actively trying to get pregnant. Cupcake was very attached to her husband, and the two of them had plans to raise their future children outside San Francisco and get jobs. Multiple arrests for parole violations continually foiled those plans. River was a woman I knew briefly in 2007 when she was seven months pregnant. She was the only woman I met who successfully got housing outside the neighborhood, and kept her baby in custody without entering drug treatment or going through a CPS intervention. Cupcake and River remained in consistent proximity to their husbands. This was unusual. Many of the other women had husbands that they referenced, as well as boyfriends and associates with whom they might be having sex, but few of these women lived with those men. None of these men had much involvement with the women's pregnancies or subsequent babies, as was demonstrated in Ramona's anger toward Duke after their son was born. Even Pano, who was out of jail the majority of the time that Lexi was pregnant in 2009, did not ever mention her pregnancy or the future of the baby she was carrying in my presence. Lexi attributed this omission to Pano's unresolved feelings and fears for the future, both connected to losing their daughter in 2004.

Concerns about the probability of hereditary disadvantages sometimes took the form of a justification for surgical interventions that ensured no future children. "Operability" is a term coined by Lawrence Cohen to describe the ways bodies of the poor are made available for surgery in the service of broader political economic ends for the wealthy.[57] Operability travels with stratified reproduction generally in efforts toward the paid or forced sterilization of addicted women and specifically among the women in this ethnography's setting. Lexi was operated on—given a hysterectomy—immediately after the second loss of a child, a son, in September 2009. The story of the ending of this pregnancy for Lexi included (1) a violent encounter with her partner, Pano; (2) her cervix opening at the daily-rent hotel where they stayed; (3) an emergency transport to the hospital in handcuffs as a 5150; (4) the birth of her "deformed" and dead baby; (5) followed immediately by a hysterectomy. At that point in the telling, I found it very difficult to assess whether or not Lexi could have given adequate informed consent for such a permanent operation. She insisted to me: "They asked me if it was what I wanted and I said yes." Lexi had expressed to me, prior to her son's death and immediately following it, that her risk—like her mother's—of the premature opening of her cervix was too high in her assessment (not based on anything she had heard from medical providers, whom she avoided). "I don't know what I would do if I lost another baby. I would probably go crazy," she had told me. During her 2009 pregnancy Lexi never accessed the indicated medical intervention to suture the cervix closed and remain on "bed rest" from five months gestation to term.

Monica retold a narrative also replete with violence, hereditary worry, and medical institutional involvement. I first met Monica in January 2007 at the homeless drop-in center. She had lived in the daily-rent hotels in the neighborhood for over fifteen years. Prior to that she had stayed at the Section 8 housing with a relative, after she ran away from her foster care situation. She smoked crack, but not all the time. She had begun to receive SSI as a child because she was judged, in her words, "slow . . . or mentally retarded." "But I have a lot of mental problems too," she said, when she described her multiple experiences with mandatory seventy-two-hour lockdown at the psychiatric ward of the local public hospital. When Monica described her childhood to me the first time, she matter-of-factly described her early physical development, abuse in her foster care, drug use, and suicidality. When Monica began to enter puberty at age nine, her biological mother, grandmother, and foster mother planned her sterilization.

OPERABILITY AS CONGENITAL PREVENTION

MONICA: And then, I was a young kid—they tied my tubes . . . you know, they cut me open, tied my tubes, and . . .

KELLY: When was that, Monica?

MONICA: I was nine years old . . . Um hmm. I was just a kid.

KELLY: Do you know why?

MONICA: They said I was getting promiscuous, like uh, you know, they don't want me having kids at a young age, because I was all—they thought I was already interested in boys, which I was not because I didn't like it—after I got molested, I didn't trust anybody for a long time, you know?

KELLY: What did they tell you about that when you were nine?

MONICA: The [doctors] said that we're doing this because your mother and your grandmother and your foster mother said you're too promiscuous . . . and that you wanna know about sex, and they don't want you getting pregnant and aborting your babies to foster care, 'cause they would take 'em away from you, 'cause of your—the way you are—you're slow . . . you have, you're mentally retarded, so they wouldn't let, allow you to keep your kids, if you had any . . . And that—ever since then, I've lost relationships because I don't feel like I'm a whole woman, you know? I've always, you know, wanted to experience what it felt like to have children . . . And so, even sometimes now, it's harder for me to get into relationships and stay in 'em because of that reason . . . Um hmm, 'cause, you know, people you meet up with . . . they want children, they want a big house, they want all these children and, you know, I can't do it, so.

Monica and I spent a lot of time together over the next couple of years. I took pictures of her so she could send them to her mother. "She wants to see how I am doing," Monica said. Sometimes she told me that her biological mother did not want her to call or write: "She doesn't want to talk to me." Other times

Monica claimed to be planning a trip to see her. Finally, in the late summer of 2009, I went with Monica to pick up her welfare check so she could buy a bus ticket to visit her mother and sister, who lived several hours south of San Francisco.

When Monica and I ran into each other at the drop-in center in October 2009, I asked Monica about her jeans. She had names written on each leg in marker—Sharpie, she told me—above her knee on each of her thighs. They were written so she could glance down and read the names while she was seated. She started to read the names to me, five on one leg, four on another. "I had my mother and sister tell me the names of all my brothers and sisters and I wrote them here so I wouldn't forget them," she says. On her recent visit, she was introduced to a sister, a sister no one had ever told her she had. "She was nice to me," Monica says about her "new" kin. "She has a job and house. She is doing good." Monica smiled when emphasizing her sister's accomplishments.

Monica's description of her relationship to her mother was not at all unusual. I found that most of the women who still had some access to their mothers would seek out frequent contact with them. In the same sitting many women would retell horrible stories of neglect and abuse as children and also emphasize the significance of their mothers (and sometimes their fathers) in their lives. One manifestation of these complex familial relations implicated pregnancy and addiction directly—when mothers, and sometimes grandmothers, aunts, and sisters, were called on to care for and raise the children of addicted, pregnant women.

Kin of Last Resort

"Kin of last resort" references relatives who are called on to take custody of pregnant women's babies and children so they are not placed in the foster care system and adopted out to strangers. Accidental or unplanned pregnancies produced forms of familial indebtedness, as many of the women—Anita, Lexi, Ramona, Crysanne, and Kitt—had to leverage familial ties due to threats of child custody loss. The family members called on to raise women's children are the "kin of last resort" because the pressures of addicted pregnancy and the threat of governmental intervention, which often meant assuming custody of the addicted women's children, cemented members of historically dysfunctional families back together.

What many women viewed as difficult and painful childhoods, especially in relation to the mothering they had received, came to be reproduced as their own children became dependent on the kindness and support of grandmothers, sisters, and aunts recruited into parenting. In Crysanne's telling, her abusive boyfriend convinced her to leave her children and join him on the street, selling and using drugs. Her description of leaving her baby had both vengeful and altruistic overtones, which captured the dynamics I often witnessed between pregnant women and kin of last resort. Crysanne said: "My mother always hated me. So, I left my baby with my mother. I go 'You know what? I'm leaving him [Crysanne's son] with you to give you a . . .' I said it nasty, 'to give you a reason to get up in the morning. You're so bored. You're probably gonna die because you have nothing to bitch about. All right, now you can worry about what he's going to eat and you can iron his socks and his underwear.'"

Upon birth, babies of addicted women often entered into legally tenuous relationships with their mothers, the state, and more distal kin until they were reordered into the custody of foster families, their mothers, or relatives. When I spoke to Anita at two months postpartum, she was not certain whether her aunt had gained custody of her daughter. She told me that she thought her daughter was with the aunt, but "I have to find out." Four months later, she told me a story about her aunt and mother trying to engage her in drug treatment so that her daughter would not be permanently adopted outside the family.

"THEY TOLD HER THAT I KEEP HAVING BABIES, AND I NEVER GO TO TREATMENT." MARCH 2010

I walk down the hallway of the Chandra Hotel and knock on the door. Anita yells, "Who?" in a menacing voice. "It's me, Anita. Kelly," I say. She lets me in.

"Kelly, you would not believe it," she says, "my son was here. My three-year-old. My aunt brought him down here. She knew where to find me. She was trying to use him to convince me to clean up [stop using drugs]. You know how she won't let me see him?"

In 2007, all of Anita's custody rights were revoked at the birth of her son because he had a positive tox screen for crack and opiates. Anita failed to enter treatment, and she lost visitation rights as well. Her aunt was awarded custody.

Anita takes a break to smoke some crack.

"What changed her mind?" I ask.

"It is my daughter [born 2009]. They [CPS] are saying that she [Anita's aunt] can't have her. They told her that I keep having babies, and I never go to treatment. [My aunt] brought my son down here to try and force me to go in [to drug treatment]. I have to do it [go to drug treatment] this time or else my daughter will be adopted out [to foster care]. She won't stay in the family. My mother is distraught—she hasn't stopped crying. I have to get to the [child custody] hearing; I have to talk to the lawyer."

Kin of last resort served to magnify guilt among addicted, pregnant women, even as these family members represented a saving grace from total child custody loss. Every time Lexi spoke about her mother caring for Lionel she described feeling "sad and guilty" that her mother should have to be caring for her son, especially considering her mother's age and failing health. This was Lexi's heartfelt experience even though her mother had forced Lexi to take care of her sisters and brothers—and their children—at a very young age. Despite this difficult family history, Lexi was the black sheep in the family as a result of her drug use, and she was forever indebted, and truly thankful, to her sisters and her mother for giving Lionel "a stable life." When Lexi told me about giving birth to her son while in custody and then later entering residential drug treatment, I asked who had custody of her son during that transition. She remarked, "My sister had him. I have a beautiful family, man. Because of my family and my CPS worker I've been blessed." Given that Lexi's mother had forced Lexi to claim the child of her sister and brother as her own, this description seems generous. Yet her mother is also the one raising Lexi's son because her relapse led her to give up custody. Ramona owed a debt to a relative who was raising her daughter, DeLoni. Kitt's mother, who had kicked Kitt out of the house when she became pregnant at thirteen, was raising her four children and using Kitt's SSI payments for child support.

Lacking custody of their children, the women rejoined the street life they had temporarily left, without further intervention from the state unless they sought to regain custody.[58] Kim Hopper first (1997) coined the term "institutional circuit" to describe the instability and transience of homeless persons as they traveled from the street to transitional hotels, jails, and shelters.[59] Both addicted, pregnant women and their babies had institutional circuits. Women traveled the circuit depending on (1) their willingness to disclose a pregnancy to service providers; (2) their interactions with the criminal justice system, which might have them pregnancy tested, court-ordered to drug treatment as a diversion to incarceration, admitted to psychiatric lockdown through a 5150, or jailed; and (3) their access to resources for staying housed and off the street. Their children, once born, spent time in custody limbo in the hospital, as wards of the state through social services, as adoptees into foster care, with their mothers in residential drug treatment, and/or adoptees of kin of last resort. Kin of last resort might be available to negotiate some form of child contact for a child's mom, contact that would be precluded if all custody was withdrawn.

Hopper suggests that unequal resource distribution under capitalism and the disintegration of extended kin support networks in postindustrial urban centers contribute to the displacement of homeless persons through institutional circuits. This argument concurs in principle with Loïc Wacquant's explanation of the *hyperghetto* of post-Fordist America. Wacquant's hyperghetto is characterized by unattainable and unsustainable wage labor and the disintegration of familial and neighborhood infrastructures that characterized, and stabilized, ghettos in the past.[60] Through these overlapping yet divergent sociological reads on urban poverty, we can locate addicted, pregnant women as those who were often seeking, sometimes with encouragement from CPS agents, to maintain relationships with families of origin. Women were hoping that kin—mothers, sisters, aunts—could raise their children. This child rearing often took place at distal locales while the women, the mothers, returned to the liminality of the daily-rent hotels.[61] As Cupcake, Lexi, Anita, and Ramona's stories all demonstrate, the custody window slammed shut quickly. It had only been conditionally propped open anyway—conditional to a woman moving into drug treatment, to her finding employment or gaining disability welfare, and to her having a place to live outside of the daily-rent hotels.

The stratified reproduction of addicted pregnancy illuminated long-standing images of the failed mother—the toxic mom—reproducing morally flawed and intellectually damaged offspring as a result of her abhorrent behaviors. Some of the pregnant women in this ethnography described partaking in such haunting future imaginings about their children, worrying over hereditary flaws that might be passed on to them because of their own behavior. More often, though, pregnant women in the daily-rent hotels sought to manage the pressures of their everyday lives of addiction and housing instability while deferring plans of action around their pregnancies. Pregnancy fit into the overall uncertainty of daily life and the ongoing, predictable disappointments that many women had experienced since childhood. Once babies arrived, women were forced to mend conflicted family dynamics and patch up old wounds if their kin of last resort were to be relied on to "save" their children from the state, since the state felt compelled to step in to "save" the babies from their mothers.

chapter 6. victim-perpetrators

Evidence, Politics, and Risk

No one wants the liability for pregnant women. No one wants them. When they get picked up from jail, the jails want them out. They don't want a miscarriage or preterm labor or birth on their hands. I can't even get a local treatment center to do a medical detox for pregnant women who need to be detoxified off alcohol. Now heroin, opiates, there are a lot of circulating rumors about detoxing too suddenly and its effects on preterm labor and miscarriage. But the research seems to be that the uterine environment for women using those drugs is not that unstable. [In contrast,] for alcohol or benzodiazepines the research is clear. An unmedicated, rapid detox can kill you. These women need a medically supervised detox for alcohol. I have to use my background as a medical provider, because I know the language to get women admitted, to get them in to the hospital for an alcohol detox. I mention several health issues. I ask if the women can be "tucked away for a while"—that is the code. When I can establish that it is medically indicated then she can get a blood workup, even get a psych evaluation while she is hospitalized. But it is a "social admit" [to the hospital] in the sense that the community-based treatment program should have taken her.
—San Francisco clinician (2008)

As the clinician quoted here indicated, addicted, pregnant women posed risk to public health systems, which produced necessary manipulations of those same systems to ensure some level of care.[1] They unavoidably interfaced with institutional systems of care and control. Whether a pregnant woman self-identified on entering drug treatment, was court-ordered to treatment (deferring incarceration), or showed up at the hospital to deliver her baby, the state was involved. The ethnographic reality of those involvements was often not a straightforward story of oppression and civil liberty violations. Rather, it was a continually renegotiated dance of assessment, cooperation, resistance, and coercion. While the jailers shackled and corralled, they also broke protocol to allow women to spend time with their babies. While the drug treatment officials called for "personal accountability," they also manipulated dysfunctional systems of public health care to ensure women received optimal prenatal care.

The pregnant women I worked with expressed both hate and admiration toward the institutional representatives who played such central roles in their family lives. This ambivalence characterized the revolving door that caught women, momentarily bringing them inside the system, only to fling them back out shortly afterward, then back in again, and then back out. This was not an institutional circuit that relied on the liminal status of addicted, pregnant women as "excess labor."[2] Rather, women were systematically reconstituted through their pregnancy from throwaway, addict sex workers into a new biologically determined category: risk incarnate. They were politically volatile, impossible-to-ignore victim-perpetrators.

Persons working in the "helping professions" were like the pregnant women they cared for and coerced: by turns hopeful and bitter, optimistic and burnt out. Addicted, pregnant women faced the real and constant fear that CPS would revoke custody of their children. While not all the women wanted to keep their children, the vast majority did (Dylan being the notable exception). What I heard unequivocally and repeatedly from the professionals closest to the women was not the rhetoric of pie-in-the-sky recovery. These professionals had no illusions about the challenges that addiction posed to their clients. What they often sought were incremental forms of stabilization. Goals included getting a woman to a "clean" birth (without a positive tox screen for illegal drug exposure), or to a birth with just a methadone detoxification for the infant, or getting a woman to birth without a CPS case, or getting a woman to stay in postpartum drug treatment long enough not to lose her baby before CPS closed the case. These professionals clung to a limited number of "success stories," presenting them like tales of incredible heroism and luck representing an almost mythic overcoming of incredible odds. In my small sample, this proved not to be understated. Only three women of the nineteen I worked with maintained custody of their children two years postpartum. All three women had navigated ways out of the daily-rent hotels. One woman was living with her husband and baby in a city south of San Francisco. Two other women were living tentatively, day-to-day, in drug treatment facilities, and transitional housing, with their babies when I completed formal fieldwork in 2011. Other women did not beat the odds.

Future possibilities that could unfold for pregnant women (or foreclose on them) were intertwined with public health institutions of care and coercion.

Various financial and affective forms of micropolitics (the politics of inter-agency deferrals of responsibility, the politics of reimbursement for health and mental health care services rendered, and the politics of hatred for addicts) came into play as the risk of an impending birth, and its potentially poor outcome, loomed large. To understand the available interventions for addicted, pregnant women and how they were used, one must first broaden the context to how these women are construed in the field of public health. This public health construction was epistemologically determinative of "pregnant addicts" as victim-perpetrators. The women who lived in the daily-rent hotels were sex workers, the majority of whom did not intend or plan for their pregnancies (with the exception of Cupcake). Sex working, drug-addicted women who become "pregnant addicts" are interpellated through a historic lens in which the "risky city" is a site of sexual depravity and vice-producing disease. The risky city is a place-determined producer of risk and diseases and of public health research and intervention. Epidemiological data that charts childhood sexual abuse, drug use, and early sexual debut paints a reproductive health picture in which unplanned pregnancy is its inevitable outcome. Addicted, pregnant women living in the daily-rent hotels provided ethnographic evidence that narrated their personal pathways to that end. In the public health infrastructure of the risky city, sex workers operationalized their stories of risk, categorizing themselves into data points that initiated interventions and shaped health policies.[3]

Seeking to decouple the victim from the perpetrator, treatment professionals often configured addicted, pregnant women into two categories: those who were taking responsibility and those who were in denial. Of course, women's motivations and actions in the everyday told a more complex story. Ethnographic evidence revealed those contradictions, as I traced how women were entangled in systems, avoided them, or escaped from them but were ultimately forced to acquiesce to institutional rules and regulations if they sought to relinquish the label "unfit." Those women who remained "unfit" returned to the daily-rent hotels—as "sex worker addicts"—unshielded yet again from the risky city.

The Risky City

The city as a site of moral degradation, licentiousness, and risk is widespread in multiple literatures that seek to describe and quantify urban landscapes and the problems of their populations. Social scientists have theorized the ways cities embody larger US government policies of structural violence, most specifically racism and classism.[4] Several ethnographic texts have offered more nuanced details of how risk is constructed and managed through everyday social and institutional relationships.[5] What informs these understandings of urban decay is the same seminal literature that informs aspects of David Harvey's Marxist understanding of neoliberalism: Friedrich Engels's writings on industrialism and the mass migration to the city of the poor from rural enclaves in the mid-nineteenth century. With this movement supposedly came "intemperance" (alcoholism) and sexual lasciviousness. Here, vice and a lack of economic opportunity are linked and enacted in the "risky city."

> Next to intemperance in the enjoyment of intoxicating liquors, one of the principal faults of English working-men is sexual license. But this, too, follows with relentless logic, with inevitable necessity out of the position of a class left to itself, with no means of making fitting use of its freedom. The bourgeoisie has left the working-class only these two pleasures, while imposing upon it a multitude of labours and hardships, and the consequence is that the working-men, in order to get something from life, concentrate their whole energy upon these two enjoyments, carry them to excess, surrender to them in the most unbridled manner. When people are placed under conditions which appeal to the brute only, what remains to them but to rebel or to succumb to utter brutality? And when, moreover, the bourgeoisie does its full share in maintaining prostitution—and how many of the 40,000 prostitutes who fill the streets of London (Alison 1840, volume 2) every evening live upon the virtuous bourgeoisie! How many of them owe it to the seduction of a bourgeois, that they must offer their bodies to the passers-by in order to live?—Surely it has least of all a right to reproach the workers with their sexual brutality.[6]

The city is made risky for bourgeois men who seek to satiate their carnal desires and quickly retreat, and risky for the working-class women and men in London who "succumb" to hardship, exploitation, and disease. These groups incur different and unequal risks.

Harvey utilizes the political and social policies that followed the bankruptcy of New York City in the mid- and late 1970s as an "iconic" case example of what can happen to citizens when "wealth is redistributed to the upper classes in the midst of a financial crisis." The results were unequivocally disastrous for the health of the poor, specifically in relation to drug use and HIV/AIDS. Harvey echoes the sentiments of Engels over a century later: "Working-class and ethnic-immigrant New York was thrust back into the shadows, to be ravaged by racism and a crack cocaine epidemic of epic proportions in the 1980s that left many young people either dead, incarcerated, or homeless, only to be bludgeoned again by the AIDS epidemic that carried over into the 1990s. Redistribution through criminal violence became one of the few serious options for the poor, and the authorities responded by criminalizing whole communities of impoverished and marginalized populations." Harvey uses the case of New York City as *the* experiment that "established the principle that . . . the role of government was to create a good business climate rather than look to the needs and well-being of the population at large."[7] This model was rapidly expanded under the Reagan and Clinton administrations, contributing to a national dismantling of US domestic social welfare programs and structural adjustment programs abroad. To Harvey the "risky city" is the geographic embodiment of the consequences of these neoliberal policies in practice.

Many public health sociologists and epidemiologists are influenced by a conceptualization of the city made risky through federal (and sometimes state and local) withdrawal. Health researchers have argued that "urban" should be theorized on its own as a "social determinant" of health by measuring the "characteristics of cities such as size, density, diversity, and complexity" in relation to health outcomes.[8] Nicholas Freudenberg and his colleagues employed public health statistics about tuberculosis infections, HIV infections, and homicides in New York City from 1975 to the early 1990s to demonstrate how the closure of public health clinics and services directly contributed to a "syndemic."[9] A syndemic is defined as "two or more epidemics, with biological determinants and social conditions interacting synergistically, that contribute to an excess burden of disease in a population."[10] Framing part of their analysis in economic terms, Freudenberg and his colleagues claim that the combined health and social costs of excess (that is, preventable) cases of tuberculosis, homicides, and HIV/AIDS cases "ranged from 54.7 billion to more than 160 billion . . . [or] 5 to 15 times greater than the total dollar savings in city expenditures during the fiscal crisis."[11] In other words, the draconian social welfare and services cuts produced a more costly disease and fiscal burden than the original crisis. The sociological construction of the probability of risk connects the impact of environmental *conditions* (the concerns of social theorists such as Engels) with their representations in the quantified individual *behaviors* of city dwellers.

Macro, meso, and micro factors are all engaged in this critical analysis.[12]

Yet an assumption of governmental withdrawal or neglect underpins these analyses. The government is not doing enough for the social welfare and, thus the health, of the poor. Another perspective, consistent with Foucault, does not locate structural vulnerability only at the point of state withdrawal. In this framing, "abandonment" in the form of government's withdrawal of social welfare is repackaged as an individuated personal responsibility for one's own poverty and disease.

It is important to attend to *how* the city is rendered risky and for whom, in specific neoliberal discourses. Following Foucault, Thomas Lemke has argued that the contractual terms of neoliberal biopolitical citizenship include a rendering of oneself as responsible for all individual and social risks.[13] Pat O'Malley, in his essay "Risk and Responsibility," claims that it is important to construe "risk" in a neoliberal context not as "indicative of an imperfectly governed world."[14] Rather, risk leads to opportunity, consistent with the rational actor, entrepreneurial model of citizenship. Here risk is being interpreted as capitalist market opportunity by neoliberals and as exclusion from markets and the social safety net by opponents of neoliberal policies. According to this logic, it is a social safety net, which social welfare liberals support, that could produce a "no-risk society."[15] Because "risk" is perceived as a free market "good," neoliberals find the overregulation of risk suspect and dangerous. Hence, the responsibility for the production of risk and its subsequent quantification play a significant role in the characterization of the interventions that governments forward to respond to urban poverty, and specifically to vice. In opposition to "safety net" welfare thinking, neoliberal interventions have failure built in.

Here we have two views of state policies and practices that share a concern over the construction of risk and its etiology, while differing in their understandings of the operations of intersections between populations and the state at the everyday level. The neo-Marxist view stresses state neglect and withdrawal as the key determinative factor in the making of persons at risk for poor health and social outcomes, arguing that structural inequalities—the unequal distribution of resources—produce poor health. Neoliberal subjectivities of risk informed by a Foucauldian reading consist of individuals who must take personal responsibility for individual and social failures in order to enter into the social contract of the neoliberal state. "Risk" here is not a negative outcome of the policies and practices of state neglect but rather is designed in, as a systematic good—creating opportunities that individuals must seize to demonstrate that they are "entrepreneurs of the self."[16] This distinction between the neo-Marxist and Foucauldian readings is useful in trying to understand how addicted, pregnant women were constructed as victim-perpetrators. In the risky city, women living in the daily-rent hotels were construed as victims of personal and social traumas and addiction; they were the contextualized embodiment of poor health outcomes stemming from impoverishment. They were also perpetrators: failed neoliberal subjects who could not take individual responsibility for (criminal) behaviors despite the availability of opportunities (drug treatment).

In Ramona's narrative of her rocky posttreatment experience in the daily-rent hotels, trying to raise her daughter, work as a sex worker, and manage her crack addiction without stable housing she revealed herself to be both a victim of her poverty and addiction and a failed mother with ongoing crack use and sex work, despite treatment access and "success."

RAMONA'S METHADONE INTAKE. DECEMBER 2009

Ramona is describing what happened with her first daughter, DeLoni, who is now seven, to a former counselor of hers [Mary] at the methadone clinic prior to her formal intake with another counselor. This explanation of the outcome is a way for Ramona to bring her old counselor up to date, to finish a story that started eight years ago when Ramona came to the clinic pregnant with DeLoni.

Ramona says to Mary: "I gave her up myself. I had to. I was trying so hard with her. You know I was. And I was clean for so long. You know that too."

The counselor shakes her head, yes. Her eye contact with Ramona is intense. Her eyes are full of concern, absolutely focused, and very sad around the edges. This counselor knows Ramona well. They have clearly been on a journey together, a journey on which this counselor was absolutely present. Ramona's head is bowed; she is fidgety. She continues, "After DeLoni was born, it was crazy. I was crazy. I was clean for a while. But then I graduated from the [drug treatment] program and I still had her with me. But I was living in the [daily-rent] hotels. And I relapsed. I would take my daughter to preschool, come back to the room, have my [sex work] tricks, smoke crack. I would hustle during the day while she was at school. The managers were always hassling me for rent. They didn't want my daughter there. I would clean everything up, pick her up [from preschool] and the evening was just me-and-her time. I wouldn't even open the door [to the hotel room]. But I couldn't keep it up. I couldn't stay on top of it. I finally had to call [names a relative] to come and take DeLoni. And it was lucky [that] I got arrested that day, the day [the relative] came to get her. Because if I had been there [in the hotel], I would not have been able to let her [DeLoni] go."

Ramona's story revealed the housing dilemmas common to addicted, pregnant women. Daily-rent hotels do not typically accept infants or children, and abstinence is a requirement in other housing arrangements for pregnant and postpartum women who have used drugs and seek to live with their children. She provided an example of trying to survive an addicted pregnancy and to care for a child while at risk. Her apt description: "It was crazy. I was crazy" links the discourse of risk in the city for drug-using sex workers and the discourse of mental health diagnosis in which this environment and its constraint makes one crazy. In admitting that she "couldn't stay on top of it," Ramona pointed toward her personal responsibility for a failed motherhood and revealed the impossibility of a successful motherhood while still housed in the daily-rent hotels.

(Ware)housing Addicted, Pregnant Women

Private, daily-rent hotels were specific sites of poor health production and reproduction.[17] The women I studied regularly stayed in the daily-rent hotels when they were not street homeless, in temporary shelters, or incarcerated. The two publicly managed, supportive housing hotels in which I had regular contact through outreach did not house any pregnant, addicted women. When I spoke to a housing official about this, he confirmed my ethnographic experience. He also echoed the sentiments of the provider quoted earlier who said about pregnant women that "no one [no institution] wants them." In relation to access to supportive housing, these women were the exception among the drug-using urban poor because an addicted pregnancy demanded abstinence in order to obtain housing. Under progressive housing and health policies in San Francisco aimed at housing the "chronically homeless mentally ill," sobriety was not a requirement to earn a room inside for persons without children. However, being a "pregnant addict" marked a woman as a

6.1. Sharps container full, with bloody syringe jammed into the top, hallway of Daya Hotel, November 2009. Photo by the author.

substance-using mother, a risk too great even for progressive policy-makers to assume responsibility. In the following example, the addicted, pregnant woman also became the "case" that is so traumatic that it produces trauma among service providers.

> KELLY: I wonder why none of the pregnant women I know are accessing supportive housing?
>
> PROVIDER: They don't have a good case manager. Or they haven't sought out those services.
>
> KELLY: But they are getting 5150'd to the hospital. They are going to the ER. They are having those interactions. They are *pregnant*.
>
> PROVIDER: There are no pregnant women in [supportive housing] buildings. You know what pregnant women become? [Pause] Mothers. Then I have to worry about their kids. I have just watched so many situations like that go *so bad*. I just can't tolerate it anymore. It is too traumatizing.

Housing First policies undergird the progressive urban health and housing initiatives in San Francisco, in which abstinence is not viewed as a necessary precursor or requirement of housing access. It would, therefore, be a mistake to assume that there is no drug use, drug dealing, or sex work that goes on in publicly funded hotels, even though many of the tenants may be controlling their drug use or be abstinent. What seems to be absent in publicly managed buildings is the extra level of economic exploitation (through visiting fee extraction) and the threat of eviction (because rent subsidies are in place, most often paid for through ssi entitlement monies).[18] While there were no pregnant women who were housed in the two publicly funded buildings I had regular contact with, it is also important to note that no women staying in those buildings *became* pregnant during the four years I was conducting fieldwork. Most of the women, in fact, who stayed in these publicly funded hotels were much older and much sicker than the younger women sex workers. This is not necessarily the case across the board in all publicly funded buildings, as one provider pointed out:

> Actually, in the building that has the highest success rate [80 percent of tenants stay housed there at least two years], there is a ton of sex work and drug use. And yet people stay housed. I am arguing the financial argument. The cost-effective argument: If you spend the money here—on beautiful new supportive housing . . . you will reduce costs. [In a national study of supportive housing sites], San Francisco is always highest on drug use. I think there are more conservative parts of the county who would see our most effective building as an abject failure, because the drug-sex economy *is* still inside.

Even though abstinence is not a housing requirement and eviction sanctions were not invoked for sex work, women in publicly funded supportive housing were not getting pregnant, and they were staying housed. As the provider points out, this makes the cost-effective argument for publicly managed, supportive housing easy to make. But it also raised the question: where can an addicted, pregnant women get housed? One provider described the paradox of housing, pregnancy, and addiction. While this provider had assumed that pregnant women would be a top priority for housing placements, this had not been her experience. This was the paradox: if a woman could successfully manage the requirements of the methadone maintenance program, she became a poor candidate for residential treatment, because she was too stable. Therefore, she had to join waiting lists for low-income housing, as opposed to "supportive housing," which is frequently allocated for single adults with no children and serious mental and physical health problems. Low-income housing waiting lists often extend beyond the life of a pregnancy. A cps case is then automatically initiated because of the woman's housing instability. The provider said:

"Pregnancy is not a 'golden ticket.' Not even for housing, which is incredible to me. Many women in the program call the housing agency and get excited by the thought of being housed only to find out that the waiting list is six months long. What are they supposed to do? They are going to deliver before that time, and they can't go back to the [daily-rent] hotels with their babies, and they can't be homeless [because then they will lose custody]." Paradoxes such as this surrounded all aspects of the institutional management of addicted pregnancy. It was, then, not a shock to discover a great deal of "hustling" as women sought to circumvent what they experienced as illogical systems.

Hustling Systems That Hustle Her

Hustling the system was an art born of necessity. It required women who use drugs to bring street survival skills into settings of public health research, health care, and service delivery in order to meet their physical, mental, and social needs. These survival skills were marked by bravado and the habitual misrepresentation of facts and circumstances. That was the "hustle." The multiple times I witnessed and documented women hustling systems, it was obvious that their hustling was generated from an interpretation that they were already being hustled by the systems themselves.

Hustling systems reflected exercises of categorization linked to funding streams that would easily dry up if all the women could access these services. Women often experienced the services and research studies that gate-kept their eligibility as exercising the same arbitrary sets of controls that hotel managers wielded with their demands for visiting fees and threats of eviction. Both denials carried with them the risk of not having money for a hit, something to eat, or a place to sleep. Hustling systems became a way for addicted, pregnant women to make visible the boundaries that were constantly being drawn for them between the worthy and the unworthy poor.

Service providers were often caught in between the granting of the desired object (housing, food, research money) and the recognition of their implicit role in enforcing rules that women would meet with deceptions. For example, one clinician who works with addicted, pregnant women told me that she expects them to lie to her. The women she worked with interpreted this provider as culturally separate, as someone who could not understand their experiences. The provider did *not* attribute the misrepresentations to a recognition that services operated *just like* the streets, however. To this provider, the lying was a reflection of survival on the streets and an unavoidable consequence of the "disease" of addiction. I asked her how she could determine whether the lying she saw on the part of an individual woman wasn't the result of a personality disorder. Personality disorders are considered to be prevalent among homeless men and women.[19] The clinicians I interviewed frequently expressed frustration at the lack of effective psychopharmacological intervention for personality disorders, such that many patients may end up with a bipolar disorder diagnosis in order to medicate them. "Antisocial personality disorder" is a particularly common diagnosis; one of its main indications is "deceitfulness, as indicated by repeated lying, use of aliases, or conning others for personal profit or pleasure."[20] I asked the provider to distinguish between lying as an indication of antisocial personality disorder versus a responsive strategy for meeting the demands of negotiating pregnancy and addiction within constrictive institutional settings. The provider stated:

> It shakes out in the end. I just try to be consistent. I anticipate that women will look at me and know that I haven't shot drugs and will believe I can't know anything about their lives. But I am a medical provider, I can offer a different perspective. And they sit and bullshit me the whole time and that's okay. I just wait it out. Eventually they see that I am here. That I am nonjudgmental. I see the lying and the hustling as part of the active addiction. It is part of the streets and part of the disease.

Ramona echoed this interpretation when her drug treatment intake counselor left the room during a session between them that I observed. She turned to me—after misrepresenting a series of her psychiatric and health symptoms to the counselor—and said, "This girl [the intake counselor] is all book." Ramona felt that the fact that the intake counselor didn't call her out on her obvious lying and dismissiveness toward the intake questions showed that the intake counselor was college educated: book-smart but street-dumb. Ramona could be seen in this situation as engaging in what Somerset Carr calls "script flipping" with and for me to demarcate her limited ability to self-authorize her mental health status in this institutional treatment setting.[21] Looking beyond the clinical encounter, Ramona and the intake counselor were manufacturing evidence about addicted, pregnant women and their physical and mental health. When these individual data points become reified in aggregate statistics, they can leverage policies, serve as the catalysts for program development. What might it mean to recognize that they can be skewed under circumstances of material constraint and as a result of power relationships which are negotiated and contested?

Or is it worse to have social policies that run counter to epidemiological data? The epidemiological literature is replete with data that shows that violence and drug use are associated and that women who use drugs experience an inordinate amount of abuse.[22] There is also a well-documented literature that demonstrates that intimate partner violence is common during pregnancy and can escalate when a woman becomes pregnant.[23] If a woman is experiencing domestic violence, however, she must lie about her drug use in order to gain temporary shelter. The addicted, pregnant woman again finds herself in a liminal space of an intervention that can only be enacted through abstinence. To maintain custody of her child, and to receive support in the domestic violence (DV) shelter in which other women and children live, she must not be using substances. Addiction conceived through the lens of neuroscience as a chronic, compulsive brain disorder fails the social reality test of the micropolitics of service delivery. Thus, women had to lie to be able to occupy the status of recognizable victim (of violence).

Benz was faced with exactly this quandary in June 2008. On an outreach shift we heard Benz yelling and throwing things in her room at the Nimish Hotel. She yelled, "That is why I don't want to be on the street anymore!" She was having a terrible fight with another woman in the hotel room. Two weeks after the fight, I received a call from an outreach worker, Mara, seeking my advice about what could be done for Benz. The field note describes how Mara, as a service person, expressed ambivalence about sending Benz into systems of care but feared for Benz's safety. However, the bottom line was that Benz would need to foreground her pregnancy and background her heroin and crack use to get housed away from her abusive boyfriend. There were no DV shelters for women who openly use drugs.

PHONE CALL ABOUT BENZ. JUNE 2008

Mara from outreach just called me for some advice. We just hung up.

Benz is pregnant. She found out two weeks ago. When we saw her after the fight that she had when she was in the Nimish [Hotel], we had thought that she was being beaten up by her boyfriend. Looks like that was going on too.

When Mara was out tonight at the Raman [Hotel] Benz said, "Hold on, I can't get up," and she opened the door and her boyfriend was there. He doesn't like Benz using drugs even though she's got an enormous heroin habit and smokes crack.

So she said she got on methadone because of the pregnancy. But apparently the methadone dose is really knocking her out. That is why she can't get up. Mara helped her up. She said Benz's head was under the bed and her legs were all twisted back. She was a total mess on the floor and she could not get herself up. Benz walked down the hall with Mara to get out of earshot of her boyfriend. Benz said that he was getting violent again.

Mara was really calling me to get permission to do more of an intervention with Benz. Mara was worried that she might overstep her bounds if she directed Benz toward treatment. This was really an interesting harm reduction moment, where Mara was feeling torn between trying to help Benz clean up and get away from the guy and also feeling like maybe that was too pushy. Mara is in drug recovery herself, and so she is sensitive about not deciding for other people what they do about their drug use. But Mara is very worried about Benz.

Mara and I discussed the situation for a while. Basically we came up with two main options, both of which probably would involve Benz lying about her drug use or her desire to stop using. (1) She can go into residential treatment, or (2) she can go to a DV shelter. Both are miserable options for someone with a huge heroin habit. Benz can get into a DV shelter because she'll jump the list due to her pregnancy. If she goes to drug treatment she doesn't have to "succeed" there. If she is afraid of her boyfriend, she could use drug treatment as a "break." She just has to work the system long enough to get a roof over her head because there are no other options.

There's nothing else for her.

As a pregnant drug-using woman she can get methadone, but in terms of the housing, to get housing, to get a situation where she's not with a violent boyfriend and in the middle of the crazy drug, sex work scene that is the Raman Hotel, she can't. She can't get out of it. She has to go into a shelter or into residential treatment, where you're not supposed to use [drugs].

Mara agreed to check with Benz to see if she wants to lie her way through [a local DV shelter] or some other program for a little while. Benz is also smoking a lot of crack, so even on methadone she has still got a big challenge. It just seems impossible for her to be able to hide her drug use. There are no good options unless she can stop using.

Benz did not go to the DV shelter or residential treatment in June 2008. Toward the end of her pregnancy, she entered a residential program when her boyfriend was facing jail time. She was able to regain custody of her baby after birth and remained in transitional drug treatment housing.

The politics of misrepresentation available to Benz were complex. Alice's problem, when we engaged with her at the Bridgit Hotel, centered on sexual health. Alice was aware that she had a sexually transmitted infection (STI) but was unable to afford the medications to resolve it. Her insurance status, the fact that she had insurance through Medi-Cal, made her somehow ineligible for the prescription she needed. After several suggestions as to where to get access to medications, another hotel tenant suggested that she game the system. As captured in the following field note, the folk wisdom again indicated that her best solution was to lie to get the medications covered.

ALICE'S STI. BRIDGIT HOTEL. MARCH 2008

Alice needs antibiotics for the STI and she can't pay for the antibiotics even though she's already been diagnosed with it. She didn't talk about where she thought she got the STI, but she is doing sex work to support her habit (and/or her boyfriend's) and to pay for their rent. Her boyfriend is in the room when we are talking and from the way she keeps looking over her shoulder you get the sense she is pretty afraid of him. We try and suggest a few places to get treatment. I don't think she's going to make it to [the clinic across town]. While we were talking, another woman tenant in the hallway interrupted and told Alice to lie. The woman said to not put down her Social Security number so the computer wouldn't figure out that Alice had Medi-Cal. Then Alice can get access to this program the woman called "Health Access California," which is only apparently for reproductive [health].

For Alice and her boyfriend, their housing depended on her being able to turn tricks. The STI was posing a serious problem. It seems unfathomable that she could receive an STI screening and positive test and still not receive a free prescription. Chances are that her medical provider and she both had no idea that her prescriptions would not be covered by her Medi-Cal. Either way, it left Alice with a diagnosis and no treatment. One week later, Alice and her boyfriend were gone, evicted, like many others from the Bridgit Hotel that week. They never returned, so I did not learn the outcome of her STI treatment.

Outside of health care, DV shelters, and drug treatment programs, public health research studies were also sites of systematic hustling. Sometimes misrepresentation appeared to be only about getting paid. But the reality of "hotel time" and its housing instability formed the subtext of all the system hustles I documented, even as women got drawn into "epidemiological time."[24] In August 2009, Lexi was temporarily homeless with her boyfriend, Pano. Lexi was five months pregnant. Pano and Lexi had been offered a coveted weekly rate at the Grey Hotel. According to Lexi, Pano agreed to put his GA welfare money on that rent. When she checked with the Grey Hotel manager, the weekly rental fee had not been paid. That meant the money had been spent on crack and Lexi would have to (sex) work to pay for the room. She was furious and fighting with Pano when I came across the two of them out on the street where they had been sleeping. "Watch my stuff for me while I'm gone!" she demanded of Pano as we left so Lexi could dose at the methadone clinic. "He is not even gonna watch my stuff, you watch. What an ASSHOLE!" Lexi said in my car. The whole trip to the clinic was a blow-by-blow description of what a liar and "dog" Pano was. At the clinic, a friend approached Lexi and me with a flyer for a study that paid $50 for a single survey visit. Lexi used my phone to call the study while we rode back to the neighborhood. She was given an appointment for the next day. She told me she had done the study about three or four times; she had just put on a different wig each time she showed up for the appointment. She laughs, "They [the study personnel] so easy to fool, 'cause 'we' [black participants] all look the same [to them].'" When we returned, Pano was back guarding her stuff. Things were tense at first, but immediately Lexi got down to business. She said to him, "You need to call this number, and get yourself an [research study] appointment. Just answer the questions yes." She coached Pano while he borrowed her phone. While Lexi was coaching Pano through the right answers to get access to the health study, she was animated (waving her arms around, talking loudly). He was contrite. This hustle had become a way for Pano to compensate for spending their weekly rental money on crack.

I had no idea what the research study was about or whether or not Lexi and Pano would indeed have been eligible for it on the basis of their behaviors. Regardless, the production of epidemiological evidence, just like the production of clinical evidence (in Ramona's case), was undermined, because its claims for scientific validity existed within a political economy of hustling and desperation.[25] I am also not suggesting that these examples implicate all public health research or clinical data. The aforementioned epidemiologic study notwithstanding, most public health researchers are savvy to the street economies in which participants live and the effect of monetary incentives from research on those economies. They respond to hustling with the same resigned patience as the clinician quoted earlier. They try to appear nonjudgmental. Then they impose more rules and security systems in order to "catch" participants trying to do the same research study twice. Further, anthropological evidence is no more immune to this hustle. I was viewed at times as someone with something to offer (food, money for a long interview, a ride to the clinic) and therefore someone to potentially befriend and/or manipulate.[26] Other times I was not: offers of food or a ride were politely refused. I had no more than the advantage of time and the method of observation with which to discern the degree of veracity women's narratives may have contained. Perhaps fortunately, unlike statistical data, anthropological data is not slave to the metric of objectivity. Perhaps unfortunately, it runs the risk of reduction to anecdote (or, worse, social performance) for the same reason.

When it came to hustling systems, CPS was one institution that many of the women outwardly feared. Lexi may have poked fun at the receptionist screening "new" appointments at the public health study, but CPS was no joke. In one description a provider gave to me, she explained the complex explanatory webs in which addicted, pregnant women find themselves caught. To this provider, the impetus for the need to lie to CPS originated from "disorganized thinking," and from not making "connections" between individual behavior and poor parenting outcomes. To the mother, the explanation stemmed from her not wanting her son to see that she had been using crack. The provider struggled to convey to me that addicted, pregnant women seem to be unable to see the rational outcomes of "cause and effect" because their social worlds are made irrational through drug use and trauma. She said:

Women do not make connections, they do not see the connections between their behaviors, the choices that they are making, their mental health conditions, and the outcomes of their pregnancies. Here is an example. I have a woman in my program who just recently got granted visitation with her son. She was very, very excited about this. She was given one hour a week to visit. When I see her the next week, she says, "I didn't go to the visit." When I ask why, she says, "Because I'm too skinny and I didn't want my son to know that I was using." She doesn't make the connection that because she was up smoking crack all night, and she doesn't eat when she smokes crack, that that is why she is too skinny. And she can do something about that. So the reason is her drug use, but she says the reason is that she is too skinny. And she has to lie to the CPS worker about why [she missed the visit] because it hurts her case when she doesn't show up. Her thinking is skewed; it is disorganized, because of her drug use, because of her trauma. It is very difficult to get to a cause-and-effect that makes sense.

Arriving at a cause-and-effect that "make sense" to both the pregnant women and the service providers was a tall order. The contradictory demands of care and coercion in this setting meant that these relationships were consistently fraught.

Pregnant, in Custody

The main avenue for addicted, pregnant women to access care and treatment was through some form of incarceration. The most frequent route was through "picking up a case" (getting arrested) for sex work and ending up with a "deferral" into drug treatment. All of the deferrals that I documented were essentially court orders. If the woman failed to show up at the treatment program, she would be incarcerated at the jail. If she took the deferral, she was bound to the rules and regulations stipulated by the drug treatment program. This does not necessarily mean residential treatment, but for many women it did. Ramona described her arrest several days before her baby was born as "bullshit," but it was indeed the intervention that got her into the hospital and on methadone. Lexi was actually in custody when her son, Lionel, was born in 2000. She was transferred to a jail ward at the local public hospital to give birth. Lexi told a story that highlighted the inhumanity of her treatment during this experience, reflecting the height of governmental

6.2. Police in front of the daily-rent hotels on Mission Street. August 2007.
Photo by the author.

controls over the bodies of the incarcerated poor. Yet within this narrative
she also highlighted a policy-changing act of resistance by her jailor. The
narrative revealed the complexity involved in the micropractices of both punishment and care toward addicted, pregnant women. Lexi retold the story to
me in March 2009, shortly after she discovered she was pregnant again:

> [My son] was born in [the city jail]. Not in [the jail]. He was born at [the
> hospital] but I was in jail. They took me [to the hospital] in custody and
> that's another thing that was so sad. Once you had a baby they immedi-
> ately take you back up to the [jail] floor. You have to be shackled up and
> taken down and you have to get an officer, a duty officer, and I didn't see
> my baby for two days. Two fucking days. And I cried and cried. You have
> a baby down in delivery and as fast as they can they get you back off to

jail, you're back up on the jail ward at [the hospital]. And the baby is in the nursery. I didn't see him for two days, for two fucking days and I was crying. 'Cause I had to have an escort. And they [the escort] wasn't doing nothing. They were just sitting around. And I'm in my hospital room [on the "jail floor"]. It was fucked up. So finally the third day I was getting ready to be escorted [back to the city jail]. They'll never tell you when you're leaving but the doctor would come in and say, "Okay, you can go back." I didn't see my baby once after I had [gave birth to] him, that was it. It was fucked up.

On my way to be transported back to [the jail], the captain—I forgot her name but she was so nice. I told her. I says, "I can't believe it," and when I told her that [I hadn't seen my baby], she said, "No. Fuck it." It's all about the count. You know, they make sure about the count [that all the prisoners are back in jail]. [The captain] fucked up the whole count at [the city jail] and everything because I wasn't there to be counted in and all that shit. But she [the captain] took me to the nursery, and we stayed down there for about eight hours. She got some pictures of him. That was the sweetest thing she ever did. I never forgot her for that. She was the sweetest thing. And I'm glad because she couldn't believe it [that Lexi had been unable to see her son]. She sat there, she held the baby. She says, "Take your time." While I sat there she did a double shift and everything. She said, "Lexi will be staying here for dinner. I'm not taking her back [to jail]. So if I gotta get written up, let me get written up." She said to me, "It's going to be all right. You get yourself better and don't come back here [to jail]." And about maybe three weeks later they opened up the [residential treatment] and I went in.

Lexi described an experience of inhumanity (her being denied access to her newborn son) that was transformed through an act of rule-breaking defiance (the captain said, "If I gotta get written up, let me get written up"). The interaction itself, and Lexi's interpretation of its consequences (motivating her to take a residential drug treatment slot), indicate how addicted, pregnant women's victim-perpetrator status is established in everyday practice. It also implicates structural policy changes for pregnant incarcerated women that could influence parenting outcomes, if even in the short term.[27]

Anita shared a similar story with me about her 2007 pregnancy with her son. By evoking her own mother, Anita was able to convince the police officers to send her to the hospital but not to take her into custody, so her mother could be present for the birth. Anita told me: "I was straight homeless. I was sleeping on this mattress on Garden Street [in the neighborhood] and I nodded out with the syringe still in me. Still sticking out of my fucking hip!" Anita "muscles" crushed-up morphine pills into her hip/buttock area or her back just below her shoulder, because she doesn't have veins that she can easily inject into anymore.

> Anyway, I started to feel like I was going into labor. So I get up, and I stumble into the alley to smoke crack. I still have the syringe hanging out of me, and I am bent over trying to take a hit, when two cops show up. Now I had a no-bail warrant out on me at this time. That means they *have* to arrest you. They *have* to take you into custody. And I say to the cop, this lady cop, I say, "You can't arrest me, please don't arrest me!" And she says, "You are eight months pregnant, in an alley smoking crack with a syringe hanging out of your ass, and a no-bail warrant. Can you give one reason why I shouldn't arrest you?" And I said, "Yes. Because I am in labor, and if you take me into custody they won't let my mom be in the delivery room with me. My mom has been at the birth of all my children. Please don't make her pay for my mistakes. She shouldn't have to pay for my mistakes." And it worked. The cop called an ambulance to take me to the hospital. It worked because the cop agreed with me. My mom shouldn't have to suffer for what I have done.

Anita, like Ramona, is taking personal responsibility for her situation ("my mistakes"), in line with the demands of her perpetrator role, and consistent with neoliberal discourse. Anita says this "worked." It may also have "worked" because the police officers recognized the primacy of Anita's medical condition (being in labor) over her criminalization (the bench warrant). It might also be that the police were enacting a denial of responsibility, worried about an at-risk pregnancy in custody, even for a short while. Like most interactions between institutions and addicted, pregnant women, empathy and punishment, care and coercion became difficult to parse from one another.

In December 2008, I ran into Danell on the street, smoking a cigarette. She was about eight months pregnant. I hadn't seen her in the hotels in a while, so I asked her where she'd been. "I got picked up [arrested and incarcerated]," she replied. "Tonight is my last night out here. I am going to the detox and then into residential." Danell had been court-ordered. Danell had "chosen" treatment over jail. The next time I saw Danell, I didn't recognize her at first. She was coming to dose at the methadone program, smiling and laughing with the other women getting out of the van that transported them from residential treatment to the methadone program once a week to pick up their take-homes (doses of methadone that are dispensed to patients to take outside of the methadone clinic). When I next saw Danell again in August 2009 her baby was with her in residential treatment. She looked happy and thrilled to show off her baby to me and Ramona, who had just checked in. Danell, like Cupcake in her earlier pregnancies, took advantage of drug treatment deferrals that offered alternatives to incarceration.

When I discussed the various options for women to gain access to housing with a health official, he raised the question of coerced residential treatment—meaning incarcerating women so that they cannot use substances during their pregnancies. Our discussion began as an exploration, a philosophical debate about the political palatability of pregnant women, who are known to be using drugs, being housed in publicly funded housing. Quickly it morphed into more fraught political and ethical domains: Is coercion in the form of incarceration ever justified to stop women using drugs while pregnant?

> KELLY: I wonder what kind of housing might work for [addicted] pregnant women.
>
> OFFICIAL: That is a very difficult population to assess. Because women who are pregnant are not necessarily ready to stop using [drugs]. It would be awful hard to advocate for harm-reduction-based pregnancy housing [meaning housing in which abstinence is not a requirement]. Gosh. That would be a tough sell. Even though I can get there because I recognize what the alternative is.

The housing official recognizes that an addicted, pregnant woman who is homeless is at much greater risk of a poor health outcome than one who is housed. Scientific data indicates that an adverse environment (such as homelessness or housing instability) can have significant additive effects on the negative fetal outcomes for babies born of women who use substances prenatally. Indeed, it is difficult to isolate the effects of drug use versus the factors of an adverse environment in these studies.

We continue talking.

> KELLY: Many people feel the ideal is a residential treatment program at least throughout the duration of the pregnancy.
>
> OFFICIAL: But would you incarcerate women to achieve that goal?

I pause. I am taken off guard by the practical nature of the question. In the world of social policy intervention, two questions are always asked at once: What to do and how to do it. If it can't be done, then it isn't practical, and should not be done. By this logic, residential treatment is irrelevant if women won't go. I decide to speak from my experience, initially avoiding the overall political and ethical dilemmas of the question.

> KELLY: I know a woman who was court-ordered [to residential treat-
> ment] who still has her kid, but . . .
> OFFICIAL: In South Carolina, there is a movement toward that, to incar-
> cerate the woman for harming her fetus.

He is taking the example to the extreme. Many southern US states, including South Carolina and Tennessee, have been aggressive in forwarding legislation to criminalize drug use during pregnancy, historically and in the present day. I respond more strongly than I actually feel.

> KELLY: Yes, I know what you are speaking of. That is a waste of time.
> OFFICIAL: But that is the legal means, because you can't incarcerate
> someone for having cocaine in their system. But an incarceration
> that feels like a drug treatment facility, not like a jail: that is an
> opportunity.
> KELLY: It's an opportunity only because it's exploiting an opportunity.
> OFFICIAL: [They say] the violation of civil liberties is justified because
> you are giving the kid the best opportunity.
> KELLY: I think that is a real slippery slope.
> OFFICIAL: All these things are slippery slopes. We are all going down
> the slide.

The conversation moved on, but I was left with a very bitter aftertaste. What are the social and moral parameters at work here? How could I rec- oncile the fact that many women reported what *they felt* were better birth outcomes (a baby on a methadone detoxification, a baby in their custody) as a result of their involvement with the criminal justice system? I thought of Danell—who was court-ordered to treatment at eight months pregnant; and Ramona's "false" arrest and detention three days before the birth of her child. Lexi's first son, whom she had custody of for two years, was born while she was incarcerated, a police officer looking on during the birth. Without the legal intervention, would any of these women feel that they would have experienced any custody of their children? Cupcake told me that she would surely have had "a crack baby" if her arrest and subsequent mandatory pregnancy test had not come back positive, forcing her into treatment. Anita, who described convincing the police not to arrest her, explained that they were the ones who got her to the hospital by calling the ambulance. Kitt, when she described her drug use during several of her pregnancies, indicated that "God helped" because she was arrested and stopped using drugs while she was pregnant as a result. Kitt said, "I've only, like, used in my pregnancy until I was like two or three months, you know, 'cause God has helped me by sending me to jail. . . . With my middle son I went to jail when I was like three months. With [my younger son], I went into jail and I went into a program so it was like three months too." Even if the tenor of our conversation was provocative, the adjudication of pregnant, addicted women made both me and the health official who was trying to push my buttons uncomfortable. It was anathema to the progressive, liberal politics of San Francisco and to notions of harm reduction that shaped policy and started our conversation. What does this say about the vital politics that surround questions of viability for addicted, pregnant women and their babies, when incarceration becomes "opportunity"? Is the criminal justice system a proxy for outreach, counseling, or programmatic services otherwise unavailable or unused?

Importantly, involvement with the criminal justice system did not have a lasting deterrent effect for any of the women in the daily-rent hotels. Danell was able to access housing out of the neighborhood due to a health condition that afforded her specific support pre- and postnatally. She attributed this disease-specific funding stream for housing to her success in keeping custody of her baby. All the other women whose arrests led to drug treatment eventually returned to drug use and to the daily-rent hotels without their children. Proponents of criminalization measures for pregnant women who use drugs have argued that these cases serve as a warning to other women.[28] I documented no such deterrent effect. Importantly, this type of rationality flies in the face of emergent scientific discourse about the etiology and course of addiction as a brain disease. Consistent with that conception of addiction, criminal justice interventions served as short-term respites that women felt helped them tremendously during a period of time. Incarceration while pregnant did not solve the problem of addiction in women's lives or resolve ongoing child custody and parenting problems associated with it.

Victim-Perpetrator

Those motherfuckers [at the drug treatment program] were taking all my
money, my whole [ssi] check! But Gloria's [the counselor] got my back.
She said she would have a bed waiting for me, whenever I was ready to
come back.
—Ramona after leaving residential treatment at five and a half months
pregnant (August 2009)

A battle was being waged through the discursive constructions of the "pregnant addict." On the one hand she was construed as a victim—of her own
brain chemistry, of her traumatic past, of her violent partner, even of her
own body as she contended with a pregnancy she did not plan and may not
have felt capable of managing. On the other hand she was also construed as
a perpetrator—as someone harming her baby through continued substance
use, through her refusal to enter or stay in drug treatment, and through her
likelihood to fail at future motherhood. Addicted, pregnant women often
constructed family members, counselors, providers, clinicians, and case managers who coerced and cared for them with the same ambivalent markers.
They perceived and described others just as others perceived and described
them: with an equal dose of hostility and admiration. For example, Ramona
went out of her way to explain to me that the pregnant women in her "crew"
(those who went through a pregnancy and drug treatment together with Ramona) fiercely protected Mary [a drug treatment counselor], defending her
as if she was their mother, even while calling her a "bitch" on several occasions. I witnessed this mix of complex relationships firsthand:

RAMONA'S METHADONE INTAKE. DECEMBER 2009

Ramona, Mary, and I are all sitting in Mary's cramped office at the
drug treatment program. It is the day of Ramona's intake. Ramona
is explaining to me how important her counselor, Mary, has been to
all the women in PPMT [postpartum methadone treatment]. Ramona
says: "We were her girls, though. You fucked with Mary, you fucked
with us!"

"People thought I was a little tough," Mary says, turning to me. This is an understatement. I have heard several women call Mary lots of names. Ramona disagrees with Mary:

"Please, Mary. You weren't tough enough!"

These constant contradictions in the attribution of blame and gratitude within interpersonal relationships also extended to women's descriptions of institutional contacts, even those that were fleeting and highly regulated, such as hospitalizations, brief stints in drug treatment, and brief incarcerations. For example, Lexi was present at the birth of Dylan's child. Lexi told me on multiple occasions that it was "unbelievable" how badly behaved Dylan was during this hospitalization. "For a full day she screamed at all the staff. She was yelling, throwing shit. I *could not* believe it," Lexi said to me. When I asked Dylan about her experience, she self-righteously told me: "I would never go to [the large public hospital]. No way. I went to [another hospital]. They treated me like a *queen*. It was fantastic." When Kitt was released from jail, she talked about voluntarily joining the drug treatment "pod" while briefly incarcerated, because there was more behavioral accountability and less drug use. Kitt told me: "In [the drug treatment program in jail] it'll [an argument] be addressed; in the other pods it wouldn't. Say if a person, I don't know if they had a bad attitude or something like that they would just have a bad attitude. But in [the program] they would like—you could bring them in and have one-on-one or something like that you know and tell them what you don't like that they're doing. The [other pods] are like some lenient places with drugs and everything and in [drug treatment] there's not too much of that type of stuff." Kitt got into physical fights regularly and was sometimes paid to beat up other girls on the street. Yet she expressed sincere appreciation for the possibility for conflict resolution offered in jail. Cupcake, remember, described herself as someone who "has trouble with authority. I don't like rules." When she commented about how she found out she was pregnant in jail at age fifteen, she stated, "I can't believe they don't automatically test all the women that get arrested. Most [women] don't know [that they are pregnant]. They should test them!" Are these examples of addicted, pregnant women coming to ape the discourses of repressive institutions? This seems plausible. But women are also consciously grappling with the fact that as "pregnant addicts" they must enact the subjectivity of both victim and perpetrator to enable social interventions and potentially keep custody of their children. They must appear both plausibly innocent and sincerely repentant. Biological understandings of craving and relapse cannot capture this dichotomous subjectivity in which willpower and a future orientation are still demanded despite the disease of addiction. A further interpretation of a provider's statement (first seen in the introduction) lends a tragic cast to the task of occupying the dual subject positions (active addict and future mother):

> That is why words like "lying" and "knowing" don't apply here—not to these patients. I see my pregnant patients smoking crack, doing all kinds of craziness. And when they lose [custody of] the kid, they are *devastated*. I mean really traumatized, *retraumatized*. And I want say [to her], "Wait a minute, *come on*. You must have seen this coming?" But she didn't. She didn't see it coming. She didn't, really, *know* it was going to happen. Not before it did. I don't know if it is holding on to hope, or just the ability to compartmentalize the addiction from everything else that is going on.

From providers' perspectives, the addicted pregnant woman was often understood as someone who had a tormented history: a backstory that made her a sympathetic victim of abuse and trauma, had got her into her current situation, and explained her behaviors. Women who lived in the daily-rent hotels were also constructed as victims of poverty who lived in dangerous and predatory social worlds. As long as the woman was construed as a victim but did not *act* like a victim (but rather a perpetrator), the relationships she could forge in various forms of treatment would not be entirely hostile and might even be cooperative. Victims by definition are blameless, not responsible; perpetrators are by definition responsible and culpable. Pregnant addicted women were asked to be both. One provider used the word "victim" reluctantly, when she described to me a scenario in which professionals intervened in what they felt was the best interest of a woman and her baby and got rewarded with a lawsuit. Careful attention to the narrative reveals that the problem of the "pregnant addict" here was not that she was a victim; victimhood is given. Rather, it was that she did not accept the role of perpetrator. The provider said:

> The victim is the hardest to work with. I don't want to use that word "victim," because it sounds like I am being unfair, but they are women who are stuck in that victim role. And it is horrible because they *are* victims; they have experienced terrible things in their lifetimes. Terrible trauma.

And yet if they can't take responsibility for what is happening right *now*, they won't be able to keep their babies. I will give an example. There is a woman who ended up at [the hospital] at 7.5 months pregnant and she told the providers that she was taking thirty Oxys [oxycodone] a day and twenty Valiums, and so the doctors did what was medically indicated for the fetus. They stopped the other opiates and put her on methadone. Methadone has long, metabolic characteristics; it breaks down over twenty-four hours, which keeps the uterine environment stable. Oxys create a high and then a withdrawal which is very unstable and potentially dangerous for the fetus. So the docs did what they were supposed to. She stayed in the hospital and delivered and was mandated to residential treatment. She had severe mental health issues and no housing. It turns out she is suing the hospital for getting her addicted to methadone. Everything that has happened, from her perspective is someone else's fault. What do you do with that?

The call toward personal responsibility becomes extremely tricky when a child is involved. This difference (the material reality and the evocation of the unborn child) marked addicted, pregnant women as difficult to treat, difficult to house, and sometimes trauma-producing to the service providers that were enlisted to respond to addicted pregnancy as a social problem. Once a woman became pregnant, even if unplanned, it was up to her to act in the best interest of her unborn child. She needed to fulfill the neoliberal promise of being an entrepreneur of herself by entering treatment, maintaining abstinence, and avoiding the state forms of adjudication which would manage her as a risky subject or criminal. Forms of state neglect and abandonment that produced her homelessness and poverty contributed to her construction as a sympathetic victim, even as her traumatic subjectivity had to be eschewed to maintain child custody. Unsurprisingly, women described themselves as, and enacted the roles of, both victims and perpetrators. And they expressed both love and hate toward those who were in place to intervene upon their lives and their babies.

conclusion

A Maternity That Suits?

Minutes before we left the hospital where Ramona's son is detoxing off methadone to drive her to residential drug treatment, she called me over. "Kelly, take out your camera. Take a picture of us now." She sobbed, "I don't want to leave him. I don't know when I will see him again." She posed herself, with her son on her lap, fussing carefully with his IV line. She was crying, yet her eyes were hollow. Her son slept peacefully, likely as a result of his continuous opioid replacement therapy. When I looked at the picture later, I was struck by the uncanny resemblance of Ramona and her son to a postmortem photograph, a memento mori. Victorian-age memento mori, like the one pictured here, were often taken after the death of a baby or young child (fig. C.1).[1] Ramona wanted to capture this moment, a moment of likely loss. She was symbolically preempting the rupture of custody, even as she was actively trying to write a different future for herself and her son by entering residential drug treatment.

The radical uncertainty of an addicted pregnancy's outcome is mediated by both the everyday realities of poverty and addiction and the techno-scientific interventions of care and control. Georges Canguilhem presented the coproduction of pathology and health as the result of responses (successes and failures) to the experience of external pressure. Such pressure is multiply construed for addicted, pregnant women. There is the pressure of the pregnancy on her body and on her baby's development: the pressure exerted by chemicals (nicotine, cocaine, opioids, alcohol) on the mother's body and the body of her fetus; the pressure to acquire food; the pressure of no sleep; the pressure of multiple sexual encounters; and the pressure of drug withdrawal. At the level of the biological, a "normal" pregnancy is quantified with rapid efficiency in the United States, but differences between normal signs and symptoms and those that indicate pathology are more difficult to discern. When Canguilhem carried his argument about environmental pressures, pathology, and health out of the petri dish and into broader society, he made an additional observation that is of particular interest here. He claimed: "Everything happens as

C.1. Memento mori daguerreotype, 1850s. Courtesy of
Michael Shanks, archaeographer.com.

if a society had 'the mortality that suits it,' the number of the dead and their
distribution into different groups expressing the importance which society
does or does not give to the protraction of life."[2] When examining pregnancy
and addiction in the daily-rent hotels, one might be tempted to wonder if a
society also has a *maternity* that suits it. The management of pregnant, addicted women can tell us a great deal about social valuation, viability, and
allowable social failure. In this ethnography, the potential viability of women's
unborn children became a complex calculus of social-institutional interaction, individual behavior, and time. Requirements of women to take individual, personal responsibility for themselves and their unborn children came
into conflict with institutional regulatory mechanisms that did not synch with
the temporal constraints of addiction and homelessness. The addicted, pregnant women I worked with struggled to square their histories, the traumas of
past pregnancies and lost custody of children, with their present moments of
institutional adjudication.

The Vital Politics of Viability

vi·a·ble

adj.

1. Capable of living, developing, or germinating under favorable conditions.
2. Capable of living outside the uterus. Used of a fetus or newborn.
3. Capable of success or continuing effectiveness; practicable: *a viable plan; a viable national economy.*

—Merriam-webster.com

How might we best theorize a vital politics of viability for the addicted, pregnant women in the daily-rent hotels? "Vital politics" references a variety of intellectual projects: from stem cell research to human genomics. The construct has been used in several scholarly conferences and books that discuss themes also emergent in this ethnography: the remaking of psychiatric illness as organic facts and the reorganization of evidence about addiction to speak to neurochemical vulnerabilities, not failure of personal will.[3]

Viability connects to several registers, including the organic, the practicable, and the philosophical. On the organic level, viability asks about fetal thriving, referencing the possibility for a living child as a result of a pregnancy. On the practicable level, viability addresses efficacy, effectiveness, and intervention. Is the plan workable? Is it realistic, given the context of its implementation? For addicted, pregnant women in this setting, I have explored a variety of public health interventions in relation to housing, drug treatment, incarceration, and welfare entitlement that attempt, with varying degrees of success, to respond to both these registers of viability. Taken together and extrapolated to the philosophical level, a vital politics of viability for addicted pregnancy asks, "What forms of life are possible here?" Placing diverse evidentiary claims about the everyday life, health, and behaviors of addicted, pregnant women in conversation allows us to address this larger question. In doing so I am advocating for the long, complex view of the social problem of pregnancy and addiction, and making a demand on the reader to acknowledge and explore the multiple ways he or she might have a relationship to the problem.

As addicted, pregnant women interfaced with institutions and institutionary figures that manage housing and health, an interwoven system of care and coercion emerged. There were multiple adjudicators in this ethnographic picture: those who profited directly off of women's risk status and behaviors (hotel owners and managers), those who waited for women to access their services (providers), those who policed women and forced them to choose between incarceration or drug treatment (the criminal justice system). In this story, those who wanted them (hotel managers and providers) could not always keep them; those who wanted to get rid of them were forced to be the main conduit into health and mental health systems. Arbitrary and ambivalent social relationships developed at these sites of adjudication, even as the stakes for all actors appeared incredibly high.

In the neoliberal context of the US welfare state, the homeless "pregnant addict" might prove to be the most evocative example of a failed entrepreneur of the self.[4] But there are two selves here: one undisciplined (the pregnant addict) and one yet to be disciplined (the child). The biological realities of both pregnancy *and* addiction collided with the social policies of drug treatment allocation and legally prescribed parenthood. The political economy driving neoliberal interventions demanded that the addicted, pregnant women take personal responsibility. This economy also ran headlong into a moral economy that contained complex dualities: woman and child, victim and perpetrator. One provider shared her experience with the many women. She carefully avoided separating women into "good" and "bad" categories. This provider reified the role of the pregnancy as a point of departure: either for a better future or a worse one. "It seems that for one group of women the pregnancy is an opportunity, a kind of 'wake-up call' to get into treatment, get their life together. For others—women who tend to come to the program later in pregnancy—they have been using throughout their whole pregnancy. The pregnancy was unplanned and unwanted. They are in abusive relationships. They are in denial about the pregnancy. They are sex workers and maybe have gotten pregnant from a trick. The pregnancy has further destabilized their already very unstable lives. They are spiraling downward."

Acceptance into intervention programs designed to help addicted, pregnant women required specific categorizations. The most frequent categorization I came to document was a strange hybrid, the criminal-volunteer: women who entered into systems of care and coercion by way of criminal justice system involvement. The terrible irony is that those women who entered into those systems had the greatest likelihood of remaining in contact with their children, at least in the short term. Those women who did not terminate their pregnancies, and also did not get court-ordered treatment, tended to have worse "outcomes." Once a woman was no longer associated with that

C.2. Project Prevention Facebook ad.

program, her status changed relative to the benefits she was allowed in the program. A potential future as a mother became foreclosed, and she returned to the "spiraling downward" social reality of the daily-rent hotels. This process often repeated, as most women in the daily-rent hotels experienced multiple addicted pregnancies.

The perceived perpetuity of addicted pregnancy leads organizations like Project Prevention, "a 501C3 nonprofit that pays drug addicts and alcoholics $300 to use long-term birth control," to advocate for social interventions that intervene at the biological level—delaying or terminating the possibility for life.[5] These solutions, considered politically and morally anathema by some who align their practices with social Darwinism, unearth a temporal problem in biological explanations of addiction. If addiction is conceived of as a chronic, relapsing disease of the brain, when can intervention efficacy be assessed? Addiction, thus conceptualized, has biological failure built in to it. So how much "clean time" is enough to condone a pregnancy or to grant child custody? For Project Prevention the rationality of not having time to wait for drug treatment success or for women to stop using drugs on their own anchors the argument for taking reproduction out of the equation completely. Not surprisingly, this logic has been criticized as a soft form of eugenics.

The director of Project Prevention, Barbara Harris, has four adopted chil-

If you believe that drugs, alcohol, and pregnancy don't mix please share this photo.

projectprevention.org

C.3. Project Prevention Facebook ad.

dren born of the same crack-addicted mother. She rejects the notion that her program is a draconian form of social engineering. Instead she proposes that financially incentivized birth control or sterilization for drug-addicted women not only helps the children who would be born destined to reproduce a life of drug abuse and poverty but also protects the addicted women from having children only to experience the pain and suffering of losing custody of them. In an interview for the BBC, Harris said: "These women have a chance every time they give birth to a child. . . . They are told if they go into drug treatment they can get their child back. They are given chance after chance after chance. . . . And drugs are more important, but at the very least we can stop them from giving birth to children whose lives may end up the same as theirs. If anybody believes that these women having multiple babies that are taken away is a good thing for these women, they are wrong." Project Prevention supports the stance that it is better to deny the woman the child up front rather than allow the child and the woman to suffer in the future. Project Prevention's public health intervention includes driving a mobile health van into poorer neighborhoods with an advertisement for cash for birth control printed on the side and disturbing pictures of infants assumed to be born of drug-addicted mothers.

While her opponents argue that resources should be spent on drug treatment instead, Harris retorts that drug treatment is a bad "gamble," with a poor return on investment. Her views are not based on opinion or experience but research (survey) evidence: "I do a survey on everyone that comes into the programme. . . . Most of them started using drugs when they were 11, 12, 13 years old. And all of them have been in and out of drug treatment programmes, in and out, in and out. So people tell me that I should be focusing on drug treatment not birth control but drug treatment is just a gamble, you know. Women go in there, they get off drugs, they go back on drugs but that doesn't keep them from getting pregnant."

The online responses to the interview covered the gamut. The four examples that follow offer a range of references, from references to the burden on society of "raising" children of drug-addicted mothers to references to multiple forms of social engineering (tax and benefits systems) and punitive social control (incarceration), to personal revelations:

> We need a sensible debate about this sort of thing. It seems to me that the women who breed the most are often the least suitable people to bring up children. The cycle goes on and society doesn't want and can't afford the results. People quite rightly call this social engineering, but the current tax and benefit system is a form of social engineering as well. This particular "experiment" states that all people who are biologically able to have children should be allowed to have children. I don't think this argument has any more validity than Project Prevention's one. Let's have a proper discussion about child rearing, rather than slinging the Eugenics accusation at anybody who dares to commit to a solution.

> Reprehensible. This is coming from the right place in her head, but is skewed by her own experience and also the general attitude in the USA that people on drugs are BAD PEOPLE. It's the same with their jail policy which has a 0 percent rehabilitation rate mainly because they don't rehabilitate offenders. It's clearly exploitation and an attempt at social engineering which will clearly fail because it does not solve the underlying socio-economic problems that drug abuse is created by or creates.

> Seven years ago I got clean after finding out I was pregnant with my first daughter. I am the only woman I've ever met that got and stayed clean for a pregnancy. I know that I am an exception to the norm. In my years of using I witnessed much pain and suffering inflicted on children with

addict parents, ranging from neglect to emotional, physical and even sexual abuse. Mrs. Harris is nothing short of a hero and the work that she's doing is truly a blessing. Addicts don't abuse substances because they innocently tried them once and became hopeless slaves. Addicts use in an attempt to compensate for a fundamental lacking and the truth is that most of them aren't going to change anytime soon, if at all. Anyone that would criticize Mrs. Harris' work obviously has little to no personal experience to speak from.[6]

The stakes are high and the politics extreme in the vital politics of viability of addicted pregnancy. As I listened to Mary (Ramona's counselor) and Ramona catch up during Ramona's intake appointment in December 2009, I was struck by an aspect of their conversation that went unremarked by the two of them. They were cycling through a mental list of names, women who had been in the drug treatment program with Ramona when her daughter, DeLoni, was born. Mary and Ramona asked each other in turns, "What happened to Shani and her daughter?" or "Did you hear about Rally?" They discussed about ten women when I begin to realize that their "outcomes" were critically divergent. The women were either mothers, having regained custody of their children through ongoing abstinence and/or sobriety, or they were dead. Pregnancy placed limits on how one could understand, and respond to, addiction as a disease and there appeared to be no middle ground, only the constant movement toward one outcome and away from the other, and back again. While the social service actors in this ethnography all adopted an ethical stance toward addicted pregnancy, the women themselves bore the differentially heavy burden of the heightened morbidity and mortality that resulted from life in the daily-rent hotels.

Of Vultures, Pregnancy, and Anthropology

The presence of the vulture concretizes impending death. It is a bad sign for the wounded and sick when they begin to circle. In this sense they embody both fear (of death) and finality (its inevitable arrival). When vultures' roles are examined in the larger hierarchy of the animal kingdom, they are doing important work: they clean up the dead. Even vultures' body chemistry is specifically engineered toward this task. Vultures have special enzymes in their stomach that allow them to digest rotting flesh without succumbing to the parasites that invade it. Their feet release a protective sweat with chemical

C.4. Poster on Mission Street, June 2008. Photo by the author.

properties that allow them to walk over and among the dead unscathed. This is why vultures can appear not only at the sight of a single dead animal in a solitary field but swarming over masses of dead bodies.

While studying women in the daily-rent hotels, and watching for the appearance and outcomes of their pregnancies over four years, I become a strange harbinger of the heightened morbidity and mortality that Ramona and Mary gestured toward, but did not openly discuss. It is obvious to point out that few medical anthropologists study success stories—the "uneventful" pregnancies of well-nourished, well-housed, nonaddicted middle-class San Francisco women, for example. Medical anthropologists tend to study things that are not working and the consequences of their failures. In line with animal vultures, social scientists of the urban poor could be accused of a morbid attraction to the wounded, sick, and dead. In this sense, my presence and interest in pregnant women's lives reflected the "public secret" of inevitably poor outcomes.[7]

Perhaps strangely, this ethnography of pregnancy and addiction appeared by "chance." It was not a topic I sought out to study when I entered the daily-rent hotels as an anthropologist, nor one I would have chosen. The circumstance, frequently repeated, of pregnancy among the women tenants in the daily-rent hotels raised the question: "What forms of life are possible here?" While I was collecting the women's narratives of their experiences, an intimacy developed between them and me. I became a witness. The narratives I have offered here should be considered with and against any other forms of evidence that shape knowledge about addicted pregnancy. My "data" reflects a complex relation to my perceived ethical responsibility to be present for the women in their pregnancies and my professional demand to feed off their situation and circumstances. My hope is to play a role, through the witnessing and the feeding, in an effort to transform pregnancy and addiction in the daily-rent hotels into something else. Vultures don't just clean up the dead. By ingesting the dead, the dead become part of them.

Is this an example of the defining characteristic of the anthropological encounter as colonial? I often experienced visceral reactions, emotional discomfort, and a sense of political and ethical betrayal while working in the daily-rent hotels with starving, drug-addicted, pregnant women. The women fought for life and resisted death in several temporal modes, and as such I analyzed them as "several in a single body."[8] In the case of addicted pregnancy, several beings were literally there, the woman and her fetus, or later child. I came to see them as living in a form of death, while also making life, through their pregnancies. The structural constraints of survival in the daily-rent hotels, the women's childhood and adult histories of violence and trauma, and their memorial practices of enlivening lost children, created forms of motherhood-in-absence. The repetition of poverty, housing instability, and addiction over lifetimes and intergenerationally sometimes felt like the inevitable poor outcomes that the vulture awaits. In her autobiography, *The Last Resort: Scenes from a Transient Hotel*, Aggie Max has a chapter called "Death." It begins: "Because poverty is boring. The endless struggle to pay the rent is boring. Because you hate the dump where you live. Why struggle to pay rent for a place to live if you are not living? As though you're already dead, and you have to pay rent on your own grave. Worse, you have to pay it to the ones who killed you. And they didn't even kill you for personal reasons, or because you were some enemy of Theirs, they just wanted to profit from your misery."[9]

In line with a Foucauldian analysis of the productive nature of power, perhaps both the colonized and colonizer are changed in encounters of knowl-

C.5. Hallway, daily-rent hotel, August 2007. Photo by the author.

edge production that anthropologists seek to evidence.[10] There are no passive witnesses, and no knowledge production that is neutral. The anthropologist is a narrative-stealing informant, an intimate, a feeder, and, even, a friend. But she does go home at the end of the day.

Evidentiary Intersections

DESIGN: Prospective, multicenter study

SETTING: 18 hospitals in the United States

RESULTS: Interviews were completed by 667 women. Of these 26.8% reported no prenatal care before admission to labor and delivery. These women were more likely to have been born in the United States, . . . [had] other children, used alcohol, and reported being unhappy.

CONCLUSION: Further research is necessary to identify non-traditional models of care to enhance outreach to women at risk for no prenatal care.[11]

CHRISTMAS DAY. 2009

I am reading some *Harry Potter* to my daughter when my cell phone rings. I think it is my second cousin. He is dying from alcoholism and a related immune disorder and has been calling for a couple of days now. According to my aunt, he is drinking again. He cannot remember that he has left several semihysterical and tragic voice messages. So he keeps calling. I sigh. I don't want to break up this moment with my daughter, so I let the call go to voicemail.

Several hours later I check the messages. It was Ramona calling from First Steps. This is the message: "Kelly, Hey. It's Ramona. Just calling to say, 'Merry Christmas!' I am still at First Steps. I started my visits with my son. He came Wednesday and Thursday. I get three hours a day, six hours total for a week. He is coming back on Monday at 2:30. So, I just wanted to call and let you know that I am doing good and I think about you every day. And I just wanted to say Merry Christmas. Okay. I love you. And give me a call here. Okay. I will be able to talk to you. All right? Have a wonderful Christmas, honey. I miss you. Tell everyone down on Mission Street that I said 'Hi.' Bye."

I call her back and get through. She sounds good. She likes the foster mom who is keeping her son—so far. "She's black," she tells me, confirming her as a good choice. She mentions a Christmas party that Duke came to, and that if I see him I need to emphasize how important it is for him to show up at the court dates, so she can have her son placed in her custody once she "phases up" in her treatment program. I never see Duke because he doesn't live in San Francisco, and isn't in the neighborhood very often. But I tell her I will let him know if I do see him. "You should see my little man, Kelly. He is getting darker [skinned] every day. He looks just like Duke! He is still a little man, though. He isn't gaining much weight. He's okay, though. He is totally detoxed now."

She mentions that Danell and her daughter are still there. We agree to talk in the new year and hang up after about twenty minutes.

Two evidentiary forms are offered here: an epidemiological abstract published in a peer-reviewed clinical journal, which includes a large sample of postpartum women, and a field note that describes a brief postpartum conversation between a woman working on her recovery and an anthropologist. How do they tell a similar story and how do they diverge? More important, why might their similarities or differences matter? The abstract describes the importance of "outreach" to women who are at risk for not having prenatal care prior to delivery; the field note narrates affection and concern shared between the two women and offers a lens into what a "nontraditional" model of care might look like. The abstract presents faceless, nameless statistical renderings of a public health problem—women with no prenatal care—in a resourced, Western capitalist society (eighteen US hospitals). The field note situates the two women as mothers who are facing wildly different parenting constraints characterized by their vastly divergent class positions and relationships to the state.

Each vignette provides evidence, a form of truth production. The anthropological field note may gain political traction through its narrative force. Any policy impact it might have often emerges when it is contextualized alongside numbers that reveal the "problem" to be "big enough" to move beyond idiosyncratic, individuated tragedies to be defined as a full-scale public health emergency.[12] This is a stark, but honest, observation about the nature of the public health enterprise on the global field. Not all problems "count": the numbers have to statistically justify research intervention. This statistical gleaning may guarantee the production of "evidence-based" scientific results while masking the unequal distribution of health resources, which then necessitate randomized controlled trials to prove the efficacy of interventions. One might ask of the epidemiological abstract: why did women report "being unhappy" as one of the statistically significant variables associated with the lack of prenatal care? What does "being unhappy" stand in for here? If the foregoing anthropological narrative provides "texture" for epidemiological renderings, are such narratives always also handmaiden to the statistical apparatuses of public health? Do these ethnographic evidentiary representations continuously replicate the "governing mentalities" of individuated risk and failure that moralistically frame health debates related to drug users?[13] Or do they unseat them?

In setting the modes of evidence production side by side in this book, I have explored their points of intersection and their points of incommensurability. I have held each evidentiary form up to discovery and to criticism, in the hope of revealing the complex politics that lie thinly veiled behind each. I argue against the "ethnographer's escape"—the tendency to smugly critique the producers of positivist evidence by depoliticizing the anthropologist's presence and presenting an omniscient narrative. In this ethnography, the anthropologist is not an unbiased reporter of ethnographic "facts," poised to pull back the curtain and reveal the foolishness of epidemiologists and the politicians they seek to influence. The foregoing abstract and narrative are both serious and strategic: one carries the weight of the compromised ethics of witnessing; another claims objectivity.

The neurocrat and the protocapitalist hotel managers also share evidentiary concerns. The evidence that matters to each is ultimately related to money. The hotel manager seeks to defer the cost of empty rooms by economically exploiting as many women as possible on a daily basis. The women recognized and were sometimes angered by the exploitative practices of charging visitor's fees and forced monthly evictions. These practices were illegal and left women displaced, transient, and at risk for poor health. The women also often expressed resignation toward these practices because they were consistent with the logic of the drug-sex economy, in which hustling often meant making money from another's misfortune. Ironically, the protocapitalist hotel managers are "proto" because their concern about profits does not match their reward. The profits will line the pockets of those who manage the master leases for the hotels, not the gatekeepers and managers who mete out punishments and privileges to the women renting rooms.

Public officials responsible for the management of mental health through neurocratic logics also need to attend to cost-effectiveness. Ensuring that drug users with mental illness can be diagnosed and documented for Supplemental Security Income (SSI) benefits is a matter of creating legible forms of disability that might also support housing stability. It is also a way for the city to be cost-effective in the provision of mental health services as part of the San Francisco safety net. Neurocrats provided a $27 million return on investment for the city and demanded a form of diagnostic recognition that could translate to care—that mental illness be equally as recognizable as physical illnesses are in the public health system. With the passing and implementation of the Affordable Care Act, the San Francisco Department of Public Health no longer has its "return on investment" argument to support SSI advocacy, because care providers have become able to bill for mental health services automatically and directly. The consequences of these policy shifts regarding SSI advocacy and mental health diagnosis for the urban poor are currently unclear. However, these shifts do demonstrate the precarity of building a benefits advocacy system on a foundation of federal defunding of addiction as a qualifying, disabling disease.

How, then, do the urban, drug-using poor garner and circulate evidence about themselves? The focus of this project has been on pregnancy and addiction, so I have attended to the forms of evidence production most relevant to pregnant women living in the daily-rent hotels. Other forms of social activism in relation to program closures and discontinued funding for homeless women's health services in general were ongoing during my ethnographic study. They included both the threatened closure of the Women's Space drop-in center (three times) and the threatened discontinuation of the outreach program (once in 2009) that I volunteered for. I attended several rallies and demonstrations between 2007 and 2011 to protest cuts in services and to increase public and media visibility about homeless women. Pregnancy was not a feature of these service demonstrations. I was even interviewed for a newspaper article about "women in the SROs" that was part of a three-article series. Interestingly, the article about women in the SROs did not discuss pregnancy or children but did address the drug-sex economy. The article about families living in the SROs did not discuss drug use.[14] Instead, it focused on underemployment among recent immigrant women and their husbands who lived with them and their children in cramped SRO rooms. The addicted, pregnant women I studied lived in the interstitial spaces between these two representations and were therefore often absent.

On the other hand the exceptional nature of the addicted pregnancy allowed it to rise to the top of the service food chain while not having a sympathetic, media-generated representation around which to rally. Services for the pregnant addict, while not perfect, were rarely cut altogether. For example, the Prenatal and Postpartum Methadone Treatment program was funded through the city's "general fund" and therefore not as susceptible to the pressures of city debt and fiscal crises, particularly those occurring in 2008–2009 during the national economic downturn. That said, addicted, pregnant women are no political constituency per se. There is no one marching in the street in defense of the "pregnant addict." Her past or continued drug use while pregnant makes her political poison, however empathetic one might feel toward an individual woman embroiled in that situation. So knowledge production about pregnancy and addiction was not a political, public construction during my ethnography. Indeed, the relative invisibility of pregnant women in the daily-rent hotels led some providers and health officials to raise their eyebrows in concern when I would mention that I had documented twenty-three pregnancies in a three-block radius from 2007 to 2010.

The truth that addicted pregnant women told about their situations was historical, biological, and maternal, including narratives of their own childhoods (the mothering they received) and assessments of their own failures to mother their children (a positive tox screen at birth, a child not in their custody). Many women who had lost or given up custody of their children carried mementos, photographs that brought to life their longing and disappointment and at the same time provided some awkward form of comfort—a connection to a past that made them recognizable to themselves. Kin of last resort sometimes had continuous contact with these women. Ramona said she spoke with her daughter DeLoni every day, and to prove it she called her on her cell phone in front of me one day while we were hanging out in her room and she was smoking crack. Other times, kin of last resort appeared in women's lives suddenly and then disappeared again, when crises related to child custody and child care arose. Each visit caused a woman's complex relationship with her family, especially her mother, to rematerialize. These relationships required delicate negotiations that consisted of equal parts guilt, blame, gratitude, and anger and often underscored a historical legacy of intergenerational poverty and drug use within families.

Biological factors were also discussed by pregnant women. Some fretted about the potential for the hereditary inheritance of behavioral, and even moral, fallibility—to them from their mothers, and from them to their children. Of the women who gave birth to live children, all had their babies tested for prenatal substance exposure at birth. This testing provided a form of biological evidence—evidence of the presence or absence of drug use during pregnancy. The results of the tox screens were used by CPS workers, service providers, and the pregnant women themselves to justify or contest forms of social adjudication. A tox screen positive for only methadone could be combined with evidence of a woman's "history" (past experiences losing child custody because of substance use) to open a CPS case and justify child removal.

Finally, addicted, pregnant women evidenced their lives maternally. The proof was sometimes the child, in the mother's arms despite the odds and however permanently or temporarily. The joy of this particular evidence trumped all others. But it was often fragile, requiring a Herculean self-discipline to maintain, and always under the watchful gaze of the state. Life was extremely uncertain for pregnant women who lived in the daily-rent hotels, and the evidence about them, including that which they produced, was unstable.

Given the multiple and circulating truth claims about pregnancy and addiction, what added value does an ethnographic approach offer? Being a medical anthropologist in this setting allows for the creation of an additional narrative, one that can follow the evidence as it travels from the laboratory, to the clinic, to the street. A serious engagement with critical anthropological methods that observe and analyze the everyday and a science studies approach toward the production of knowledge can offer a unique lens into the complexity of pregnancy and addiction within this social world. This is not an omniscient story of passive witnessing, of mere documentation and associated critique. Here the social scientist becomes woven, sometimes unwittingly, into the fabric of the story.

Time Seals All Wounds . . . Until They Reopen—Lexi

"It is all bad, Kelly, all bad," Lexi says to me as she is trying to get into my car. She can't do so without a lot of pain. She winces.

"I lost the baby, and . . ." Her voice trails off. She says softly, "I think it was something I did. I don't know. The same thing happened. [Her cervix opened prematurely.] But see, Pano and I were fighting and it was such a mess. Then the police came and when I got to the hospital, it was horrible. The baby wasn't right. He was deformed, and, oh my God." She stops. Lexi is numb, staring out the window as we drive back to her hotel.

"I am so sorry Lexi," I say.

I don't ask any questions, so she continues. "This was two days ago. I called my sister and then I found out that Lionel [her six-year-old son], that my mother is in the hospital and Lionel is coming down here on the bus tonight! So I gotta get my [hotel] room paid for and get his papers and I have to take care of *him*, because this is a test. This is a test for me, because I ain't gonna have no more babies now. They took it all out [performed a hysterectomy]. So I gotta do right by Lionel and my family. I need to pay for the room and clean it up, and buy him some food, 'cause he is coming tonight. I didn't tell them [her family] what happened to the baby. This is a test for me, and I need to just take care of this today [Lionel and her rent] and then I will let them know."

The present in this ethnography was linked most closely to the temporality of pregnancy. Pregnancy time marked the progression toward a resolution of uncertain futures or their foreclosure. Time often seemed to repeat. Histories (of neglectful and abusive childhoods, of past children lost to the state or dead) were relived, while each pregnancy offered (the often unfulfilled) opportunity to change a life course. Understanding the multiple temporalities at stake in the everyday lives of addicted, pregnant women was essential to synthesize the wide-ranging narratives and behaviors that I documented during my participant observation. Temporality was also central in the widespread diagnosis of PTSD and bipolar disorder. The cumulative vulnerabilities of the past—born of neglect, abuse, loss, and grief—combined with the violent and chaotic drug economies of the daily-rent hotels to produce symptoms in the present. As the symptoms of these histories lingered over time, rage, sadness, and irritability were diagnosed as psychiatric illnesses and medicated pharmaceutically.

Addict time, pregnancy time, and hotel time exerted competing pressures on women. Memorial and biological time affected the ways they were able to project futures for themselves as mothers. The institutional involvements enacted during jail and treatment time intervened in and disrupted the lives of addicted, pregnant women, offering possibilities for access to services while imposing the carceral logic of adjudication. Epidemiological time sought to introduce scientifically valid temporal parameters in order to quantify the complex intersection of women's individual behaviors and socio-structural experiences. Their pasts, their childhoods with their biological families, foster families, and institutional "families," constantly injected the present moments of pregnancy with weighty significance.

Shifting the Scene of the Crime

How do we sort the victims from the perpetrators in a landscape of violence and generations of suffering?[15] For addicted, pregnant women who embody the victim/perpetrator dichotomy, the scene of the crime is constantly shifting from brain to behavior, from deprived social histories to PTSD, from manic income generation in support of drug addiction and staying housed to bipolar disorder, from the daily-rent hotels to the hospital to the residential treatment facility and back to the hotels. Blame and responsibility are constituted and reconstituted as a woman moves through these various "locations." Observing what addicted, pregnant women did—their individual and social behaviors— revealed the political economic constraints of place. These locations could range from progressive and not-so-progressive neoliberal public health intervention sites (hospitals, residential treatment facilities, advocacy programs, jails) to privately owned, daily-rent hotels. Each location played a temporary role in stabilizing or destabilizing women's vulnerability to residential transience, food insecurity, and poor health outcomes while pregnant.

Some women told narratives of movement from a family home to an SSI home when they described the linkages between their childhood experiences and their current mental health diagnoses. Monica linked her suicidality, drug use, and anxiety to her childhood molestation, sterilization, and subsequent rapes. Kitt linked her bipolar disorder to a forced abortion and confession to her father. Lexi (and her boyfriend, Pano) linked her bipolar disorder to experiences of childhood molestation and being forced to raise her sister's child. Some women told narratives of moving from the street to the hospital. Anita was taken directly from street homelessness to labor and delivery. Ramona was arrested sitting on the ground at the Sixteenth Street BART plaza and taken to a hospital, where she was able to stay and give birth to a baby free of crack and stabilized on methadone. Danell and Benz both entered drug treatment in advance of the birth of their children, swapping monitoring in drug treatment for hospital-based adjudication.

Ramona did not escape this fate of hospital-based detection of substance use: her baby was tested and a CPS case opened. She was mandated into drug treatment, and her son went into foster care. Her entrance into residential treatment reconstituted her from a failed addict to a recovering mother. Lexi, Dylan, and Anita all traveled, several times, directly from the hospital back to the daily-rent hotels. Lexi experienced the traumatic deaths of two of her children while she was approximately six months pregnant and saw all of the social benefits she had been given while pregnant (access to methadone, case management, a chance for housing) evaporate when her biological status changed her back into merely an addict. Another woman, Rocky, described her journey differently. She told me she was "called back." Having gotten into drug treatment and gained custody of her son, she returned to drug use at the daily-rent hotels.

As addicted, pregnant women were displaced between these multiple locations, they experienced ontological shifts that shaped how they were visible as mothers and as addicts, as victims and as perpetrators. It was difficult to assess whether these shifts would be long-lasting or would be only temporary deferrals. Would history repeat itself, or could she land in a stable home? The fact that several of the women had experienced periods of drug treatment, sobriety, and mothering, followed by relapse and child custody loss, cast an unwelcome shadow on the efforts of Danell and Benz, as first-time mothers, seeking to maintain child custody. The frequent and repetitive ontological shifting of addicted pregnancy marked the state of abstinent mothering as tenuous and revealed the contradictions of acknowledging addiction as a chronic relapsing biological condition while demanding immediate and permanent abstinence as a condition of parenting.

Mental Health and Addiction: Categorical Convergence?

Scientific renderings of addiction and mental illness appear to be experiencing a convergence. Discourse is recentering on the brain as the wellspring of relevant information about behavior and motivation. How do addicted, pregnant women both embody and disrupt this convergence? Construing mental illness and addiction as organic brain diseases shaped moral discourses about pregnancy and addiction and provided necessary subtext in the diagnosis and treatment of homeless women. Neurocratic practices biomedicalized the social realities of poverty and underemployment, specifically capturing the rage and despair many homeless women experience through the diagnostic "fit" of

PTSD and bipolar disorder. The collective pharmaceuticalization of addiction and mental illness was manifest in the widespread diagnosis and treatment of these illnesses with atypical antipsychotic medications.[16] Thus convergence was instrumental, and it served many masters. Neurocratic practices spoke to the necessity for both social recognition and cost reimbursement within the health care safety net. Pharmaceutical companies offered atypical antipsychotic medications that glossed over the problematic clinical reality of the diagnosis of PTSD and bipolar disorder symptoms in women who are actively using stimulants and hustling in social environments that necessitated hypervigilance and mania in order to work, eat, and stay housed.

It is unclear what the future will hold regarding the convergence of mental illness and addiction, especially in light of the inclusion in the Affordable Care Act (ACA) of the Mental Health Parity and Addiction Equity Act (H.R. 1424).[17] This parity law mandates that insurance companies—private and public—that provide mental health and substance abuse services must compensate treatment plans for mental health and substance abuse conditions on par with physical health conditions. Perhaps more important than scans showing the addicted brain on the cover of *Time* or exponentially increasing public testimonial about substance use and abuse, H.R. 1424 is, in fact, the policy instantiation of the biomedicalization of addiction.[18] Currently caught in the political maelstrom of the Affordable Care Act, the regulatory practices, including the amount at which and degree to which chronic mental health conditions will be covered, have yet to be written on the federal level.[19] However, H.R. 1424 is expected to move forward with the ACA, meaning that local systems of neurocratic practice in place to ensure urban poor persons in San Francisco—including the women living in the daily-rent hotels—do not fall out of the health care safety net might be rendered fiscally unnecessary through federal health care accessibility. The processes of implementation of these health care reform policies and their outcomes are currently unclear.

The disease of "addiction," construed as compulsivity, has proliferated in such a way as to absorb multiple problematic behaviors—not just alcohol and drugs but also food, exercise, sex, gambling, and the use of technology. The National Institute of Drug Abuse is optimistic that scientific discourse will push the envelope of our understanding of addiction as a brain disease through improved MRI technologies and better animal studies.[20] There is a redemptive narrative at work, in which the objectivity of science might better identify and respond to complex social and emotional entanglements produced by addiction and producing addiction in the first place.[21] The hope is that the brain disease model could unburden many families: many mothers who, like the "schizophrenogenic" mothers of the past, incur blame and responsibility for their children's failed lives. This model could also liberate addicted people themselves from guilt and shame.

We are, perhaps, a long way from that point. But it is interesting that even bench scientists, those whose laboratory experiments continue to add to the growing literature of neurological addiction science, waver at the loss of autonomy that might become the logical extension of the brain disease thesis. While biological explanations of addiction's etiology and course are seductive on some registers, the autonomy and "agency" to command our life choices is difficult to resign. This abdication of control to genetics, to the subcortex, or even to the pull of threatening social environments (such as those of the daily-rent hotels) is personally repugnant. It also reflects a significant breach in the social contract. One neurologist of addiction I interviewed spent several hours explaining to me the intricacies of what is known about drugs, behaviors, and the brain. Shortly before our tour of the rat lab, where various rodents were attached to wires, fed illicit substances intravenously, and monitored, he paused to make this comment:

> "Abuse" is not a biological term. Addiction is. Addiction is in the brain. It is behavior you cannot stop doing. Once you start getting into the actual neural mechanisms of it, all of that goes away. You stop making the value judgments. Science has nothing to do with value judgments. It really doesn't. What people try to do is that they try and use science to support their values. You see politicians do that all the time. I like being a scientist because I really want to get at explanations and I want to get around the confusing metaphors and narratives that people use. But the biggest problem that I run into is that I say, "The brain is doing it." And they say, "You mean the person is not responsible?" And I say, "Yeah, that is what I mean, they are not responsible." Well, if you do away with the concept of personal responsibility, the culture disintegrates. We need it. But it is just not scientifically based. Not if you are a pure scientist. I would say that it has not been established that there are any scientifically validated value judgments. That is what I mean when I say that willpower is just another form of neural activity. Let's stop worrying about it.

And yet the worry continues, representing our dual desires to explain addiction as compulsivity and to make it stop. In an issue of the *British Journal of Addiction*, a debate ensued over the publication of an article titled "The

10 Most Important Things Known about Addiction." The article revealed a rivalry between therapeutic and scientific camps in addiction health research that mirrored earlier debates between psychoanalytic and psychiatric orientations toward mental illness.[22] The article attempted to synthesize the brain science and behavioral modification treatment perspectives. It called for "unity" between "warring factions" to ease the suffering caused by addiction:

> This paper brings together a body of knowledge across multiple domains and arranged as a list of 10 things known about addiction. . . . The 10 things are:
>
> (1) Addiction is fundamentally about compulsive behaviour;
> (2) Compulsive drug seeking is initiated outside of consciousness;
> (3) Addiction is about 50% heritable and complexity abounds;
> (4) Most people with addictions who present for help have other psychiatric problems as well;
> (5) Addiction is a chronic relapsing disorder in the majority of people who present for help;
> (6) Different psychotherapies appear to produce similar treatment outcomes;
> (7) "Come back when you're motivated" is no longer an acceptable therapeutic response;
> (8) The more individualized and broad-based the treatment a person with addiction receives, the better the outcome;
> (9) Epiphanies are hard to manufacture; and
> (10) Change takes time.[23]

The abstract is far-reaching and concise: items 1 and 2 place addiction squarely in the organic realm: addiction involves compulsive behavior that is "outside of consciousness" and therefore outside of reasoned behavior, outside of control. Item 4 references the fact that addiction and psychiatric disorders are overlapping and thus difficult to distinguish from one another. Items 3, 5, 6, 7, and 8 all underscore the variability of addiction at the individual level. They argue against a specific "recipe" for the treatment of addiction and highlight that "motivation" is not an appropriate moral metric for judging addicted people or their need for treatment. Item 9 is the perfect blending of the moral (the spiritual devastation that drug addiction brings to individuals and families) and the industry of treatment. Epiphanies—personal, scientific, religious, or philosophical breakthroughs that lead to fundamental change—are difficult to "manufacture." Last, item 10 references the complex relationship between addiction and temporality. "Change takes time." But who has time? Not treatment professionals who are burnt out on women missing appointments and disappearing from services, only to resurface pregnant again and perpetually strung out. Not policy-makers who seek cost-effective (rational, timely, efficacious) interventions with quick and lasting results. And, least of all, addicted, pregnant women whose biological clocks are ticking ever closer to delivery each moment while they struggle with their drug use and hustle to make the rent.

The Labor and Delivery of Public Policy

> *What is problematic, then, is not the good versus bad intentions informing [policy] processes . . . but the contexts and forms in which such intentions are asserted, along with their unintended consequences.*
> —C. Kingfisher, "Discursive Constructions of Homelessness in a Small City in the Canadian Prairies" (2007)

Public policy about addicted pregnancy is labored. During my period of ethnographic fieldwork, a national economic crisis occurred that altered the stakes of housing and health policies in San Francisco. The belt-tightening that resulted from this crisis changed how health officials discussed evidence for supportive housing public policy-making. In 2007, when I first interviewed a health and housing official, he insisted that "numbers don't build buildings; stories do." At that time he was arguing that public officials were swayed by testimony, by the kind of vignettes that a medical anthropologist might produce, as much as if not more than by statistics about the health benefits of housing for the urban poor. The reasons for this were multiple. Epidemiological research studies took too long and lacked the "human element" that conveyed the importance of housing in people's lives. Policy-makers also often didn't understand numbers. Narratives, people's stories, were easier to relate to, he argued. By late 2009 his viewpoint was one of fiscal constraint. He said: "My budget is about cost. I like to think of it this way: I take one person—one drug user who is out on the street with a bunch of health problems and active substance use. My budget is whatever costs that person accrues yearly in the emergency room, and the psych ward, minus the cost to house that person for one year and defer those costly service visits. That is my budget. That is what I have to work with."

I am not implying that housing and health policy was made regardless of cost prior to the economic meltdown; I am merely pointing to the changing context and forms of evidence that were leveraged in these different time points. The general political and economic climate that exists in San Francisco is progressive and liberal, with a solid safety net in place to care for the mental and physical health of the poor and uninsured written into city law. Harm reduction efforts to house homeless mentally ill people and to prioritize addicted, pregnant women for treatment and services are broadly supported. Given that these progressive, structural interventions were in place, I found it disconcerting that most women were not accessing them. Rather, they were often entering drug treatment through interactions with the criminal justice system. While programs for addicted, pregnant women were supported and even protected from budget cuts, and services existed specifically to engage women who were addicted and pregnant into care in order to *avoid* CPS involvement and retain child custody, most women from the daily-rent hotels didn't go until they were forced to by court order. Furthermore, some women credited certain interactions with the criminal justice system as those which secure later child custody.

These claims on the part of addicted, pregnant women flew in the face of my own judgments about the criminalization of women drug users. They forced me to self-reflect on my own political views, views that were tested when the events I observed fell outside of my comfort zone. The ongoing criminalization of women in the daily-rent hotels disrupted their ability to conduct sex work, criminalized their addictions, and was never directed toward the hotel managers who illegally exploited women on a daily basis. Yet at crisis points during many women's pregnancies, an arrest and court order was what got them out of the hotels and closer to gaining custody of their babies. Were the allied relationships with police, and other adjudicators, that many women described some form of Stockholm syndrome, where the captive bonds with, and ultimately defends, her capturer? Were they simply a reflection of the extent of the women's lumpen social status?[24] It would be inaccurate to describe the women's interaction with the criminal justice system as reformative. Many of the women, such as Kitt and Cupcake, cycled in and out of the jail throughout pregnancies and young adulthood. Some women attributed certain interventions of the police, and criminal justice system representatives—especially those who operated outside of official protocol as was seen with both Lexi and Anita—providing better mothering outcomes than the women felt would have happened otherwise. But these outcomes didn't last. It forces one to ask: what is the criminal justice system standing in for here? What forms of outreach and care are unfunded or underfunded so that community policing and incarceration are a reproductive respite for addicted pregnant women?

Services exist for addicted, pregnant women in San Francisco, yet they are underutilized or inconsistently utilized without court mandate. Supportive housing initiatives exist for homeless women in San Francisco, yet none of the pregnant women I studied in the daily-rent hotels were accessing those programs. Facing this quandary that I feel unable to solve, I make demands on my discipline to bear witness to pregnancy and addiction as it is located in the socially compromised everyday realities of women's lives. Anthropology that seeks to comment on publicly adjudicated social problems needs to turn a critical eye on itself. What role can anthropological evidence play here? A conversation I had with a housing policy-maker highlighted the tensions between an interventionist's orientation toward the social problem of homeless, addicted, pregnant women and the witness's stance.

WHAT'S WORSE? NOVEMBER 2009

I am having lunch with a friend, colleague, and longtime interlocutor. I have let it slip during our conversation that it is very hard for me, personally, as a mother, to bear witness to pregnant women smoking crack. She asks me what I do when I see a pregnant woman smoking crack and I say, "I don't know. Sometimes I just want to kill her."

Later in the conversation she says, "Kelly, I have to tell you, you seem really burnt out. I don't think I have ever heard you say you wanted to kill one of your women before. What are you doing to take care of yourself?"

I laugh uneasily; "I am trying to finish this up."

She says, "To me, what's hard is lack of gratitude. Me and my staff work so hard, and try and make it work, try and keep people housed, keep them from dying. There is no gratitude. It may be ego but sometimes I feel I need that, that acknowledgment of my work."

"That is so messed up, because I get thanked all the time. Women are always so grateful to me. I get so much love. And sometimes it makes me feel so cheap. Here is you, offering medical care, offering housing. You have something, some skill that *could* be useful. I have nothing to offer," I complain.

"I think having someone to hear your story can be very beneficial . . ."
My skeptical face stops her short from finishing.

"Blah, blah, blah," she says in reaction to my raised eyebrows. "Well, at least you aren't in the position of offering an intervention, of defending an intervention, that might not be working, one that might be the wrong thing. That is a horrible feeling."

"Peddling snake oil?" I question.

"Exactly. That's the fear. That's worse [than being an anthropologist]."

We exchange glances. We have both been doing our versions of "this work" for over fifteen years in San Francisco. This is an honest conversation.

As we grab our coats, she says, "What I don't understand is that there doesn't seem to be any less of them. No less misery. We have housed thousands of homeless people in this city—a huge number. Yet when I look at the streets, it seems the same. I don't believe they are coming from the East Bay to use up San Francisco's resources, but I just don't get it. How can there be more?"

This conversation reflects the honest exasperation that service providers/policy-makers, pregnant, addicted women, and anthropologists alike can feel when they have an up-close relationship with addicted pregnancy. All of these actors experience forms of ethical and structural constraint when trying to make the decision about the policy or health care intervention, change the behavior that is attracting the adjudication, or get the story "right." The effort to respond, and its risks, can produce judgment, burnout, anger, and resignation. How do we hold a space for the problematic behaviors of all of these actors—the poor policy-making, the ongoing drug use, the social scientific vulturism—while also maintaining a focus on the structural conditions (the perception of resource scarcity, the rising gentrification, the inadequacy of drug treatment modalities, the criminalization of addiction, the intergenerational poverty) that produce the behaviors, bind these actors together, and prolong suffering? There are no easy enemies in addicted pregnancy, and no ready-made solutions at hand.

As my interlocutor kindly pointed out, "Having someone hear your story can be very beneficial." But what is the utility of an ethnographic approach to addicted pregnancy for health policy and care? The vantage point of an anthropologist in this setting is unique. I was able to travel with women from the daily-rent hotels to medical and drug treatment appointments, to hospital intensive care units that cared for their babies, and (for many women) back to the hotels. Traveling along and recording the multiple ways pregnancy and addiction is recognized, becomes known, and gets intervened upon can help reveal where care succeeds and where it fails. Showing pictures of the daily-rent hotels to drug treatment providers, psychiatrists, and policy-makers, as I often did during my fieldwork, can illuminate the conditions of daily living that are made dim and sanitized through statistical renderings. Stories can help keep housing policies made under conditions of fiscal constraint from losing sight of the people they are charged to house. Finally, this ethnography takes seriously all the social actors who are called on to address pregnancy and addiction, including addicted, pregnant women, their care providers, and policy-makers. With that seriousness, the possibility for capturing a "vertical slice"[25] showing the complexity and intractability of addicted pregnancy emerges and then circulates with hope toward better understanding and support for all actors involved.

The Reproduction of Poverty

> *The boundary between collective trauma and individual trauma is as difficult to discern as is the passing of historical trauma from one generation to the next.*
> —D. Fassin and R. Rechtman, *The Empire of Trauma* (2009)

Addicted pregnancy, full of plight and possibility, unfolded as a collective and individual traumatic drama.[26] A pregnant addicted woman living in a daily-rent hotel embodies social failure—somewhere in her history things went horribly wrong: In her brain? In her childhood? With her family? A result of all the drugs? Too much abuse? Not enough social intervention—or not the right one at the right time? She is now struggling with addiction—really struggling and losing every day—and with impending motherhood, staying at and (sex) working in the daily-rent hotels amid social conflict, violence, and the daily economic exploitation. She becomes pregnant, keeps using drugs, has a child, and loses custody. Or, she becomes pregnant, uses drugs, enters treatment, and then regains custody. It is difficult to rely on any temporal cross-section in the life of an individual woman in this story. One inescapably feels that the cycle of housing instability, violence, and neglect is merely being temporarily disrupted by pregnancy. Pregnancy among most women

I studied did not reconfigure their life course, at least not for long. As the statistics point out, the majority of women who use drugs before and during pregnancy return to drug use postpartum.[27] Pregnancy did not bring them out of poverty, and addiction often drew them back to the hotels after birth.

My desire to report that Ramona remained in drug treatment, graduated, and now has custody of her son is almost overwhelming. But that is not what happened. Ramona was kicked out of her drug treatment program in March, three months after her Christmas phone call to me. According to Ramona, after an off-site visit getting her methadone take-home doses from the clinic, she returned without receipts for the money she had taken with her. Ramona says she bought diapers and lost the receipt. Her residential drug treatment counselor accused her of buying crack. A loud and heated verbal fight followed in which Ramona called the counselor a "bitch" and was kicked out. Ramona called me from a daily-rent hotel in tears and very high. She said: "I was doing so well. I was so happy there. I was seeing my son. And that bitch took at all away from me." Ramona's crack use escalated, and she returned to heroin use at the hotels instead of methadone treatment at the Prenatal and Postpartum Methadone Treatment program. The morning after Ramona had been placed in temporary housing prior to her child custody trial, I arrived at her hotel to take her to her child custody hearing. She was too exhausted, socially defeated, and hungover to show up in court, and she permanently lost custody in June 2010.

Whether we construe addiction as a condition exacerbated by a woman's social position of poverty and housing instability when they become pregnant and/or as biological disease over which they have little control, it was an act of sheer resurrection to escape the pull back into her pre-pregnant social world. Several women (Danell, Benz, River) accomplished that feat. It is hard to know if, or for how long, it will last. Lexi and Anita's narratives also described moments of mothering victory—two years clean and sober with Lionel for Lexi, two children born drug-free for Anita. What followed for Lexi and Anita was the opposite social reality—children dying and children lost to custody because of drug use. One provider emphasized the importance of being ready when the right time came:

> You know we work with a lot of women who have lost baby after baby after baby to the foster care system, to CPS. And you know they will come in [pregnant] at one point and this will be the time. And they have a healthy baby, and they keep their baby. I got a call from one of those

clients around the holidays; her son is now five going to kindergarten. She is doing great, has maintained her housing. No more drug use, after probably twenty years of being a prostitute, using drugs on the street. No one would have ever thought she would have made it.

This provider urges us to understand that the doors for help and support should never be slammed shut on addicted, pregnant women. The story of Anita's child custody hearing bears witness to how complicated a feat it can be for a woman to walk through those doors, when drug addiction is raging, the daily-rent hotels are violent and familial, and institutional relationships are fraught.

ANITA'S TRIP TO COURT. CHANDRA HOTEL. MARCH 2010

I arrive at the Chandra Hotel to pick up Anita for her daughter's custody hearing at about 8:20 a.m. We are supposed to be at court at 9:00, and we need to swing by and pick up her mother, who lives a couple of blocks away. Anita's aunt has been refused custody of Anita's six-month-old daughter. Anita says this is because "I keep having babies, and they [CPS] are afraid that my family will keep taking them for me. Because I don't get it together [go into treatment]." I also suspect that because Anita's aunt has eight children under her care already, including Anita's three-year-old, CPS is reluctant to add one more. The custody hearing today is to decide whether her daughter will go for permanent adoption, which would permanently terminate any custody claims Anita or other members of her family could make on her.

When I knock on the door, Anita says, "Shit. She is here *already*." She seems surprised that it is already time to go. She opens the door and I come in. There is a guy in her room named Darren. He is sitting very close to the TV watching an episode of *ER*. Ironically, it is the one where one of the show's doctor stars falls, goes into labor, and has a difficult and dangerous birth followed by an emergency hysterectomy. We are all watching the show, and it lends a sense of urgency to the eerie, dark scene in the hotel room. The curtains are drawn; the bed has no sheets on it. I am not sure that Anita has slept at all. Darren doesn't say a word, and doesn't move much. Anita also seems absorbed and stunned to silence.

Then, as if waking up suddenly, Anita starts cleaning up the room a bit. There are needles spilled all over the bed, and all the contents of Anita's purse have been dumped out on the floor. I sit in a chair, whose cover is ripped up and stuffing is leaking out of it. There are clothes everywhere, piled under the desk, to the right of the door, and by the TV. Anita stops to sit down and smoke some crack. She then tries to find some pants that don't have stains on them and a jacket. As she reaches over the bed, I notice that the abscess on her back left shoulder has opened and is bleeding down her back. I point this out, and she tries to mop up the blood with some toilet paper. A few minutes later I say, "Anita, honey, you're really bleeding. We should bandage that up." I look around and see some gauze still in the wrapper and some tape on the desk. I do a quick and haphazard job of covering the wound.

We watch more ER. The father of the baby is sent to ICU, but it looks like the baby will be OK.

After a short while I mention the time. She says, "Don't worry, they [the court hearings] never start on time. Do you have your phone?" she asks. "Call my mom and see if she is there." Anita gives me the number and I dial. No answer. "Just let it ring," Anita instructs me. After awhile I hang up. "She already left," says Anita. "They don't think I am going to make it, because I didn't go to the methadone program." Anita had plans to go to methadone, so she could show the judge that she is making an effort in drug treatment. She didn't go.

She keeps looking for her coat, and cleaning up all the needles into a plastic bucket. She asks me if I would take some pictures of the huge hole in the floor underneath her bed that cold air is coming through. "Watch out for the needles. Don't go on the bed—they are everywhere," she tells me. I move the bed a bit and see the hole and take several pictures of it. I open the curtain to look at the air shaft. "So, is this where Nancy fell?" I ask. "Yeah," Anita says, sighing. "The paramedics had to break down my window to get to her." A week earlier one of the women who stayed upstairs, Nancy, fell, or was pushed, out of the window as she was trying to escape from someone in a drug deal gone wrong. She broke her back and became paralyzed.

Anita goes down the hall to settle up some business and get more crack. She whispers specific instructions to Darren. "Do not leave my door open," she commands. She has left her next hit of morphine

c.6. Anita packs her things for court: a comb, a cross, and a crack pipe, March 2010. Photo by the author.

loaded in a syringe on the desk and is afraid someone will steal it while she is at the hearing. Finally we are ready to go. We start to drive toward the courthouse, and she suddenly motions to me to turn around. We go to a local drop-in, where she picks up a methadone voucher. She feels this might help her case if she shows it to the judge. After having moved slowly in her hotel room, Anita is now agitated about the time and worried about getting there.

On the rest of the ride down, Anita explains that her mother has always been there for her, through all her pregnancies. She reiterates that it was not until her father passed away that any of her children were "born dirty" [with a tox screen positive for illicit drugs]. Her father did blame her drug use for the stillborn death of one of her children with a birth defect. But Anita explains that she went into premature labor and the doctors wanted the baby to be bigger so they could perform an operation on her [the baby] to correct the birth defect. According to Anita, it was her father's mother, who refused to leave a relative's birthday party to go back for Anita's forgotten medication, that caused her daughter's death. "I begged my grandmother to go back [and get her medication], but she didn't want to use up the gas. So of course I went into labor again. Both me and my mother agree that it was that mean bitch who killed my daughter. If she had gone back, she would have lived." As we rush to the hearing Anita stops to put on a hat her grandmother—the same woman whom she blames for her daughter's death—made for her when she was five. "Maybe the hat will bring me good luck [in my custody case]," she tells me. "There was a time that the woman was nice to me."

We arrive forty-five minutes late for the hearing. Anita is now panicked, looking in all the courtrooms for her aunt and her mother, while I wait in line at information. When we reach the desk, Anita starts to cry. She says her name, and that she hopes the hearing isn't over. We find out that it is over. We go to courtroom number 4 anyway. Her mother and her sister are not there, but the CPS lawyer is there. She explains to Anita that she cannot discuss the case because Anita has her own lawyer, but that the decision has been postponed until June. The CPS lawyer tells Anita to find her lawyer out in the hall. The CPS staff are helpful and attentive. Anita asks the CPS lawyer, "Will it make a difference if I am in treatment, now?" As we leave the small courtroom, Anita says she does not want to find her lawyer, she wants to leave.

Walking to the car Anita says, mostly to herself, "Okay, so I just need to get into a program by June. Okay." In the parking elevator, I ask Anita what she is going to do now. "Smoke crack," she says with a sheepish grin. But then she immediately retorts in a tougher voice, "You asked."

It is strange that in the midst of all the shifting signifiers of category and causation characterizing the production of knowledge in this domain, somehow "pregnant addict" still remains immediately recognizable; there is a mental picture to conjure up. Anita embodies it here. Yet behind the media portrayals and the numbers, prior to the diagnoses, and in the everyday, a much more complex and contradictory set of explanations emerged. These fractured narratives, full of inconsistencies, corrections, and thoughtful pauses, were ushered forth from the army of professionals struggling, sincerely and ethically, with how to understand and *respond* to addicted pregnancy. These fractured narratives mirrored those of many addicted, pregnant women themselves, who performed their own self-reflexive categorization and causation exercises as they sought to understand their lives.

The stakes and consequences of these necessary exercises in knowledge production and circulation make political and ethical demands on all involved. A critical examination of evidence production is crucial to broaden our understanding of the seemingly intractable problems that surround addicted pregnancy here: repeated rape and assault; smoking endless amounts of crack cocaine; hostile, overworked clinicians casting a blind eye on women's suffering; activists producing pictures of those the government has left out of its urban planning. There are certainly many ways to tell the stories of addicted, pregnant women. Yet we cannot lose sight of who falls faster and harder when the evidence gets too muddled and the stories begins to lose whatever ability to generate empathy they may have had.

Even so, it would be a mistake to understand addicted, pregnant women only as victims, because in doing so, one can ignorantly endorse the paradigms of the worthy and the unworthy poor, silencing alternative possible narratives. An addicted, pregnant woman is a producer of evidence who can narrate her own story. She has a theory, an explanation, or an opinion at least, about why it is turning out this way. It is when she or her baby ends up in the morgue (a behavioral health statistic transformed into a death statistic) that it is blatantly obvious: one story can be silenced in a manner others cannot be. Evidence production and circulation matter because how we know what we know about a social problem matters. We need to be critically inclusive and self-reflexive in our understanding and then bring that full weight to bear on "useless suffering," in the multiplicity of forms in which its truth comes to light.[28]

appendix. demographics and methods

Notes on Methods

I conducted four years of ethnographic research with women living, on and off, in the daily-rent hotels that spanned a three-by-three-block radius in the Mission District of San Francisco. I first began fieldwork in the daily-rent hotels in June 2007, working a Tuesday night shift that conducted outreach in four hotels, later switching to Monday evenings to work in five other hotels, and then back to Tuesday nights again. I conducted participant observation in a total of fifteen hotels, the majority of which were privately owned, daily-rent hotels. Although this book reflects the experiences of women renting rooms in daily-rent hotels in the Mission District, I had other concurrent ethnographic research projects in the field at the time that allowed me to conduct participant observation in additional private and publicly funded hotels in the Tenderloin, Civic Center, and Sixth Street Corridor neighborhoods of San Francisco.

When I began to focus on the daily-rent hotels, I decided to leave the drop-in center (Women's Space) as my main site of participant observation, and I only attended the center in the company of women with whom I was ethnographically engaged or for policy or procedural trainings relevant to my topic. I did not discontinue my role with the outreach program, because it gave me access to the daily-rent hotels. I sometimes approached women in the hotels, sometimes on the street, and described my project to them. Those willing to provide informed consent became a part of my core cohort. Overall, both the larger and the core cohort of addicted, pregnant women mirrored the demographics of women in the daily-rent hotels. The women who rented daily-rent hotel rooms, at that time, were ethnically diverse, with about one-third being African-American, one-third white, and one-third Latina. I have encountered in these rooms very few Asian women or women who identified themselves as Native American. Only a handful (five) of all the women (about seventy-five) I encountered during participant observation in hotels were monolingual Spanish speakers (unlike many of the younger men), although many women I knew were bilingual, speaking both Spanish and English.

When conducting participant observation with the women, I used a variety of data collection techniques, including participant observation of the places where the women lived and worked; one-to-one taped interviews; walking tours of the neighborhood and housing environments narrated by the women; accompanying of the women, with their permission, to health and social service appointments; documenting of the women's interactions with other institutional bodies (medical staff, drug treatment providers, police, entitlement counselors, eviction court, and family court); observation of drug and sex work venues; documenting of the women's participation in activist, community, political, and other public activities; and photo-ethnography. I traveled with women tenants of the daily-rent hotels from the drop-in center program to the streets, to local restaurants, on neighborhood walks, and to methadone clinics and other medical appointments throughout my four years of fieldwork. My multisited approach was intentional. First, it reflected the everyday movements of women who might have "dropped in" to shelters, and other day programs, but did not sleep there. Second, it was an attempt to disrupt the limits that emplacement can create in an ethnographic perspective. Shelters and drug treatment facilities could become overdetermined spaces for the construction of identity among the women. Addicted, pregnant women were on the move, their subjectivity changing in accordance to the variable institutional settings and built environments where knowledge was being produced about and by them.

Although I did not compensate women for participant observation activities, I was able to reimburse a handful of women (thirteen) for longer, qualitative interviews. The women I selected for these interviews varied throughout the four years of my project. Initially, I interviewed several women in 2007 and then stopped, focusing on participant observation instead. Through this participant observation, I discovered what appeared to me to be a high number of pregnancies occurring among women in daily-rent hotels. As my project shifted to focus on the experience of pregnancy and addiction, I reserved the longer qualitative interviews for pregnant or recently postpartum women. Women who participated in these interviews were compensated $20 for their time, consistent with the political economy of ongoing public health studies that take place among urban poor, homeless populations on San Francisco.

Initially I informed the women I spoke with that I was an anthropologist working on "a book" about their experiences living in daily-rent hotels. I explained that I was a student, getting my doctorate in medical anthropology. Consistent with the Internal Review Board procedures of the Committee of Human Research that I was mandated to follow as part of the state and federally funded research studies, and as a student at my university, I was authorized to use an information sheet explaining my project and a signed consent form for those women I selected for the longer qualitative interviews. I was also authorized to gain consent for photos. Women could decide whether they consented to photos being identifiable (e.g., of their faces, etc.) and/or nonidentifiable (e.g., of the condition of their rooms in hotels). Despite this permission being granted, no identifiable photos have been used herein. Most women responded favorably and with interest to being informed about my project; some neutrally dismissed the information sheet. Other women sometimes asked, "What does an anthropologist do?" or "Don't you study bones?" I would reply that I study everyday life, and women's experiences living in the hotels. Regardless of my continual restatement of my role, many women mistook me for a case manager or social worker, because this was a more recognizable social role (especially for a white woman taking a keen interest in their everyday lives).

Table App.1. Characteristics of women with pregnancies in the daily-rent hotels, 2007–2009

PSEUDONYM	RACE/ETHNICITY	AGE	YEAR OF PREGNANCY
Anita	Latina	late 30s	2007; 2009
Bella	African-American	mid-20s	2009
Benz	African-American	mid-20s	2009
Cupcake	White	mid-30s	2008; 2009
Danell	African-American	mid-20s	2009
Dylan	White	late 20s	2007; 2009
Kitt	African-American	mid-30s	2007
Lexi	African-American	late 30s	2009
Luisa	Latina	mid-30s	2008
Marlena	African-American	mid-30s	2009
Marta	White	late 20s	2008
Monique	African-American	mid-20s	2007
Noah	White	mid-20s	2007
Ramona	White/Latina	mid-30s	2007; 2009
Rebecca	White	early 20s	2008
River	White	early 20s	2007
Rocky	Latina	mid-20s	2009
Scoop	Latina	early 20s	2008
Tara	White	early 20s	2008

Table App.2. Other women and men who appear in the ethnography

PSEUDONYM	GENDER	RACE/ETHNICITY	AGE
Alexandra	Female	African-American	mid-50s
Alice	Female	White	late 20s
Axel	Male	African-American	late 40s
CJ	Male	unknown	unknown
Crysanne	Female	White	mid-60s
Duke	Male	African-American	early 30s
Gregory	Male	White	early 60s
Jackie	Female	White	mid-40s
Mara	Female	White	early 30s
Marco	Male	African-American	mid-30s
Marcus	Male	African-American	mid-50s
Maria	Female	Latina	early 40s
May	Female	White	mid-60s
Michael	Male	unknown	unknown
Monica	Female	White	mid-60s
Nancy	Female	White	early 30s
Pano	Male	Latino	late 40s
Rally	Female	unknown	unknown
Ruth	Female	White	late 20s
Shani	Female	unknown	unknown
Sophia	Female	Latina	mid-20s
Stacey	Female	Latina	late 20s
Wilson	Male	African-American	mid-60s
Wisdom	Female	African-American	mid-60s

Table App.3. Hotel details

PSEUDONYM	OWNERSHIP	OUTREACH SITE?	APPROXIMATE NUMBER OF ROOMS
Bridgit	Private	Yes	85
Chandra	Private	Yes	25
Daly	Private	Yes	20
Daya	Private	Yes	25
European	Private	No	25
Globe	Private	No	50
Grey	Private	Yes	40
Hotel 66	Private	No	100
Kennedy	Public	No	100
Marque	Public	Yes	30
Metropica	Private	No	100
Nimish	Private	Yes	25
Raman	Private	Yes	50
Roberts	Private	No	30
Visha	Private	Yes	20

notes

Introduction

1　All names for hotels are pseudonyms, as are the names of all women, their partners, and their children. In some cases I have changed the gender and/or specific profession of other interviewees in order to mask their identities. I have also altered details in women's stories in order to make them less identifiable. For example, city names may be changed, and family members' titles may be changed (aunt instead of grandmother, etc.), when the general meaning of the narrative is not significantly altered as a result of the change.

2　The vast majority, although not all, of the hotel managers I interacted with during my fieldwork were from the State of Gujarat in western India.

3　"5150" is the police code for a mandatory arrest, followed by a seventy-two-hour mandatory lockdown—psychiatric hospitalization for harm to self or harm to another.

4　First Steps is a pseudonym.

5　The women in this ethnographic study used a variety of substances, and most were polysubstance users. These substances included stimulants (methamphetamine and crack cocaine) and opiates/opioids like heroin and opioid-based pain medications (e.g., "pain killers" such as synthetic morphine, Codeine, Vicodin, and Dilaudid). Opiates/opioids were accessed through prescription, bought off the street, or administered through a drug substitution drug treatment facility (e.g., methadone clinic). Some women also drank alcohol, although this was less common. The most prevalent and frequently used substance in the daily-rent hotels was crack cocaine. Almost all of the women whom I worked with closely smoked cigarettes.

6　Nora Volkow, National Institute on Drug Abuse, *Comorbidity: Addiction and Other Mental Illnesses*, NIDA Research Report Series.

7　U.S. Substance Abuse and Mental Health Services Administration, *Results from the 2010 National Survey on Drug Use and Health: National Findings*. http://archive .samhsa.gov/data/NSDUH/2k10nsduh/2k10results.htm#2.6, accessed March 15, 2015.

8　Patrick et al., "Neonatal Abstinence Syndrome and Associated Health Care Expenditures," 1934.

9　Szabo, "Number of Painkiller-Addicted Newborns Triples in 10 Years," 1.

10　U.S. Substance Abuse and Mental Health Services Administration, Office of Applied Studies, *The NSDUH Report: Substance Use among Women during Pregnancy and Following Childbirth*; Carpenter, "Nature of the Problem and State of the Field."

11 Bessa et al., "Underreporting of Use of Cocaine and Marijuana during the Third Trimester of Gestation among Pregnant Adolescents"; Chasnoff et al., "The Prevalence of Illicit-Drug or Alcohol Use during Pregnancy and Discrepancies in Mandatory Reporting in Pinellas County, Florida."

12 Guttmacher Institute, *State Policies in Brief*.

13 National Institute on Drug Abuse, *Prenatal Exposure to Drugs of Abuse*.

14 Eckholm, "Case Explores Rights of Fetus versus Mother."

15 See Flavin, *Our Bodies, Our Crimes*. Also see the National Advocates for Pregnant Women website, http://www.advocatesforpregnantwomen.org/issues/pregnancy _and_drug_use_the_facts/, accessed March 15, 2015.

16 Cooney, "Drug Addiction, Personhood, and the War on Women."

17 P. K. Muhuri and J. C. Gfroerer, "Substance Use among Women"; Ondersma, Svikis, and Schuster, "Computer-Based Brief Intervention."

18 Gentrification (and its associated debates) in this neighborhood is an ongoing phenomenon and a broader topic that deserves a thorough ethnographic treatment in its own right. I focus on how the changing political economy of the neighborhood formed a backdrop that added specific pressures to the experience of pregnancy and addiction on these blocks. A more thorough, separate ethnography needs to be done to assess the complex nature of the debates over public and private space, access to affordable housing, community development, community activism, and city politics. For example, several organizations, including the Plaza16 coalition, have recently put forth specific demands for limits on real estate in the neighborhood in response to a market-rate, ten-story condominium project proposed in the neighborhood. See Plaza16.org; Kamiya, "Omaha Beach in the Mission"; and Wong, "The Battle of 16th and Mission."

19 See Hernandez, "A Violent Year for Mission SROs."

20 Women's Space is a pseudonym.

21 Scheper-Hughes, *Death without Weeping*; and Bourgois et al., "The Everyday Violence of Hepatitis C."

22 "Urban" in real estate and marketing terminology is typically code for an area that is densely populated, crime-ridden, and/or populated by people of color.

23 See Wong, "DropBox, Air BnB, and the Fight over San Francisco's Public Spaces"; and Golightly, "San Francisco's Mission District: The Controversial Gentrification."

24 During this period, there has been a political pushback against gentrification, some of which was deemed largely ineffective in the local media. For example, in a recent anti-gentrification block party that took place at the Sixteenth Street BART plaza, protesters took a baseball bat to a "Google Bus piñata." This form of protest has then had a pushback of its own in the form of public commentary arguing that the Mission has historically been a neighborhood of continuous change in its ethnic and economic character over the years. One blog post offers an excellent example of the tenor: "I was a 23 year old gay latino when I moved here [to the Mission District] in 1976. Then the Mission was finishing its transition from an Irish, Italian, latino neighborhood to a predominantly latino

neighborhood. The new generation of Irish and Italians just wanted to move to the burbs. Think Sunset, Daly City. I remember sitting in the Rialto Diner across from the New Mission Cinema and listening to the old Irish couple complain about the hood changing for the worst, "The KFC on Valencia is owned by latinos now." "Serramonte Monte was like Little Manila Saturday." I loved it sitting right at the counter browner than my burger's bun. Anyway, East of Mission and 24th St. have changed very dramatically lately and not necessarily for the worst. The important thing is that institutions like La Galeria de la Raza, the Mission Cultural Center for Latino Arts, Precita Eyes be maintained to inform this ever transient neighborhood that there is a history and culture here that predates [a new, higher end restaurant]." http://missionlocal.org/2010/07/concerned-citizen-wants-city-to-fix-hipster-gentrification/, accessed March 15, 2015.

25 See Jones, "Clean Up the Plaza Run"; and Wong, "Battle of 16th and Mission." The website of Clean Up the Plaza reads: "We are a coalition of Residents, Merchants, and Visitors who use the 16 Mission Bart Station in our daily travels. The area around the Plaza on these corners is in deplorable condition. We have lived in danger and with the blight of this corner for too long. Our neighborhood deserves better access to safe, clean and walkable transportation corridors." Signed by Gil Chavez, Gwen Kaplan, Dr. David Sanchez Jr., Carmen Castillo, Jon Gainza, Anca Stratianu, Lawrence Smith, Jackson Smith, and Manuel Carmona. See http://cleanuptheplaza.com/, accessed March 15, 2015.

26 Alix Lutnick helpfully uses the term "third-party involvement" to describe the multiplicity of roles for persons other than the sex worker him- or herself, in sex exchange transactions, including roles historically labelled "pimping" and "pandering." See Lutnick, *Beyond Victims and Villains*.

27 One article highlighted the overall policing strategy in neighborhood by quoting Capt. Greg Corrales: "'When drug arrests are up, all other crimes are down. . . . The bottom line is we will make the Mission District safer for all residents and tourists. . . . When you get drug users and drug dealers off the streets, you also get an auto burglar, a thief, you're getting people who are committing a lot of other crimes,' said Capt. Greg Corrales of the Mission Police Station. 'The whole goal of getting drug dealers off the street is to make the Mission District a safe place for everyone to live.'" Carr, "Police Set Goals for 2010."

28 Even with this degree of police presence, I had very little direct contact with police. One evening in 2008, an undercover officer approached me during an outreach shift to ask what we were passing out; he then pulled Danell out of line to question her parole status. This interaction was uncomfortable and somewhat exceptional, but that also reflected the periods of time I conducted ethnography: many of the arrests for drugs possession and sales occur in the very late evening and early morning hours.

29 See Plaza16.org; Kamiya, "Omaha Beach in the Mission"; and Wong, "Battle of 16th and Mission."

30 Philippe Bourgois and Jeff Schonberg's ethnography *Righteous Dopefiend* (2009),

about homeless heroin addicts, focused on a specific homeless encampment, under a freeway and further outside major, commercial city traffic, and ended with a discussion of the unintended outcomes experienced by many of their ethnographic participants who were able to find housing in government-subsidized hotel rooms. Hooper (2003), investigating homeless men in 1979–1982, for example, focused either on men who were in male-only dormitory and single-room hotels run by the Social Security Administration or those who were "sleeping rough" (street homeless). Several ethnographies of homelessness have been conducted in shelters—settings that have direct bearing on how mental illness among the homeless clientele has been interpolated by staff and contested by anthropologists. Robert Desjarlais (1994) argued that "experience" in shelters was constituted by sensory responses to a series of interpersonal relations established in the shelter. This experience reflected an attempt to "stay calm" and self-regulate in light of the monotony of everyday life as a homeless person and the political economy of street-based exchanges. Desjarlais, "Struggling Along." Vincent Lyon-Callo's (2000) analysis of the medicalization of the homeless implicates the homeless shelter staff in creating an environment in which individual pathology, rather than structural violence, is implicated as the causal agent in homelessness. To Lyon-Callo, the "sheltering industry's" "helping practices" are guilty of reproducing deviant subjectivities. He states: "Within the dominant medicalized conceptual framework, it becomes common sense to understand the coping strategies of people surviving in homeless shelters as symptoms and evidence of mental illness. These people are thus understood as passive victims of biological disorders rather than situated social agents" (Lyon-Callo, "Medicalizing Homelessness," 331). Amir Marvasti's (2003) work, which was also shelter based, sought to use the voices of homeless persons to exemplify how homeless identities were textually constructed from societal, personal, and historical factors. Marvasti, *Being Homeless*. Catherine Kingfisher (2007) also focused on the narrative construction of the category of homeless. However, she chose to "study up" (Nader, "Up the Anthropologist") by examining how the political actors (politicians, service providers, activists) debated the placement and parameters of a new homeless shelter in a small Canadian city. Like Marvasti and Lyon-Callo, Kingfisher was interested in exploring the ways individualizing, medicalizing practices reflected a neoliberal political agenda which "invite[s], prompt[s], or coerce[s] individuals to work on and transform themselves" (Kingfisher, "Discursive Constructions of Homelessness," 102). Similarly, Darin Weinberg (2005) situated his ethnography in two treatment facilities serving dual diagnosis patients—those diagnosed with a mental illness and a substance use disorder. Choosing treatment facilities as ethnographic spaces of habitation gave Weinberg the opportunity to address "how putative mental health problems have been *experienced* and *managed* when they have been found to afflict homeless, impoverished, and/or otherwise culturally marginalized members of the community" (Weinberg, *Of Others Inside*, 10). Few ethnographies of homelessness have focused on privately managed hotels, on women, or on pregnant women. In 1989 Anne Christiano and Ida Susser reported on their ethnographic research conducted with "homeless pregnant women" who lived in a residential hotel. This study focused on low-income Latina and African-American women's awareness of their risks for HIV infection. The study did not offer a broad analysis of the dynamics of housing and gender but did describe the role of crowding, illegal drug use, and sex work occurring in those built environments. A. Christiano and I. Susser, "Knowledge and Perceptions of HIV Infection among Homeless Pregnant Women." Alisse Waterston (1999) describes two years of ethnographic engagement with women stigmatized by mental illness and homelessness. Waterston offers a powerful ethnographic engagement with the everyday by documenting women's narratives of "what it is like to live on the street and how it feels to lose your mind, about the taste of crack cocaine and the sweetness of friendship" (Waterston, *Love, Sorrow, and Rage*, 19). Tanya Luhrmann's (2008) study with homeless women focused on a daytime drop-in center serving women who stayed in publicly funded shelters in the Uptown neighborhood of Chicago. Luhrmann, "'The Street Will Drive You Crazy': Why Homeless Psychotic Women in the Institutional Circuit in the United States Often Say No to Offers of Help." Both Waterston and Luhrmann's ethnographic engagements with homeless women are most similar to my own, yet neither was ethnographically situated in the world of privately owned and managed daily-rent hotels nor focused on reproduction. Maria Epele (2002) has conducted ethnographic work among Latina injection drug users who often spent nights in daily-rent hotels in the Mission District of San Francisco, focused on HIV risk, injection drug use, embodiment, gendered violence, and political economy. She does not analyze the hotel rooms as specific sites of production for these practices, likely because her ethnography was completed in the late 1990s, prior to progressive housing initiatives in which public institutions (the San Francisco Department of Public Health and the San Francisco Health and Human Service Agency) assumed the master lease of several previously privately managed buildings in the Mission District, creating a starker contrast between publicly and privately managed hotel rooms and buildings. Epele, "Gender, Violence and HIV"; and Epele, "Excess, Scarcity and Desire among Drug-Using Sex Workers."

31 Hopper et al., "'Homelessness, Severe Mental Illness, and the Institutional Circuit.'" See Carr, "'Ethnography of an HIV Hotel,'" for a lengthy description of health service integration for HIV-infected persons in a single-room occupancy (SRO) hotel in San Francisco.

32 There has been some ethnographic research on brothels in Nevada, but although private, they are highly regulated by the state.

33 I began as a qualitative public health researcher in 1994 working on a study of methadone maintenance treatment access and risk for HIV infection funded by the National Institutes of Health. I have continued to study drug use, health, and socio-structural factors on over eighteen different qualitative studies that

recruited active drug users in the San Francisco Bay Area and throughout the United States. Although my ethnographic project of pregnancy and addiction was independent of those other research studies, it was certainly informed by my multiple decades of work with urban poor women and men who use illicit substances. In addition, I was a cofounder and site coordinator for the Women's Needle Exchange Program, which opened in 1995 in the Mission District, and I have continued to volunteer for syringe exchange programs and at the drop-in center for homeless women in the Mission on and off from 1995 to the present. Other harm reduction roles I have occupied include being an outreach worker in the daily-rent hotels, which I discuss extensively herein.

34 Here I am influenced by Cori Hayden's (2007) discussion of "taking as giving," in which both science and politics become leveraged to transform relationships between researchers and research subjects and establish the goal of research itself as mutually beneficial. See Hayden, "Taking as Giving."

35 Although I traveled with women to different locations in the city and interviewed city policy-makers about health and welfare issues, the city of San Francisco was not my ethnographic site per se. By the same token, the Mission District is diverse and very large, and my ethnography focused a small portion of it, the daily-rent hotels. For an interesting examination of cities as whole objects of study, and the importance of an examination of the "whole city" in addressing urban health disparities, see Fullilove, *Urban Alchemy*.

36 For another discussion on the decision to exclude or include photographs of socially marginalized persons, see Bourgois and Schonberg, *Righteous Dopefiend*.

37 See Brodwin, *Everyday Ethics*, for a discussion of the distinction between traditional bioethics and "everyday ethics" in situ. Also see Zigon and Throop (2014) for a discussion of an anthropology of moral experience that is attuned to the "nitty-gritty complexity of actual persons interacting with one another" and recognizes that "morality cannot simply be equated with normative social behavior" (Zigon and Throop, "Moral Experience," 1, 2).

38 Here I am drawing directly on Laura Nader's methodological entreaty to examine a "vertical slice" of any social problem. See Nader, "Up the Anthropologist," 292.

Chapter 1: Consumption and Insecurity

1 "Cotton fever" is the common street name for a medical condition people who inject drugs often report. Cotton fever includes the "acute onset of fever and myalgia after injecting heroin reclaimed from previously used cotton filters. Although the causative mechanisms are unknown, the syndrome does appear to have a benign, self-limiting course." Shragg, "'Cotton Fever' in Narcotic Addicts," 279–280.

2 Definitions accessed from wordnetweb.princeton.edu/perl/webwn, accessed March 15, 2015.

3 Sections of this chapter have been previously published. See Knight et al., "Single Room Occupancy (SRO) Hotels as Mental Health Risk Environments."

4 See Brodwin (2013) and Metzl (2009) for broader discussions of US deinstitution-alization, its controversies, and its impacts on psychiatric care. Brodwin, *Every-day Ethics*; and Metzl, *The Protest Psychosis*.

5 See C. Willse for a critique of the underlying economic rationale of social pro-grams seeking to house chronically homeless men and women. Willse, "Neo-liberal Biopolitics and the Invention of Chronic Homelessness."

6 At the same time as the redevelopment of SRO housing stock by Housing and Urban Health, welfare reforms to San Francisco General Assistance (GA) funding produced a voter-mandated policy called "Care Not Cash," which redirected wel-fare monies from recipient payments to rent payments. Recipients' GA payments were reduced from approximately $400 per month to approximately $50, and if the recipient could "prove homelessness" through an extended shelter stay or frequent documentation of visits to the GA office, an SRO room would be secured for a longer-term basis and rent paid directly from GA welfare payments. "Care Not Cash" rooms can be located in a range of housing stock from well-managed, safe, and clean buildings to poorly managed and chaotic environments.

7 After my study was completed, one woman gained housing through a supportive housing program.

8 P. Groth, *Living Downtown*, cited in Central City SRO Collaborative, San Fran-cisco, *History of SROs in San Francisco*, n.d., http://www.ccsro.org/pages/history.htm, accessed March 15, 2015.

9 Central City SRO Collaborative, San Francisco, *History of SROs in San Francisco*.

10 See also Lazarus et al., "Risky Health Environments"; and Shannon et al., "The Impact of Unregulated Single Room Occupancy Hotels on Health Status of Illicit Drug Users in Vancouver."

11 Alix Lutnick helpfully uses the term "third-party involvement" to describe the multiplicity of roles for persons other than the sex worker him- or herself, in sex exchange transactions, including roles historically labelled "pimping" and "pandering." See Lutnick, *Beyond Victims and Villains*.

12 The Federal Strategic Plan to Prevent and End Homelessness recognized support-ive housing as an evidence-based HIV prevention and health care intervention for homeless/unstably housed persons. The United States Interagency Council on Homelessness, *Opening Doors*. Also see Riley et al., "Basic Subsistence Needs and Overall Health among Human Immunodeficiency Virus–Infected Homeless and Unstably Housed Women"; Riley et al., "Social, Structural and Behavioral Deter-minants of Overall Health Status in a Cohort of Homeless and Unstably Housed HIV-Infected Men"; Karaca, Wong, and Mutter, *Characteristics of Homeless and Non-homeless Individuals Using Inpatient and Emergency Department Services*; Aday, "Health Status of Vulnerable Populations"; and National Coalition for the Homeless, *Health Care and Homelessness*.

13 Gelberg and Linn, "Demographic Differences in Health Status of Homeless Adults"; Hwang, "Homelessness and Health"; Gelberg et al., "Health, Homeless-ness, and Poverty"; Robertson and Cousineau, "Health Status and Access to Health

Services among the Urban Homeless"; Fazel et al., "The Prevalence of Mental Disorders among the Homeless in Western Countries"; Beijer, Wolf, and Fazel, "Prevalence of Tuberculosis, Hepatitis C Virus, and HIV in Homeless People"; and Lebrun-Harris et al., "Health Status and Health Care Experiences among Homeless Patients in Federally Supported Health Centers."

14 This phenomenon among homeless heroin-addicted men has been extensively documented by Philippe Bourgois and Jeffrey Schonberg in their book *Righteous Dopefiend*.

15 Hopper et al., "Homelessness, Severe Mental Illness, and the Institutional Circuit."

16 Davey-Rothwell, German, and Latkin, "Residential Transience and Depression."

17 German, Davey, and Latkin, "Residential Transience and HIV Risk Behaviors among Injection Drug Users."

18 Rhodes et al., "The Social Structural Production of HIV Risk among Injecting Drug Users."

19 Kushel et al., "No Door to Lock: Victimization among Homeless and Marginally Housed Persons."

20 Knight et al., "Single Room Occupancy (SRO) Hotels."

21 Riley et al., "Recent Violence in a Highly Co-morbid Community-Based Sample of Homeless and Unstably Housed Women."

22 See Nancy Scheper-Hughes, *Death without Weeping*; and Kalofonos, "'All I Eat Is ARVs.'"

23 Weiser et al., "Food Insecurity as a Barrier to Sustained Antiretroviral Therapy Adherence in Uganda"; Roberts et al., "Factors Associated with the Health Status of Internally Displaced Persons in Northern Uganda"; and Kalofonos, "'All I Eat Is ARVs.'"

24 Weiser et al., "Food Insecurity among Homeless and Marginally Housed Individuals Living with HIV/AIDS in San Francisco."

25 Vogenthaler et al., "Food Insufficiency among HIV-Infected Crack-Cocaine Users in Atlanta and Miami"; and Melchior et al., "Mental Health Context of Food Insecurity."

26 Harrison and Sidebottom, "Systematic Prenatal Screening for Psychosocial Risks."

27 See Riley, "Basic Subsistence Needs and Overall Health."

28 Lester, "Long-Term Effects of Prenatal Substance Exposure on Children," webinar, sponsored by National Abandoned Infants Assistance Resource Center, University of California, Berkeley, February 26, 2013, http://aia.berkeley.edu/training /online/webinars/2013series/, accessed March 15, 2015. See chapter 5 for a more detailed description of the adversity index.

29 The dynamic described here of feeding pregnant women food with low nutritional value in the guise of service provision is reminiscent of Scheper-Hughes's description of her role in proliferating Nestle baby formula to the pregnant, poor women in northern Brazil. See Scheper-Hughes, *Death without Weeping*.

30 Although all the women I worked with had cell phones, many were not smart-phones with data-enabled access to the Internet, due to the cost. In addition, cell phones were highly commodified in the drug-sex economy of the daily-rent ho-tels. Thus cell phones were often stolen and sold or traded for drugs. Cell phones were often deactivated due to unpaid bills.

Chapter 2: Addicted Pregnancy and Time

1 Johannes Fabian has argued against a "schizogenic" notion of time—one that favors physical time: time as linear, topological progression—because it can mask the importance of the intersubjective power relations at work in the present. These power relations are essential in the cultural work of time-making. They reveal, through the production of discourse, "the specific way in which actors create and produce beliefs, values, and other means of social life." Fabian's call for attention to the way social life is discursively constructed through social relations in the present offers an intellectual frame for how addicted pregnant women in the daily-rent hotels navigated the temporal demands of everyday life. Fabian, *Time and the Other*, 21, 24.

2 Tanya Luhrmann has offered a perspective on homeless women's ability to narrate their own lives. She claims that women's descriptions of their history (the past) and their current situations (their present) have narrative holes. Pieces of the story are missing as the cumulative result of years of drug use, perhaps mental illness, and the repeated experience of "social defeat" on the streets. Luhrmann, "Social Defeat and the Culture of Chronicity."

3 This encounter mirrored what Sue Estroff documented so expertly in her eth-nography *Making It Crazy*: being "crazy" in a given social interaction may be beneficial, even necessary. Estroff, *Making It Crazy*.

4 See Snow et al., "The Myth of Pervasive Mental Illness among the Homeless"; Lyon-Callo, "Medicalizing Homelessness"; Marvasti, *Being Homeless*; Bourgois and Schonberg, *Righteous Dopefiend*; Luhrmann, "Social Defeat and the Culture of Chronicity"; Weinberg, *Of Others Inside*; and Estroff, *Making It Crazy*, for a va-riety of perspectives of the question of categorization and the homeless in relation to mental illness.

5 In describing the social world of the Canaque, Maurice Leenhardt took as his starting point an open view toward the otherness of experience. The transforma-tions wrought by colonial encounters with Western, Christian views of identity, rationality, and the self brought into relief alternative ways of understanding time, experience, and context. He wrote: "Identity acts in man's mind like the deforming mirrors which bewilder passersby in arcades. We must now study the notion of time. Only this can give a measure of coherence to the mass of observations we have lying before us." Leenhardt, *Do Kamo*, 74.

6 Philippe Bourgois and Jeff Schonberg's ethnography of homeless heroin addicts

in San Francisco took place over a ten-year period. They were able, through this *longue durée* analysis, to observe the impact of the passing of years on informants' reconstructions of their history and current drug use practices. One field note, by Schonberg, captures both the ethnographic outsider's experience of the redundancy and monotony of studying addicts and the way history intrudes into the addicted present: "I've been away for three months and, as usual, nothing whatsoever has changed in the Edgewater scene. Carter and Tina are about to smoke crack. . . . Tina excitedly grabs a large, plastic garbage bag and begins pulling out dolls retrieved from the toy factory's dumpster. They are, with one exception, all black, and Tina has christened them with the names of her daughters." Bourgois and Schonberg, *Righteous Dopefiend*, 206.

7 See Nancy Campbell's discussion of "living the subcortical life" in "Toward a Critical Neuroscience of 'Addiction.'"

8 I was able, through partial support by an ethnographic study of women, housing, and HIV risk, to compensate women for longer, life-history-oriented interviews. Women were given $20 for a completed, taped interview.

9 For an excellent analysis of "addiction talk," see Carr, *Scripting Addiction*.

10 See chapter 1 for a more detailed historical examination of progressive housing policies and the political economy of rental charges in San Francisco.

11 See chapter 3 for a lengthy description of federal changes in welfare entitlements benefit eligibility and their local policy impacts on mental health care and treatment in San Francisco.

12 Gaulden et al., "Menstrual Abnormalities Associated with Heroin Addiction."

13 Kolman, "New Police Chief Targets Drugs and Prostitution."

14 See chapter 6 for an in-depth discussion of pregnant, addicted women's experiences with policing and incarceration. Also see Sufrin, "Jailcare: The Safety Net of a U.S. Women's Jail."

15 This "pregnancy" ended up being false.

16 Lutnick and Cohan, "Criminalization, Legalization, or Decriminalization of Sex Work"; and Klausner, "Decriminalize Prostitution."

17 Folk, scientific, and media-generated beliefs about prenatal drug exposure are discussed at length in chapter 5.

18 See chapter 6 for a discussion of women's experiences with health research studies and the construction of public health data.

19 See Porter, *The Rise of Statistical Thinking 1820–1900*, and *Trust in Numbers*; and Bowker and Star, *Sorting Things Out*.

20 See Marshall, "The Development of the Severity of Violence Against Women Scale."

21 Knight et al., "Single Room Occupancy (SRO) Hotels as Mental Health Risk Environments among Impoverished Women"; and Riley et al., "Recent Violence in a Highly Co-morbid Community-Based Sample of Homeless and Unstably Housed Women."

22 Kath Weston, in her interesting and challenging philosophical exploration of gen-

der and time, describes the "violence of counting," linked to industrialization, in which "fluid social relations" become fixed and social injustice masked, and naturalized, by statistical renderings. She writes: "Our time travels open with an investigation into the violence of counting. As industrialization took hold in different areas of the world, an 'avalanche of numbers' [citing Hacking, 1991] generated by shining new bureaucracies promised to tame chance by calculating probabilities. First to be aggregated by these technologies were the landless bodies pouring into the cities from the countryside. The king's subjects, poorhouse residents, and the dead, all sorted into closed categories and counted. In the current era of nation-states and transnational corporations, number fetishism continues to lend fluid social relations the appearance of fixity and to cloak unjust social arrangements with an aura of the inevitable." Weston, *Gender in Real Time*, 23.

23 Strathern, "New Accountabilities."

24 These numbers refer to the scale of the assessment of neonatal abstinence syndrome. There are different scales used for this assessment, including the Finnegan scale and the Lipsitz scale, and additional assessments. Finnegan et al., "Neonatal Abstinence Syndrome"; Lipsitz, "A Proposed Narcotic Withdrawal Score for Use with Newborn Infants"; and Jansson, Velez, and Harrow, "The Opioid Exposed Newborn." It is not clear which scale or scales Ramona is referring to here, or whether different scales were used in the two births she is describing to Mary.

25 See Flavin, *Our Bodies, Our Crimes*; Murphy and Rosenbaum, *Pregnant Women on Drugs*.

26 For example, a recent study on the impacts of prenatal exposure to methamphetamine recruited cohorts of pregnant women in the United States and New Zealand in order to test this hypothesis. This study found that women in New Zealand, a country that does not remove children from a mother's custody as a result of prenatal exposure to illicit drugs, had consistently healthier babies than the American cohort, even though the children had the same level of drug exposure in utero. This finding led the authors to argue that "given the considerable differences in governmental and healthcare responses to maternal drug use across countries . . . and the nearly identical data collection processes employed, this comparison represents a unique and informative way to account for these traditional confounds (e.g., inadequate prenatal and postnatal care, poverty, out-of-home placement due to maternal drug use) in prenatal drug exposure research." See Abar et al., "Cross-National Comparison of Prenatal Methamphetamine Exposure on Infant and Early Child Physical Growth"; and Wu et al., "Predictors of Inadequate Prenatal Care in Methamphetamine-Using Mothers in New Zealand and the United States." Also see National Institute on Drug Abuse, *Prenatal Exposure to Drugs of Abuse*, May 2011.

27 See chapter 5 for a discussion of the historical construction of prenatal substance use exposure risk through scientific research and the media, and its current circulation.

28 See Watkins-Hayes, *The New Welfare Bureaucrats*, for a discussion on bureaucratic reasoning, decision-making, and professional identity among welfare workers.

29 Naomi Weinstein of Phoenix House's center of addiction and family writes that

drug treatment and child welfare services are two conflicting systems: one has the parent's well-being in mind, and the other is charged to protect the child. Weinstein argues that the stakes for public scrutiny on the part of CPS workers also contribute to differential assessments of risk, to which treatment systems are not held accountable. Interestingly, she makes the additional point that many treatment professionals may have also had their pregnancies previously adjudicated, leading to an anger and frustration similar to that which Ramona expressed at her methadone intake appointment about being caught in biomedical time. Weinstein writes: "Treatment and child welfare don't usually get along too well. In treatment, the client is an adult and your sympathies and work are to advocate for the client. In child welfare, the social worker is concerned with the child. That leads to conflict, because parents and children may not have the same interests. Then there's media scrutiny. Every single thing ACS [New York state child protective services] does has the potential to land on the front page and for people on the case to get fired. Treatment people don't understand why ACS is so cautious. If a mother in a treatment program relapses and harms her child, ACS will be blamed by the media, but no one wonders what that treatment agency was doing. Finally, many treatment professionals were once addicts who had their children removed in the past. They haven't gotten past that, for good reason. There's been a lot of hate on both sides. We're trying to fix that, so parents in treatment are not caught between two conflicting systems." Quotation from Weinstein, "Conflict Resolution," in *Rise*, 8. See also Barrow and Laborde, "Invisible Mothers."

30 Here I borrow from Veena Das for a conceptualization of "the everyday" that theorizes the ordinary as a series of acts and words in which "turning back evokes not so much the idea of a return, as a turning back to inhabit the same space now marked as a space of destruction, in which you must live again." See Das, *Life and Words*, 62.

31 The practice of creating tokens of separation between poor women and their infants and children is not new. In the Foundling Museum in London there is an archive of "foundling tokens"—coins, buttons, and small pieces of cloth or ribbon that mothers and fathers would leave with their infants and small children when abandoning them to the state in the nineteenth century. The hope was that these tokens would make children identifiable to parents when circumstances changed and they were able to collect them back from the orphanage, especially since children were given new names when they entered the foundling system. See http://www.foundlingmuseum.org.uk/collections/the-foundling-hospital-collection/, accessed March 15, 2015.

32 In her discussion opposing the interpretations of the Antigone story by Hegel and Lacan, Das asks, "What is it to bear witness to the criminality of the societal rule that consigns the uniqueness of being to eternal forgetfulness through a descent into everyday life—to not simply articulate loss through a dramatic gesture of defiance but to inhabit the world, or inhabit it *again*, in a gesture of mourning?" Das, *Life and Words*, 62.

33 Butler, *Giving an Account of Oneself*.

34 See Carr, *Scripting Addiction*; Fassin and Rechtman, *The Empire of Trauma*; and Ticktin, "Where Ethics and Politics Meet."

35 From an earlier ethnographic moment, Maurice Leenhardt described the planting of trees for newborn children in the following way: "The tree, planted the day the child is born, in the hole where they bury the umbilical cord, may indeed have a reality similar to the reality of the child's life. The Caledonian custom of sending a stranger away from the village with the words, 'Your Tree is not here,' is persuasive evidence that the tree confers social and civic authority on a man." This passage by Leenhardt caught my attention because of its powerful reference to symbolic children. In Leenhardt's analysis of the social world of the Canaque, trees are not technically a symbol, in the sense of being a representation of the child. The tree is in fact the child himself. Leenhardt, *Do Kamo*, 19.

36 Allan Young has written: "PTSD is a disease of time. The disorder's distinctive pathology is that it permits the past (memory) to relive itself in the present, in the form of intrusive images and thoughts and in the patient's compulsion to replay old events. The space occupied by PTSD in the DSM-III classificatory system depends on this temporal-causal relation: etiological event → symptoms. Without it, PTSD's symptoms are indistinguishable from syndromes that belong to other classifications. The relation has practical implications also, since it is the basis on which PTSD qualifies as a "service-connected" disability within the Veterans Administration Medical System. (A service-connected designation is a precondition for getting access to treatment and compensation.) There are numerous clinical cases that resemble PTSD in every respect except that time runs in the wrong direction, that is, from present back to the past . . . [and] there is no effective way to distinguish these [two types of] cases. . . . PTSD knowledge workers have responded . . . by developing technologies that provide the disorder's otherwise invisible pathogenic process with a visible presence." Young, *The Harmony of Illusions*, 7.

37 See the conclusion for more detail about this custody interaction between Anita, her son, and her aunt.

38 See chapter 5 for a discussion of how addicted pregnancy can reengage many women with families of origin, re-cementing tenuous kinship bonds that may have been strained or severed as a result of women's difficult childhood experiences.

39 In her multiple, eloquent writings about political and social ramifications of the Partition of India and Pakistan, Veena Das describes rumor as one way the events of community violence are constructed in language, so words can be expressed about them. She writes: "I begin with outlining the incident and then show how language and event constituted each other, gathering the past and making it present in a contracted form. I am not making an argument that language itself had the power to *make* these grievous events out of nothing, but rather that memories that may have lain inert came to life in the form of rumors. Enmeshed into local histories of conflict, such rumors became part and parcel of scenes of devastating

local violence." I raise Das's analysis of rumor, language, and event as a way to help understand my own ethnographic present and presence with the pregnant addicts I came to know and tried to understand. Das, *Life and Words*, 109. Also see Briggs and Mantini-Briggs, *Stories in the Time of Cholera*.

40 Haraway, "Situated Knowledges."

41 Despite how often I heard stories from women about being beaten up and abused by their boyfriends, and the number of black eyes I have seen, it was actually rare to come across a couple in the midst of violent conflict on the outreach shift. This was probably due, in part, to the fact that outreach was conducted during limited hours (6–8 p.m.).

42 Fabian (1983) demands that anthropology focus phenomenological attention toward the discursive relations between all the subjects who are engaged in knowledge production in the present—during their encounters. Such attention could counter "a persistent and systematic tendency to place the referent of anthropology in a time other than the present of the producer of anthropological discourse." Fabian, *Time and the Other*, 31.

43 Brackette Williams, "The Public I/Eye."

44 See Clarke, Marno, Fosket, Fishman, and Shim, *Biomedicalization*; also Rapp, *Testing Women, Testing the Fetus*.

Chapter 3: Neurocratic Futures in the Disability Economy

1 The US Substance Abuse and Mental Health Services Administration describes comorbidity in the following way: "Individuals are classified as having SMI (Serious Mental Illness) if at some time during the past year they had a mental, behavioral, or emotional disorder that met criteria specified in the *Diagnostic and Statistical Manual of Mental Disorders, 4th ed.* (DSM-IV), and that resulted in functional impairment that substantially interfered with or limited one or more major life activities. . . . Individuals with either alcohol or drug dependence or abuse are said to have a substance use disorder. Individuals with both SMI and a substance use disorder are said to have co-occurring SMI and a substance use disorder." U.S. Substance Abuse and Mental Health Services Administration, Office of Applied Studies, *The NSDUH Report*. Also see U.S. National Institute on Drug Abuse, *Comorbidity*.

2 U.S. Substance Abuse and Mental Health Services Administration, Office of Applied Studies, *The NSDUH Report*.

3 Biehl describes his project as an exploration of "the institutionalization of AIDS in urban poor settings. I chart the concrete ways in which politics and personhood are being configured through the rational-technical management of AIDS." Biehl, *Will to Live*, 101.

4 I am borrowing the term *biomedicalization* from A. E. Clarke and colleagues, who describe it as "the increasingly complex, multisited, multidirectional processes of medicalization, both extended and reconstituted through the new social forms of

highly techno-scientific biomedicine. The historical shift from medicalization to biomedicalization is one from control over biomedical phenomena to transformations of them. Five key interactive processes both engender biomedicalization and are produced through it: (1) the political economic reconstitution of the vast sector of biomedicine; (2) the focus on health itself and the elaboration of risk and surveillance biomedicines; (3) the increasingly technological and scientific nature of biomedicine; (4) transformations in how biomedical knowledges are produced, distributed, and consumed, and in medical information management; and (5) transformations of bodies to include new properties and the production of new individual and collective technoscientific identities." See Clarke et al., "Biomedicalization"; and Clarke et al., *Biomedicalization*.

5 National Public Radio reporter Chana Joffe-Walt has gained attention and critique for her journalistic analyses of the rise in the numbers of US adults and children claiming disability eligibility and winning disability entitlement benefits cases. Joffe-Walt's focus was not on mental health conditions or the urban nonworking poor. See "490: Trends with Benefits," on *This American Life*, National Public Radio, March 22, 2013; Lennard Davis, "NPR Reporter Chana Joffe-Walt Gets Disability Wrong," *Huffington Post*, March 29, 2013; E. H. Groch-Begley, "*This American Life* Features Error-Riddled Story on Disability and Children," March 22, 2013, http://mediamatters.org/mobile/research/2013/03/22/this-american-life -features-error-riddled-story/193215, accessed March 15, 2015, for fact checking of Joffe-Walt's analysis. Also see Hansen, Bourgois, and Drucker, "Pathologizing Poverty."

6 For a review of writing in the anthropology of disability, see Ginsburg and Rapp, "Disability Worlds." For an analysis of disability categorization and projects of state-making, see Kohrman, "Why Am I Not Disabled?" For a historical analysis of disability in relation to medicine, poverty and public space, and reproduction, see respectively Linker, "On the Borderland of Medical and Disability History"; Schweik, *The Ugly Laws*; and Reagan, *Dangerous Pregnancies*.

7 See Estroff, *Making It Crazy*, for a landmark ethnographic exploration into how mental illness is construed bureaucratically and socially in sites where homeless and poor persons utilize services.

8 See Fassin and Rechtman, *The Empire of Trauma*, and Young, *Harmony of Illusions*, for social histories of traumatic stress and PTSD; and Martin, *Bipolar Expeditions*, for the biosocial history of bipolar disorder.

9 See El-Bassel et al., "HIV and Intimate Partner Violence among Methadone-Maintained Women in New York City"; Nyamathi, Leake, and Gelberg, "Sheltered versus Nonsheltered Homeless Women"; Bassuk, Melnick, and Browne, "Responding to the Needs of Low-Income and Homeless Women Who Are Survivors of Family Violence"; Browne and Bassuk, "Intimate Violence in the Lives of Homeless and Poor Housed Women"; Goodman, Dutton, and Harris, "The Relationship between Violence Dimensions and Symptom Severity among Homeless, Mentally Ill Women"; Theall, Sterk, and Elifson, "Past and New Victimization among Af-

rican American Female Drug Users Who Participated in an HIV Risk-Reduction Intervention"; Wenzel, Koegel, and Gelberg, "Antecedents of Physical and Sexual Victimization among Homeless Women"; Kushel et al., "No Door to Lock: Victimization among Homeless and Marginally Housed Persons"; Wenzel et al., "Toward a More Comprehensive Understanding of Violence against Impoverished Women"; Gelberg et al., "Health, Homelessness, and Poverty"; Thompson et al., "Partner Violence, Social Support, and Distress among Inner-City African American Women"; and James, Johnson, and Raghavan, "'I Couldn't Go Anywhere.'"

10 Chan, Dennis, and Funk, "Prevalence and Comorbidity of Major Internalizing and Externalizing Problems among Adolescents and Adults Presenting to Substance Abuse Treatment."

11 Quoted from National Institute on Drug Abuse, *Comorbidity: Addiction and Other Mental Illnesses*.

12 Kennedy and King, "Access to Benefits for Persons with Disabilities Who Were Experiencing Homelessness."

13 See U.S. Department of Housing and Urban Development, *The 2010 Annual Homeless Assessment Report to Congress*; Tabol, Drebing, and Rosenheck, "Studies of 'Supported' and 'Supportive' Housing."

14 Degenhardt et al., "Estimation Burden of Disease Attributable to Illicit Drug Use and Mental Disorders." Also see Prince et al., "No Health without Mental Health."

15 See Shumway, Boccellari, O'Brien, and Okin, "Cost-Effectiveness of Clinical Case Management for ED Frequent Users."

16 See Brodwin, *Everyday Ethics*, for a more extensive discussion of representative payees.

17 Barber, *Supplemental Security Income Recipients for Whom the Alcoholism and Drug Addiction Provisions Apply*. For a more in-depth discussion of the social and policy history of SSI and its relationship to larger criminalization movements as part of the War on Drugs, see Bluthenthal et al., "Collateral Damage in the War on Drugs."

18 See Wacquant, *Punishing the Poor*; and Alexander, *The New Jim Crow*.

19 See Dorgan, "Addicts Feed Habits with U.S. Hand Outs"; Fitzgerald, "America's Shocking Disability Scam"; Rust, "Social Security Scam"; Seligman, "The SSI Follies"; Walsh, "A Partisan Agenda for Cutting the Roles of Government, Labor"; and Weaver, "Welfare Reform Is Likely to Leave This Monster Intact."

20 Satel, "Hooked: Addicts on Welfare." Satel, "When Disability Benefits Make Patients Sicker."

21 Shaner et al., "Disability Income, Cocaine Use, and Repeated Hospitalization among Schizophrenic Cocaine Abusers."

22 http://www.socialsecurity.gov/disability/professionals/bluebook/AdultListings .htm, accessed March 15, 2015.

23 Schmidt, *Effects of Welfare Reform on the Supplemental Security Income (SSI) Program*.

24 Myself (then a HIV/AIDS qualitative researcher) and group of activists, service

providers, sex workers, epidemiologists, and doctors started the first women-only needle exchange program in San Francisco's Mission District in 1995. I served as the program's volunteer site coordinator from 1995 to 1997.

25 See Crane, Quirk, and van der Straten, "'Come Back When You're Dying.'"

26 San Francisco (City and County) Department of Public Health, *Return on Investment: How SSI Advocacy Became a Standard of Practice in San Francisco* (2004, revision, San Francisco: San Francisco Department of Public Health, 2008).

27 San Francisco (City and County) Department of Public Health, *Return on Investment*. See Joel Braslow for the relationship between discourses of recovery in mental health care and neoliberal social policies. Braslow, "The Manufacture of Recovery."

28 Note that the I-V axial system has been removed from the most current iteration of the DSM, the *DSM-5*, which was not yet published when this interview took place.

29 The *DSM-5* had not yet been published when this training took place.

30 Nicholas Rose has spoken of new "technologies of truth"—ways of counting, categorizing, and making visible—which have given birth to our "neurochemical selves." Technologies of truth have created broad changes in our conception of the human in the wake of emergent biological psychiatry: "The new style of thought in biological psychiatry not only establishes what counts as an explanation, it establishes what there is to explain. The deep psychological space that opened in the twentieth century has flattened out. In this new account of personhood, psychiatry no longer distinguishes between organic and functional disorders. It no longer concerns itself with the mind and the psyche. . . . This is a shift in human ontology—in the kinds of persons we take ourselves to be. It entails a new way of seeing, judging, and acting on human normality and abnormality. It enables us to be governed in new ways. And it enables us to govern ourselves differently." Rose, *The Politics of Life Itself*, 192.

31 Workfare is another form of city welfare in which welfare payment are linked to doing menial work or being in job training programs, also a result of late 1990s welfare reforms. See Wacquant, *Punishing the Poor*, for a more in-depth discussion of US welfare policies and employment insecurity.

Chapter 4: Street Psychiatrics and New Configurations of Madness

1 See Paul Linde for a nuanced view of the organization of care in an emergency psychiatry unit. Linde, *Danger to Self*. Also see Rhodes, *Emptying Beds*.

2 "Mental retardation" according to Monica, diagnosed in childhood.

3 Falck et al., "The Epidemiology of Physical Attack and Rape among Crack-Using Women"; Hedtke et al., "A Longitudinal Investigation of Interpersonal Violence in Relation to Mental Health and Substance Use"; Ullman, Townsend, Starzynski, and Long, "Correlates of Comorbid PTSD and Polysubstance Use in Sexual Assault Victims"; and Wechsberg et al., "Violence, Homelessness, and HIV Risk among Crack-Using African-American Women."

4 See chapter 2 for a detailed analysis of the temporal registers of addicted pregnancy for women in the daily-rent hotels.

5 See chapter 3 for a description of neurocratic practices.

6 See Snow et al., "The Myth of Pervasive Mental Illness among the Homeless." For a variety on perspectives of the question of categorization and the homeless in relation to mental illness, see Lyon-Callo, "Medicalizing Homelessness"; Marvasti, *Being Homeless*; Bourgois and Schonberg, *Righteous Dopefiend*; Luhrmann, "Social Defeat and the Culture of Chronicity"; Weinberg, *Of Others Inside*; and Estroff, *Making It Crazy*.

7 See Riley et al., "Recent Violence in a Community-Based Sample of Homeless and Unstably Housed Women with High Levels of Psychiatric Comorbidity."

8 A list of atypical antipsychotic medications from the FDA website: aripiprazole (marketed as Abilify); asenapine maleate (marketed as Saphris); clozapine (marketed as Clozaril); iloperidone (marketed as Fanapt); lurasidone (marketed as Latuda); olanzapine (marketed as Zyprexa); olanzapine/fluoxetine (marketed as Symbyax); paliperidone (marketed as Invega); quetiapine (marketed as Seroquel); risperidone (marketed as Risperdal); ziprasidone (marketed as Geodon), http://www.fda.gov/Drugs/DrugSafety/PostmarketDrugSafetyInformationfor PatientsandProviders/ucm094303.htm, accessed March 15, 2015. Also see Dumit, *Drugs for Life*; and Metzl, *Prozac on the Couch*.

9 Martin, *Bipolar Expeditions*, 46.

10 See chapter 2 for a detailed description of addict time.

11 Fassin and Rechtman, *The Empire of Trauma*, xi.

12 "Most historians suggest that changes in collective sensibilities—i.e., in the way in which trauma and more particularly the victims of trauma are depicted—come about as a result of scientific developments. But in fact the direction of the causal relationship is far from one way. There is a moral genealogy running parallel to the scientific development. It derives from the collective process by which a society defines its values and norms, and embodies them in individual subjects." Fassin and Rechtman, *Empire of Trauma*, 30.

13 See Holmes and Ponte, "En-case-ing the Patient"; and Davenport, "Witnessing and the Medical Gaze" for discussions of how structural factors that impact the physical and mental health of patients are made visible and erased during clinical encounters.

14 Literally, in the form of psychiatrist Roger Spitzer, who was instrumental in the development of the DSM-III and in PTSD as a disease recognized within it. Young, *Harmony of Illusions*, 89, 101, and 104–105.

15 Fleck, *Genesis and Development of a Scientific Fact*, 28.

16 Lawrence Cohen has theorized that the high occurrence of family debt in Indian neighborhoods with many poor kidney sellers is not merely a result of "naturalized states of poverty." Indebtedness does not only produce the circumstances under which selling a kidney becomes the only option for survival, but neighborhoods full of kidney sellers also produce a thriving debtor's economy. Cohen

states: "The argument here is that the decision to sell may be set for debtors by their lenders, who advance money through an embodied calculus of collateral value. In other words, the aggressiveness with which moneylenders call in debts may correlate with whether a debtor lives in an area that has become a kidney zone. If so, the decision whether or not to sell is a response not simply to some naturalized state of poverty, but to a debt crisis that might not have happened if the option to sell were not present." Cohen, "Where It Hurts," 152.

17 What trauma did and was made to do among women in the daily-rent hotels provided another ethnographic rendering of Fassin and Rechtman's claim: "Trauma is not confined to the psychiatric vocabulary; it is embedded in everyday usage." Where my ethnographic rendering differs from the examples offered in *The Empire of Trauma* and also from Veena Das's work on social suffering in the aftermath of the Partition is in the complex relationship between event and the construction of trauma in my ethnographic setting. This is not because "trauma," so conceptualized, is individually idiosyncratic among women, and not a collective experience. As Fassin and Rechtman point out, the "politics of trauma" requires a bridging of the individual and collective: "The politics of trauma [are defined by the fact that] the collective event supplies the substance of the trauma which will be articulated in individual experience; in return individual suffering bears witness to the traumatic aspect of the collective dramas." Fassin and Rechtman, *Empire of Trauma*, 18. The ethnographic difference in my work centered on a qualitative and temporal economy of scale.

18 See Smith, Smith, and Earp, "Beyond the Measurement Trap"; Saxe and Wolfe, "Gender and Post-traumatic Stress Disorder," in *Post-Traumatic Stress Disorder*; Jenkins, "Sexual Abuse: A Process, Not an Event"; and Wasco, "Conceptualizing the Harm Done by Rape," for discussions of problematic epidemiological renderings of trauma and event.

19 In contrast to Angela Garcia's description of unending addiction and melancholia among New Mexican heroin users, the affective climate among addicted women in daily-rent hotels registered as the routinized, constant stress of potential and real victimization. See Garcia, *The Pastoral Clinic*.

20 See chapter 3.

21 Fassin and Rechtman conclude their analysis of the conceptualization and circulation of trauma discourse by saying, "We believe that the truth about trauma lies not in the psyche, the mind, or the brain, but in the moral economy of contemporary society." Fassin and Rechtman, *Empire of Trauma*, 276.

22 Methadone maintenance programs frequently urine test patients for methadone, cocaine, prescription pain killers, and other drugs.

23 Wisner, Perel, and Findling, "Antidepressant Treatment during Breast-Feeding"; and Greden, "Treatment of Recurrent Depression."

24 Wisner, Perel, and Findling, "Antidepressant Treatment during Breast-Feeding."

25 Jones and Smith, "Puerperal Psychosis: Identifying and Caring for Women at Risk."

26 See Ginsburg and Rapp, *Conceiving the New World Order*. See also chapter 5.

27 Colfax et al., "Amphetamine-Group Substances and HIV."

28 See Bourgois, "The Moral Economies of Homeless Heroin Addicts."

29 See German, Davey, and Latkin, "Residential Transience and HIV Risk Behaviors among Injection Drug Users"; and Davey-Rothwell, German, and Latkin, "Residential Transience and Depression." See chapter 1 for a detailed discussion of residential transience.

30 I am borrowing this term from Hacking and from Young. See Hacking, *Mad Travellers*; and Young, "America's Transient Mental Illness," in *Subjectivity*.

Chapter 5: Stratified Reproduction and Kin of Last Resort

1 The Substance Abuse and Crime Prevention Act, also known as Proposition 36, was passed by 61 percent of California voters on November 7, 2000. This vote permanently changed state law to allow first- and second-time nonviolent, simple drug possession offenders the opportunity to receive substance abuse treatment instead of incarceration. Proposition 36 went into effect on July 1, 2001, with $120 million for treatment services allocated annually for five years. According to the Drug Policy Alliance: "In its first seven years, Prop. 36 graduated 84,000 participants, saved the state nearly $2 billion, expanded treatment capacity by 132 percent and reduced the number of drug offenders in prison. Despite Prop. 36's demonstrated cost savings and public safety record, funding decisions ten years later confirm that treatment in California remains secondary to punishment. Over a four-year period, California entirely eliminated treatment funding for Prop. 36—from a high of $145 million in 2007–08 to nothing in 2010–11." Drug Policy Alliance website, http://www.drugpolicy.org/departments-and-state-offices/california/proposition-36-victory, accessed March 15, 2015.

2 Ginsburg and Rapp, *Conceiving the New World Order*, 1.

3 Ginsburg and Rapp, *Conceiving the New World Order*, 3.

4 See for example Scheper-Hughes, *Death without Weeping*; Ginsburg and Rapp, *Conceiving the New World Order*.

5 See Schoen, *Choice and Coercion*; Larson, *Sex, Race and Science*; Reilly, *The Surgical Solution*; Davis, *Women, Race, and Class*; Dreifus, "Sterilizing the Poor," in *Seizing Our Bodies*; and Pickens, "The Sterilization Movement."

6 Waller, "LaBruzzo: Sterilization Plan Fights Poverty: Tying Poor Women's Tubes Could Help Taxpayers, Legislator Says," *New Orleans Times-Picayune*, September 24, 2008.

7 Campbell, *Using Women*, 1.

8 Campbell, *Using Women*, 1, 35.

9 Campbell, *Using Women*, 138.

10 *Born Hooked: Confronting the Impact of Perinatal Substance Abuse*, Hearing before the Select Committee on Children, Youth, and Families, House of Representatives, 101st Cong., 1st sess., April 27, 1989, ERIC no. ED314920. Abstract: "This

hearing was called to develop a better understanding of the damage to women and their babies resulting from substance abuse during pregnancy. The hearing transcript addresses prevalence and trends, impacts on mothers and children, impacts on health care costs, impacts on the child welfare system, legal and health policy issues, intervention strategies, and policy recommendations. The document contains statements, letters, and supplemental materials from: (1) Congressional Representatives Thomas Bliley, Jr., Ronald Machtley, George Miller, Nancy Pelosi, Charles Rangel, and Curt Weldon; (2) nurses, doctors, child development specialists, health educators, hospital directors, and substance abuse specialists; (3) attorneys; and (4) a representative of the National Council of Juvenile and Family Court Judges. Included are the findings from a telephone survey of 14 public and 4 private hospitals in 15 cities, and article reprints from a newsletter and two medical journals."

11 Campbell, *Using Women*, 139, 183.

12 Campbell, *Using Women*, 191.

13 National Institute on Drug Abuse–funded studies entitled "An Ethnographic Study of Pregnancy and Drug Use" (Rosenbaum and Murphy 1991–94); "An Ethnography of Victimization, Pregnancy and Drug Use" (Murphy 1995–98).

14 Murphy and Sales borrow the concept of "ideological offensives from 'Vincent Navarro, a medical sociologist who analyzed trends in national and international health care provision [and] reminds us that a radical reconstructing of a social welfare system . . . cannot take place only by repression but has to rely on active ideological offensive that could create a new consensus around a new set of values, beliefs, and practices" (1986, p. 26). Quoted in Murphy and Sales, "Pregnant Drug Users."

15 Public Law No. 104–193.

16 See Pollack and Reuter, "Welfare Receipt and Substance-Abuse Treatment among Low-Income Mothers"; National Abandoned Infants Assistance Resource Center, *AIA Fact Sheet: Prenatal Substance Use Exposure*, 2012, http://aia.berkeley.edu, accessed March 15, 2015.

17 Harvey, *Brief History of Neoliberalism*, 23, 31.

18 At the population level, Harvey argues that the "financialization of everything" led to the harsh reality: "In the event of a conflict between Main Street and Wall Street, the latter was always favored." This is eerily reminiscent of circulating questions about why the US Treasury released the majority of the $750 billion bailout monies to banks as opposed to spending the money to prevent housing foreclosures on "Main Street." In other words, Americans, and others, are facing a crash course in the mechanisms and forms of accountability that exist in a neoliberal, finance-driven economic collapse. In this sense Harvey's descriptions of Mexico's experience with structural adjustment resonate with the current US context. Vincanne Adams has offered an updated analysis of this neoliberalizing effect among Hurricane Katrina survivors struggling to rebuild, which indicates that this process has intensified rather than abated since its inception in the

1990s. See Harvey, *Brief History of Neoliberalism*, and Adams, *Markets of Sorrow, Labors of Faith*.

19 Harvey, *Brief History of Neoliberalism*, 53.

20 Lexi reported having an incompetent cervix. "Incompetent cervix" is a medical term: "A cervix (the structure at the bottom of the uterus) that is incompetent is abnormally weak, and therefore it can gradually widen during pregnancy. Left untreated, this can result in repeated pregnancy losses or premature delivery." http://medical-dictionary.thefreedictionary.com/Incompetent+Cervix, accessed March 15, 2015. Also see http://www.mayoclinic.org/diseases-conditions/incompetent-cervix/basics/definition/con-20035375, accessed March 15, 2015. I did not access the medical records from Lexi's birth to assess what medical professionals attributed as the cause of the infant's death.

21 See Barry, Osbourne, and Rose, *Foucault and Political Reason*.

22 Murphy and Sales, "Pregnant Drug Users."

23 I borrow the construct of biological citizenship and the definition of "social suffering" from Petryna, who draws a connection between pain and suffering as a manifestation on the one hand of a personal experience/history and on the other of social context. The mediation between the embodied and the social comes to "illustrate the extent to which explanations and claims of health and their failures are understood within the scientific, economic, and political domains in which they are coming to be addressed." Petryna, *Life Exposed*, 14–15.

24 In Flavin's account, addicted pregnancy demonstrates "how the criminal justice system responds to the threat that women's sexuality and reproductive behaviors pose to the dominant order." Flavin argues that neither addiction nor pregnancy is a crime, but rather the act of remaining pregnant is being adjudicated: "Neither being addicted nor being pregnant is a crime. Some law enforcement officials and prosecutors, operating under false assumptions that a woman's drug dependency is inevitably and irreversibly harming her unborn child, have persisted in pursuing charges against pregnant women. They define the problem as being one of a woman who uses drugs while she is pregnant. The problem is more accurately defined as being one of a woman becoming pregnant and remaining pregnant. If a woman who is already addicted to drugs becomes pregnant, the only way she can be assured of avoiding criminal charges is to get an abortion. In other words, it is a woman's decision to continue her pregnancy that is being criminalized, more so than the fact of her addiction and continued drug use." Flavin, *Our Bodies, Our Crimes*, 5. See also Calhoun, "The Criminalization of Bad Mothers."

25 Guttmacher Institute, *State Policies in Brief: Substance Abuse during Pregnancy*. Fact sheet (New York: Guttmacher Institute, March 1, 2015). http://www.guttmacher.org/statecenter/spibs/spib_SADP.pdf, accessed March 15, 2015.

26 R. Newman (contact) and forty clinician coauthors. "Open Letter to the Media and Policy Makers Regarding Alarmist and Inaccurate Reporting on Prescription Opiate Use by Pregnant Women" (March 13, 2013). http://advocatesforpregnant women.org/issues/pregnancy_and_drug_use_the_facts/experts_urge_media

_to_end_inaccurate_reporting_on_prescription_opiate_use_by_pregnant_women
.php, accessed March 15, 2015.

27 Nora Volkow, director of the National Institute of Drug Abuse, quoted in *Co-morbidity: Addiction and Other Mental Illnesses*, NIDA Research Report Series, NIH pub. no. 08–5771 (Rockville, MD: U.S. Dept. of Health and Human Services, National Institutes of Health, National Institute on Drug Abuse, 2008), http://www.oregon.gov/oha/amh/co-occurring/co-morbidity.pdf, accessed March 15, 2015. See Valverde, *Diseases of the Will*.

28 See also Garriott, "'You Can Always Tell Who Is Using Meth," in *Addiction Trajectories*, for a discussion of how scientific knowledge about addiction is incorporated into the logics of criminalization, thus "complicating easy dichotomies between treatment and punishment, sickness and badness, retribution and rehabilitation" among methamphetamine addicts in West Virginia (215).

29 Term attributed to Michel-Rolph Trouillot; Trouillot, "Anthropology and the Savage Slot," chap. 1 in *Global Transformations*.

30 Chasnoff, Landress, and Barrett, "The Prevalence of Illicit-Drug or Alcohol Use during Pregnancy and Discrepancies in Mandatory Reporting in Pinellas County, Florida." Campbell, *Using Women*, chap. 7. Alexander, *The New Jim Crow*.

31 Lillie-Blanton, Anthony, and Schuster, "Probing the Meaning of Racial/Ethnic Group Comparisons in Crack Cocaine Smoking."

32 As discussed in the introduction, the sample of women I worked with in this study was ethnically diverse. The female tenants in the daily hotels, and the smaller sample of women whose pregnancies I followed, were approximately one-third white, one-third African-American, and one-third Latina. Also see Table A.1, this volume.

33 See Havens et al., "Factors Associated with Substance Use during Pregnancy"; Lester et al., "The Maternal Lifestyle Study."

34 See Frank et al., "Growth, Development, and Behavior in Early Childhood Following Prenatal Cocaine Exposure"; Chavkin, "Cocaine and Pregnancy—Time to Look at the Evidence"; and Aronson, "Cocaine," in *Meyler's Side Effects of Psychiatric Drugs*.

35 Crack babies are a point of origin for the modern tale of drug-exposed babies; however, as Nancy Campbell points out, the history of surveillance of pregnant women's drug and alcohol consumption precedes the "crack epidemic" of the 1980s. See *Using Women*. "Meth babies" refers to infants prenatally exposed to methamphetamine, and "oxybabies" to infants prenatally exposed to the prescription opioid analgesic medication Oxycontin (oxycodone).

36 See Calhoun, "Criminalization of Bad Mothers."

37 Okie, "Crack Babies: The Epidemic That Wasn't."

38 Fitzgerald, "'Crack Baby' Study Ends with Unexpected but Clear Result."

39 Okie, "Crack Babies."

40 See Lester et al., "Maternal Lifestyle Study; National Abandoned Infants Assistance Resource Center," *AIA Fact Sheet*.

41 See Wacquant's discussion of folk categories in urban ethnography in Wacquant, *Urban Outcasts*.

42 See Campbell, *Using Women*, chap. 7, for a discussion of drug policy implications of this political discourse.

43 Murphy and Sales, "Pregnant Drug Users."

44 Nancy Scheper-Hughes argued persuasively two decades ago that maternal love is susceptible to social and economic environments that place limits on its affordability, its price. Maternal love is malleable, flexible, and socially constructed. Explained ethnographically by Scheper-Hughes, maternal love is not a universal human form but rather a luxury to which the poor and hungry residents of Bom Jesus in northeastern Brazil were not privy during Scheper-Hughes's anthropological work there. Arguably, one of the most significant interventions that her book *Death without Weeping* makes is her insistence that this fact was eminently obvious—using a common-sense logic—to the pregnant women of Bom Jesus. It required multiple repetitions and interactions for the Western anthropologist to recognize lack of maternal love as something other than individuated pathology.

45 Donohue, Cevasco, and Rosenthal, "A Decade of Direct-to-Consumer Advertising of Prescription Drugs."

46 See Acker, *Creating the American Junkie*; and Campbell, *Using Women*.

47 Campbell, *Using Women*, 65.

48 Tanya Luhrmann has argued that residual shame in the psychiatric community over blaming and stigmatizing so many mothers for a disease that is now considered primarily organic in nature has largely contributed to the eager acceptability of the biomedicialization of that mental illness. Luhrmann, "Social Defeat and the Culture of Chronicity."

49 As Campbell writes, "Dysfunctional families may be seen as an outcome of social practices, or as the sum of the pathological individuals within them. As a nation we prefer the latter explanation, locating 'problematic mothering' as the source of our dysfunctionalities." *Using Women*, 168.

50 See Barnard and McKeganey, "The Impact of Parental Problem Drug Use on Children"; and O'Connor, Kogan, and Findlay, "Prenatal Alcohol Exposure and Attachment Behavior in Children."

51 See Asanbe and Lockert, "Cognitive Abilities of African American Children with Prenatal Cocaine/Polydrug Exposure"; Behnke, Eyler, Warner, Garvan, Hou, and Wobie, "Outcome from a Prospective Longitudinal Study of Prenatal Cocaine Use: Preschool Development at 3 Years of Age."

52 Insel and Quirion, "Psychiatry as a Clinical Neuroscience Discipline."

53 Video on the website of the Homeless Prenatal Program of San Francisco, http://homelessprenatal.org, accessed March 15, 2015.

54 B. Lester, "Long-Term Effects of Prenatal Substance Exposure on Children," webinar sponsored by the National Abandoned Infants Assistance Resource Center, University of California, Berkeley, February 26, 2013. http://aia.berkeley.edu, accessed March 15, 2015.

55 Lester and Padbury, "Third Pathophysiology of Prenatal Cocaine Exposure."

56 Because my role did not involve systematically testing women for pregnancy in the hotels, I cannot be certain that I was aware of all the pregnancies that occurred—although, as part of the outreach effort, I did give out pregnancy tests on demand and I was able to interview several women in the ethnography as a result of giving them the test. Still, I am sure there were several women who may have tested positive and terminated the pregnancy early on. Kitt was the only women who discussed her abortion with me, and she deferred the procedure until relatively late in her pregnancy (twenty weeks).

57 Cohen, "Operability, Bioavailability, and Exception," in *Global Assemblages*.

58 According to the Substance Use and Mental Health Service Administration data, while most pregnant women decrease their intake of addictive substances during pregnancy, most also increase their use after birth: "The rates of past month illicit drug, alcohol, and tobacco use among recent mothers were higher than the rates of pregnant women and similar to the rates for nonpregnant women. For example, among women aged 15 to 44, the rate of past month illicit drug use for recent mothers (9 percent) was similar to the rate among nonpregnant women (10 percent), with both groups reporting a higher rate of past month illicit drug use than pregnant women (3 percent). The data presented . . . suggest that women aged 15 to 44 use alcohol, tobacco, and illicit drugs less during pregnancy, but increase their substance use after giving birth." Substance Use and Mental Health Service Administration, *Pregnancy and Substance Use*, National Survey on Drug Use and Health Report, January 2, 2004.

59 Hopper et al., "Homelessness, Severe Mental Illness, and the Institutional Circuit."

60 Wacquant, *Urban Outcasts*.

61 Hopper uses the construct "liminality," which references the "dicey uncertainty of transitional states" to understand how homelessness is a process of in-between living, not an end in and of itself. "Liminality" is an anthropological, not sociological, concept that was coined by Van Gennup (a Belgian folklorist) at the turn of the twentieth century, using the Latin/Roman word for "threshold." Liminality was taken up by Victor Turner to describe rituals that remove the person from one social state and move the person through a transition into another one. To Hopper, the social problem of homelessness is not a question of laziness or addiction. Rather, homeless persons are those who are redundant in labor markets and lacking support for that redundancy. Hopper writes: "Reframing homelessness as the problem of redundant people, lacking sufficient resources (money or kin) to secure housing, redirects our assessment of the social response to homelessness. It may make better sense to think of 'regular access to a conventional dwelling' more as *work* than *residence*, in ways analogous to those used by economists in measuring 'regular access to a conventional job.'" Hopper, *Reckoning with Homelessness*, 19.

Chapter 6: Victim-Perpetrators

1 A "social admit" is short for "social [hospital] admission." For a period of time in the 2000s, it was common practice for providers to "socially admit" patients to the hospital whom clinicians knew were homeless. The social admit ensured that the medical conditions that had led to the hospitalization did not become much worse due to homelessness. It could also "buy time" to try and acquire housing and other social services for the patient. Hospital administrators recognized the high short-term health care costs associated with this practice and formally disallowed it.

2 Hopper et al., "Homelessness, Severe Mental Illness, and the Institutional Circuit."

3 Knight, "The Public Life of Sex Work."

4 There are divergent interpretations of the concept of "structural violence." This literature draws on the conception of structural violence as neglect. One definition—which many public health sociologists adopt—discusses increased morbidity and mortality as life spans are reduced when people are socially dominated, politically oppressed, or economically exploited. "Sickness is a result of structural violence: neither culture nor pure individual will is at fault; rather, historically given (and often economically driven) processes and forces conspire to constrain individual agency. Structural violence is visited upon all those whose social status denies them access to the fruits of scientific and social progress." Farmer, *Infections and Inequality*, 14. Also see Wacquant, "Violence from Above," 30. See Massey and Denton, *American Apartheid*; and Wilson, *The Truly Disadvantaged*.

5 See Bourgois, *In Search of Respect*; Bourgois and Schonberg, *Righteous Dopefiend*; and Wacquant, *Urban Outcasts*.

6 Engels, *Conditions of the Working Class in England in 1844*, 158.

7 Harvey, *A Brief History of Neoliberalism*, 45, 56, 48.

8 Vlahov et al., "Urban as a Determinant of Health," 116.

9 Medical anthropologist Merrill Singer originally developed the concept of a syndemic. See Singer and Clair, "Syndemics and Public Health: Reconceptualizing Disease in Bio-Social Context."

10 Freudenberg et al., "The Impact of New York City's 1975 Fiscal Crisis," 424.

11 Freudenburg et al., "The Impact of New York City's 1975 Fiscal Crisis," 430.

12 See Rhodes et al. for a discussion of the interplay between macro, meso, and micro factors in public health studies of risk among people who inject drugs. Rhodes et al., "The Social Structural Production of HIV Risk among Injecting Drug Users."

13 Lemke, "'The Birth of Biopolitics,'" 201; and Foucault, *The Birth of Biopolitics*, 144. See also Wendy Brown for a broader discussion of the impact of neoliberal rationality on our understandings of freedom, equality, and solidarity, as well as our democratic participation in the political process. Brown, *Undoing the Demos*.

14 O'Malley, "Risk and Responsibility," in *Foucault and Political Reason*, 204.

15 O'Malley, "Risk and Responsibility," 203, citing Y. Aharoni, *The No-Risk Society*.

16 In his lectures *The Birth of Biopolitics*, Foucault argues that neoliberalism does

not equate with benign neglect; neoliberalism marks the emergence of a new form of *Homo oeconomicus*, "the entrepreneur of himself" (221). Criminality becomes yet another market to American neoliberals, and risk is further privatized. See Knight, "The Public Life of Sex Work."

17 Some of the findings in this section have been published elsewhere. See Knight et al., "Single Room Occupancy."

18 See chapter 1 for a discussion of the political economy of privately owned versus publicly managed hotels.

19 North et al., "A Diagnostic Comparison of Homeless and Nonhomeless Patients in an Urban Mental Health Clinic"; and North, Smith, and Spitznagel, "Is Antisocial Personality a Valid Diagnosis among the Homeless?"

20 American Psychiatric Association, *DSMIV-TR, Quick Reference* (Washington, DC: APA Press, 2000), Cluster B Personality Disorders, 301.7, Antisocial Personality Disorder, 291.

21 In her ethnography Somerset Carr explores the ways drug-addicted women are enlisted into specific forms of therapeutic discourse. She argues that "since the specialists' evaluative powers are linked with the capacity to distribute basic goods and resources, [patients'] ritual performance—that is, the way you speak in the course of your treatment—has far reaching material and symbolic consequences." See Carr, *Scripting Addiction*, chap. 6.

22 See Burke et al., "Intimate Partner Violence, Substance Use, and HIV among Low-Income Women: Taking a Closer Look"; El-Bassel et al., "HIV and Intimate Partner Violence among Methadone-Maintained Women in New York City"; Wechsberg et al., "Violence, Homelessness, and HIV Risk among Crack-Using African-American Women"; Nyamathi, Leake, and Gelberg, "Sheltered versus Nonsheltered Homeless Women Differences in Health, Behavior, Victimization, and Utilization of Care"; Theall, Sterk, and Elifson, "Past and New Victimization among African American Female Drug Users Who Participated in an HIV Risk-Reduction Intervention"; El-Bassel et al., "Correlates of Partner Violence among Female Street-Based Sex Workers"; Wenzel, Koegel, and Gelberg, "Antecedents of Physical and Sexual Victimization among Homeless Women"; and Wenzel et al., "Physical Violence against Impoverished Women."

23 Curry, "The Interrelationships between Abuse, Substance Use, and Psychosocial Stress during Pregnancy"; Norton et al., "Battering in Pregnancy"; McFarlane, Parker, and Soeken, "Abuse during Pregnancy"; Coker, Sanderson, and Dong, "Partner Violence during Pregnancy and Risk of Adverse Pregnancy Outcomes"; Bullock et al., "Retrospective Study of the Association of Stress and Smoking during Pregnancy in Rural Women"; and Gelles, "Violence and Pregnancy."

24 See chapter 2 for a description of epidemiological time.

25 See also Bourgois, "The Moral Economies of Homeless Heroin Addicts," for a description of how the moral economy of drug and needle sharing within social networks of homeless heroin addicts contradicts their reported behaviors to anthropologists and on health surveys.

26 See Eaton, "A Brazzaville Friendship."
27 See Surfrin, "Jailcare: The Safety Net of a U.S. Women's Jail."
28 See Calhoun, "The Criminalization of Bad Mothers."

Conclusion

1 "Memento mori" translates from Latin as "remember (that you have) to die," http://
www.oxforddictionaries.com/definition/english/memento-mori, accessed March 15,
2015. "The origins of memento mori photographs can be traced back nearly to
the beginning of photography itself. During the nineteenth century, post-mortem
portraits were used to acknowledge and mourn the death of a loved one, especially a baby or child. All social classes engaged in the practice, which became
more widespread after the introduction of the daguerreotype in 1839. The subjects of the photos were generally arranged to appear as if peacefully asleep, all
their earthly suffering ended. Displayed prominently in the household alongside
other family photographs, the portraits helped heal grieving hearts by preserving
some trace of the deceased." Tetens, "Group Revives Victorian Custom of Post-
mortem Portraiture to Help Grieving Parents," February 15, 2007, http://victorian
peeper.blogspot.com/2007/02/group-revives-custom-of-post-mortem.html, accessed March 15, 2015. See also Burns and Burns, *Sleeping Beauty II*; and Meinwald, *Memento Mori: Death and Photography in 19th Century America*, http://
vv.arts.ucla.edu/terminals/meinwald/meinwald1.html, accessed March 15, 2015.
2 Canguilhem, *The Normal and the Pathological*, 161.
3 See Rose, "Neurochemical Selves," in *The Politics of Life Itself*.
4 Foucault discusses a politics of life, social policy, and the assurance of a minimum
of health in *The Birth of Biopolitics*. Foucault argues that social policy "cannot
have equality as its objective" but must instead only authorize the insurance of a
"vital minimum" from those who have the most economic resources in society
to those who are permanently or temporarily disabled. Foucault acknowledges
that assessing the "vital minimum" is, of course, subjective. In neoliberal political
settings, these social policies serve to divorce the state from any responsibility
for individual or collective risk management in what Foucault calls a "privatized
social policy." Drawing from Dankwart Rustow's notion that social policies create
a "Vitalpolitik" or a "politics of life," Foucault describes vital politics as "not a
matter of constructing a social fabric in which the individual would be in direct
contact with nature, but of constructing a social fabric in which precisely the
basic units would have the form of enterprise, for what is private property if not
enterprise?" (*The Birth of Biopolitics*, 242). Individuals in society are managed
not in relation to nature but in relation to entrepreneurial and private ownership.
Those who fail to cling to this social fabric must be disciplined to become more
successful "entrepreneurs of self," according to Foucault.
5 Project Prevention's Facebook page description, https://www.facebook.com/
pages/Project-Prevention/, accessed March 15, 2015.

6 Jane Beresford, "Should Drug Addicts Be Paid to Be Sterilized?," online commentary, BBC *News Magazine*, February 8, 2010, http://news.bbc.co.uk/2/hi/uk_news /magazine/8500285.stm, accessed March 15, 2015; identifying names have been removed from the online posts.

7 Taussig, *The Magic of the State*.

8 In his writing about modernity in Africa, Achille Mbembe describes a "necropolitics." In the postcolony, the colonized must delegate death to and against an "other," or defer it. Mbembe writes: "How is it possible to live while going to death, while being somehow already dead? And how can one *live in death*, be already dead, while being-there—while having not necessarily left the world or being part of the spectre—and when the shadow that overhangs existence has not disappeared, but on the contrary weighs ever more heavily? . . . First, by being, literally, *several in a single body*. 'We are twelve in my body. We are packed like sardines.' In other words, the *being* that I am exists each time in *several modes*—or, let us say, several beings, which, although sometimes mutually exclusive, are nevertheless inside one another. . . . This virtually constant passage from the single to the multiple must be performed in the very compartments of ordinary life, as circumstance and events occur. . . . One still needs to know how to recognize oneself in these multiples, notably when they give out signals, lurch, liquefy, or do monstrous things. . . . In the postcolony, it is power to delegate oneself that . . . enables one to delegate one's death to another, or at least to constantly defer it, until the final rendezvous. It follows that death, in its essence, can very well, each time, not be mine, my death; the other can die in my stead." Mbembe, *On the Postcolony*, 201–202.

9 Aggie Max, *The Last Resort: Scenes from a Transient Hotel*, 116.

10 Foucault writes: "So the question is not: Why do some people want to be dominant? What do they want? What is their overall strategy? The question is this: What happens at the moment of, at the level of the procedure of subjugation, or in the continuous and uninterrupted processes that subjugate bodies, direct gestures and regulate forms of behavior? In other words, rather than asking ourselves what the sovereign looks like from on high, we should be trying to discover how multiple bodies, forces, energies, matters, desires, thoughts and so on are gradually progressively, actually, and materially constituted as subjects, or as the subject." Foucault, *History of Sexuality*, 124–125. For Joan Comaroff the "continuities and discontinuities of the modern Tshindi world" are only accessible through a historical analysis that reveals that the "articulation" of the relationship between global systems and local formations, "while inherently contradictory and unequal, is not universally determining" (*Body of Power, Spirit of Resistance*, 155). Comaroff finds the Zionist movement among the Tshindi particularly illustrative of the ways the body is the ground of social suffering and of healing, that religion can arrive initially wearing the face of spiritual imperialism—to impart colonist ideologies of exploitation and dependence—and, in a future guise, come to criticize those ideologies. She writes that the "desired transformations focus

upon 'healing' as a mode of repairing the tormented body and through it, the oppressive social order itself. Thus the signs of physical discord are simultaneously the signifiers of an aberrant world" (*Body of Power, Spirit of Resistance*, 9).

11 Potter et al., "Factors Associated with Prenatal Care Use among Peripartum Women in the Mother-Infant Rapid Intervention and Delivery Study."

12 Vincanne Adams has commented about the hierarchies of attention attributed to public health problems according to their statistical power. When participating in a clinical trial of a technology to decrease maternal mortality, Adams was part of a research team who were told there would not be enough maternal death in their region of study to merit funding for their research project. Adams et al., "The Challenge of Cross-Cultural Clinical Trials Research."

13 Campbell, *Using Women.*

14 Carr, "Women Seek Stability in the sros"; Goodby and Minters, "A Family Home in an sro."

15 Nancy Scheper-Hughes famously asked "Who's the Killer?" in her essay exploring the trial of three boys for the murder of a young white female antiapartheid activist (Amy Biehl) in a South African township riot. In a conversation between anthropologist Scheper-Hughes and Nona Goso, a defense lawyer, during the murder trial in South Africa, Scheper-Hughes asks: "What can you tell me about the defendants?" And Goso replies: "In every sense, they are children . . . in fact, lovely children, like any other. Under normal circumstances, they would have had a wonderful, normal life. But they are children of apartheid. Most come from broken homes and from deprived families where no one is working. Education is out of the question. . . . They have experienced everything, been exposed to everything." Scheper-Hughes, "'Who's the Killer?,'" 56.

16 Many psychoanalysts could not, in their wildest nightmares, have predicted in 1985 that by 2005, 27 million people in the United States (or 10 percent of the population) would be taking antidepressant medications. "Better" drugs changed the market, and physicians have become inundated with pressure to prescribe them. The increase in media-generated images and public discourse about depression is thought to have combatted social stigma about the condition and to have contributed to the doubling of medication rates. We have observed similar shifts occurring in the publicly mediated representations of addiction, demonstrated through popular culture programs and confessional works produced for public consumption. See Liz Szabo, "Number of Americans Taking Anti-depressants Doubles," *USA Today*, August 9, 2009; Dumit, *Drugs for Life*; Metzl, *Prozac on the Couch*; and Moreno et al., "Feeling Bad on Facebook."

17 H.R. 1424, the Paul Wellstone and Pete Domenici Mental Health Parity and Addiction Equity Act was a piece of legislation that was subtly attached to the $700 billion bank bailout legislation, the Troubled Assets Recovery Program, and was signed into law by President George W. Bush on October 3, 2008. Mental health care parity may have been voted in under the radar of public debate, but its implications for the health care treatment of millions of Americans with substance

use disorders are potentially profound. Prince et al., "No Health without Mental Health."

18 See Nash, "Addicted." The mediated spectacle of the public confession of drug and alcohol addiction is now commonplace in the United States. From politicians to writers and to entertainers and reality show guests, everyone appears to have an addiction struggle to share with the American public. They offer their "stories" up for public consumption with the implicit understanding that both blame (for personal failures) and sympathy (for the fact that they are "diseased") will be on offer. Addiction is near to us as we see family members, friends, and coworkers struggle with it. We watch extremely popular and lauded television shows, such as the The Wire or Breaking Bad, barely registering that the stories told and the protagonists' struggles reveal our desire to have a relationship with illicit drugs and addiction that is both familiar and alienated. Sympathetic, public confessions of addiction struggles are de rigueur in current American public culture. A local example comes from San Francisco mayor Gavin Newsom's public admission of alcoholism and rehabilitation. See Knight, Vega, and Matier, "Newsom Seeks Treatment for Alcohol Abuse." A website listing hundreds of celebrity addicts, whose names include J. Paul Getty Jr., Eminem, Daryl Strawberry, Prince Harry, Mary Tyler Moore, and Tonya Harding, is circulating in the public domain because "drug and alcohol addiction knows no boundaries when it comes to social classes, wealth, ethnicity or status. Addiction is a part of every group of people everywhere" (http://www.drugalcohol-rehab.com/famous-addicts.htm, accessed March 15, 2015). The hugely popular reality TV program Intervention, on the A&E cable network, which won the 2009 Emmy Award for Outstanding Reality Series, charts the personal and family lives of everyday Americans who are struggling with drug and alcohol addiction, as well as "other compulsive disorders" (http://www.aetv.com, accessed March 15, 2015). The public perception appears to be that addiction can affect anyone's brain and ruin anyone's life.

19 See Abelson, "On the Threshold of Obamacare, Warily."

20 National Institute of Drug Abuse, Drugs, Brains, and Behavior: The Science of Addiction, NIH pub. no. 07–5605.

21 See Raikhel and Garriott, Addiction Trajectories.

22 See Lakoff, Pharmaceutical Reason; Luhrmann, Of Two Minds; and Luhrmann, "Social Defeat and the Culture of Chronicity," for discussion of these tensions in the field of psychology/psychiatry in Argentina and the United States, respectively.

23 Sellman, "The 10 Most Important Things Known about Addiction."

24 See Bourgois and Schonberg, Righteous Dopefiend.

25 See Nader, "Up the Anthropologist: Perspectives Gained from Studying Up," in Reinventing Anthropology.

26 The epigraph to this section is from Fassin and Rechtman, The Empire of Trauma, 284.

27 U.S. Substance Use and Mental Health Service Administration, Pregnancy and Substance Use, National Survey on Drug Use and Health Report, January 2, 2004.

28 Levinas, Entre Nous.

bibliography

Books and Journal Articles

Abar, B., L. L. LaGasse, T. Wouldes, C. Derauf, E. Newman, R. Shah, L. M. Smith, A. M. Arria, M. A. Huestis, S. DellaGrotta, L. M. Dansereau, T. Wilcox, C. R. Neal, B. M. Lester. "Cross-National Comparison of Prenatal Methamphetamine Exposure on Infant and Early Child Physical Growth: A Natural Experiment." *Prevention Science* 15(5) (2014): 767–776.

Acker, C. J. *Creating the American Junkie: Addiction Research in the Classic Era of Narcotic Control*. Baltimore: John Hopkins University Press, 2002.

Adams, V. *Markets of Sorrow, Labors of Faith: New Orleans in the Wake of Katrina*. Durham, NC: Duke University Press, 2013.

Aday, Lu Ann. "Health Status of Vulnerable Populations." *Annual Review of Public Health* 15 (1994): 487–509.

Aharoni, Y. *The No-Risk Society*. Chatham, NJ: Chatham House, 1981.

Alexander, M. *The New Jim Crow: Mass Incarceration in the Age of Colorblindness*. New York: The New Press, 2011.

Aronson, J. K. "Cocaine." In *Meyler's Side Effects of Psychiatric Drugs*. Amsterdam: Elsevier Science, 2008.

Asanbe, C. B., and E. Lockert. "Cognitive Abilities of African American Children with Prenatal Cocaine/Polydrug Exposure." *Journal of Health Care for the Poor and Underserved* 17(2) (2006): 400–412.

Barnard, M., and L. McKeganey. "The Impact of Parental Problem Drug Use on Children: What Is the Problem and What Can Be Done to Help?" *Addiction* 99(5) (2004): 552–559.

Barrow, S. M., and Nicole D. Laborde. "Invisible Mothers: Parenting by Homeless Women Separated from their Children." *Gender Issues* 25 (2008): 157–172.

Barry, A., T. Osbourne, and N. Rose. *Foucault and Political Reason: Liberalism, Neoliberalism and Rationalities of Government*. Chicago: University of Chicago Press, 1996.

Bassuk, E. L., S. Melnick, and A. Browne. "Responding to the Needs of Low-Income and Homeless Women Who Are Survivors of Family Violence." *Journal of the American Medical Women's Association* 53(2) (1998): 57–64.

Behnke, M., F. D. Eyler, T. D. Warner, C. W. Garvan, W. Hou, and K. Wobie. "Outcome from a Prospective Longitudinal Study of Prenatal Cocaine Use: Preschool Development at 3 Years of Age." *Journal of Pediatric Psychology* 31(1) (2006): 41–49.

Beijer, U., A. Wolf, and S. Fazel. "Prevalence of Tuberculosis, Hepatitis C Virus, and HIV in Homeless People: A Systematic Review and Meta-Analysis." *Lancet: Infectious Diseases* 12(11) (November 2012): 859–870.

Bessa, M. A., S. S. Mitsuhiro, E. Chalem, M. M. Barros, R. Guinsburg, and R. Laranjeira. "Underreporting of Use of Cocaine and Marijuana during the Third Trimester of Gestation among Pregnant Adolescents." *Addictive Behaviors* 35(3) (2010): 266–269.

Biehl, J. *Will to Live: AIDS Therapies and the Politics of Survival.* Princeton: Princeton University Press, 2009.

Bluthenthal, R. N., J. Lorvick, A. H. Kral, and E. A. Erringer. "Collateral Damage in the War on Drugs: HIV Risk Behaviors among Injection Drug Users." *International Journal of Drug Policy* 10 (1999): 25–38.

Bourgois, P. *In Search of Respect: Selling Crack in El Barrio.* Cambridge: Cambridge University Press, 1995.

Bourgois, P. "The Moral Economies of Homeless Heroin Addicts: Confronting Ethnography, HIV Risk, and Everyday Violence in San Francisco Shooting Encampments." *Substance Use and Misuse* 33(11) (1998): 2323–2351.

Bourgois, P., and J. Schonberg. *Righteous Dopefiend.* Berkeley: University of California Press, 2009.

Bourgois, P., B. Prince, and A. Moss. "The Everyday Violence and the Gender of Hepatitis C among Young Women Who Inject Drugs in San Francisco." *Human Organization* 63(3) (2004): 253–264.

Bowker, Geoffrey, and Susan Leigh Star. *Sorting Things Out: Classification and Its Consequences.* Cambridge, MA: MIT Press, 1999.

Boyd, S. *From Witches to Crack Moms: Women, Drug Law, and Policy.* Durham, NC: Carolina Academic Press, 2006.

Boyd, S. *Mothers and Illicit Drugs: Transcending the Myths.* Toronto: University of Toronto Press, 1999.

Braslow, J. T. "The Manufacture of Recovery." *Annual Review of Clinical Psychology* 9 (2013): 781–809.

Briggs, C. L., and C. Mantini-Briggs. *Stories in the Time of Cholera: Racial Profiling during a Medical Nightmare.* Berkeley: University of California Press, 2003.

Brodwin, Paul. *Everyday Ethics: Voices from the Front Line of Community Psychiatry.* Berkeley: University of California Press, 2013.

Brown, W. *Undoing the Demos: Neoliberalism's Stealth Revolution.* New York: Zone Books, 2015.

Browne, A., and S. S. Bassuk. "Intimate Violence in the Lives of Homeless and Poor Housed Women: Prevalence and Patterns in an Ethnically Diverse Sample." *American Journal of Orthopsychiatry* 67(2) (1997): 261–278.

Bullock, L. F. C., J. L. C. Mears, C. Woodcock, and R. Record. "Retrospective Study of the Association of Stress and Smoking during Pregnancy in Rural Women." *Addictive Behaviors* 26 (2001): 405–413.

Burke, J. G., L. K. Thieman, A. C. Gielen, P. O'Campo, and K. A. McDonnell. "Intimate Partner Violence, Substance Use, and HIV among Low-Income Women: Taking a Closer Look." *Violence Against Women* 11(9) (2005): 1140–1161.

Burns, S. B., and E. A. Burns. *Sleeping Beauty II: Grief, Bereavement in Memorial Photography: American and European Traditions*. New York: Burns Archive Press, 2002.

Butler, J. *Giving an Account of Oneself*. New York: Fordham University Press, 2005.

Campbell, N. D. *Using Women: Gender, Drug Policy, and Social Justice*. New York: Routledge, 2001.

Canguilhem, G. *The Normal and the Pathological*. 1966; reprint, Cambridge, MA: Zone Books, 1989.

Caplan, P. *They Say You're Crazy: How the World's Most Powerful Psychiatrists Decide Who's Normal*. New York: Addison-Wesley, 1995.

Carr, G. "Ethnography of an HIV Hotel." *Journal of the Association of Nurses in AIDS Care* 7(2) (1996): 35–42.

Carr, S. *Scripting Addiction: The Politics of Therapeutic Talk and American Sobriety*. Princeton: Princeton University Press, 2010.

Chan, Y. F., M. L. Dennis, and R. L. Funk. "Prevalence and Comorbidity of Major Internalizing and Externalizing Problems among Adolescents and Adults Presenting to Substance Abuse Treatment." *Journal of Substance Abuse Treatment* 34(1) (2008): 14–24.

Chasnoff, I. J., H. J. Landress, and M. E. Barrett. "The Prevalence of Illicit-Drug or Alcohol Use during Pregnancy and Discrepancies in Mandatory Reporting in Pinellas County, Florida." *New England Journal of Medicine* 322(17) (1990): 1202–1206.

Chavkin, W. "Cocaine and Pregnancy—Time to Look at the Evidence." *Journal of the American Medical Association*. 285(12) (2001): 1626–1628.

Christiano, A., and I. Susser. "Knowledge and Perceptions of HIV Infection among Homeless Pregnant Women." *Journal of Nurse Midwifery* 34(6) (1989): 318–322.

Clarke, A. E., L. Mamo, J. R. Fosket, J. R. Fishman, and J. K. Shim. *Biomedicalization: Technoscience, Health, and Illness in the United States*. Durham, NC: Duke University Press, 2010.

Clarke, A. E., J. K. Shim, L. Mamo, J. R. Fosket, and J. R. Fishman. "Biomedicalization: Technoscientific Transformations of Health, Illness, and U.S. Biomedicine." *American Sociological Review* 68(2) (2003): 161–194.

Cohen, L. "Operability, Bioavailability, and Exception." In *Global Assemblages*, ed. A. Ong and S. Collier, 79–90. Oxford: Blackwell, 2004.

Cohen, L. "Where It Hurts: Indian Material for an Ethics of Organ Transplantation." *Daedalus* 128(4) (1999): 135–165.

Coker, A. L., M. Sanderson, and B. Dong. "Partner Violence during Pregnancy and Risk of Adverse Pregnancy Outcomes." *Paediatric Perinatal Epidemiology* 18 (2004): 260–269.

Colfax, G., G. Santos, P. Chu, E. Vittinghoff, A. Pluddemann, S. Kumar, and C. Hart. "Amphetamine-Group Substances and HIV." *Lancet* 376(9739) (2010): 458–474.

Comaroff, J. *Body of Power, Spirit of Resistance*. Chicago: University of Chicago Press, 1985.

Crane, J., K. Quirk, and A. van der Straten. "'Come Back When You're Dying': The Commodification of AIDS among California's Urban Poor." *Social Science and Medicine* 55 (2002): 1115–1127.

Curry, M. A. "The Interrelationships between Abuse, Substance Use, and Psychosocial Stress during Pregnancy." *Journal of Obstetrics, Gynecology, and Neonatal Nursing* 27 (1998): 692–699.

Das, A. K., M. Olfson, M. J. Gameroff, D. J. Pilowsky, C. Blanco, A. Feder, R. Gross, Y. Neria, R. Lantigua, S. Shea, and M. M. Weissman. "Screening for Bipolar Disorder in a Primary Care Practice." *Journal of the American Medical Association* 293(8) (2005): 956–963.

Das, V. *Life and Words: Violence and the Descent into the Ordinary.* Berkeley: University of California Press, 2007.

Davenport, B. A. "Witnessing and the Medical Gaze: How Medical Students Learn to See at a Free Clinic for the Homeless." *Medical Anthropology Quarterly* 14(3) (2000): 310–327.

Davey-Rothwell, M. A., D. German, and C. Latkin. "Residential Transience and Depression: Does the Relationship Exist for Men and Women?" *Journal of Urban Health* 85(5) (2008): 707–716.

Davis, A. Y. *Women, Race, and Class.* New York: Vintage Press, 1981.

Degenhardt, L., H. Whiteford, W. Hall, and T. Vos. "Estimation Burden of Disease Attributable to Illicit Drug Use and Mental Disorders: What Is 'Global Burden of Disease 2005' and Why Does It Matter?" *Addiction* 104(9) (2009): 1466–1471.

Desjarlais, R. "Struggling Along: The Possibilities for Experience among the Homeless Mentally Ill." *American Anthropologist* 96(4) (1994): 886–901.

Donohue, J. M., M. Cevasco, and M. B. Rosenthal. "A Decade of Direct-to-Consumer Advertising of Prescription Drugs." *New England Journal of Medicine* 357 (2007): 673–681.

Dreifus, C. "Sterilizing the Poor." In *Seizing Our Bodies: The Politics of Women's Health.* New York: Vintage Books, 1977.

Ducq, H., I. Guesdon, and J. L. Roelandt. "Mental Health of Homeless Persons: Critical Review of the Anglo-Saxon Literature." *Encephale* 23(6) (1997): 420–430. In French.

Dumit, J. *Drugs for Life: How Pharmaceutical Companies Define Our Health.* Durham, NC: Duke University Press, 2012.

Eaton, D. "A Brazzaville Friendship." *Ethnography* 1(2) (2000): 239–256.

El-Bassel, N., S. S. Witte, T. Wada, L. Gilbert, and J. Wallace. "Correlates of Partner Violence among Female Street-Based Sex Workers: Substance Abuse, History of Childhood Abuse, and HIV Risks." *AIDS Care and STDs* 15(1) (2001): 41–51.

El-Bassel, N., L. Gilbert, E. Wu, H. Go, and J. Hill. "HIV and Intimate Partner Violence among Methadone-Maintained Women in New York City." *Social Science and Medicine* 61(1) (2005): 171–183.

Engels, F. *Conditions of the Working Class in England in 1844.* 1845; reprint, Charleston, SC: BiblioBazaar, 2007.

Epele, M. E. "Excess, Scarcity and Desire among Drug-Using Sex Workers." Reprinted in *Commodifying Bodies*, ed. N. Scheper-Hughes and L. Wacquant, 161–179. London: Sage, 2002.

Epele, M. E. "Gender, Violence and HIV: Women's Survival in the Streets." *International Journal of Comparative Cross-Cultural Research* 26(1) (2002): 33–54.

Estroff, Sue E. *Making It Crazy: An Ethnography of Psychiatric Clients in an American Community*. Berkeley: University of California Press, 1981.

Fabian, J. *Time and the Other: How Anthropology Makes Its Object*. New York: Columbia University Press, 1983.

Falck, R. S., J. Wang, R. G. Carlson, and H. A. Siegal. "The Epidemiology of Physical Attack and Rape among Crack-Using Women." *Violence and Victims* 16(1) (February 2001): 79–89.

Farmer, P. *Infections and Inequality: The Modern Plagues*. Berkeley: University of California Press, 1999.

Fassin, D., and R. Rechtman. *The Empire of Trauma: An Inquiry into the Condition of Victimhood*. Princeton: Princeton University Press, 2009.

Fazel, S., V. Khosla, H. Doll, and J. Geddes. "The Prevalence of Mental Disorders among the Homeless in Western Countries: Systematic Review and Meta-regression Analysis." *PLoS Medicine* 5(12) (December 2, 2008): e225.

Finnegan, L. P., J. F. Connaughton, Jr., R. E. Kron, and J. P. Emich. "Neonatal Abstinence Syndrome: Assessment and Management." *Addictive Diseases* 2(1–2) (1975): 141–158.

Flavin, J. *Our Bodies, Our Crimes: The Policing of Women's Reproduction in America*. New York: New York University Press, 2009.

Fleck, L. *Genesis and Development of a Scientific Fact*. Chicago: University of Chicago Press, 1935.

Foucault, M. *The Birth of Biopolitics: Lectures at the College de France, 1978–79*. Translated by Graham Burchell. New York and London: Palgrave Macmillan, 2008.

Foucault, M. *History of Sexuality*. Vol. 1, *An Introduction*. Translated by Robert Hurley. 1978; reprint, New York: Vintage Books, 1990.

Frank, D. A., M. Augustyn, W. G. Knight, T. Pell, and B. Zuckerman. "Growth, Development, and Behavior in Early Childhood following Prenatal Cocaine Exposure: A Systematic Review." *Journal of the American Medical Association* 285(12) (2001): 1613–1625.

Freudenberg, N., M. Fahs, S. Galeo, and A. Greenberg. "The Impact of New York City's 1975 Fiscal Crisis on the Tuberculosis, HIV, and Homicide Syndemic." *American Journal of Public Health* 96(3) (2006): 424–434.

Fullilove, M. *Urban Alchemy: Restoring Joy in America's Sorted-Out Cities*. New York: New Village Press, 2013.

Garcia, A. *The Pastoral Clinic: Addiction and Dispossession along the Rio Grande*. Berkeley: University of California Press, 2010.

Garriott, W. "'You Can Always Tell Who Is Using Meth': Methamphetamine Addiction and the Semiotics of Criminal Difference." In *Addiction Trajectories*, ed. E. Raikhel and W. Garriott, 213–237. Durham, NC: Duke University Press, 2013.

Gaulden, E. C., D. C. Littlefield, O. E. Putoff, and A. L. Sievert. "Menstrual Abnormalities Associated with Heroin Addiction." *American Journal of Obstetrics and Gynecology* 90 (1964): 155–160.

Gelberg, L., and L. S. Linn. "Demographic Differences in Health Status of Homeless Adults." *Journal of General Internal Medicine* 7(6) (November–December 1992): 601–608.

Gelberg, L., L. S. Linn, R. P. Usatine, and M. H. Smith. "Health, Homelessness, and Poverty: A Study of Clinic Users." *Archives of Internal Medicine* 150(11) (1990): 2325–2330.

Gelles, R. J. "Violence and Pregnancy: Are Pregnant Women at Greater Risk of Abuse?" *Journal of Marriage and the Family* 50 (1998): 841–847.

German, D., M. A. Davey, and C. A. Latkin. "Residential Transience and HIV Risk Behaviors among Injection Drug Users." Supplement (11) *AIDS and Behavior* 6 (2007): 21–30.

Ginsburg, F., and R. Rapp. *Conceiving the New World Order: The Global Politics of Reproduction*. Berkeley: University of California Press, 1995.

Ginsburg, F., and R. Rapp. "Disability Worlds." *Annual Review of Anthropology* 42 (2013): 53–68.

Goodman, L. A., M. A. Dutton, and M. Harris. "The Relationship between Violence Dimensions and Symptom Severity among Homeless, Mentally Ill Women." *Journal of Traumatic Stress* 10(1) (1997): 51–70.

Greden, J. F. "Clinical Prevention of Recurrent Depression." In *Treatment of Recurrent Depression*, ed. J. R. Greden, 143–170. *Review of Psychiatry* 20(5). Washington, DC: American Psychiatric Publishing, 2001.

Groth, P. *Living Downtown: The History of Residential Hotels in the United States*. Berkeley: University of California Press, 1989.

Hacking, I. *Mad Travellers: Reflections on the Reality of Transient Mental Illness*. Charlottesville: University Press of Virginia, 1998.

Hacking, I. *The Taming of Chance*. Cambridge: Cambridge University Press, 1991.

Hansen, H., P. Bourgois, and E. Drucker. "Pathologizing Poverty: New Forms of Diagnosis, Disability, and Structural Stigma under Welfare Reform." *Social Science and Medicine* 103 (2014): 67–83.

Haraway, D. "Situated Knowledges: The Science Question in Feminism and the Privilege of Partial Perspective." *Feminist Studies* 14 (1988): 575–599.

Harrison, P. A., and A. C. Sidebottom. "Systematic Prenatal Screening for Psychosocial Risks." *Journal of Health Care for the Poor and Underserved* 19(1) (2008): 258–276.

Harvey, D. *A Brief History of Neoliberalism*. Oxford: Oxford University Press, 2005.

Havens, J. R., L. A. Simmons, L. M. Shannon, and W. F. Hansen. "Factors Associated with Substance Use during Pregnancy: Results from a National Sample." *Drug and Alcohol Dependence* 99(1–3) (2009): 89–95.

Hayden, C. "Taking as Giving: Bioscience, Exchange, and the Politics of Benefit-Sharing." *Social Studies of Science* 37(5) (2007): 729–758.

Holmes, S. M., and M. Ponte. "En-case-ing the Patient: Disciplining Uncertainty in

Medical Student Patient Presentations." *Culture, Medicine and Psychiatry* 35(2) (2011): 163–182.

Hopper, K. *Reckoning with Homelessness.* Ithaca: Cornell University Press, 2003.

Hopper, K., et al. "Homelessness, Severe Mental Illness, and the Institutional Circuit." *Psychiatric Services* 48 (1997): 659–665.

Hwang, S. W. "Homelessness and Health." *Canadian Medical Association Journal / Journal de l'Association medicale canadienne* 164(2) (January 23, 2001): 229–233.

Insel, T. R., and T. Quirion. "Psychiatry as a Clinical Neuroscience Discipline." *Journal of the American Medical Association* 29(4) (2005): 2221–2224.

James, S., J. Johnson, and C. Raghavan. "'I Couldn't Go Anywhere.'" *Violence against Women* 10(9) (2004): 991–1014.

Jansson, L. M., M. Velez, and C. Harrow. "The Opioid Exposed Newborn: Assessment and Pharmacologic Management." *Journal of Opioid Management* 5(1) (2009): 47–55.

Jenkins, S. "Sexual Abuse: A Process, Not an Event." *Psychiatry, Psychology and Law* 4(1) (1997): 65–71.

Jones, I., and S. Smith. "Puerperal Psychosis: Identifying and Caring for Women at Risk." *Advances in Psychiatric Treatment* 15 (2009): 411–418.

Kalofonos, I. "'All I Eat Is ARVs': Paradoxes of AIDS Treatment Programs in Central Mozambique." *Medical Anthropology Quarterly* 24(3) (September 2010): 363–380.

Kingfisher, C. "Discursive Constructions of Homelessness in a Small City on the Canadian Prairies: Notes on Destructuration, Individualization, and the Production of (Raced and Gendered) Unmarked Categories." *American Ethnologist* 34(1) (2007): 91–107.

Knight, K. R. "The Public Life of Sex Work: Risk, Politics, and Public Health." *Western Humanities Review* (fall 2012): 55–76.

Knight, K. R., A. M. Lopez, M. Shumway, M. Comfort, J. Cohen, and E. B. Riley. "Single Room Occupancy (SRO) Hotels as Mental Health Risk Environments among Impoverished Women: The Intersection of Policy, Drug Use, Trauma and Urban Space." *International Journal of Drug Policy* 25(3) (2013): 556–561.

Kohrman, M. "Why Am I Not Disabled? Making State Subjects, Making Statistics in Post-Mao China." *Medical Anthropology Quarterly* 17(1) (2003): 5–24.

Kushel, M. B., J. E. Evans, S. Perry, M. J. Robertson, and A. Moss. "No Door to Lock: Victimization among Homeless and Marginally Housed Persons." *Archives of Internal Medicine* 163(20) (2003): 2492–2499.

Lakoff, A. *Pharmaceutical Reason: Knowledge and Value in Global Psychiatry.* Cambridge: Cambridge University Press, 2005.

Larson, E. J. *Sex, Race and Science: Eugenics in the Deep South.* Baltimore: John Hopkins University Press, 1995.

Lazarus, L., J. Chettiar, K. Deering, R. Nabess, and K. Shannon. "Risky Health Environments: Women Sex Workers' Struggles to Find Safe, Secure and Nonexploitative Housing in Canada's Poorest Postal Code." *Social Science and Medicine* 73(11) (2011): 1600–1607.

Lebrun-Harris, L. A., T. P. Baggett, D. M. Jenkins, A. Sripipatana, R. Sharma, A. S. Hayashi, C. A. Daly, and Q. Ngo-Metzger. "Health Status and Health Care Experiences among Homeless Patients in Federally Supported Health Centers: Findings from the 2009 Patient Survey." *Health Services Research* 48(3) (June 2013): 992–1017.

Leenhardt, M. *Do Kamo: Person and Myth in the Melanesian World.* 1947; reprint, Chicago: University of Chicago Press, 1979.

Lemke, T. "'The Birth of Biopolitics': Michel Foucault's Lecture at the College de France on Neoliberal Governmentality." *Economy and Society* 30(2) (2001): 190–207.

Lester, B., E. Tronick, L. Gasse, and R. Seifer. "The Maternal Lifestyle Study: Effects of Substance Exposure during Pregnancy on Neurodevelopmental Outcomes in 1-Month-Old Infants." *Pediatrics* 110(6) (2002): 1182–1192.

Lester, B. M., and J. F. Padbury. "Third Pathophysiology of Prenatal Cocaine Exposure." *Developmental Neuroscience* 31(1–2) (2009): 23–35. doi: 10.1159/000207491.

Levinas, E. *Entre Nous.* New York: Columbia University Press, 1998.

Lillie-Blanton, M., J. C. Anthony, and C. R. Schuster. "Probing the Meaning of Racial/Ethnic Group Comparisons in Crack Cocaine Smoking." *Journal of American Medical Association* 269(8) (1993): 993–997.

Linde, P. *Danger to Self: On the Front Line with an ER Psychiatrist.* Berkeley: University of California Press 2011.

Linker, B. "On the Borderland of Medical and Disability History: A Survey of the Fields." *Bulletin of the History of Medicine* 87(4) (winter 2013): 499–535.

Lipsitz, P. J. "A Proposed Narcotic Withdrawal Score for Use with Newborn Infants: A Pragmatic Evaluation of Its Efficacy." *Clinical Pediatrics* 14 (1975): 592–594.

Luhrmann, T. M. *Of Two Minds: An Anthropologist Looks at American Psychiatry.* New York: Vintage Books, 2000.

Luhrmann, T. M. "Social Defeat and the Culture of Chronicity: Or, Why Schizophrenia Does So Well Over There and So Badly Here." *Culture, Medicine and Psychiatry* 31 (2007): 135–172.

Luhrmann, T. M. "'The Street Will Drive You Crazy': Why Homeless Psychotic Women in the Institutional Circuit in the United States Often Say No to Offers of Help." *American Journal of Psychiatry* 165(1) (2008): 15–20.

Lutnick, A. *Beyond Victims and Villains: The Complex Issue of Domestic Minor Sex Trafficking.* New York: Columbia University Press, 2016.

Lutnick, A., and D. Cohan. "Criminalization, Legalization or Decriminalization of Sex Work: What Female Sex Workers Say in San Francisco, USA." *Reproductive Health Matters* 17(34) (2009): 38–46.

Lyon-Callo, V. "Medicalizing Homelessness: The Production of Self-Blame and Self-Governing with Homeless Shelters." *Medical Anthropology Quarterly* 14(3) (2000): 328–345.

Marshall, L. L. "The Development of the Severity of Violence Against Women Scale." *Journal of Family Violence* 7(2) (1992): 103–121.

Martin, E. *Bipolar Expeditions: Mania and Depression in American Culture*. Princeton: Princeton University Press, 2007.

Marvasti, A. B. *Being Homeless: Textual and Narrative Constructions*. Lanham, MD: Lexington Books, 2003.

Massey, D., and N. Denton. *American Apartheid: Segregation and the Making of the Underclass*. Cambridge, MA: Harvard University Press, 1993.

Max, A. *The Last Resort: Scenes from a Transient Hotel*. San Francisco: Chronicle Books, 1997.

Mbembe, A. *On the Postcolony*. Berkeley: University of California Press, 2001.

McFarlane, J., B. Parker, and K. Soeken. "Abuse during Pregnancy: Associations with Maternal Health and Infant Birth Weight." *Nursing Research* 45 (1996): 37–42.

Melchior, M., A. Caspi, L. M. Howard, A. P. Ambler, H. Bolton, N. Mountain, and T. E. Moffitt. "Mental Health Context of Food Insecurity: A Representative Cohort of Families with Young Children." *Pediatrics* 124(4) (2009): e564–572.

Metzl, J. M. *Prozac on the Couch: Prescribing Gender in the Era of Wonder Drugs*. Durham, NC: Duke University Press, 2003.

Metzl, J. M. *The Protest Psychosis: How Schizophrenia Became a Black Disease*. Boston: Beacon Press, 2009.

Miller, C. L., D. R. Bangsberg, D. M. Tuller, J. Senkungu, A. Kawuma, E. A. Frongillo, and S. D. Weiser. "Food Insecurity and Sexual Risk in an HIV Endemic Community in Uganda." *AIDS and Behavior* 15(7) 2011: 1512–1519.

Miller, P., and N. Rose. *Governing the Present: Administering Economic, Social and Personal Life*. Malden, MA: Polity Press, 2008.

Moreno, M. A., L. A. Jelenchick, K. G. Egan, E. Cox, E. Young, K. E. Gannon, and K. Becker. "Feeling Bad on Facebook: Depression Disclosures by College Students on a Social Networking Site." *Depression and Anxiety* 28(6) (June 2011): 447–455.

Murphy, S., and M. Rosenbaum. *Pregnant Women on Drugs: Combating Stereotypes and Stigma*. New Brunswick: Rutgers University Press, 1999.

Murphy, S., and P. Sales. "Pregnant Drug Users: Scapegoats of the Reagan/Bush and Clinton Era Economics." *Social Justice: A Journal of Crime, Conflict and World Order* 28(4) (2001): 72–95.

Nader, L. "Up the Anthropologist: Perspectives Gained from Studying Up." In *Reinventing Anthropology*, ed. D. Hymes, 284–311. New York: Vintage Books, 1972.

North, C. S., E. M. Smith, and E. L. Spitznagel. "Is Antisocial Personality a Valid Diagnosis among the Homeless?" *American Journal of Psychiatry* 50(4) (1993): 578–583.

North, C. S., S. J. Thompson, D. E. Pollio, D. A. Ricci, and E. M. Smith. "A Diagnostic Comparison of Homeless and Nonhomeless Patients in an Urban Mental Health Clinic." *Social Psychiatry and Social Epidemiology* 32(4) (1997): 236–240.

Norton, L. B., J. F. Peipert, S. Zierler, B. Lima, and L. Hume. "Battering in Pregnancy: An Assessment of Two Screening Methods." *Obstetrics and Gynecology* 85 (1995): 321–325.

Nyamathi, A. M., B. Leake, and L. Gelberg. "Sheltered versus Nonsheltered Homeless

Women: Differences in Health, Behavior, Victimization, and Utilization of Care." *Journal of General Internal Medicine* 15(8) (2000): 565–572.

O'Malley, P. "Risk and Responsibility." In *Foucault and Political Reason: Liberalism, Neo-liberalism and Rationalities of Government*, ed. A. Barry, T. Osbourne, and N. Rose, 180–205. Chicago: University of Chicago Press, 1996.

Ondersma, S. J., D. S. Svikis, and C. R. Schuster. "Computer-Based Brief Intervention: A Randomized Trial with Postpartum Women." *American Journal of Preventive Medicine* 32(3) (2007): 231–238.

Patrick, S. W., S. R. E. Schumacher, B. D. Benneyworth, E. E. Krans, J. M. McAllister, and M. M. Davis. "Neonatal Abstinence Syndrome and Associated Health Care Expenditures: United States, 2000–2009." *Journal of the American Medical Association* 307(18) (2012): 1934–1940.

Petryna, A. *Life Exposed: Biological Citizenship after Chernobyl*. Princeton: Princeton University Press, 2002.

Pickens, D. K. "The Sterilization Movement: The Search for Purity in Mind and State." *Phylon* 28 (spring 1967): 78–94.

Pollack, H. A., and P. Reuter. "Welfare Receipt and Substance-Abuse Treatment among Low-Income Mothers: The Impact of Welfare Reform." *American Journal of Public Health* 96(11) (2006): 2024–2031.

Porter, T. *The Rise of Statistical Thinking, 1820–1900*. Princeton: Princeton University Press, 1986.

Porter, T. *Trust in Numbers*. Princeton: Princeton University Press, 1996.

Potter, J. E., M. Pereyra, M. Lampe, Y. Rivero, S. P. Danner, M. H. Cohen, A. Bradley-Byers, M. P. Webber, S. R. Nesheim, M. J. O'Sullivan, and D. J. Jamieson. "Factors Associated with Prenatal Care Use among Peripartum Women in the Mother-Infant Rapid Intervention at Delivery Study." *Journal of Obstetric, Gynecological and Neonatal Nursing* 38(5) (2009): 534–543.

Prince, M., V. Patel, S. Saxena, M. Maj, J. Maselko, M. Phillips, and A. Rahmon. "No Health without Mental Health." *Lancet* 370 (2007): 859–877.

Raikhel, E., and W. Garriott, eds. *Addiction Trajectories*. Durham, NC: Duke University Press, 2013.

Rapp, R. *Testing Women, Testing the Fetus: The Social Impact of Amniocentesis in America*. New York: Routledge, 2000.

Reagan, L. *Dangerous Pregnancies: Mothers, Disabilities, and Abortion in Modern America*. Berkeley: University of California, 2010.

Reilly, P. R. *The Surgical Solution: A History of Involuntary Sterilization in the United States*. Baltimore: John Hopkins University Press, 1991.

Rhodes, L. *Emptying Beds: The Work of an Emergency Psychiatry Unit*. Berkeley: University of California Press, 1991.

Rhodes, T., M. Singer, P. Bourgois, S. R. Friedman, and S. A. Strathdee. "The Social Structural Production of HIV Risk among Injecting Drug Users." *Social Science and Medicine* 61(5) (2005): 1026–1044.

Riley, E. D., J. Cohen, K. R. Knight, A. Weber, K. Marson, and M. Shumway. "Recent Violence in a Highly Co-Morbid Community-Based Sample of Homeless and Unstably Housed Women." *American Journal of Public Health* 104(9) (2014): 1657–1663.

Riley, E. D., K. Moore, J. L. Sorensen, J. P. Tulsky, D. R. Bangsberg, and T. B. Neilands. "Basic Subsistence Needs and Overall Health among Human Immunodeficiency Virus–Infected Homeless and Unstably Housed Women." *American Journal of Epidemiology* 174(5) (2011): 515–522.

Riley, E. D., T. B. Neilands, K. Moore, J. Cohen, D. R. Bangsberg, and D. Havlir. "Social, Structural and Behavioral Determinants of Overall Health Status in a Cohort of Homeless and Unstably Housed HIV-Infected Men." *PLoS One* 7(4) (2012): e35207.

Roberts, B., K. F. Ocaka, J. Browne, T. Oyok, and E. Sondorp. "Factors Associated with the Health Status of Internally Displaced Persons in Northern Uganda." *Journal of Epidemiology and Community Health* 63(3) (2009): 227–232.

Robertson, M. J., and M. R. Cousineau. "Health Status and Access to Health Services among the Urban Homeless." *American Journal of Public Health* 76(5) (May 1986): 561–563.

Rose, N. *The Politics of Life Itself: Biomedicine, Power, and Subjectivity in the Twenty-First Century.* Princeton: Princeton University Press, 2007.

Satel, S. L. "When Disability Benefits Make Patients Sicker." *New England Journal of Medicine* 333 (1995): 794–796.

Saxe, G., and J. Wolfe. "Gender and Post-traumatic Stress Disorder." In *Post-Traumatic Stress Disorder: A Comprehensive Text*, ed. P. Saigh and J. Bremmer, 160–179. Needham Heights, MA: Allyn and Bacon, 1999.

Scheper-Hughes, N. *Death without Weeping: The Violence of Everyday Life in Brazil.* Berkeley: University of California Press, 1992.

Scheper-Hughes, N. "Who's the Killer? Popular Justice and Human Rights in a South African Squatter Camp." *Social Justice* 22(3) (1995): 143–164.

Schoen, J. *Choice and Coercion: Birth Control, Sterilization, and Abortion in Public Health and Welfare.* Chapel Hill: University of North Carolina Press, 2005.

Schweik, S. *The Ugly Laws: Disability in Public.* New York: New York University Press, 2009.

Sellman, D. "The 10 Most Important Things Known about Addiction." *Addiction* 105(1) (2010): 6–13.

Shaner, A., T. C. Eckman, L. J. Roberts, J. N. Wilkins, D. E. Tucker, J. W. Tsuang, and J. Mintz. "Disability Income, Cocaine Use, and Repeated Hospitalization among Schizophrenic Cocaine Abusers: A Government-Sponsored Revolving Door?" *New England Journal of Medicine* 333 (1995): 777–783.

Shannon, K., T. Ishida, C. Lai, and M. Tyndall. "The Impact of Unregulated Single Room Occupancy Hotels on Health Status of Illicit Drug Users in Vancouver." *International Journal of Drug Policy* 17(2) (2006): 107–114.

Shragg, T. "'Cotton Fever' in Narcotic Addicts." *Journal of the American College of Emergency Physicians* 7(7) (1978): 279–280.

Shumway, M., A. Boccellari, K. O'Brien, and R. L. Okin. "Cost-Effectiveness of Clinical Case Management for ER Frequent Users: Results of a Randomized Trial." *American Journal of Emergency Medicine* 6(2) (2008): 155–164.

Singer, M., and S. Clair. "Syndemics and Public Health: Reconceptualizing Disease in Bio-social Context." *Medical Anthropology Quarterly* 17 (2003): 423–441.

Smith, P., J. Smith, and J. Earp. "Beyond the Measurement Trap: A Reconstructed Conceptualization and Measurement of Women Battering." *Psychology of Women Quarterly* 23 (1999): 177–193.

Snow, D. A., S. G. Baker, L. Anderson, and M. Martin. "The Myth of Pervasive Mental Illness among the Homeless." *Social Problems* 33(5) (1986): 407–423.

Strathern, M. "New Accountabilities: Anthropological Studies in Audit, Ethics and the Academy." In *Audit Cultures: Anthropological Studies in Accountability, Ethics and the Academy*, ed. M. Strathern, 1–18. New York: Routledge, 2000.

Sufrin, C. "Jailcare: The Safety Net of a U.S. Women's Jail." Ph.D. dissertation, University of California, San Francisco, 2014.

Tabol, C., C. Drebing, and R. Rosenheck. "Studies of 'Supported' and 'Supportive' Housing: A Comprehensive Review of Model Descriptions and Measurement." *Evaluation and Program Planning* 33(4) (November 2010): 446–456.

Taussig, M. *The Magic of the State*. New York: Routledge, 1997.

Theall, K. P., C. E. Sterk, and K. W. Elifson. "Past and New Victimization among African American Female Drug Users Who Participated in an HIV Risk-Reduction Intervention." *Journal of Sex Research* 41(4) (2004): 400–407.

Thompson, M. P., J. B. Kingree, A. Rashid, R. Puett, D. Jacobs, and A. Matthews. "Partner Violence, Social Support, and Distress among Inner-City African American Women." *American Journal of Community Psychology* 28(1) (2000): 127–143.

Ticktin, M. "Where Ethics and Politics Meet: The Violence of Humanitarianism in France." *American Ethnologist* 33(1) (2006): 33–49.

Trouillot, M. *Global Transformations: Anthropology and the Modern World*. New York: Palgrave, 2003.

Valverde, M. *Diseases of the Will: Alcohol and the Dilemmas of Freedom*. Cambridge: Cambridge University Press, 1998.

Vlahov, D., N. Freudenberg, F. Proietti, D. Ospad, A. Quinn, V. Nandi, and S. Galeo. "Urban as a Determinant of Health." *Journal of Urban Health* 84(1) (2007): 116–126.

Vogenthaler, N. S., C. Hadley, S. J. Lewis, A. E. Rodriguez, L. R. Metsch, and C. Del Rio. "Food Insufficiency among HIV-Infected Crack-Cocaine Users in Atlanta and Miami." *Public Health Nutrition* 15 (2010): 1–7.

Wacquant, L. *Punishing the Poor: The Neoliberal Government of Social Insecurity*. Durham, NC: Duke University Press, 2009.

Wacquant, L. *Urban Outcasts: A Comparative Sociology of Advanced Marginality*. Cambridge: Polity Press, 2008.

Wasco, S. M. "Conceptualizing the Harm Done by Rape: Applications of Trauma Theory to Experiences of Sexual Assault." *Trauma Violence Abuse* 4(4) (2003): 309–322.

Waterston, A. *Love, Sorrow and Rage: Destitute Women in a Manhattan Residence*. Philadelphia: Temple University Press, 1999.

Watkins-Hayes, C. *The New Welfare Bureaucrats: Entanglements of Race, Class, and Policy Reform*. Chicago: University of Chicago Press, 2009.

Wechsberg, W. M., W. K. Lam, W. Zule, G. Hall, R. Middlesteadt, and J. Edwards. "Violence, Homelessness, and HIV Risk among Crack-Using African-American Women." *Substance Use and Misuse* 38(3–6) (2003): 669–700.

Weinberg, D. *Of Others Inside: Insanity, Addiction, and Belonging in America*. Philadelphia: Temple University Press, 2005.

Weiser, S. D., D. R. Bangsberg, S. Kegeles, K. Ragland, M. B. Kushel, and E. A. Frongillo. "Food Insecurity among Homeless and Marginally Housed Individuals Living with HIV/AIDS in San Francisco." *AIDS and Behavior* 13(5) (2009): 841–848.

Weiser, S. D., D. M. Tuller, E. A. Frongillo, J. Senkungu, N. Mukiibi, and D. R. Bangsberg. "Food Insecurity as a Barrier to Sustained Antiretroviral Therapy Adherence in Uganda." *PLoS One* 5(4) (2010): e10340.

Wenzel, S. L., P. Koegel, and L. Gelberg. "Antecedents of Physical and Sexual Victimization among Homeless Women: A Comparison to Homeless Men." *American Journal of Community Psychology* 28(3) (2000): 367–390.

Wenzel, S. L., J. S. Tucker, M. N. Elliot, G. N. Marshall, and S. L. Williamson. "Physical Violence against Impoverished Women: A Longitudinal Analysis of Risk and Protective Factors." *Women's Health Issues* 14(5) (2004): 144–145.

Wenzel, S. L., J. S. Tucker, K. Hambarsoomian, and M. N. Elliot. "Toward a More Comprehensive Understanding of Violence against Impoverished Women." *Journal of Interpersonal Violence* 21(6) (2006): 820–839.

Weston, K. *Gender in Real Time: Power and Transience in a Visual Age*. New York: Routledge, 2002.

Williams, B. "The Public I/Eye: Conducting Fieldwork to Do Homework on Homelessness and Begging in Two U.S. Cities." *Current Anthropology* 36(1) (1995): 25–51.

Willse, C. "Neo-liberal Biopolitics and the Invention of Chronic Homelessness." *Economy and Society* 39(2) (2010): 155–184.

Wilson, W. J. *The Truly Disadvantaged: The Inner City, the Underclass, and Public Policy*. Chicago: University of Chicago Press, 1987.

Wisner, K. L., J. M. Perel, and R. L. Findling. "Antidepressant Treatment during Breast-Feeding." *American Journal of Psychiatry* 153 (1996): 1132–1137.

Wu, M., L. L. LaGasse, T. A. Wouldes, A. M. Arria, T. Wilcox, C. Derauf, E. Newman, R. Shah, L. M. Smith, M. A. Huestis, S. DellaGrotta, and B. M. Lester. "Predictors of Inadequate Prenatal Care in Methamphetamine-Using Mothers in New Zealand and the United States." *Maternal and Child Health Journal* 17 (2013): 566–575.

Young, A. "America's Transient Mental Illness: A Brief History of the Self-Traumatized Perpetrator." In *Subjectivity: Ethnographic Investigations*, ed. J. Biehl, B. Good, and A. Kleinman. Berkeley: University of California Press, 2007.

Young, A. *The Harmony of Illusions: Inventing Post-traumatic Stress Disorder*. Princeton: Princeton University Press, 1995.

Zigon, J., and C. J. Throop. "Moral Experience: Introduction." *Ethos* 42(1) (2014): 1–15.

Media Articles and Governmental/Nonprofit Reports

Abelson, R. "On the Threshold of Obamacare, Warily: When It Comes to Mental Health Coverage, a Long Line of Patients Is Still Waiting." *New York Times*, September 29, 2013.

Agency for Health Care Research and Quality. HCUP *Fact Book 8: Serving the Uninsured: Safety-Net Hospitals, 2003*. Rockville, MD: Agency for Health Care Research and Quality, 2007.

American Psychiatric Association. DSM-IV-TR, *Quick Reference*. Washington, DC: APA Press, 2000.

Barber, S. L. *Supplemental Security Income Recipients for Whom the Alcoholism and Drug Addiction Provisions Apply (DAA Recipients)*. Washington, DC: Office of Program Benefits, Social Security Administration, 1996.

Beresford, J. "Should Drug Addicts Be Paid to Be Sterilized?" BBC *News Magazine*, February 8, 2010.

Born Hooked: Confronting the Impact of Perinatal Substance Abuse. Hearing before the Select Committee on Children, Youth, and Families. House of Representatives, 101st Congress, 1st sess. April 27, 1989. ERIC no. ED314920.

Calhoun, A. "The Criminalization of Bad Mothers." *New York Times*, April 25, 2012.

Care Not Cash Overview and Progress Report. Prepared for the Ten-Year Implementation Council. San Francisco: San Francisco Department of Human Services, 2005.

Carpenter, L. "Nature of the Problem and State of the Field." Presentation at the National AIA Resource Center Substance Exposed Newborns Conference, Alexandria, VA. June 2010. Quoted in National Abandoned Infants Assistance Resource Center. AIA *Fact Sheet: Prenatal Substance Use Exposure*. 2012. http://aia.berkeley.edu, accessed March 15, 2015.

Carr, V. "Police Set Goals for 2010." *Mission Loc@1*, January 8, 2010.

Carr, V. "Women Seek Stability in the SROs." *Mission Loc@1*, January 9, 2010.

Central City SRO Collaborative, San Francisco. *History of SROs in San Francisco*. http://www.ccsro.org/pages/history.htm, accessed March 15, 2015.

Cooney, K. "Drug Addiction, Personhood, and the War on Women." *Time*. April 26, 2012.

Dorgan, M. "Addicts Feed Habits with U.S. Hand Outs." *San Jose Mercury News*, December 19, 1993.

Duenwald, M. "A Conversation With: Nora Volkow; A Scientist's Lifetime of Study into the Mysteries of Addiction." *New York Times*, August 19, 2003.

Eckholm, E. "Case Explores Rights of Fetus versus Mother." *New York Times*, October 23, 2013.

Fitzgerald, R. "America's Shocking Disability Scam." *Reader's Digest*, August 1994.

Fitzgerald, R. "'Crack Baby' Study Ends with Unexpected but Clear Result." *Philadelphia Inquirer*, July 22, 2013.

Golightly, L. "San Francisco's Mission District: The Controversial Gentrification." *Global Site Plans: Branding for Environmental Design*, August 27, 2014.

Goodby, N., and B. Minters. "A Family Home in an SRO." *Mission Loc@l*, January 5, 2010.

Guttmacher Institute. *State Policies in Brief: Substance Abuse during Pregnancy*. Fact sheet. New York: Guttmacher Institute, March 1, 2015. http://www.guttmacher.org/statecenter/spibs/spib_SADP.pdf, accessed March 15, 2015.

Hernandez, R. "A Violent Year for Mission SROs." December 9, 2010. http://mission local.org/2010/12/a-violent-year-for-mission-sros/, accessed March 15, 2015.

Jones, Steve T. "Clean Up the Plaza Run by Political Consultant with Ties to Developers." *San Francisco Bay Guardian Online*. www.sfbg.com, accessed March 15, 2015.

Kamiya, Gary. "Omaha Beach in the Mission: Cue the Mother of All San Francisco Real Estate Battles." *San Francisco Magazine*, November 20, 2013.

Karaca, Z., H. Wong, and R. Mutter. *Characteristics of Homeless and Non-homeless Individuals Using Inpatient and Emergency Department Services, 2008*. Statistical brief no. 152. Rockville, MD: Agency for Healthcare Research and Quality (US), 2013.

Kennedy, E., and L. King. "Access to Benefits for Persons with Disabilities Who Were Experiencing Homelessness: An Evaluation of the Benefits Entitlement Services Team Demonstration Project." *Social Security Bulletin* 74(4) (2014).

Klausner, J. D. "Decriminalize Prostitution—Vote Yes on K." *San Francisco Chronicle*, September 8, 2008.

Knight, H., C. M. Vega, and P. Matier. "Newsom Seeks Treatment for Alcohol Abuse." *San Francisco Chronicle*, February 5, 2007.

Kolman, P. "New Police Chief Targets Drugs and Prostitution." *Mission Loc@l*, December 15, 2009.

Meinwald, Dan. *Memento Mori: Death and Photography in 19th Century America*. N.d. http://vv.arts.ucla.edu/terminals/meinwald/meinwald1.html. March 15, 2015.

Nash, M. J. "Addicted." *Time*, May 5, 1997.

National Abandoned Infants Assistance Resource Center. *AIA Fact Sheet: Prenatal Substance Use Exposure*. 2012. http://aia.berkeley.edu, accessed March 15, 2015.

National Coalition for the Homeless. *Health Care and Homelessness*. National Coalition for the Homeless, July 2009. http://www.nationalhomeless.org/factsheets/health.html, accessed March 15, 2015.

National Institute on Drug Abuse. *Comorbidity: Addiction and Other Mental Illnesses*. NIDA Research Report Series. NIH pub. no. 08–5771. Rockville, MD: U.S. Dept. of Health and Human Services, National Institutes of Health, National Institute on Drug Abuse, 2008.

National Institute on Drug Abuse. *Drugs, Brains, and Behavior: The Science of Addiction*. NIH pub. no. 07-5605. April 2007. http://www.drugabuse.gov/publications/drugs-brains-behavior-science-addiction/, accessed March 15, 2015.

National Institute on Drug Abuse. *NIDA InfoFacts: Understanding Drug Abuse and Ad-

diction. September 2007. http://cchealth.org/aod/pdf/fact_sheet_understanding _drug_addiction.pdf, accessed March 15, 2015.

National Institute on Drug Abuse. *Prenatal Exposure to Drugs of Abuse*. May 2011. http://www.drugabuse.gov/sites/default/files/prenatal.pdf, accessed March 15, 2015.

Okie, S. "Crack Babies: The Epidemic That Wasn't." *New York Times*, January 26, 2009.

Rust, M. "Social Security Scam: Uncle Sam as Enabler." *Insight*, April 11, 1994.

San Francisco (City and County) Department of Public Health. *Return on Investment: How SSI Advocacy Became a Standard of Practice in San Francisco* (2004). Revision, San Francisco: San Francisco Department of Public Health, 2008.

Satel, S. L. "Hooked: Addicts on Welfare." *New Republic*, May 30, 1994.

Schmidt, L. *Effects of Welfare Reform on the Supplemental Security Income (SSI) Program*. National Poverty Center Policy Brief No. 4. Gerald R. Ford School of Public Policy, University of Michigan 2004.

Seligman, D. "The SSI Follies." *Fortune*, June 13, 1994.

Substance Abuse and Mental Health Services Administration, Office of Applied Studies. *Pregnancy and Substance Use*. National Survey on Drug Use and Health Report. January 2, 2004. http://www.ou.edu/cwtraining/assets/pdf/handouts/1009 /pregnancy.pdf, accessed March 15, 2015.

Substance Abuse and Mental Health Services Administration. *Results from the 2010 National Survey on Drug Use and Health: National Findings*. http://archive.samhsa .gov/data/NSDUH/2k10nsduh/2k10results.htm#2.6 accessed March 15, 2015.

Substance Abuse and Mental Health Services Administration, Office of Applied Studies. *The NSDUH Report: Adults with Co-Occurring Serious Mental Illness and a Substance Use Disorder*. Rockville, MD: Department of Health and Human Services, June 23, 2004. http://dmh.mo.gov/docs/mentalillness/nsduhreport.pdf, accessed March 15, 2015.

Substance Abuse and Mental Health Services Administration, Office of Applied Studies. *The NSDUH Report: Women with Co-Occurring Serious Mental Illness and a Substance Use Disorder*. Rockville, MD: Department of Health and Human Services, August 20, 2004.

Substance Abuse and Mental Health Services Administration, Office of Applied Studies. *The NSDUH Report: Substance Use among Women during Pregnancy and Following Childbirth*. Rockville, MD: Department of Health and Human Services, May 21, 2009.

Szabo, L. "Number of Americans Taking Anti-depressants Doubles." *USA Today*, August 9, 2009.

Szabo, L. "Number of Painkiller-Addicted Newborns Triples in 10 Years." *USA News and World Report*, May 1, 2012.

Tetens, K. "Group Revives Victorian Custom of Post-mortem Portraiture to Help Grieving Parents," February 15, 2007. http://victorianpeeper.blogspot.com/2007 /02/group-revives-custom-of-post-mortem.html accessed March 15, 2015.

U.S. Department of Housing and Urban Development. *The 2010 Annual Homeless Assessment Report to Congress*. Washington, DC: U.S. Department of Housing and Urban Development, 2010.

U.S. Interagency Council on Homelessness. *Opening Doors: Federal Strategic Plan to Prevent and End Homelessness*. 2010. https://wwwich.gov/PDF/Opening Dooors_2010_FSPPreventEndHomeless.pdf, accessed March 15, 2015.

Waller, M. "LaBruzzo: Sterilization Plan Fights Poverty: Tying Poor Women's Tubes Could Help Taxpayers, Legislator Says." *New Orleans Times-Picayune*, September 24, 2008.

Walsh, E. "A Partisan Agenda for Cutting the Roles of Government, Labor." *Washington Post*, October 8, 1994.

Weaver, C. L. "Welfare Reform Is Likely to Leave This Monster Intact." *Wall Street Journal*, April 6, 1994.

Weinstein, N. "Conflict Resolution." *Rise: Stories by and for Parents Affected by the Child Welfare System* (fall 2005), www.risemagazine.org, accessed March 15, 2015.

Wong, J. C. "The Battle of 16th and Mission: Inside the Campaign to 'Clean-Up' the Plaza and Build Luxury Housing." 48hillsonline.org, accessed March 15, 2015.

Wong, J. C. "DropBox, Air BnB, and the Fight over San Francisco's Public Spaces." *New York Times*, October 23, 2014.

index

abortion, 68–70, 210–11, 271n56
Adams, Vincanne, 267n18, 276n12
addicted (as term), 7–8
addicted pregnancy, 11–14, 87, 206–39; adversity index of stressors during, 61, 169–73, 199; biological citizenship achieved through, 158, 267n23; as child abuse, 12, 159; construction of victim-perpetrators for, 180–85, 202–5, 209, 224–25, 276n15; criminalization of, 12–13, 78–82, 155–56, 158–60, 200–201, 209–13, 230–31, 268n24; demographics of study participants with, 240–41, 243–45t; drug treatment during, 5, 72, 89–90, 102, 151–52, 157–58, 178, 198–201, 230–31; fathers' involvement with, 170–71; food insecurity of, 61–67; housing insecurity of, 40, 47, 58–61, 185–88; intimate partner abuse and, 190–92; morbidity and mortality of, 213–17; neurocratic case management of, 30–31, 105–6, 144–50, 158, 219–20, 225–26; political invisibility of, 14–15, 218–22; politics of viability for, 208–13; prenatal drug exposure during, 12–13, 61, 63, 89, 155–60, 159–64, 271n58; prenatal health care for, 53, 61, 83, 89; public health costs of, 146–49, 229–30; racialized and sexualized constructions of, 154–64; rates of, 11–12; return to drug use and sex work after, 12, 146–47, 234–39; risks of detox for, 178; social admits

for, 178, 272n1; substances used in, 72, 160–64, 247n5; temporal constraints of, 8–11, 68–101, 141–42, 223, 259n39, 260n42; termination of pregnancy for, 68–70, 209–11, 271n56. *See also* children; drug-sex economies

addiction and drug use: among recent mothers, 146–47, 175–76, 271n58; comorbidity with mental illness of, 7–8, 37, 71, 103–10, 121–24, 225–26, 260n1, 276n17; criminalization of, 109, 151, 266n1, 269n27; definition of, 160; eligibility for ssi benefits for, 106–10, 123–24; neurobiology of, 106–7, 144–45, 160, 164–69, 226–29; ontological shifts of, 12–13, 70–71, 225; potential invisibility of, 14–15; public confession of, 277n18; temporal constraints of, 72–74, 134–36, 223, 255n6, 255n8; toxic moms and, 164–69, 221–22, 270n44, 270nn48–49. *See also* treatment

addict time, 72–74, 134–36, 223, 255n6, 255n8

adversity index, 61, 169–73, 199

Affordable Care Act (ACA), 220, 226

Aid to Families with Dependent Children (AFDC), 157

alcohol abuse, 72, 130, 162, 247n5; detox risks for, 178; fetal alcohol spectrum disorder (FASD) and, 167

anthropology. *See* ethnography of addicted pregnancy

drug-sex economies, 12–21; addictive substances used in, 130, 247n5; children in proximity to, 46–47; commodification of cell phones in, 118, 254n30; earnings of sex-workers in, 49; food insecurity in, 61–63, 61–67; gentrifying neighborhoods of, 15–20, 29, 248n18, 248n22; HIV risk behaviors in, 59–60, 102, 146–47; hustling systems in, 188–95, 273n21; invisibility of, 14–15; local responses to, 18–19, 20f; moral economies of debt in, 37, 49–51; policing of, 17–18, 249nn27–28; residential transience in, 58–61, 67, 149; resistance to health care in, 53–55, 127, 254n14; risky city paradigm of, 181–85, 272n4, 272n13; third-party involvement in, 49, 249n26, 253n11; violence and abuse in, 98–99, 190–92, 260n41. See also addicted pregnancy; daily-rent hotels
drug siloing, 162
drug treatment. See treatment
drug use. See addiction and drug use
dysfunctional families, 165, 169–70, 174–75, 270n49

The Empire of Trauma (Fassin and Rechtman), 136–37, 265n17
Engels, Friedrich, 181–82
entrepreneurs of the self, 183–85, 205, 209, 272n16, 274n4. See also neoliberalism; personal responsibility
Epele, Maria, 251n30
epidemiological categorization: of food insecurity, 61–63; of housing instability, 58–61; temporal constraints of, 85–86, 100–101, 193–94, 224
epidemiological time, 85–86, 100–101, 193–94, 224
Estroff, Sue, 255n3
ethnography of addicted pregnancy, 22–32; being hustled in, 194; compensation for interviews in, 241; ethical commitment of, 28, 29–30, 232, 252n37; evidentiary forms of truth production in, 217–22, 239, 276n12; field notes and photographs in, 28–29; geographic location of, 29; methods used in, 240–42; multiple roles of ethnographer in, 26–28, 62–63, 251–52nn33–35, 271n56; multisited approach in, 241; narrative texture provided by, 10, 23–24, 154–55, 215, 217–23, 231–39; study of poor outcomes in, 213–17, 275n8; temporal constraints of situated knowledge in, 97–101, 223, 259n39, 260n42
eugenics, 210–13. See also forced sterilization
Everyday Ethics (Brodwin), 252n37

Fabian, Johannes, 255n1, 260n42
Fassin, Didier, 136–37, 265n17
fetal alcohol spectrum disorder (FASD), 167
fetal drug exposure. See prenatal drug exposure
fetal rights movement, 12, 154–55, 159–60
5150 psychiatric hospitalizations, 23, 105f, 125–26, 186, 247n3
Flavin, Jeanne, 158–59, 268n24
Fleck, Ludwik, 141
food insecurity, 61–67
forced sterilization, 152f, 153, 171–73, 210–13
Foucault, Michel: on the nature of power, 215–17; on neoliberal technologies of the self, 157–58, 183–84, 272n16; on vital politics, 274n4
free food programs, 64
Freudenberg, Nicholas, 182

gaffle, 18
"Gender, Violence and HIV" (Epele), 251n30

of poverty in, 103, 225–26, 260n4; biomedical time of, 8, 86–90; criminalization of addicted pregnancy in, 12–13, 78–82, 155–56, 158–60, 268n24; diagnosis of mental illness in, 103–4, 110–15, 118–24, 128, 130, 132, 158, 220; disability as qualifier for SSI in, 106–10; drug enforcement policies of, 109, 150; forced sterilization and, 152f, 153, 171–73; hustling the system and, 188–95, 273n21; leveraging of material support through, 121–24; neurocratic facilitation of, 10, 103–7, 111–12, 158, 219–20, 225–26; progressive housing programs of, 37–43, 76, 185–88, 231, 253n6, 253n12; Proposition 36 and, 151, 266n1; on rep payee services, 113–14; on residential transience, 58–61, 67; risky city landscape of, 180–85, 272n4, 272n13; social engineering in, 210–13; stratified reproduction in, 154–60; temporal constraints and, 9–11

public shelters, 20, 51, 98–99, 190–92

public SRO housing, 37–43; access restrictions on, 40–43, 185–88, 253n7; costs and payment policies of, 40, 41, 49, 76, 127; measures of efficacy of, 40, 44; social and physical health services at, 41, 143; turnover at, 187

Rapp, Rayna, 153

rates of addicted pregnancy in the United States, 11–12

Reagan, Ronald, 182

Rechtman, Richard, 136–37, 265n17

rep payee system, 113–14

reproduction. *See* children; stratified reproduction

residential transience, 58–61, 67, 149

Righteous Dopefiend (Bourgois and Schonberg), 249–50n30, 254n14, 255n6

"Risk and Responsiblity" (O'Malley), 183

risky city paradigm, 180–85, 272n4, 272n13

Rose, Nicholas, 263n30

Rosenbaum, Marsha, 156

Sales, Paloma, 156, 157–58, 164, 267n14

San Francisco: Care Not Cash policy of, 102–3, 253n6; costs of addicted pregnancy in, 229–30; General Assistance (GA) of, 75, 253n6; gentrification of, 15–20, 29, 248n22; homelessness in, 37–38; progressive housing programs of, 37–43, 185–88, 231, 253n6; recession of 2008 and, 229; workfare program of, 263n31. *See also* Mission District; public health systems; public policy

San Francisco Department of Public Health, 108, 111–15

Scheper-Hughes, Nancy, 254n29, 270n44, 276n15

schizogenic notion of time, 255n1

schizophrenia, 104; atypical antipsychotic medications for, 133–34; schizophrenogenic mothers and, 165, 227

Schonberg, Jeff, 249–50n30, 254n14, 255n6

selective serotonin reuptake inhibitors (SSRI), 134

self-medication for mental illness, 128–30

serious mental illness (SMI), 103. *See also* mental illness

sexually transmitted infections (STIs), 68, 192–93

sex work. *See* drug-sex economies

Singer, Merrill, 272n9

Sixteenth and Mission corridor. *See* Mission District

Sixteenth Street BART plaza, 12f, 14–15, 64f, 65; clean-up campaigns for, 15, 249n25; protesting gentrification at, 19, 20f, 248n24
social admits, 178, 272n1
social science vulturism, 22–28, 67, 213–17, 232, 252n34
Social Security Administration (SSA), 144
Social Security Disability Insurance (SSDI), 108–15
Social Security Income (SSI), 41–43, 75–76, 102–3, 127; disability claims under, 104, 108, 116, 261n5; drug addiction and eligibility for, 106–10, 123–24; general eligibility requirements for, 108; levels of impairment (Blue Book) categories of, 116–18; mental illness and eligibility for, 110–15, 118–24, 128, 130, 132, 158, 220; physical illness and eligibility for, 115–18, 121; retroactive payments of, 114
speed. *See* methamphetamine; stimulants
Spitzer, Roger, 264n14
SRO (definition), 37, 40–41, 43, 67. *See also* daily-rent hotels; public SRO housing
stimulants, 128–30, 141–42, 247n5; bipolar disorder and, 134–36; healthcare resources for use of, 146–49. *See also* crack cocaine
stratified reproduction, 146, 151–77; assumptions about child development outcomes and, 164–69, 176–77; crack babies and, 161–64, 269n35; family ties in, 173–77; forced sterilization and operability in, 152f, 153, 171–73, 210–13; neoliberal constructions of addicted pregnancy and, 154–60, 176–77; science of prenatal substance exposure and, 160–61
street psychiatry, 125–50; atypical anti-

psychotic medications and, 132–36, 150, 164, 264n8; bipolar disorder and, 131–36, 149–50; neurocratic pregnancy and, 144–50; PTSD and, 131, 136–44, 149–50, 158, 264n12, 264n16; self-diagnosis in, 130; self-medication in, 128–30
"The Street Will Drive You Crazy" (Luhrmann), 251n30
structural violence, 181, 272n4
"Struggling Along" (Desjarlais), 250n30
Substance Abuse and Crime Prevention Act (Proposition 36), 151, 266n1
substance use disorder, 103. *See also* addiction
supportive housing, 187–88. *See also* public SRO housing
Susser, Ida, 251n30
syndemics, 182–84, 272n9
synthetic morphine, 247n5

technologies of truth, 122, 263n30. *See also* neurocratic case management
temporal constraints of addicted pregnancy, 8–11, 68–101, 141–42, 222–24, 255nn1–3; of addict time, 72–74, 134–36, 223, 255n6, 255n8; of biomedical time, 86–90, 223, 257n29; construction of PTSD and, 95, 223, 259n36; of epidemiological time, 85–86, 100–101, 193–94, 224; of ethnographic situated knowledge, 97–101, 223, 259n39, 260n42; of hotel time, 75–78, 146, 193, 223; of jail time, 78–82, 223–24; of life time, 96–97; of memorial time, 90–96, 223; of pregnancy time, 77–78, 223; of treatment time, 82–86, 223–24; of twenty-one day policies, 68–70
"The 10 Most Important Things Known about Addiction," 227–29
tenancy rights, 47–48
Throop, C. Jason, 252n37

tobacco, 130, 162, 247n5

toxic moms, 164–69, 221–22, 270n44, 270nn48–49

trauma, 141–42, 265n17, 265n21; homelessness and, 128–31, 137–39, 141–42, 265n17, 265n19, 265n21; loss of child custody and, 92, 202, 205–6, 207f, 221. *See also* posttraumatic stress disorder (PTSD)

treatment, 13–14; for addicted pregnancy, 5, 72, 89–90, 102, 151–52, 157–58, 178, 198–201, 217–18, 230–31, 247n4; for crack addiction, 83, 147–48; criminal-volunteers for, 209–13; for depression, 276n16; as disruption of addict time, 74; expectations of personal responsibility and, 149, 227–28; in jail, 79–81, 195–201; for mental illness, 7–8, 105, 128–30, 132, 133–36, 145, 150, 164, 226, 264n8; for opiate/opioid addiction, 83–84, 147, 265n22; pregnancy time and, 77–78; Proposition 36 and, 151, 266n1; risks of, 178. *See also* criminalization

treatment time, 82–86, 223–24

Troubled Assets Recovery Program (TARP), 276n17

Turner, Victor, 271n71

twenty-one day policy, 47–48, 51, 58–59, 69–70

"Up the Anthropologist" (Nader), 250n30, 252n38

Using Women: Gender, Drug Policy, and Social Justice (Campbell), 154–56

US Substance Abuse and Mental Health Services Administration, 103

Van Gennup, Arnold, 271n71

vertical slice, 233

Veterans' Administration PTSD treatment, 142

viability. *See* politics of viability

Vicodin, 247n5

victim-perpetrators, 180, 184–85, 202–5, 209, 224–25, 276n15

violence, 6, 22, 248n19; by intimate partners, 98–99, 190–92, 260n41; PTSD as normative response to, 137–39; temporal measurement of, 86, 256n22

vital politics, 208, 213, 274n4. *See also* politics of viability

Volkow, Nora, 106–7, 161, 164

vultures and vulturism, 22–26, 213–17

Wacquant, Loïc, 176

War on Drugs campaign, 150

Waterston, Alisse, 251n30

Weinberg, Darin, 250n30

Weinstein, Naomi, 257n29

welfare entitlements: of AFDC, 157; of General Assistance benefits, 75, 157, 253n6; hotel time and, 75–76; reforms of the 1990s in, 156–60, 182–84, 267n14; of SSI benefits, 41–43, 75–76. *See also* public SRO housing

welfare queens, 156–57, 267n14

Wellstone, Paul, 276n17

Weston, Kath, 256n22

Williams, Brackette, 100

Women Infants and Children (WIC), 65f, 66

Women's Needle Exchange Program, 251nn33, 262n24

Young, Allan, 95, 140–41, 259n36

Zigon, Jarrett, 252n37